Private Law Remedies

PRINCIPLES OF PRIVATE LAW

The principles underpinning private law reflect some of the oldest and most enduring legal concepts. As the structure of our society grows ever more complex, so do the agreements that govern the interactions between its constituent individuals and private entities. The Principles of Private Law series provides rigorous yet accessible, analytical overviews of the laws regulating the private sphere.

Leading authorities in the field take a structured approach to cover core concepts such as remedies, damages, restitution and negligence, as well as others including agency, succession and product liability. Titles in the series offer a firm and thought-provoking grounding for scholars and postgraduate students, as well as for practicing lawyers and policymakers.

For a full list of Edward Elgar published titles, including the titles in this series, visit our website at www.e-elgar.com.

Private Law Remedies

Katy Barnett

Professor of Law, University of Melbourne, Australia

Sirko Harder

Reader in Law, University of Sussex, UK

PRINCIPLES OF PRIVATE LAW

Edward Elgar
PUBLISHING

Cheltenham, UK • Northampton, MA, USA

Published by
Edward Elgar Publishing Limited
The Lypiatts
15 Lansdown Road
Cheltenham
Glos GL50 2JA
UK

Edward Elgar Publishing, Inc.
William Pratt House
9 Dewey Court
Northampton
Massachusetts 01060
USA

Authorised representative in the EU for GPSR queries only: Easy Access System Europe – Mustamäe tee 50, 10621 Tallinn, Estonia, gpsr.requests@easproject.com

A catalogue record for this book
is available from the British Library

Library of Congress Control Number: 2025938979

This book is available electronically in the **Elgar**online
Law subject collection
https://doi.org/10.4337/9781035316021

MIX
Paper | Supporting responsible forestry
FSC® C014540

ISBN 978 1 0353 1601 4 (cased)
ISBN 978 1 0353 1602 1 (eBook)
ISBN 978 1 0353 7005 4 (ePub)

Printed and bound in the UK by Short Run Press Ltd, Exeter EX2 7LW

Contents

Preface

The law of remedies contains the rules that determine how a court can respond to a wrong. This includes the availability of compensation for loss, disgorgement of gain, coercive and other remedies, as well as the measure of money awards. This book covers remedies for civil (private law) wrongs such as breach of contract, breach of fiduciary duty, breach of trust, and tort.

Courts pronounce rules in relation to the specific causes of action upon which they adjudicate. This includes rules on remedies. Thus, in actions for breach of contract, the courts have shaped the remedies for breach of contract; in actions for breach of fiduciary duty, the courts have shaped the remedies for breach of fiduciary duty; etc. Textbooks on a particular area of law (contract, equity, tort, trust) cover the remedies for that area. It might, therefore, be thought that the law of remedies is fragmented.

However, it is important to look at the rules on private law remedies as a whole. While there are specific rules for individual wrongs, there are many commonalities. When a particular remedies issue arises for the first time for a particular wrong, it may be useful to consider how that issue has been resolved for other wrongs. The court may adopt or reject that solution, depending on whether it is aligned with the rationale of the liability in question. Either way, the court's decision is more informed than it would be if the solution for other wrongs were ignored.

Two events have had a particular impact on the law of damages. The first is the abolition of juries in civil proceedings. Juries used to fix the amount of damages. The calculation was not transparent, and appellate courts could intervene only in exceptional circumstances. Judges are required to explain how they have arrived at the amount awarded, and appellate courts can scrutinise those reasons. A large number of refined rules have developed and continue to develop.

The other event is the recognition in *Henderson v Merrett Syndicates Ltd* [1995] 2 AC 145 that a professional who delivers a service under a contract and is under a contractual duty of care may also be under a tortious duty of care, resulting in concurrent liability in contract and negligence if the duty is breached. Courts have since been required to calculate the amount of damages in both causes of action for the same breach, which has put a spotlight on the differences between them in relation to the measure of damages, particularly in relation to contributory negligence and remoteness of loss. Some convergence of the rules has occurred to ensure that a particular position in one cause of action is not undermined by the claimant's choice to pursue the concurrent cause of action.

Our aim with this book is to provide an overview of private law remedies, focussing on commonalities between causes of action. We structure the remedies not primarily according to causes of action, but according to the function of the remedy, whatever the cause of action. The function of a remedy can be compensation for loss, coercion, vindication, disgorgement of gain, or restitution (in the sense of giving back something). This enables us to compare the remedies for various wrongs in relation to a particular function. We appreciate that some remedies may have multiple functions, and our division is ultimately a pragmatic one.

We provide an introduction to the general principles and key debates in the area of private law remedies. Our focus is on the law of England and Wales, although we mention differences in some other common law jurisdictions where appropriate. Our book is meant for everyone seeking to understand private law remedies in England and Wales, including students, practitioners, judges, academics, and overseas lawyers.

Considering the limits of space, we have left out some matters that are of less relevance in a commercial context. In particular, we do not cover the various items of loss recoverable in an action for defamation or personal injury. However, cases involving personal injury are considered in relation to general principles such as causation and loss of chance.

The primary responsibility for Chapters 2 to 6 lay with Sirko, and the primary responsibility for the other chapters lay with Katy, but the text is very much a joint work. We have considered material available to us before 30 November 2024.

Katy would like to thank her family (Scott, Eloise, Josh, and Hamish) for their support. She is particularly grateful for the proofreading skills of Marina Loane. She would also like to thank her students at Melbourne Law School, who have made her think about how to present the law of remedies more clearly to a diverse audience, and her Masters co-lecturers, Professor Paul S Davies from UCL and Associate Professor Wayne Jocic from Melbourne Law School. Finally, she also wants to thank Sirko for being an amazing co-author.

Sirko would like to thank his family (Huan, Oliver, and Alina) for their constant support. He also wants to thank Katy for doing brilliant work on this book in challenging times for her.

We both would like to thank Amber Watts of Edward Elgar for approaching us to write this book, and the staff of Edward Elgar for their care in preparing this text.

Katy Barnett
Sirko Harder
November 2024

1. Introduction to *Private Law Remedies*

INTRODUCTION TO REMEDIES LAW

This chapter outlines key concepts, including the history of remedies law, what a remedy is, how remedies work, what the theoretical debates are, and what the functions of remedies in private law are.

While the focus of this book will be on the common law of England, we will, at times, also refer to the law in other common law jurisdictions to illustrate our discussion.[1]

It is important for civilian readers to note that the common law legal system is not a system that has arisen by design; it has no overarching Code. Rather, it is a system that has evolved, over a long period of time: from its origins in twelfth-century medieval England to the present day. It has been adopted in many Commonwealth and former Commonwealth jurisdictions, including the United States, Canada, Australia, New Zealand, Hong Kong, and Singapore. Consequently, there is no consistent direction to the law, and the system has evolved to fit different circumstances, times, and places. Moreover, historically, different courts have dealt with different matters and remedies. The long shadows cast by this history can still be seen in the law today.

In *Letang v Cooper*, Diplock LJ noted that, historically, in English law, remedies were often considered before any analysis of primary rights and obligations because of the way in which common law court procedure focused on the causes of action.[2] As long as a claimant could make out a particular 'form of action', they could then obtain a remedy. The English Kings established the Royal Courts to apply the common law and operated according to a system of writs which stipulated particular processes for particular causes of action, and particular remedial consequences flowed from that choice.[3] This led lawyers

---

1 The decisions of superior courts in other common law countries such as Australia, New Zealand and Canada are not binding upon the United Kingdom courts but may be persuasive.

2 *Letang v Cooper* [1965] 1 QB 232, 243.

3 Frederick W Maitland, *The Forms of Action at Common Law: A Course of Lectures* (CUP 1958) 1–5.

to focus on the remedy they wanted for their clients, and work backward to fit the facts of a given case within the form of action.[4] Hence, Diplock LJ went on to observe that 'a cause of action is simply a factual situation the existence of which entitles one person to obtain from the court a remedy against another person'.[5] If the claimant could not fit their case into any of the forms of action, then they were not entitled to any remedy.[6] Thus, it is sometimes said, *ubi jus, ibi remedium* ('where there is a right there is a remedy'). The inflexibility of the forms of action helps to explain why a parallel court system developed alongside the Royal Courts, namely, the Court of Chancery.

Even now, Tettenborn has observed that, for a common lawyer, 'we must always remember that legal advice is, at bottom, simply advice as to the remedy likely to be available (or unavailable) to the client'.[7]

It is pivotal to understand the history of common law before one can really understand remedies granted in the English common law system; hence, the history will be discussed first. Those aware of the history can skip to the discussion of the nature of a remedy.

HISTORY

English law has developed organically, in a non-linear fashion.

The term 'common law' has two meanings. One meaning is general: common law means a system of law derived from the English system which relies on judicial decision making and case-by-case analysis, rather than a Code. A common law system has been exported to many former colonies of the British Empire. The other meaning is specific: common law means that body of law which was originally derived from England's medieval Royal Courts, to be contrasted with the body of law derived from the Court of Chancery (known as 'equity').

The origins of the common law can be traced back to the great harmonisation of the Royal Courts which took place during the reign of Henry II of

---

[4] Even in the thirteenth century, Henry de Bracton, a jurist and commentator, noted '*Non potest quis sine brevi agere*' ('no one can sue without a writ'): Henry de Bracton, *On the Laws and Customs of England* ['*De legibus et consuetudinibus Angliæ*'], transl. SE Thorne, 4 vols (Harvard University Press, 1968–1977) f 413b.

[5] *Letang v Cooper* [1965] 1 QB 232, 242–43.

[6] Frederick W Maitland, *The Forms of Action at Common Law: A Course of Lectures* (CUP 1958) 5.

[7] Andrew Tettenborn, 'Remedies: A Neglected Contribution' [1999] Denning LJ 41, 41.

England (1154–1189).[8] Prior to this, manorial lords had enforced their own justice in their own manorial courts according to local custom. Henry II created Royal Courts and ordered them to amalgamate all the regional traditions and apply a 'common law' (with any regional idiosyncrasies in custom to be ignored). This law continued to develop on a case-by-case basis. As noted above, the forms of action were all-important: the facts had to be fitted into the relevant forms in order for a claimant to achieve a remedy. The clerks responsible for drafting the forms of action would allow some innovations, meaning that more and more forms of action developed. However, often claimants were hamstrung by the oddities of the forms of action, having to utilise 'legal fictions' to ensure that their claims fitted within the forms.[9]

There were significant issues with the formulaic nature of the writs of the Royal Courts, and consequently, parties appealed to the ultimate authority, the Monarch, for unfair and rigid decisions to be overturned. Gradually, the King (or Queen) began to hand these decisions off to his or her Lord Chancellor, a churchman trained in canon law (ecclesiastical law governing Christian Churches). The Lord Chancellor was responsible for the Chancery, an administrative office staffed by clerks who produced and recorded official documentation such as Royal Charters. The religious background and training of the Chancellors meant that they tended to act according to conscience.

The result was that an entirely parallel court system, the Court of Chancery, with its own separate rules and procedures, developed alongside the Royal Courts. Among other things, it was inquisitorial, not adversarial. At first, the Court of Chancery only stepped in to remediate any unfairness of the common law forms of action; however, it later came to develop its own body of law. This is not without precedent. It may help any readers trained in Roman law to think of the equitable law of the Court of Chancery as equivalent to the Praetorian Edict (*ius honorarium*), the more flexible discretionary body of praetorian law which developed to mitigate the inflexibility of the civil law (*ius civile*).[10]

---

8 John Baker, *An Introduction to English Legal History* (5th edn, OUP 2019) 16–35.

9 For example, the nascent common law of contract was stifled by the limitations placed on the praecipe writ of covenant, which allowed for the enforcement of contractual-style promises. In the fourteenth century, the Royal Courts held that it was necessary to have a deed under seal for the praecipe writ of covenant to apply. Because most commercial bargains did not fulfil this requirement, the writ was not used to enforce bargains. Instead, the Royal Courts had to use debt (with penal bonds and performance bonds) and the writ of assumpsit (originally a writ dealing with trespass) to enforce contractual-style promises.

10 Paul du Plessis, *Borkowski's Textbook on Roman Law* (6th edn, OUP 2020) [2.2.2.4] 35.

The presence of two different sets of decision-makers operating according to different rules led to complexity and conflict at times. In the early seventeenth century, it was decided that equity would always prevail over common law.[11] This remains the case today. However, the Court of Chancery was reluctant to trespass too much on the territory of the Royal Courts and only tended to intervene to change a common law remedial decision where common law rules were unable to effect an 'adequate' remedy.

Hence, there are in fact two historical bases for the present common law in a wide sense (namely, judge-made law): the common law in a narrow sense (which derives from the law that the Royal Courts used to apply); and equity (which derives from the law that the Courts of Chancery used to apply). The shadows of this historical division can still be seen in the law today, particularly in the area of remedies.

By the seventeenth century, at common law, for causes of action in tort and the collection of causes of action which later became modern contract, compensatory damages were usually the presumptive remedy. This remains, by and large, the rule today. For tort and contract, it is still presumed (to a lesser or greater degree) that the remedial response is compensatory damages, and any other remedy is exceptional. However, as we will see, in some situations, specific relief (ie, specific performance or an injunction) will be readily granted, particularly in relation to interests in real (or immovable) property.

Historically, tort (the law of civil wrongs) and the law of criminal wrongs were also intertwined. Even now, some common law torts have criminal equivalents (eg, criminal assault versus tortious assault). Until the eighteenth century, the victim of a criminal offence privately prosecuted the wrongdoer; in modern times, on the other hand, it has been the state which has prosecuted the wrongdoer for such offences. The historical lack of separation between tort and criminal law has given rise to some oddities. In tort, a claimant can seek exemplary damages (called 'punitive damages' in the United States) which seek to punish the defendant for the wrong committed. The extent to which such damages should be available outside tort (or even, outside a narrowly defined set of circumstances within tort) remains controversial.

Conversely, the Courts of Chancery typically dealt with every remedy except compensation. The Court of Chancery was also more discretionary than the common law courts (reflecting the conscience-based approach) and had its own rules of evidence, procedure, and terminology. For example, a 'defence' in common law is called a 'bar to relief' in equity, and the bars to relief are typically highly discretionary.

---

11 *Earl of Oxford's Case* (1615) 1 Ch Rep 1, (1615) 21 ER 485.

For claims that arose purely in the Court of Chancery (also called equity's original jurisdiction), the courts were ready to compel parties to perform obligations, strip profits from wrongdoers (accounts of profits), and award remedies that undid transactions (rescission) or attached remedies to property, even in the hands of third parties (through constructive trusts or liens). In this way, the remedial hierarchy was the inverse of the common law courts.

However, historically, the Court of Chancery did not generally award compensation. While equitable compensation is now available for breaches of equitable obligations, such as breaches of fiduciary duty or breaches of confidence, the idea of compensating for wrongdoing has come late to this body of law.

For common law causes of action, the Court of Chancery would sometimes step in, but only if damages were inadequate, in which case a remedy such as specific performance (ie, an order compelling performance of a contract) or an injunction might be awarded. This was known as equity's auxiliary jurisdiction.

In the end, the Court of Chancery became very slow and inefficient.[12] There was also a problem with circuitry of actions, created by the dual courts running side by side. Suppose, for example, a claimant had a contract for the sale of land (which is generally specifically performable) and went to the Court of Chancery to gain a decree of specific performance. However, because equitable remedies are discretionary, the Court of Chancery declined to award specific performance (for example, there might be unreasonable delay on the claimant's part, which prejudiced the defendant). The claimant would then have to go to the common law courts and start all over again, using common law forms of action and procedures, to seek damages.

There were some attempted fixes, including statutes allowing the common law courts to award injunctions, and statutes allowing the Court of Chancery to award damages in lieu of an injunction (Lord Cairns' Act, dealt with in Chapter 7).

Ultimately, however, the fixes did not work, and in the 1870s, the English legislature fused the administration of the courts with the Judicature Acts.[13] In other words, Parliament abolished the two separate court systems with different procedures and rules of evidence running side by side. The Judicature Acts allowed a single judge in the one court system to apply both the rules of

[12] A situation famously described by the author Charles Dickens: Charles Dickens, 'The Martyrs of Chancery' (1851) 2 *Household Words* 251; Charles Dickens, 'The Martyrs of Chancery: Second Article' (1851) 2 *Household Words* 493; Charles Dickens, *Bleak House* (1853).

[13] The principal among these were the Supreme Court of Judicature Act 1873 (36 & 37 Vict. c. 66) and the Supreme Court of Judicature Act 1875 (38 & 39 Vict. c. 77).

common law and equity and ensured that the same rules of evidence and procedure applied. However, equity still prevailed over the common law.[14]

In Ashburner's *Principles of Equity*, the effect of the Judicature Acts upon common law and equity was said to be that 'the two streams of jurisdiction, though they run in the same channel, run side by side and do not mingle their waters'.[15] Lord Diplock commented in *United Scientific Holdings Ltd v Burnley Borough Council*:

> My Lords, by 1977 this metaphor has in my view become both mischievous and deceptive. ...As at the confluence of the Rhône and Saône, it may be possible for a short distance to discern the source from which each part of the combined stream came, but there comes a point at which this ceases to be possible. If Professor Ashburner's fluvial metaphor is to be retained at all, the waters of the confluent streams of law and equity have surely mingled now.[16]

Nonetheless, although there has been a greater tendency to borrow from one body of law and apply the remedial principles to another, the separation between the two bodies of principles still subsists to a degree.

Because of this, and the fact that remedies awarded continue to differ, it remains important to know whether a particular cause of action was originally a common law cause of action or an equitable cause of action.

Equity developed a number of legal concepts which may be unfamiliar to civilians, and common lawyers may benefit from a refresher. Primary among those concepts are the trust and the fiduciary duty, both of which arose in equity's original jurisdiction.

In the modern era, statutes have had an increasing influence on the development of the law generally and upon the ability to award remedies. Consequently, when looking at the law, it is necessary to consider judge-made law (both common law and equity decisions) and statute (made by Parliament, but then interpreted by the courts).

An important part of the common law method is the case: a decision based on particular facts, with particular reasoning given by the judge or judges. For non-common lawyers, it might be startling to learn that there needs to be no unanimity between judges: judges can differ in their reasoning and can disagree entirely on the outcome of a case. In the event of disagreement, however, there is generally an odd-numbered bench so that the majority of judges must agree on the outcome.

---

14 Supreme Court of Judicature Act 1873 (UK) (36 & 37 Vict, c. 66) s 25(11).

15 Walter Ashburner and Denis Browne, *Ashburner's Principles of Equity* (2nd edn, Butterworths 1933) 18.

16 [1978] AC 904, 924–25.

Table 1.1 A table comparing common law and equitable remedies

Common law	Equity
Customary judge-made law common to England	Law originally developed by Lord Chancellor (generally clergyman): inspired by canon law
Strict and inflexible	Discretionary
Common law causes of action:	Equitable causes of action:
• Contract • Tort • Unjust Enrichment • Debt	• Breach of trust • Breach of fiduciary duty • Breach of confidence
Common law remedies:	Equitable remedies:
• Compensatory damages • Exemplary damages in tort • But if common law damages are inadequate, may seek specific performance through equity's auxiliary jurisdiction	• Account of profits • Specific relief (specific performance and injunctions) • Proprietary relief (constructive trusts etc) • Equitable compensation

Despite the fascination which case law holds for common lawyers (and possibly others), it is also important not to forget statute. Unlike a Code, however, the intervention of statute tends to be more piecemeal.

WHAT IS A REMEDY?

Colloquially, we might think of a remedy as a 'cure' or a way of ameliorating a wrong.[17] However, it is necessary to be more specific when discussing the legal nature of remedies. Lawyers have used the term 'remedy' in a variety of different ways, including to describe a cause of action, a substantive right, a court order, a means of enforcing a court order, and a final outcome of litigation.[18]

Another way of conceptualising legal remedies is to see them as a response to civil wrongdoing.[19] According to this view, a remedy confers a 'right' on the claimant because the claimant then has the ability to enforce a correlative 'duty'. Hence, the scholar John Austin argued that remedies are 'secondary rights', which only arise when there is a violation of a 'primary right'

---

17 Rafal Zakrzewski, *Remedies Reclassified* (OUP 2005) 8–9.

18 ibid 10–22.

19 See, eg, *Attorney-General v Blake* [2001] 1 AC 268, 284 (Lord Nicholls).

Table 1.2 A table outlining the elements of the trust and the fiduciary duty

The trust	The fiduciary duty
A trustee holds legal title to property for the benefit of the beneficiary who (traditionally) holds equitable title. 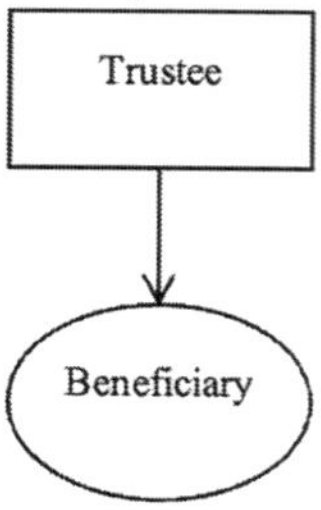	A fiduciary owes duties not to conflict and not to profit to the beneficiary: • Inner circle: trustee-beneficiary, agent-principal, testator-beneficiary, employee-employer, partner-partner etc. • Fact based fiduciary obligations can arise if one party makes an undertaking to another.

recognised by the law.[20] Austin proposed that primary rights serve the purposes of the law and do not arise from wrongdoing or violation of other rights. Secondary rights, on the other hand, arise from wrongdoing or violation of other rights and are conferred to protect and enforce the primary right; they presume that obedience to the law is not perfect because otherwise there would be no violations of the law. On this view, remedies are simply a response to wrongdoing or violation of rights.

As Austin notes, remedies give 'teeth to the obligations imposed by law: "I have no right, independently of the injunction or prohibition which declares that some given act, forbearance or omission, would be a violation of my right; nor would the act or forbearance be a violation of my right, unless my right and the corresponding duty were clothed with a sanction, criminal or civil."'[21] Thus, he argues, in this sense there is truth in the maxim *ubi jus ibi remedium* mentioned earlier ('when there is a right there is a remedy').

Lord Diplock accepted an Austinian view of contract damages in *Photo Production Ltd v Securicor Transport Ltd*:

> Every failure to perform a primary obligation is a breach of contract. The secondary obligation on the part of the contract breaker to which it gives rise by implication of the common law is to pay monetary compensation to the other party for the

---

20 John Austin, 'Lecture XLV' in Robert Campbell and John Murray (eds), *Lectures in Jurisprudence, Or the Philosophy of Positive Law* (Vol 2, 1885) 760.

21 ibid 794–95.

> loss sustained by him in consequence of the breach; but, with two exceptions, the primary obligations of both parties so far as they have not yet been fully performed remain unchanged. This secondary obligation to pay compensation (damages) for non-performance of primary obligations I will call the "general secondary obligation". [22]

There are difficulties with separating out rights and remedies in this way, as Austin concedes. This is because there are several instances in common law systems where the primary right cannot be described without reference to the injury and the availability of a remedy. Although there are more, two brief examples will be given here.

First, for some torts, damage is the gist of the cause of action—in other words, it is necessary to show damage in order to make out the primary duty itself—including for malicious falsehood, passing off, and negligence. The primary duty is defined in terms of a duty not to cause harm. Second, it has also been argued that the restitution of a mistaken transfer is also not susceptible to an Austinian analysis, because mistaken payment is not a breach of duty.[23]

Therefore, Austin's definition is too narrow, as it does not cover certain court-ordered responses to events that are not based on wrongdoing but nonetheless give rise to a remedial response, such as unjust enrichment.

In the context of unjust enrichment, Peter Birks distinguished between 'wrongs' (breaches of duty including tort, breach of contract, breach of fiduciary duty, and breach of confidence) and contrasted them with causes of action such as unjust enrichment, which he called 'not-wrongs'.[24] In Birks' view, the range of remedial responses available for courts in relation to wrongs was wider than that for not-wrongs; the remedial responses for 'not-wrongs' were limited to reversing the effects of the transfer.[25]

Rafal Zakrzewski, meanwhile, defines remedies as 'the rights immediately arising from certain judicial commands and statements which aim to redress a pre-suit grievance, usually an actual or threatened infringement of a substantive right'.[26]

---

22 [1980] AC 827, 848–49. See Brice Dickson, 'The Contribution of Lord Diplock to the Law of Contract' (1989) 9 OJLS 441.

23 Norman Witzleb, Elise Bant, Simone Degeling and Kit Barker, *Remedies: Commentary and Materials* (7th edn, LBC 2020) [1.20]. Cf Kit Barker, 'Rescuing Remedialism in Unjust Enrichment: Why Remedies are Right' (1998) 57 Camb LJ 301, 320–22, arguing that the rights-remedy distinction can still be applied to mistaken payments.

24 Peter Birks, 'Rights, Wrongs and Remedies' (2000) 20 OJLS 1, 25–36.

25 ibid 38.

26 Rafal Zakrzewski, *Remedies Reclassified* (OUP 2005) 2. See also Stephen A Smith, 'Why Courts Make Orders (And What This Tells Us About Damages)'

Although most of the remedies discussed in this book fit within Zakrzewski's definition, some 'remedies' are perhaps better conceived of as 'permission' by the court for claimants to respond to wrongs in certain ways ('self-help remedies') or as procedural mechanisms (interlocutory injunctions, freezing orders, and other similar remedies).

Stephen Smith argues that we must distinguish between substantive rights and remedial rights.[27] Remedial rights are a response to, or a consequence of, a ruling by a court on a question of substantive rights. Smith identifies three categories of remedial rights, each of which flows from the preceding right:[28]

1. Action-rights: respond to the successful establishment of a cause of action.
2. Court-ordered rights: created by order of a judge in response to an action-right.
3. Enforcement-rights: the means by which a court or government body ensures that the court-ordered rights are enforced or complied with.

Under this analysis, post-judgment remedies would be a species of 'enforcement right'.

Ultimately, we can conclude that a remedy in the legal sense is a court order seeking to redress or respond to a claimant's grievance, where the grievance often involves the infringement of a primary right. However, as we have seen, it is difficult to separate the primary right, the secondary right, and the procedural rights necessary for the enforcement of the secondary rights.

The Relationship Between the Right and the Remedy

If the remedy responds to the infringement of a right, and in some sense is a reflection of the primary right, there is a question as to whether the remedy must mirror the right, and to what extent it must do so.

There are two extremes in this debate. On the one hand, a court could consider the array of available remedies and pick whichever remedy the judge thought was most appropriate to ensure justice, on a discretionary basis. This is called a 'dualist' view.[29] The advantage of this approach is that the judge has flexibility in the way she responds to the grievance and can tailor the remedy

(2011) 64 CLP 51; Stephen A Smith, 'Duties, Liabilities and Damages' (2012) 125 Harv L Rev 1727.

27 Stephen A Smith, *Rights, Wrongs, and Injustices* (OUP 2019) 77–80.

28 ibid 80–87.

29 See, eg, Grant Hammond, 'Rethinking Remedies: The Changing Nature of the Conception of the Relationship between Legal and Equitable Remedies' in Jeffrey Berryman (ed), *Remedies: Issues and Perspectives* (Carswell 1991) ch 4.

accordingly. She is not constrained by rigid categories which may prevent justice from being done. However, there are disadvantages to this approach too. First, there is the certainty problem: it is difficult to predict what remedy might be awarded if there is a great deal of discretion, and difficult to advise. Second, there is the rule of law problem: different judges may exercise discretion differently in otherwise similar cases, which means that litigants are not treated equally, and individual prejudices may dictate the responses to disputes.

On the other hand, the other extreme is to have a very rigid system, where the remedy reflects the right, and there is very little discretion. This is called 'monism' and reflects the traditional English approach. This has the advantage of certainty, but the lack of flexibility may give rise to injustice, just as with the old common law pleading system.

The ideal is to have what David Wright has called a 'sticky' relationship between right and remedy.[30] In other words, it is reasonably predictable what the default remedy for a breach of contract will be at common law (expectation damages), but if damages are not appropriate, there is a structured discretion whereby other remedies can be awarded, according to identified criteria. This is the preferred approach of the authors.

There remains a question of how we organise and discuss remedies. As noted at the outset of this chapter, common law remedies (in the broad sense) are inflected by their historical background, and whether they emanate from the common law or equitable courts. However, some English scholars have questioned whether the common law and equitable divide should continue to dictate the responses to grievances.

The primary challenge to the historical view of remedies has been the scholarship regarding unjust enrichment. Peter Birks sought to reformulate and understand common law remedies in a way which reflected Roman law principles. Birks was a 'monist', as his analysis of common law remedies was predicated on the view that certain causative events triggered a particular remedy. Hence, he said, '[t]he secondary obligation to pay compensatory damages is … the same thing as the right, looked at from the other end'.[31]

However, Birks thought that the traditional common law way of categorising remedies by historical causes of action (eg, according to 'contract', 'tort', etc.) was incorrect. He and other scholars sought to devise a taxonomy of

---

[30] David Wright, *Remedies* (2nd edn, Federation Press 2014) 8–9; David Wright, 'Wrong and Remedy: A Sticky Relationship' [2001] Sing J Leg Stud 1.

[31] Peter Birks, 'Definition and Division: A Meditation on Institutes 3.13' in Peter Birks (ed), *The Classification of Obligations* (Clarendon 1997) 24.

the common law causes of action, based on Roman law (which had categories based on delict, contract, quasi-contract, and quasi-delict in the time of Justinian).[32]

Birks argued that there were also four categories in the common law, namely:

1. wrongs;
2. consent;
3. unjust enrichment; and
4. 'other'.

He placed tort and equitable wrongs (such as breach of trust or breach of fiduciary duty) in the category of 'wrongs', arguing that the remedy was triggered in each instance by wrongdoing. He placed contract and express trusts (trusts created by the agreement of parties) in the category of 'consent' and argued that the remedy was triggered by the consent of the parties. Unjust enrichment had not historically been recognised as a coherent form of action in the common law, and hence Birks' elevation of it to stand alongside wrongs and contract was controversial. Importantly, this taxonomy cuts across the historical distinctions between common law and equity discussed at the outset of this chapter and encourages us to de-emphasise the historical differences.

Birks argued that 'like cases should be treated alike'. He encouraged courts and scholars to analogise wrongs in tort and equity because they had the same 'trigger' (namely, wrongdoing). For example, if exemplary damages are available in tort, it follows that exemplary damages should also be available for equitable wrongdoing because the two have the same trigger (wrongdoing). Similarly, Birks emphasised the similarity of contract and the express trust, on the basis that both arise by consent. Therefore, given that an account of profits (a gain-based award) is available for breach of trust, it should also be available for breach of contract because each arises by consent. Andrew Burrows, now a judge on the United Kingdom Supreme Court, has argued for a greater coherence between common law and equitable remedies using a Birksian schema.[33]

We make particular mention of Birks's analysis because it has proved influential, particularly in England and Wales. It has been less influential in some other parts of the common law world, such as Australia.

---

32 Paul J du Plessis, *Borkowski's Textbook on Roman Law* (6th edn, OUP 2020) [9.1.2.3] 256–57.

33 Andrew Burrows, 'We Do This at Common Law but That in Equity' (2002) 22 OJLS 1.

A FUNCTIONAL APPROACH TO REMEDIES

This book will take a functional approach, looking at the dominant goals of different remedies. The general goal will be identified, and individual remedies that share that goal will be discussed. We divide remedies according to the following general functions:

1. compensation;
2. compulsion;
3. deterrence;
4. vindication (including punishment);[34] and
5. restitution.

Rafal Zakrzewski has criticised functional approaches, suggesting that the use of 'compulsion' or similar as a goal should not be included in a series including 'compensation', 'punishment' and 'restitution', because it is taxonomically incoherent.[35] He suggests instead that a distinction should be made between 'replicative remedies' (which replicate primary rights or secondary rights) and 'transformative remedies' (which create a new legal relationship different to that which existed before trial). Ying Khai Liew has suggested that a further category of 'reflective remedies' should be added to Zakrzewski's taxonomy (these, like replicative remedies, give effect to secondary rights, but are more discretionary).[36]

Under this analysis, payment of a debt or specific performance is a replicative remedy as is an award of compensatory damages for tort, for example.[37] A remedial constructive trust is a transformative remedy which creates a new right altogether,[38] but as discussed in Chapter 11, English law does not recognise such trusts. Under Liew's system, the sliding scale of remedial response to equitable estoppel (which can range from specific performance to equitable compensation) would be a reflective remedy.[39]

Despite the fact that a functional scheme does not sit well with this kind of theoretical taxonomy, we proceed with a functional analysis because

---

[34] Vindication and punishment are separate goals, but we treat them together, because they are intertwined. We use the term vindication in the sense suggested in Jason NE Varuhas, 'The Concept of "Vindication" in the Law of Torts: Rights, Interests and Damages' (2014) 34 OJLS 253, 258.

[35] Rafal Zakrzewski, *Remedies Reclassified* (OUP 2005) 68–75.

[36] Ying Khai Liew, *Rationalising Constructive Trusts* (Hart 2017) 20–23.

[37] Rafal Zakrzewski, *Remedies Reclassified* (OUP 2005) 75–84.

[38] ibid 214–15.

[39] Ying Khai Liew, *Rationalising Constructive Trusts* (Hart 2017) 22–23.

it is pragmatic and reflects the way in which the law operates in practice. Compensatory damages are a default award for common law actions, so we consider them first. If damages are inadequate, the court may compel performance, which is why remedies that compel are considered directly after compensation. We then move to the more unusual vindicatory remedies, which seek to recognise the importance of certain rights. Next, we consider remedies that seek to deter, such as the account of profits, which is only exceptionally available at common law. The equitable hierarchical structure is the inverse of this, but it is helpful with a practical book to present the areas of law in a way that maps practice to a degree and gives a clear shape to the law.

In what follows, the functional structure of this book is discussed, along with some theoretical approaches which may be relevant to the remedy or area in question. We have not been able to divide remedies perfectly between these categories. Lord Cairns' Act damages present particular difficulties, as they have been argued to perform multiple functions (including compensation and prevention of unjust enrichment). They can also be seen as a monetarised version of specific relief and are therefore placed with specific performance and injunctions in this book.

One remedy which we discuss in the book does not fit neatly within a functional scheme. Proprietary remedies fulfil more than one function, and there is no general rule for when they will be awarded, so they are considered in a separate chapter, Chapter 11.

Chapters 2, 3, 4, 5 and 6: Compensation for Loss

Chapters 2 and 3 consider the general principles of remedies that seek to compensate for loss. It is necessary to consider compensation at the outset because of its prevalence and importance in private law. Often, a claimant's central concern is that they have lost something because of the defendant's breach. Chapter 2 explores general rules governing the assessment of compensation that are not unique to one cause of action, and which are common at least for common law causes of action. Chapter 3 explores the general rules governing the attribution of responsibility, which are common, at least, to all common law causes of action. Chapters 4, 5, and 6 explore the specific rules for breach of contract, tort, and equitable obligations, respectively.

On a theoretical basis, some scholars, such as Ernest Weinrib, argue that the only legitimate situation in which a court can intervene in a private law dispute is when there has been a gain on the part of one person and a loss at the expense of the other.[40] Weinrib uses the theoretical accounts of Aristotle and Immanuel Kant to define 'loss' and 'gain' in normative terms. The core of private law compensation is said to be corrective justice, with remedies granted by the court to return the parties to equality. The dispute in question must be restricted to a strictly bilateral private transaction. According to this theory, there is no room in the law for remedies that have concerns 'extrinsic' to correcting the plaintiff's loss at the defendant's hands. Remedies which have deterrent or punitive functions are focused on matters outside the claimant's loss (deterrence of other parties in the future, punishing the defendant) and are therefore illegitimate. Weinrib's theories have proved influential in his home jurisdiction of Canada and in some sections of the English private law academy.

Compensatory damages are also favoured, particularly as a remedy for breach of contract, by scholars who take a law-and-economics approach, but for very different reasons from the corrective justice scholars. Richard Posner, an American academic and a former judge, argues that it is societally beneficial to allow a defendant to efficiently breach his contract where he could contract more profitably with a third party other than the claimant.[41] A remedy which compels performance would deter 'efficient breach', but damages do not, because everyone is placed in the optimal position. This theory has proved highly influential in the United States. It has not been influential in other regions of the common law world. In fact, courts in Australia and New Zealand have unequivocally rejected efficient breach theory as a rationale for how the common law of contract and its remedies operate.[42] English courts appear to have ignored it. To a civilian reader, the lack of emphasis on *pacta sunt servanda* ('agreements must be kept') exemplified by efficient breach theory may be startling.

Eric Descheemaeker has suggested, for tort law, that all losses, including those suffered by corporations, ultimately represent a loss of happiness and

---

40 See, eg, Ernest Weinrib, 'The Gains and Losses of Corrective Justice' (1994) 44 Duke LJ 277; Ernest Weinrib, 'Restitutionary Damages as Corrective Justice' (2001) 1 Theo Inq Law 1; Ernest Weinrib, 'Corrective Justice in a Nutshell' (2002) 52 UTLJ 349; Ernest Weinrib, 'Punishment and Disgorgement as Contract Remedies' (2003) 78 Chi-Kent L Rev 55; Ernest Weinrib, *The Idea of Private Law* (2nd edn, OUP 2012); Ernest Weinrib, *Corrective Justice* (OUP 2012).

41 Richard Posner, *Economic Analysis of Law* (9th edn, Aspen 2014) §4.10.

42 *Butler v Countrywide Finance Ltd* [1993] 3 NZLR 623, 635; *Zhu v Treasurer of the State of New South Wales* [2004] HCA 56, (2004) 218 CLR 530 [129]; *Tabcorp Holdings Ltd v Bowen Investments Pty Ltd* [2009] HCA 8, (2009) 236 CLR 272 [13].

that the use of market values for pecuniary loss is a stabilised measure of loss of happiness.[43]

Several scholars (discussed in greater detail below) have advanced theories regarding substitutionary (or substitutive) money awards for various kinds of civil wrong, which are said to be distinguishable from normal compensatory damages for pecuniary loss. While there are differences between these theories, the common core of these analyses is a distinction between compensatory money awards, which are said to compensate for factual and consequential loss caused by a civil wrong, and another type of award, which is said to be a substitute for the fulfilment of the wrongdoer's primary obligation and is not concerned with the compensation of factual loss. Crucially, a substitutionary award is said to be available even if the wrong has caused no factual loss, and it is also said that it is not subject to the rules of remoteness and mitigation.

In the context of breach of contract, we mention the theories of three scholars. Stephen Smith argues that damages reflecting the amount of cost of cure of a breach of contract, as opposed to diminution in value, do not compensate for loss suffered but constitute a form of substitute specific performance. He argues that cost of cure should be available for every breach of contract unless rectification will not be undertaken, or the cost of repair is wholly disproportionate to the value of the loss, or the claimant is seeking the award in bad faith.[44] Robert Stevens argues that substitutionary damages represent the value of the infringed right to performance. Unlike Stephen Smith, he does not see the cost of cure as the necessary measure. Instead, he argues that the difference in value between the performance contracted for and that provided plays a substitutionary role.[45] David Winterton argues that substitutionary damages substitute not for the right to performance but for performance itself. Their measure is generally the minimum cost of substitute performance (repair or replacement) whether or not the plaintiff intends to cure the breach, but where

---

[43] Eric Descheemaeker, 'Pecuniary and Non-Pecuniary Loss: A Reinterpretation' (2022) 138 LQR 79.

[44] Stephen A Smith, *Contract Theory* (OUP 2004) 420–23; Stephen A Smith, 'Substitutionary Damages' in CEF Rickett (ed), *Justifying Private Law Remedies* (Hart 2008) 100–05 (where the theory is advanced for the loss of property or services in general); Stephen A Smith, *Rights, Wrongs, and Injustices* (OUP 2019) 172–76.

[45] Robert Stevens, 'Damages and the Right to Performance: A Golden Victory or Not?' in Jason W Neyers, Richard Bronaugh and Stephen GA Pitel (eds), *Exploring Contract Law* (Hart 2009) 171–74.

that cost is unquantifiable or unreasonable, the price of release from further performance is the next-best substitute for performance.[46]

In the context of tort damages, Robert Stevens argues that substitutionary damages are the next-best substitute for the primary right infringed. These are assessed objectively as at the time of the infringement and are available even if there is no loss to the plaintiff or gain to the defendant. By contrast, consequential loss is assessed subjectively as at the time of judgment, and the recovery of consequential loss is subject to limitations that do not apply to the substitutive award, such as remoteness of loss.[47]

In the context of the misapplication of trust property by a trustee, Steven Elliott and others distinguish two types of money awards. One is an award of 'reparative compensation' for loss caused by the breach of trust. Its measure is the difference between the beneficiary's actual position and the position the beneficiary would have occupied but for the wrong. The other type of award is 'substitutive compensation', which requires the balancing of the account with the trustee's own money where the property cannot be returned in specie. This award is measured by the property's objective value, and is available regardless of whether the beneficiary's overall financial position is diminished or improved by the deprivation of the property.[48]

Each of the substitutionary theories relies primarily upon English cases in which a purportedly compensatory award was made in excess of the actual factual loss suffered by the claimant.

The substitutionary theories have been supported by Edelman J in the High Court of Australia.[49] In *Lewis v Australian Capital Territory*, his Honour distinguished between compensation to rectify a wrongful act and compensation for the consequences of a wrong, and stated that compensation to rectify a wrongful act was available even if no actual loss was suffered.[50] Similarly, in *Moore v Scenic Tours Pty Ltd*, Edelman J distinguished between two kinds of

---

46 David Winterton, 'Money Awards Substituting for Performance' [2012] LMCLQ 446, 450–51; David Winterton, *Money Awards in Contract Law* (Hart 2015).

47 Robert Stevens, *Torts and Rights* (OUP 2007) 60.

48 Steven B Elliott, 'Remoteness Criteria in Equity' (2002) 65 Mod LR 588, 590; Steven B Elliott and Charles Mitchell, 'Remedies for Dishonest Assistance' (2004) 67 Mod LR 16, 23–34; James Edelman and Steven B Elliott, 'Money Remedies against Trustees' (2004) 18 TLI 116, 116–25; Paul Matthews, Charles Mitchell, Jonathan Harris and Sinéad Agnew, *Underhill and Hayton Law Relating to Trusts and Trustees* (20th edn, LexisNexis 2020) [87.7]–[87.11].

49 Prior to his judicial career, James Edelman was a Professor of the Law of Obligations at the University of Oxford.

50 [2020] HCA 26, (2020) 271 CLR 192 [140]–[150].

contractual damages: those based directly on the performance interest (which are not concerned with actual loss); and contractual damages for consequential loss.[51]

Otherwise, the substitutionary theories have not received express judicial approval in the common law world. Moreover, the theories have been criticised; Robert Stevens's theory in particular has been said to conflict with the conventional understanding of damages and the law on mitigation.[52]

More fundamentally, substitutionary theories have been said to fail to justify the award of money in response to the occurrence of a civil wrong irrespective of the consequences of the wrong.[53] They do not explain why the consequences of a wrong cannot be adequately remedied by, for example, compensating loss caused by the wrong or stripping the wrongdoer of profit made through the wrong. Where a civil wrong has not generated any consequences and it is necessary for a court to recognise that a wrong has occurred, this can be done through a declaration by the court or, where available, an award of nominal damages. Indeed, substitutionary theories have been said to fail to account for the availability of nominal damages.[54]

Before moving on from compensation, one final point should be made. While compensation is pivotal to the private law remedial landscape, Birks decried the 'false monopoly of compensation' in private law and argued that one should not be misled into thinking that compensatory remedies are the only remedies available for private law wrongs.[55] The following remedies indicate that there are many different functions for private law remedies.

Chapter 7: Coercive Remedies

Chapter 7 considers specific performance, injunctions and other remedies which compel performance of the primary obligation. A defendant may be either compelled to do a positive act or compelled not to do a specific act. In

---

51 [2020] HCA 17, (2020) 268 CLR 326 [63]–[67].

52 Andrew Burrows, 'Are "Damages on the Wrotham Park Basis" Compensatory, Restitutionary or Neither?' in Djakhongir Saidov and Ralph Cunnington (eds), *Contract Damages: Domestic and International Perspectives* (Hart 2008) 181–83.

53 See Charlie Webb, 'Justifying Damages' in Jason W Neyers, Richard Bronaugh and Stephen GA Pitel (eds), *Exploring Contract Law* (Hart 2009) 167–68.

54 Andrew Burrows, 'Are "Damages on the Wrotham Park Basis" Compensatory, Restitutionary or Neither?' in Djakhongir Saidov and Ralph Cunnington (eds), *Contract Damages: Domestic and International Perspectives* (Hart 2008) 184–85.

55 Peter Birks, 'The Law of Restitution at the End of an Epoch' (1999) 28 UWALR 52, 54.

common law causes of action such as tort and contract, typically, specific relief (namely, specific performance of a contract or an injunction) is awarded only where compensatory damages are inadequate; hence, it makes logical sense to consider this category of remedy after considering compensatory damages.

Chapter 7 also considers monetary awards made in lieu of an injunction pursuant to Lord Cairns' Act as they represent a monetised form of specific relief.

Compelling a defendant to do what they ought to do (or to desist from doing what they ought not to do) is the ultimate vindication of the claimant's primary right. Some rights-based scholars, such as Robert Stevens, argue that tort law can generally be understood as a vindication of the claimant's rights infringed by the defendant, rather than as compensation for foreseeable loss.[56] Other rights-based scholars have extended this theory to other areas of law.[57]

It is useful to consider the extent to which private law operates as a mechanism for vindicating the claimant's rights. Courts are often concerned to award the 'next-best' remedy to the primary right itself; however, they balance this against other considerations. For example, even though compensatory damages for breach of contract represent a less perfect remedy for a failure to perform than specific relief, they are the preferred remedy (as long as they provide an adequate substitute for performance) because they are less intrusive to the defendant.

Similarly, Lord Cairns' Act damages are sometimes awarded in lieu of an injunction or specific performance precisely because it is not appropriate to compel the defendant to do a particular thing, but it is still appropriate that the claimant receive some monetary sum in lieu of the specific relief. However, Lord Cairns' Act damages also have other functions which make them difficult to categorise. They are placed in this section simply because of their kinship with specific relief more generally.

Chapter 8: Vindicatory Remedies

Chapter 8 considers remedies with a vindicatory function, such as 'reasonable fee' awards, self-help remedies, exemplary damages, aggravated damages, apologies, declarations, and nominal damages.

Vindication of rights (in a broad sense) is the overarching aim of all private remedies if we take vindication to mean a making good of, and recognition of, the claimant's rights.[58] For a claimant's rights to be recognised, they must have an adequate remedy. For example, in *Ashby v White*, Holt CJ said:

---

[56] Robert Stevens, *Torts and Rights* (OUP 2007).

[57] See, eg, Ben McFarlane, *The Structure of Property Law* (Hart 2008).

[58] Stephen Smith has argued that this is the only function of damages awards: Stephen A Smith, 'Duties, Liabilities and Damages' (2012) 125 Harv L Rev 1727,

> If the plaintiff has a right, he must of necessity have a means to vindicate and maintain it, and a remedy if he is injured in the exercise or enjoyment of it; and, indeed, it is a vain thing to imagine a right without a remedy; for want of right and want of remedy are reciprocal.[59]

However, it has been said that it is unclear what is meant by 'vindication'.[60] Jason Varuhas has argued for a more specific sense of vindication, where the law attests to, affirms, and reinforces the importance and inherent value of particular interests.[61] He argues that vindication is particularly evident in the torts actionable per se (ie, without the need to prove loss), which protect interests such as bodily integrity,[62] property rights,[63] reputation,[64] economic interests[65] and fair process.[66]

The categorisation of 'reasonable fee' awards had been contested. Now that the United Kingdom Supreme Court has decided in *One Step Support Pty Ltd v Morris-Garner* that 'reasonable fee' awards of various kinds operate to vindicate private law rights,[67] these are included in Chapter 8.

Also included are remedies which allow one to make one's own rights good, such as nominal damages,[68] remedies which seek to punish the defendant, such as exemplary damages,[69] and remedies which seek to assuage the claimant or to recognise the distressing impact of the defendant's conduct on the

---

1728. See also Jason Varuhas, 'The Concept of "Vindication" in the Law of Torts: Rights, Interests and Damages' (2014) 34 OJLS 253, 258.

59 (1703) 2 Ld Raym 938; 92 ER 126, 136. For a more recent expression of a similar sentiment, see *Chester v Afshar* [2004] UKHL 41, [2005] 1 AC 134 [87] (Lord Hope): 'The function of the law is to enable rights to be vindicated and to provide remedies when duties have been breached'.

60 Kit Barker, 'Private and Public: The Mixed Concept of Vindication in Torts and Private Law' in Stephen Pitel, Jason Neyers and Erika Chamberlain (eds), *Tort Law: Challenging Orthodoxy* (Hart 2013) 59.

61 Jason Varuhas, 'The Concept of "Vindication" in the Law of Torts: Rights, Interests and Damages' (2014) 34 OJLS 253, 258.

62 eg, Assault, battery, false imprisonment.

63 eg, Trespass to land, wrongful interference with goods.

64 eg, Defamation.

65 eg, Interference with contractual relations, intimidation, passing off.

66 Misfeasance in public office.

67 [2018] UKSC 20, [2019] AC 649. See also *Turf Club Auto Emporium Pte Ltd v Yeo Boong Hua* [2018] SGCA 44, [2018] 2 SLR 655.

68 Jason Varuhas, 'The Concept of "Vindication" in the Law of Torts: Rights, Interests and Damages' (2014) 34 OJLS 253, 290.

69 ibid.

claimant, such as aggravated damages.[70] All these remedies involve the legal affirmation of the importance and value of certain interests.

Of course, exemplary damages have a clear punitive aspect as well. As noted earlier, generally, punishment is regarded as a matter of criminal law and not private law. As a result, some scholars have argued that considerations of punishment should not be part of private law at all.[71] Ultimately, it seems that exemplary damages are here to stay; the main issues are whether they can be awarded for causes of action other than tort, and the extent to which they are available in tort itself, particularly in English law.

Chapter 9: Disgorgement of Gain

Chapter 9 considers accounts of profit and disgorgement. In equity, the account of profit is the remedy of choice where a defaulting fiduciary has made a profit as a result of their breach, and it is available subject to discretionary considerations. By contrast, gain-based awards have not been openly available for common law wrongs and are generally available only if compensatory damages are inadequate and specific relief is unavailable. We consider the availability of allowances for work and skill, and the operation of discretionary factors and bars to relief.

The primary rationale of gain-based remedies has been identified as deterrence and prophylaxis of breach by a range of scholars.[72] Deterrence does not operate to resolve the precise dispute in question. Instead, deterrence considers the future conduct of the specific defendant (specific deterrence) and the future

---

70 ibid 284.

71 Ernest Weinrib, 'Punishment and Disgorgement as Contract Remedies' (2003) 78 Chi-Kent L Rev 55, 86–87; Allan Beever, 'The Structure of Aggravated and Exemplary Damages' (2003) 23 OJLS 87; Stephen Todd, 'A New Zealand Perspective on Exemplary Damages' (2004) 33 CLWR 255. Cf Robert Stevens, *Torts and Rights* (OUP 2007) 85; James Edelman, *Gain-Based Damages – Contract, Tort, Equity and Intellectual Property* (Hart 2002) 19; Ralph Cunnington, 'Should Punitive Damages be Part of the Judicial Arsenal in Contract Cases?' (2006) 26 LS 369.

72 James Edelman, *Gain-Based Damages – Contract, Tort, Equity and Intellectual Property* (Hart 2002) 83–86; Irit Samet, 'Guarding the Fiduciary's Conscience – A Justification of a Stringent Profit-Stripping Rule' (2008) 28 OJLS 763; Sarah Worthington, 'Reconsidering Disgorgement for Wrongs' (1999) 62 Mod LR 218; Matthew Conaglen, *Fiduciary Loyalty: Protecting the Due Performance of Non-Fiduciary Duties* (Hart 2010); Robert Cooter and Bradley Freedman, 'The Fiduciary Relationship: Its Economic Character and Legal Consequences' (1991) 66 NYULR 1045; Peter Devonshire, *Account of Profits* (Thomson Reuters 2013) 58–59.

conduct of other potential defendants (general deterrence) and responds to those possibilities. By stripping the defendant of his gain (or part of his gain), the defendant (and other potential wrongdoers) will be deterred from engaging in similar conduct in the future. Deterrence and efficient encouragement of adherence to the law appeals to law-and-economics scholars.

Chapter 10: Restitution and Giving Back

Chapter 10 considers personal remedies for unjust enrichment. It also considers the defences to a claim for restitutionary remedies, and the overlap between unjust enrichment law and contract law.

These remedies have at their heart the rationale of prevention of unjust enrichment. Unjust enrichment has come to prominence in recent years with a blossoming of restitutionary scholars in England and Wales. These scholars have identified the action for unjust enrichment as an important cause of action in private law concealed by notions such as 'quasi-contract'. They see its proper recognition as reshaping private law generally.

It can be difficult to distinguish between the cause of action and the remedy. Chapter 10 briefly examines the nature of the restitutionary causes of action in order to explain the remedies available.

Chapter 10 also considers rescission of contracts and other transfers, including common law and equitable rescission, the requirement of restitutio in integrum, election, partial rescission, bars to rescission and the possible proprietary consequences of rescission.

Rescission follows unjust enrichment because there is a kinship between unjust enrichment and the way in which rescission operates to unwind transfers, particularly given the presence of vitiating factors. An understanding of unjust enrichment informs an understanding of rescission, because both involve vitiating factors leading to the reversal of transactions. Even though rescission is placed under the broader rationale of restitution and giving back, some aspects of rescission (particularly common law rescission) arguably have a self-help aspect.

Chapter 11: Proprietary Remedies

Chapter 11 considers proprietary remedies. There are several forms of proprietary remedy (the constructive trust, the proprietary power, and the lien), but courts have not traditionally exercised the choice between these remedies in a principled manner.

We consider proprietary remedies in the contexts of equitable wrongdoing, perfection, unconscionability, unjust enrichment and rescission, linking rescission to the discussion in Chapter 10.

Chapter 11 notes the operation of discretionary factors and bars to relief in this area because proprietary remedies are by and large creatures of equity. Finally, Chapter 11 discusses the need for more defined and certain criteria for the availability of proprietary remedies.

CONCLUSION

In writing this book, we have tried to ensure that our discussion of private law remedies has a logical flow, and that recurring issues are dealt with clearly in each chapter. As in our previous writings on this topic, our intention is to create a coherent functional narrative of remedies which explains the law to a variety of audiences ranging from the newcomer to the specialist.

2. Assessment of compensation: general principles

INTRODUCTION

The victim of a civil wrong may generally claim compensation for the resulting loss. When the courts pronounce rules as to the assessment of such compensation, they often do so in respect of a particular cause of action. But there are many commonalities. This chapter examines the rules that are common to at least contract and tort.

THE COMPENSATORY PRINCIPLE AND THE IDENTIFICATION OF THE WRONG

The assessment of compensation for a civil wrong involves a comparison of the claimant's actual position with the position the claimant would have been in had the wrong not occurred. This comparison must be made as at a particular date, which may be the date of the wrong, the date of the trial, or a date in between those. The date of assessment will be discussed later in this chapter.

In order to determine the claimant's hypothetical position in the absence of the wrong, the court needs to go back to the time just before the wrong and remove the wrong in that hypothetical world. This requires the identification of the wrong the defendant committed. It is obvious in most cases, but care must be taken in some circumstances.

In particular, where the defendant made a false statement of fact which induced the claimant to enter into a contract with the defendant, the question arises whether the hypothetical world with which the actual world is to be compared is a world in which the statement was not made or a world in which the statement was true. In other words, the question is whether the claimant is compensated for the loss suffered as a result of changing her position in reliance on the statement (reliance loss) or for the loss she has suffered as a result of not being in the position she expected to be in on the basis of the represented facts (expectation loss).[1] Expectation loss can be compensated only where the mere fact that the statement was false constitutes a wrong, which requires that the defendant gave a contractual guarantee that the statement be true.[2] Otherwise, only the making of the statement may be a wrong (the tort of deceit or negligence if the defendant acted with the required degree of culpability), and only reliance loss may be compensated.[3]

Once the comparison of the claimant's actual and hypothetical positions has been undertaken, the compensatory principle comes into play. It comprises two rules, each of which has exceptions: all losses attributable to the wrong must be compensated, and the amount of damages must not exceed the amount of those losses.[4]

The first rule requires the compensation of all losses attributable to the wrong.[5] The comparison of the claimant's actual and hypothetical positions has identified those losses that would not have been suffered had the wrong not occurred. However, in order to be recoverable, such a loss must, in a normative exercise, be attributable to the wrong. An item of loss is not recoverable where it is regarded as too remote or where it has been suffered only because the claimant unreasonably failed to avoid it. Those matters will be discussed in Chapter 3.

Some heads of loss are not recoverable in a particular cause of action, at least as a general rule.[6] For example, as explained in Chapter 4, non-pecuniary loss is not generally recoverable in an action for breach of contract, although there are considerable exceptions. In the tort of negligence, the exclusion of

---

1 The expectation measure is better for the claimant where the contract would have been a profitable one had the defendant's statement been true; otherwise, the reliance measure is better for the claimant. See GH Treitel, 'Damages for Deceit' (1969) 32 Mod LR 556, 558–59.

2 This depends upon the parties' intention objectively ascertained: *Heilbut, Symons & Co v Buckleton* [1913] AC 30.

3 eg, *McConnel v Wright* [1903] 1 Ch 546, 554–55 (Lord Collins MR); *Khakshouri v Jimenez* [2017] EWHC 3392 (QB) [138]–[139].

4 'The court in applying the compensatory principle is charged with avoiding under-compensation and also over-compensation. Justice is not achieved if a claimant receives less or more than its actual loss': *Sainsbury's Supermarkets Ltd v Visa Europe Services LLC* [2020] UKSC 24, [2020] 4 All ER 807 [217]. See generally David McLauchlan, 'Some Damages Dilemmas in Private Law' (2021) 52 VUWLR 875.

5 See *Robinson v Harman* (1848) 1 Exch 850, 855 (for contract); *Livingstone v Rawyards Coal Co* (1880) 5 App Cas 25, 39 (for tort).

6 It has been said that the recoverability of a head of loss must be established before the compensatory principle is applied: *Amaca Pty Ltd v Latz* [2018] HCA 22, (2018) 264 CLR 505 [41] (Kiefel CJ and Keane J).

compensation for a particular type of damage is often achieved by denying a duty of care, thus preventing a civil wrong from arising in the first place.[7] For example, in the absence of physical injury, there is no liability in negligence for mental harm short of a recognised psychiatric illness.[8]

The second rule of the compensatory principle prohibits over-compensation. This rule too has exceptions, in three respects. First, over-compensation is accepted where the only alternative on the facts is under-compensation.[9] Second, while the determination of the loss is generally subjective in that it considers the claimant's individual circumstances and not the typical claimant, some individual circumstances may be ignored for pragmatic reasons,[10] creating the potential for over-compensation. For example, as explained in Chapters 4 and 5, the cost of having certain property repaired may be awarded to a claimant who may not intend to have the property repaired. Finally, the second rule requires that account be taken of benefits that the claimant received as a result of the wrong. However, as discussed later in this chapter, some types of benefit will be ignored for policy reasons.

Since both parts of the compensatory principle have exceptions, Fell and Field suggest an alternative to the actual loss account: 'a claimant will be compensated for the loss for which it is *reasonable* to require the defendant to compensate them (whether or not the claimant actually suffered that loss'.[11] Fell and Field are correct in stating that their account of the law 'squarely acknowledges the normative dimension to questions of compensation'.[12] But their account is not less complex than the actual loss account, as the determination of what loss a defendant can reasonably be required to compensate ultimately involves an application of the two parts of the compensatory principle and their exceptions.

---

7 See Donal Nolan, 'Damage in the English Law of Negligence' (2013) 4 JETL 259, 264.

8 eg, *Alcock v Chief Constable of South Yorkshire Police* [1992] 1 AC 310, 401, 416; *Page v Smith* [1996] AC 155, 167. In cases of wrongful death, people who had a particular relationship with the deceased can claim a fixed sum as bereavement damages under the Fatal Accidents Act 1976, s 1A.

9 *Swift v Carpenter* [2020] EWCA Civ 1295, [2021] QB 339 [206].

10 For a critical discussion of the courts' tendency to disregard subjective features, see Eric Descheemaeker, 'The Standardisation of Tort Damages' (2021) 84 Mod LR 2.

11 Andrew Fell and Iain Field, 'The Actual Loss Illusion' (2024) 83 Camb LJ 301, 330 (emphasis in original).

12 ibid.

LOSSES AND BENEFITS

Pecuniary and Non-Pecuniary Loss

Loss may be defined as an undesired consequence.[13] It may be pecuniary or non-pecuniary.[14]

A pecuniary loss exists where the claimant's financial position is worse than it would have been had the wrong not occurred. The claimant may have incurred expenses, for example, for medical treatment or for the repair of property, or not received a financial benefit that would have been received had the wrong not occurred. It is not always straightforward to ascertain the amount of a pecuniary loss. But once the amount has been established, it generally provides the amount of damages. Special considerations apply where, while the amount of an alleged pecuniary loss is established, there is uncertainty as to whether the loss would have been avoided had the wrong not occurred; this will be discussed later in this chapter.

A civil wrong may cause undesired consequences that are not of a financial nature, at least where the victim is a natural person. For example, physical injury may cause pain, defamation may cause loss of reputation, and some wrongs may cause anxiety, disappointment, and distress. Such an 'unpleasant emotional reaction'[15] must be distinguished from psychiatric harm, which is pathological and constitutes personal injury.

Mental distress resulting from injury to a protected interest can often be compensated in tort.[16] When damages for mental distress are recoverable in tort, 'the type of mental harm that may be compensated is not limited to distress in its narrow sense of anxiety or anguish. Other unpleasant emotional reactions such as sorrow, disappointment, shame, humiliation, anger,

---

[13] James Edelman, 'The Meaning of Loss and Enrichment' in Robert Chambers, Charles Mitchell and James Penner (eds), *Philosophical Foundations of the Law of Unjust Enrichment* (OUP 2009) 212–16.

[14] For the interesting suggestion (for tort law) that all losses, including those suffered by corporations, are ultimately losses of happiness, and that the use of market values for pecuniary loss is a stabilised measure of loss of happiness, see Eric Descheemaeker, 'Pecuniary and Non-Pecuniary Loss: A Reinterpretation' (2022) 138 LQR 79.

[15] Peter Handford, *Tort Liability for Mental Harm* (3rd edn, LBC 2017) 140.

[16] *George v Cannell* [2024] UKSC 19, [2024] 3 WLR 153 [100]–[101]. For a discussion, see Eric Descheemaeker, 'Rationalising Recovery for Emotional Harm in Tort Law' (2018) 134 LQR 602.

annoyance and indignation are included within its scope'.[17] By contrast, non-pecuniary loss cannot be compensated in equity except in actions for breach of confidence. Compensation for non-pecuniary loss is also generally barred in contract, but there are considerable exceptions.[18] The details are discussed separately for each type of wrong in Chapters 4–6.

Two objections might be raised against an award of damages in respect of non-pecuniary detriments. The first is that no amount of money can place the claimant in the position as if the detriment had not been suffered. It is not possible to buy a substitute in the market, as can be done for many pecuniary detriments. However, people are willing to spend money to be free from unpleasant emotions, and the law does recognise that non-pecuniary detriments constitute loss.[19] While 'compensation' may 'not [be] a wholly apt expression',[20] an award of money is 'the best that can be done'.[21]

Another objection that might be raised is that it is difficult to express non-pecuniary detriments in monetary terms. Reasonable minds may differ significantly about the appropriate sum to be awarded for a particular episode of pain or distress. However, this difficulty should not stand in the way of giving effect to the compensatory principle.[22] When it is difficult to ascertain the amount of pecuniary loss, the courts do not deny compensation but do their best to estimate the loss. What is important is that like cases are treated alike.[23] It is therefore desirable to develop some tariff for non-pecuniary losses, which has been achieved in personal injury cases.[24]

---

[17] *George v Cannell* [2024] UKSC 19, [2024] 3 WLR 153 [91] (Lord Leggatt JSC, with whom Lord Hodge DPSC and Lord Richards JSC agreed).

[18] In *Simmons v Castle* [2012] EWCA Civ 1288, [2013] 1 WLR 1239, it was laid down that the amount of damages for non-pecuniary loss in any civil claim was to increase by 10% from 1 April 2013.

[19] cf Peter Birks, 'Harassment and Hubris: The Right to an Equality of Respect' (1997) 32 Irish Jurist (NS) 1, 25 fn 82: 'Mental distress is harm, but to say that it is a "loss" courts the danger of its being understood as a compensable pecuniary detriment, which it is not; and the fact that it is not then begins to suggest that it is not the proper subject of any award at all.'

[20] James Goudkamp and Donal Nolan, *Winfield and Jolowicz on Tort* (20th edn, Sweet & Maxwell 2020) [23–010].

[21] *Parry v Cleaver* [1970] AC 1, 22 (Lord Morris). Sometimes, an apology by the defendant may be an effective remedy. But an apology cannot be ordered by a court. Apologies are discussed in Ch 8.

[22] *Owners of the Steamship Mediana v Owners, Master and Crew of the Lightship Comet (The Mediana)* [1900] AC 113, 116–17 (Lord Halsbury LC).

[23] *Milner v Carnival plc* [2010] EWCA Civ 389 [38].

[24] See Judicial College, *Guidelines for the Assessment of General Damages in Personal Injury Cases* (17th edn, OUP 2024).

A corporation can suffer loss of reputation, but not pain or distress.[25] In *Crédit Suisse v Beegas Nominees Ltd*,[26] where the premises rented by a bank were in a state of disrepair, Lindsay J awarded the bank £40,000 for 'the inconvenience suffered by staff and customers' as a result of the defect. Subsequently, in *Electricity Supply Nominees Ltd v National Magazine Co Ltd*,[27] Judge Hicks QC rejected the notion that a corporation can suffer inconvenience or recover damages for the discomfort and distress suffered by its staff and customers, but he held that a corporate lessee can recover damages for diminution in value of the tenancy.

Cost of Cure and Diminution in Value

There are generally two ways of determining the existence and amount of financial loss when a physical state of affairs is not as it would be without the wrong. Examples include negligent damage to a chattel or land and the failure to carry out work on a chattel or land in accordance with contractual specifications. Where it is possible to rectify the problem (ie, to create the physical state of affairs that would exist had the wrong not occurred), the claimant could engage a third party to carry out the relevant work. But the third party will charge a fee. This will be called the cost of cure.

The cost of cure could be regarded as the loss suffered by the claimant. It is the cost of *physically* placing the claimant in the position as if the wrong had not occurred. The fact that a third party has paid for or done the repairs without charging the claimant does not remove an entitlement to cost-of-cure damages otherwise existing, if the third party intended to benefit the claimant and not the defendant.[28] Where an award of cost of cure is made, the claimant is not obliged to actually have the cure effected (unless the claimant has given an undertaking to the court to that effect). Claimants can spend their damages in any way they like.[29] However, the claimant's intention (at the time of the

---

25 *Regus (UK) Ltd v Epcot Solutions Ltd* [2008] EWCA Civ 361, [2009] 1 All ER (Comm) 586 [31]–[32]; *Ventouris v Trevor Rex Mountain, The Italia Express (No 2)* [1992] 2 Lloyd's Rep 281, 293; *Electricity Supply Nominees Ltd v National Magazine Co Ltd* [1999] 1 EGLR 130, 134.

26 [1994] 4 All ER 803, 828.

27 [1999] 1 EGLR 130, 134–35. For circumstances where a party to a contract can recover loss suffered by a non-party, see Ch 4.

28 *The Endeavour* (1890) 6 Asp MC 511, 512; *Jones v Stroud District Council* [1986] 1 WLR 1141, 1150–51; *Burdis v Livsey* [2002] EWCA Civ 510, [2003] QB 36 [96]-[102].

29 *Ruxley Electronics and Construction Ltd v Forsyth* [1996] AC 344, 359, 372.

trial) to have the cure effected is sometimes a prerequisite of an award of cost of cure.

Alternatively, the actual value of the chattel or land could be compared with the value it would have if the wrong had not occurred. If there is no difference, it could be said that no loss has been suffered. If the actual value is below the hypothetical value, the difference (usually called diminution in value) could be regarded as the loss. An award of diminution in value would place the claimant *financially* in the position as if the wrong had not occurred.

Diminution in value should not generally be awarded where it exceeds the cost of cure. An award of the cost of cure enables the claimant to have the rectification work carried out and thus increase the value of the property. Any diminution in value that will remain after rectification work has been carried out should be added to the cost of cure.[30]

However, the cost of cure usually exceeds the diminution in value. Sometimes, there is no diminution in value at all. Suppose that a new building is not constructed in accordance with the contractual specifications, but it is otherwise free from defects, and the deviation does not affect the value of the land. In those circumstances, a legal system needs to decide whether it protects the claimant's interest in being physically placed in the position as if the wrong had not occurred, or whether it limits the claimant to being financially placed in the position as if the wrong had not occurred. The details will be discussed separately for contract and tort in Chapters 4 and 5.

Different scholars subscribe to different conceptualisations of awards of cost of cure and diminution in value. Robert Stevens argues that an award of diminution in value is a substitute for the right to performance and not concerned with the compensation of loss, whereas the cost of cure represents consequential loss and is recoverable only subject to limitations such as mitigation and remoteness.[31] Conversely, other scholars maintain that a cost-of-cure award for breach of contract gives effect to the performance interest, whereas an award of diminution in value merely compensates consequential loss.[32] The courts regard both types of award as being concerned with the compensation of loss,

---

30 *Harrison v Shepherd Homes Ltd* [2011] EWHC 1811 (TCC), (2011) 27 Const LJ 709 [264].

31 Robert Stevens, 'Damages and the Right to Performance: A *Golden Victory* or Not?' in Jason W Neyers, Richard Bronaugh and Stephen GA Pitel (eds), *Exploring Contract Law* (Hart 2009) 190–92.

32 Brian Coote, 'Contract Damages, *Ruxley*, and the Performance Interest' (1997) 56 Camb LJ 537, 557; Stephen A Smith, 'Substitutionary Damages' in Charles EF Rickett (ed), *Justifying Private Law Remedies* (Hart 2008) 93; Charlie Webb, 'Performance and Compensation: An Analysis of Contract Damages and Contractual Obligation' (2006) 26 OJLS 41, 48–49, 57–61; David Winterton,

and we take the view (for contract law) that both types of award seek to provide an adequate monetary substitute for performance.[33]

New For Old

The repair or replacement of damaged or defective property may place the claimant in a better position than without the wrong. Suppose that the defendant has negligently damaged the claimant's tractor, which was six years old and was expected to last for another four years. The claimant has bought a brand-new tractor of the same make and model as the destroyed one. The new tractor is expected to last for ten years. If the full cost of the new tractor is awarded as damages, the claimant will be better off than without the defendant's wrongdoing.

In those circumstances, it must first be determined whether the repair or replacement that has been undertaken (or is intended to be undertaken) can properly be regarded as no more than the remedying of the consequences of the wrong or whether it constitutes an upgrade going beyond a merely remedial measure. In the latter case, the claimant's decision to undertake an upgrade constitutes an intervening act,[34] and the costs and benefits of it are on the claimant's own account.[35] However, the claimant remains entitled to an award in the amount of the cost of merely remedying the consequences of the wrong.[36]

A good illustration is the Australian case *Gagner Pty Ltd v Canturi Corporation Pty Ltd*.[37] Water escaping from the defendant's restaurant

---

'Money Awards Substituting for Performance' [2012] LMCLQ 446, 450–51; David Winterton, *Money Awards in Contract Law* (Hart 2015).

[33] See Katy Barnett, 'Great Expectations: A Dissection of Expectation Damages in Contract in Australia and England' (2016) 33 JCL 1.

[34] See *Skandia Property (UK) Ltd v Thames Water Utilities Ltd* [1999] BLR 338, 344. Intervening acts are discussed in Ch 3.

[35] See, in the insurance context, *Endurance Corporate Capital Ltd v Sartex Quilts & Textiles Ltd* [2020] EWCA Civ 308, [2020] 2 All ER (Comm) 1050 [90], adopted for the damages context in *Taylor v Jones* [2024] EWCA Civ 170, (2024) 213 Con LR 1 [60].

[36] See *Harbutt's 'Plasticine' Ltd v Wayne Tank and Pump Co Ltd* [1970] 1 QB 447, 468, 473, 476; *Scott Wilson Kirkpatrick & Partners v Ministry of Defence* [2000] BLR 20 [28]–[33]; *McGlinn v Waltham Contractors Ltd (No 3)* [2007] EWHC 149 (TCC), (2007) 111 Con LR 1 [845].

[37] [2009] NSWCA 413, (2009) 262 ALR 691. Another example from Australia is *State Transport Authority v Twiteco Pty Ltd* (1984) Aust Torts Reports 80–596: A 70-year-old railway bridge was substantially damaged. Its owner decided to install a new model capable of bearing heavier trains and requiring less maintenance. The owner was awarded the cost of reconstructing the old bridge.

damaged 10 percent of the floor in the plaintiff's jewellery store on the floor below. A repair of the damaged part of the floor would have taken 10 days. The plaintiff decided to refurbish the whole floor, which required the jewellery store to be closed for 29 days. The plaintiff was awarded the cost of repairing only the damaged part of the floor and loss of business for 10 days.

It is not always easy to determine whether a particular measure constitutes an upgrade or can still be regarded as no more than the remedying of the consequences of the wrong.[38] In particular, where an old building has been destroyed and needs to be rebuilt, the materials and construction techniques of today will be superior to those prevailing when the old building was erected. But this does not by itself constitute a voluntary upgrade, as there is no choice but to use today's materials and construction techniques. Current building regulations may even require this. An upgrade may exist where a different technique not required by building regulations is used because it has become best practice.[39]

Where the repair or replacement can properly be regarded as the remedying of the consequences of the wrong and not an upgrade, the assessment of damages starts with the cost of the repair or replacement. However, as discussed in the next section, benefits flowing from an action of the claimant aimed at mitigating loss are usually taken into account in the assessment of damages. Thus, where the repair or replacement of damaged or defective property has yielded a cash benefit for the claimant (ie, the claimant has received money or saved an expenditure), this must usually be taken into account.[40] In *British Westinghouse Electric and Manufacturing Co Ltd v Underground Electric Railways Company of London Ltd*,[41] where defective turbines were replaced with turbines of a new generation that consumed much less coal, the saved cost of coal was deducted from the cost of the new turbines.

The principle of deducting benefits resulting from a mitigating measure becomes problematic where the benefit is abstract in that the claimant merely has a new item instead of an old one without deriving any cash benefits from

---

38 The claimant is not required to adopt a measure that is not sufficiently reliable: *Moore v DER Ltd* [1971] 1 WLR 1476 (the owner of an 18-month-old Rover that had been destroyed was entitled to buy a new Rover rather than an 18-month-old Rover as he needed a reliable car for professional purposes).

39 *Scott Wilson Kirkpatrick & Partners v Ministry of Defence* [2000] BLR 20 [28]–[33]. See, in the insurance context, *Tonkin v UK Insurance Ltd* [2006] EWHC 1120 (TCC), [2006] 2 All ER (Comm) 550 [357]–[358], [361].

40 *Voaden v Champion* [2002] EWCA Civ 89, [2002] 1 Lloyd's Rep 623 [85]; *Taylor v Jones* [2024] EWCA Civ 170, (2024) 213 Con LR 1 [60].

41 [1912] AC 673. The case is discussed in the next section.

this fact. If the full cost of the remedial measure is not awarded, the claimant will, in cash terms, be undercompensated.

After initially making a 'new for old' deduction,[42] the English courts have in more recent times rejected such a deduction, first in cases of tortious damage to ships,[43] then also in cases of tortious damage to real property,[44] damage to a chattel in breach of contract,[45] and damage to real property in breach of contract.[46] In a case in which a breach of contract resulted in the destruction of a factory whose owner claimed damages for the cost of having it rebuilt, Widgery LJ explained that he did not accept 'that the plaintiffs must give credit under the heading of "betterment" for the fact that their new factory is modern in design and materials. To do so would be the equivalent of forcing the plaintiffs to invest their money in the modernising of their plant which might be highly inconvenient for them'.[47]

Some judges and commentators in other Commonwealth jurisdictions have suggested that a betterment discount should be made but that the claimant should be compensated for the cost of the capital investment, ie, the value of the use of the capital or the cost of borrowing it.[48] However, this approach is still problematic as the defendant's wrong forced the claimant to make a capital investment that the claimant did not intend to make at that time or at all. The modern English approach is preferable.

---

42 *Lukin v Godsall* (1795) Peake Add Cases 15; 170 ER 178; *Hide v Thornborough* (1846) 2 C & K 250; 175 ER 103; *Yates v Dunster* (1855) 11 Ex 15; 156 ER 726.

43 *The Gazelle* (1844) 2 W Rob 279; 166 ER 759; *The Pactolus* (1856) Swab 173; 166 ER 1079.

44 *Hollebone v Midhurst and Fernhurst Builders* [1968] 1 Lloyd's Rep 38; *Haysman v Mrs Rogers Films Ltd* [2008] EWHC 2494 (QB); *Taylor v Jones* [2024] EWCA Civ 170, (2024) 213 Con LR 1 [60].

45 *Bacon v Cooper (Metals) Ltd* [1982] 1 All ER 397 (rotor of machine for fragmenting steel).

46 *Harbutt's 'Plasticine' Ltd v Wayne Tank and Pump Co Ltd* [1970] 1 QB 447, 468, 473, 476.

47 ibid 473.

48 *James Street Hardware and Furniture Co Ltd v Spizziri* (1987) 62 OR (2d) 385, 404; *J & B Caldwell Ltd v Logan House Retirement Home Ltd* [1999] 2 NZLR 99, 107; Catherine Penhallurick, 'The Principle of "Betterment" in Damages for Contract and Tort' (2002) 22 Aust Bar Rev 109, 117–18; Stephen M Waddams, *The Law of Damages* (5th edn, Canada Law Book 2012) [1.2790].

Benefits Flowing from Post-Wrong Actions of the Claimant

A wrong may cause the claimant to take an action that generates a benefit for the claimant that the claimant would not have received without that action. Such a benefit is taken into account in the assessment of damages unless it is collateral.

A benefit is usually taken into account where the purpose of the claimant's action was to mitigate loss. This applies even where it would have been reasonable for the claimant not to take that action. This principle is usually regarded as one of the rules of mitigation, ie, that there is no recovery for avoided loss. However, it can also be seen as part of the principle of compensation that advantages that are sufficiently connected to the wrong are deducted from the damages for consequential loss.[49] While the defendant bears the legal onus on this issue,[50] the claimant may have an evidential onus.[51]

The leading authority for the deductibility of benefits arising from a mitigating action is *British Westinghouse Electric and Manufacturing Co Ltd v Underground Electric Railways Company of London Ltd*.[52] The defendant supplied steam turbines to the plaintiff railway company and guaranteed that they would consume a certain amount of coal. The turbines consumed much more coal than guaranteed. The plaintiff used the turbines for a few years but then replaced them with different turbines which, because of technological advances, were much more efficient than the defendant's turbines, even if the latter had conformed to the contract. The House of Lords held that, in calculating the plaintiff's damages, the benefits derived by the plaintiff from the superiority of the substitute turbines had to be deducted from the cost of installing them. Viscount Haldane LC, speaking for the House, said that 'when in the course of his business [the plaintiff] has taken action arising out of the transaction, which action has diminished his loss, the effect in actual diminution of the loss he has suffered may be taken into account even though there was no duty on him to act'.[53]

The same rule applies in tort. An example is *Bacciottini v Gotelee and Goldsmith (a firm)*.[54] In May 2007, the claimants purchased a property for development. They would not have done so but for their solicitors' negligent failure to advise them of a planning restriction preventing residential use.

---

[49] See *Talacko v Talacko* [2021] HCA 15, (2021) 272 CLR 478 [57].

[50] *Sainsbury's Supermarkets Ltd v Visa Europe Services LLC* [2020] UKSC 24, [2020] 4 All ER 807 [211].

[51] ibid [216].

[52] [1912] AC 673.

[53] ibid 689.

[54] [2016] EWCA Civ 170, [2016] 4 WLR 98.

Subsequently, the claimants procured the removal of the restriction by the local authority. They claimed damages in the amount of £100,000 as the difference between the actual value of the property in May 2007 and the value it would have had in May 2007 if the planning restriction had not then existed. The Court of Appeal upheld the trial judge's decision to award only £250 as the cost of the application for the removal of the planning restriction. The Court emphasised that the outcome was independent of whether a failure by the claimants to apply for a removal of the planning restriction would have constituted a failure to mitigate loss,[55] although the Court took the view that it would have been.[56]

Where the action of the claimant that generated the benefit was not aimed at mitigating loss, the benefit is taken into account only if it can be properly attributed to the wrong. The demarcation line is difficult to define with precision. It is not sufficient that the benefit would not have accrued but for the wrong.[57] The courts have made a distinction between a benefit that is 'part of a continuous transaction' of which the wrong was the inception,[58] and a benefit that has arisen from an independent decision of the claimant[59] and is *res inter alios acta*.[60] A benefit resulting from a post-wrong action of the claimant may be ignored where the action had the potential to produce a loss and the defendant would not have been liable for such loss.[61]

The last factor was important in *Fulton Shipping Inc of Panama v Globalia Business Travel SAU of Spain*.[62] A charterparty that was due to end in 2009

---

[55] ibid [60].

[56] ibid [59].

[57] *Lavarack v Woods of Colchester Ltd* [1967] 1 QB 278, 290, 300; *Assetco plc v Grant Thornton UK LLP* [2019] EWHC 150 (Comm), [2019] Bus LR 2291 [895].

[58] eg, *Hussey v Eels* [1990] 2 QB 227 (CA) 241 (Mustill LJ speaking for the court); *Needler Financial Services v Taber* [2002] 3 All ER 501 [24] (Sir Andrew Morritt VC).

[59] eg, *Koch Marine Inc v D'Amica Societa di Navigazione arl (The Elena d'Amico)* [1980] 1 Lloyd's Rep 75, 89; *Thai Airways International Public Co Ltd v KI Holdings Co Ltd* [2015] EWHC 1250 (Comm), [2016] 1 All ER (Comm) 675 [46].

[60] *British Westinghouse Electric and Manufacturing Co Ltd v Underground Electric Railways Company of London Ltd* [1912] AC 673, 691; *Swynson Ltd v Lowick Rose LLP* [2017] UKSC 32, [2018] AC 313 [11]. The Latin phrase *res inter alios acta* means 'a thing done between others' and denotes that the transaction does not concern the defendant.

[61] *AKAS Jamal v Moolla Dawood, Sons & Co* [1916] 1 AC 175, 179; *Assetco plc v Grant Thornton UK LLP* [2019] EWHC 150 (Comm), [2019] Bus LR 2291 [904].

[62] [2017] UKSC 43, [2017] 1 WLR 2581.

was repudiated by the charterer in 2007. Since there was no available chartering market at the time, the owner sold the vessel for about US$23.8m. The owner claimed damages for the loss of profit during the remaining two years of the charterparty, amounting to around €7.5m. In 2009, the value of the vessel was only US$7m. Thus, the owner had received a substantial benefit from being able to sell the vessel two years earlier. The Supreme Court held that this benefit was to be ignored in the assessment of damages. The Court observed that the market value of the vessel could have risen between 2007 and 2009, in which case the owner could not have claimed for that difference; for the same reason, the owner did not need to account for the benefit gained by the fall in the market value.[63] The decision has been criticised on the ground that the owner had no real choice but to sell the vessel.[64] However, as the Supreme Court pointed out, this would only mean that the repudiation was the factual cause of the sale; it does not follow that the sale is to be attributed to the repudiation.[65]

An uncontroversial example of a collateral benefit is a betting or lottery win that a victim of fraud made with money received from the fraudster.[66] In *Tuke v Hood*, where this example was given, the Court of Appeal also stated that where the defendant fraudulently induced the claimant to exchange one luxury car for another (unfavourably for the claimant) and the value of both cars has since risen, the increase in value of the car the claimant received is to be ignored even if the increase in value of the car the claimant lost is taken into account.[67] This is unconvincing. If the increase in value of the car lost is not regarded as too remote (which is convincing), the increase in value of the car received cannot be collateral.[68]

---

63 ibid [33].

64 David McLauchlan and Andrew Summers, 'Mitigation and Causation of Benefits: Fulton v Globalia (The New Flamenco)' [2018] LMCLQ 171. See also Andrew Burrows, *Remedies for Torts, Breach of Contract, and Equitable Wrongs* (4th edn, OUP 2019) 151–52.

65 [2017] UKSC 43, [2017] 1 WLR 2581 [33]. See also *Dominion Mosaics and Tile Co Ltd v Trafalgar Trucking Co Ltd* [1990] 2 All ER 246, 252, where the destruction of the plaintiff's business premises forced the plaintiff to acquire new premises, which rose in value. The increase in value was ignored in the assessment of damages.

66 *Tuke v Hood* [2022] EWCA Civ 23, [2022] QB 659 [47].

67 ibid [37].

68 The Court held that the time value of money received by a victim of fraud is ignored in the assessment of damages. For a discussion, see Sirko Harder, 'The Valuation Date of Benefits Received by a Victim of Fraud' (2024) 3 Stetson Bus LR 35.

Other Benefits Arising From a Wrong

The previous section concerns the benefits resulting from a post-wrong action of the claimant. A wrong may generate benefits for the claimant in other ways too. For example, the claimant may receive payments under an insurance contract or assistance from third parties.

'The general rule is that where the claimant has received some benefit attributable to the events which caused his loss, it must be taken into account in assessing damages, unless it is collateral.'[69] Thus, where a fire negligently destroyed a disused building on a site that its owner had already intended to redevelop, the saved cost of clearing the site was taken into account in the assessment of damages.[70]

The exception for collateral benefits is crucial. A benefit does not reduce the amount of damages simply because it would not have accrued but for the wrong. The deductibility of a benefit involves a normative judgement based on policy considerations.

Payments under an insurance contract taken out by the claimant[71] are ignored in the assessment of damages.[72] In many cases, the insurer will be subrogated to the insured's claim against the wrongdoer.[73] In those cases, the claimant would be undercompensated if the insurance payment were deducted from the damages. But insurance payments are ignored in the assessment of damages even where there is no subrogation.[74] The rule has been justified on the ground that the defendant should not benefit from the thrift and foresight of the claimant.[75] It has been objected that a wrongdoer benefits from the injured person's thrift and foresight where it prevents the injury in the first place (by wearing a protective helmet, for example).[76] However, the non-deductibility of

---

69 *Titua International Ltd v De Villiers Surveyors Ltd* [2017] UKSC 77, [2017] 1 WLR 4627 [12] (Lord Sumption JSC speaking for the Court).

70 *CR Taylor (Wholesale) Ltd v Hepworths Ltd* [1977] 1 WLR 659, 670.

71 Payments under an insurance contract taken out by the claimant's employer are deducted from the amount of damages: *Gaca v Pirelli General plc* [2004] EWCA Civ 373, [2004] 1 WLR 2683.

72 eg, *Bradburn v Great Western Railway Co* (1874) LR 10 Ex 1; *Hodgson v Trapp* [1989] AC 807, 819.

73 Subrogation is standard for indemnity insurance, where the insurer promises to indemnify the insured against a particular item of loss. Subrogation is not standard for contingency insurance, where the insurer promises to pay an agreed amount on the happening of a specified event.

74 *Hunt v Severs* [1994] 2 AC 350, 358.

75 *Browning v War Office* [1963] 1 QB 750, 763 (Donovan LJ).

76 Kenneth D Cooper-Stephenson, *Personal Injury Damages in Canada* (2nd edn, Carswell 1996) 579.

insurance payments gives people an incentive to cater for certain contingencies themselves, reducing the need for social security benefits.

The deductibility of payments made by a third party to the claimant in response to the wrong depends upon whether the third party intended to benefit the wrongdoer. Charitable gifts are not deducted as they are not intended to benefit the wrongdoer.[77] Similarly, the claimant can claim the commercial cost of repairing property damaged by the defendant even though a third party has gratuitously carried out the repair,[78] or paid for the repair.[79] 'It would be revolting to the ordinary man's sense of justice, and therefore contrary to public policy, that the sufferer should have his damages reduced so that he would gain nothing from the benevolence of his friends or relations or of the public at large, and that the only gainer would be the wrongdoer.'[80]

A payment from one third party to another, which ultimately reached the claimant, was present in *Swynson Ltd v Lowick Rose LLP*.[81] The claimant, a lending company, made three loans to a borrower, relying on a negligent report prepared by the defendant firm of accountants. When the borrower defaulted, Mr Hunt, who owned and controlled the claimant, lent money to the borrower, which (as intended by Mr Hunt) was used to repay two of the three loans given by the claimant. The Supreme Court held that this payment was not collateral and therefore reduced the claimant's loss, for three reasons: the transaction discharged the very liability whose existence represented the claimant's loss; the agreements between the claimant and the borrower and between Mr Hunt and the borrower were distinct transactions, each of which was made for valuable consideration; Mr Hunt's loan was not an act of mitigation because it was not an act of the claimant and was not attributable to the defendant's breach of duty.[82]

---

77 eg, *Parry v Cleaver* [1970] AC 1, 14, 31, 39, 50; *Hodgson v Trapp* [1989] AC 807, 819–20; *Hunt v Severs* [1994] 2 AC 350, 358.

78 *Powercor Australia Ltd v Thomas* [2012] VSCA 87, (2012) 43 VR 220 [74]–[91].

79 ibid [42]; *Jones v Stroud District Council* [1986] 1 WLR 1141, 1150–51.

80 *Parry v Cleaver* [1970] AC 1, 14 (Lord Reid).

81 [2017] UKSC 32, [2018] AC 313.

82 ibid [13].

THE RESOLUTION OF UNCERTAINTY AND LOSS OF A CHANCE

Introduction

In order to obtain substantial damages, the claimant must satisfy the court as to the fact that loss has been suffered and the quantum of that loss. This depends upon what has happened (past loss) or will happen (future loss), and it also depends upon what would have happened had the wrong not occurred. While the claimant bears the onus of proof, the law does not require absolute certainty as to the relevant events.[83] Absolute certainty rarely exists. 'The restoration by way of compensation is therefore accomplished to a large extent by the exercise of a sound imagination and the practice of the broad axe.'[84] Where it is clear that some loss has been suffered, the court cannot deny substantial damages only because the assessment of the loss is difficult.[85] The court must make the best attempt to evaluate the various chances involved unless they amount to no more than remote speculation.[86]

Often, the existence and amount of loss depend upon the occurrence or non-occurrence of a particular event or a limited number of particular events.[87] It may be a past event, a future event, or a hypothetical event. Lack of knowledge may create uncertainty as to the occurrence of a particular event. Such epistemic uncertainty can be resolved in two different ways. One possibility is to determine the matter on the balance of probabilities.[88] The court makes a finding as to whether the occurrence or the non-occurrence of the event is more likely, and the more likely scenario forms the basis of assessing loss. It is all or nothing. The other possibility is to calculate damages in proportion to the degree of probability of the event's occurrence. The higher the probability that an event favouring the claimant would have occurred but for the defendant's

---

83 *Parabola Investments Ltd v Browallia Cal Ltd* [2010] EWCA Civ 486, [2011] QB 477 [22].

84 *Watson, Laidlaw & Co Ltd v Pott, Cassels & Williamson* (1914) SC (HL) 18, 29–30 (Lord Shaw).

85 *Chaplin v Hicks* [1911] 2 KB 786, 792 (Vaughan Williams LJ).

86 *Parabola Investments Ltd v Browallia Cal Ltd* [2010] EWCA Civ 486, [2011] QB 477 [23]; *Vasiliou v Hajigeorgiou* [2010] EWCA Civ 1475 [25].

87 eg, the formation or continuation of a contract between the claimant and a particular third party, as in *Jackson v Royal Bank of Scotland* [2005] UKHL 3, [2005] 1 WLR 377.

88 For an insightful discussion of the civil standard of proof, see George Leggatt, 'Black Marbles, Blue Buses and Yellow Submarines: An Essay on the Civil Standard and Burden of Proof' (2024) 140 LQR 570.

wrong, the higher the amount of damages; the lower the probability, the lower the amount. It is a sliding scale.

'In determining what did happen in the past a court decides on the balance of probabilities. Anything that is more probable than not it treats as certain.'[89] By contrast, the degree-of-probability approach applies to future events. As Lord Reid observed in *Davies v Taylor*: 'You can prove that a past event happened, but you cannot prove that a future event will happen and I do not think that the law is so foolish as to suppose that you can. All that you can do is to evaluate the chance.'[90]

For hypothetical events, it is necessary to distinguish various categories of case, at least at common law.[91] Uncertainty as to whether personal injury would still have been suffered without the wrong is always determined on the balance of probabilities.[92] By contrast, the degree-of-probability approach applies where it is uncertain whether a particular item of consequential loss suffered by a personal injury claimant would still have been suffered had the personal injury not been sustained.[93] In cases of pure economic loss, uncertainty as to what the claimant would have done is resolved on the balance of probabilities, the degree-of-probability approach applies to hypothetical conduct of third parties, and both approaches have been applied to hypothetical lawful conduct of the defendant. The details will be discussed below.

Where the degree-of-probability approach applies to particular hypothetical events, the claimant is said to recover for the loss of a chance. It has been said that 'the law treats the loss of a chance of a favourable outcome

---

89 *Mallett v McMonagle* [1970] AC 166, 176 (Lord Diplock). See also *Davies v Taylor* [1974] AC 207, 213 (Lord Reid); *Allied Maples Group Ltd v Simmons & Simmons (a firm)* [1995] 1 WLR 1602, 1610; *Milton Keynes Borough Council v Nulty* [2013] EWCA Civ 15, [2013] 1 WLR 1183 [37].

90 [1974] AC 207, 213. See also *Mallett v McMonagle* [1970] AC 166, 176 (Lord Diplock); *Allied Maples Group Ltd v Simmons & Simmons (a firm)* [1995] 1 WLR 1602, 1610.

91 In Australia, these rules have also been applied to misleading or deceptive conduct under statute (the leading case being *Sellars v Adelaide Petroleum NL* (1994) 179 CLR 332) and – in some cases (*Ramsay v BigTinCan Pty Ltd* [2014] NSWCA 324, (2014) 101 ACSR 415 [71], [123]; *Anderson v Canaccord Genuity Financial Ltd* [2023] NSWCA 294 [347]–[413]) – to equitable compensation.

92 The same should apply to uncertainty as to whether particular property would still have been damaged without the wrong; see Andrew Burrows, *Remedies for Torts, Breach of Contract, and Equitable Wrongs* (4th edn, OUP 2019) 61 fn 12.

93 The same applies to uncertainty as to whether a particular item of loss would still have been suffered had the claimant's property not been damaged or destroyed: *Blue Circle Industries plc v Ministry of Defence* [1999] Ch 289, 315.

as compensatable damage in itself'.[94] This conceptualisation can reconcile the application of the degree-of-probability approach with the requirement of factual causation to be established on the balance of probabilities.[95] All that the claimant must establish on the balance of probabilities to prove factual causation is that the defendant's wrong caused the claimant to lose a real and substantial chance (even if less than even) of avoiding a loss or making a profit; the valuation of the chance is a question for the quantification of loss.[96] The degree-of-probability approach does not as such apply in the quantification process. Where it is clear that the claimant has lost some business, the court will estimate the lost profit; there is no room for a further discount to reflect the chance that no profit might have been made.[97]

The concept of loss of a chance as a discrete item of loss may give the impression that the claimant has a choice between claiming damages for the ultimate loss (ie, the loss that would be identified if the occurrence of an event favourable to the claimant is regarded as certain) and the loss of the chance of avoiding the ultimate loss. It might be thought that where the chance is 50 percent or less, the claimant may choose to claim damages for the loss of the chance, and where the chance is more than 50 percent, the claimant may claim damages for the ultimate loss which can be established on the balance of probabilities. But such a rule could not be justified,[98] and it is not the law. Where the degree-of-probability approach applies to the type of uncertain event, it applies to chances above and below 50 percent.[99]

Pure Economic Loss

In cases of pure economic loss (ie, cases not involving damage to the claimant's property or injury to the claimant's person), there is a distinction between

---

[94] *Barker v Chorus UK Ltd* [2006] UKHL 20, [2006] 2 AC 572 [36] (Lord Hoffmann).

[95] See James Edelman, *McGregor on Damages* (21st edn, Sweet & Maxwell 2021) [10-048]. Factual causation is considered in Ch 3.

[96] *Wellesley Partners LLP v Withers LLP* [2015] EWCA Civ 1146, [2016] Ch 529 [99]; *McGill v Sports and Entertainment Media Group* [2016] EWCA Civ 1063, [2017] 1 WLR 989 [60].

[97] *Owners of the Ship Front Ace v Owners of the Vicky 1* [2008] EWCA Civ 101, [2008] 2 All ER (Comm) 42 [71]–[73]; *Vasiliou v Hajigeorgiou* [2010] EWCA Civ 1475 [22]–[28], [44].

[98] Carolyn Sappideen et al, *Fleming's The Law of Torts* (11th edn, Lawbook Co 2024) [9.170].

[99] For an in-depth discussion of whether probabilistic liability is ever justified, see Sandy Steel, *Proof of Causation in Tort Law* (CUP 2015) 339–65.

hypothetical conduct of the claimant and hypothetical conduct of a third party: the balance-of-probabilities approach applies to the former, whereas the degree-of-probability approach applies to the latter.[100] This distinction was first pronounced by the Court of Appeal in *Allied Maples Group Ltd v Simmons & Simmons (a firm)*.[101] The Supreme Court confirmed the distinction in *Perry v Raleys Solicitors*,[102] which – like *Allied Maples* – involved negligence on the part of solicitors. Lord Briggs JSC, speaking for the Court, stated:

> To the extent (if at all) that the question whether the client would have been better off depends upon what the client would have done upon receipt of competent advice, this must be proved by the claimant upon the balance of probabilities. To the extent that the supposed beneficial outcome depends upon what others would have done, this depends upon a loss of chance evaluation.[103]

A good illustration of these rules is *Wellesley Partners LLP v Withers LLP*.[104] The claimant headhunting firm instructed the defendant solicitors to draft an agreement with new partners, including an investor. The investor was to have the option to withdraw half its capital after 42 months. As a result of the defendants' negligence in drafting the agreement, the investor had the option to withdraw half its capital *within* the first 41 months. The investor exercised that option. The claimant sought damages for the loss of mandates from Nomura, a US bank. The claimant contended that it would have used the money from the investor to open an office in the US and would then have obtained mandates from Nomura. The Court of Appeal stated that the claimant needed to show, on the balance of probabilities, that but for the defendants' negligence, it would have opened an office in the US; once that was shown, the Court would evaluate the chance of Nomura awarding mandates to the claimant.[105]

While the distinction between hypothetical conduct of the claimant and hypothetical conduct of a third party is now firmly established, nothing was said in the leading cases on the rationale of the distinction. In other cases and in the literature, the rationale has been seen in the consideration that claimants can be expected to adduce persuasive evidence about their own hypothetical conduct, whereas it may be difficult to adduce evidence about the hypothetical

---

[100] The degree-of-probability approach probably applies to the question of whether the claimant would have passed a particular exam; see *Lillington v Ministry of Defence* [2015] EWCA Civ 775 [4].

[101] [1995] 1 WLR 1602, 1610–14.

[102] [2019] UKSC 5, [2020] AC 352.

[103] ibid [20].

[104] [2015] EWCA Civ 1146, [2016] Ch 529.

[105] ibid [100].

conduct of a third party who may not be before the court.[106] However, the degree-of-probability approach is applied to the hypothetical conduct even of a third party who has given evidence,[107] and the claimant may be unable to give evidence or may give self-serving evidence.[108]

There are two other types of hypothetical events: conduct of the defendant and a natural event. Hypothetical conduct of the defendant is considered separately below. There is little authority on natural events; an evaluation of chances seems more appropriate.

Where there is only one event to which the degree-of-probability approach applies, the damages are usually calculated by multiplying the chance of the event occurring by the amount of loss that would have been avoided (or the amount of profit that would have been made) had the event occurred. It makes no difference if hypothetical conduct of the claimant is also relevant. This will be established on the balance of probabilities and regarded as certain. The court is not required to, and usually will not, assign a particular percentage figure to that chance.

Where there are two dependent events to which the degree-of-probability approach applies, the chances of each event occurring must be multiplied, and the result multiplied with the amount of loss that would have been avoided had both events occurred. In *Phillips & Co v Whatley*, where negligence on the part of legal practitioners caused the claimant to become unable to bring a damages claim against a former employer which had become insolvent, there was a 70 percent chance that the claim would have been successful but only a 40 percent chance that the former employer's insurer would have satisfied such a judgment (because the insurer was informed too late of the claim), resulting in an overall lost chance of 28 percent.[109] In some other cases involving the loss of a claim, the courts multiplied the chances of establishing separate prerequisites of the claim, for example, breach of duty and causation.[110]

---

106 *Gregg v Scott* [2002] EWCA Civ 1471, [2003] Lloyd's Rep Med 105 [71] (Mance LJ); *Palliser Ltd v Fate Ltd* [2019] EWHC 43 (QB) [27]; James Edelman, *McGregor on Damages* (21st edn, Sweet & Maxwell 2021) [10–065].

107 *Wellesley Partners LLP v Withers LLP* [2015] EWCA Civ 1146, [2016] Ch 529 [112]–[122]; *Tom Hoskins plc v EMW Law (a firm)* [2010] EWHC 479 (Ch) [126].

108 Lord Neuberger, 'Loss of a Chance and Causation' (2008) 24 Prof Negl 206, 213.

109 [2007] UKPC 28, [2008] Lloyd's Rep IR 111 [47]. See also *Talisman Property Co (UK) Ltd v Norton Rose* [2006] EWCA Civ 1104, [2006] 3 EGLR 59 [57]–[58].

110 *Sharpe v Addison* [2003] EWCA Civ 1189, [2004] PNLR 23 [34]–[35]; *Haithwaite v Thomson Snell & Passmore* [2009] EWHC 647 (QB), [2010] Lloyd's

Where there are more than two events to which the degree-of-probability approach applies, it may be too artificial to assign a percentage figure to the chance of each event occurring and then multiply those figures.[111] Instead, the court may simply assign an overall percentage to the whole set of events.[112]

Personal Injury

In cases of personal injury, two categories of uncertainty must be distinguished.

The court evaluates chances where it is uncertain whether a particular item of loss resulting from personal injury would still have been suffered if the personal injury had not been sustained. Damages in the amount of a proportion of the loss were awarded, for example, where it was uncertain whether and when the claimant would have suffered a similar injury as a result of a pre-existing condition,[113] or whether the claimant would have achieved a particular significant career advancement.[114]

The uncertainty just mentioned must be distinguished from uncertainty as to whether the personal injury would still have been sustained had the wrong not occurred. A majority of jurisdictions in the United States have embraced the concept of a lost chance of avoiding personal injury and permit a proportionate damages award,[115] the most prominent case being *Matsuyama v*

Rep PN 98 [131]–[133].

[111] This was, however, done in *Joyce v Bowman Law Ltd* [2010] EWHC 251 (Ch), [2010] PNLR 22 [111]–[115].

[112] *Tom Hoskins plc v EMW Law (a firm)* [2010] EWHC 479 (Ch), [2010] ECC 20 [133]–[135]; *Di Matteo v Marcus Lee & Co* [2010] EWHC 312 (QB) [9], [10], [61], [67].

[113] eg, *Smithurst v Sealant Construction Services Ltd* [2011] EWCA Civ 1277, [2012] Med LR 258 [9]–[13]. A prominent Australian case illustrating this rule is *Malec v JC Hutton Pty Ltd* (1990) 169 CLR 638. See also *Gregg v Scott* [2005] UKHL 2, [2005] 2 AC 176 [11] (Lord Hoffmann). Cf *Hotson v East Berkshire Health Authority* [1987] AC 750, 793 (Lord Ackner).

[114] eg, *Doyle v Wallace* [1998] PIQR Q146, Q148-Q150; *Langford v Hebran* [2001] EWCA Civ 361, [2001] PIQR Q13; *Smith v Collett* [2009] EWCA Civ 583. Where there was no prospect of significant career advancement, the court takes the amount of lost earnings in the expected profession and applies a discount for the vicissitudes of life; see, eg, *Herring v Ministry of Defence* [2003] EWCA Civ 528, [2004] 1 All ER 44.

[115] For a list of cases from 26 states, see Jed Kurzban, Lauren Gallagher, and Samira Arabnia, 'It is Time for Florida Courts to Revisit Gooding' (2017) 91 Florida Bar J 9, fn 8. Irish law seems to be the same; see *Philp v Ryan* [2004] IESC 105, [2004] 4 IR 241.

Birnbaum.[116] The opposite approach of resolving the uncertainty on the balance of probabilities and rejecting the concept of a lost chance in this context has been adopted by the Supreme Court of Canada,[117] the High Court of Australia,[118] and also by the House of Lords in two cases.

In *Hotson v East Berkshire Health Authority*,[119] the plaintiff, then aged 13, fell from a tree and suffered an acute traumatic fracture of the left femoral epiphysis. He was not correctly treated in hospital for five days and suffered avascular necrosis. The trial judge found that there was a 75 percent chance that the boy would have developed the avascular necrosis from the fall anyway and awarded damages for the loss of a 25 percent chance of full recovery. The House of Lords dismissed the claim on the ground that the plaintiff was required to establish on the balance of probabilities that the delay in treatment had at least materially contributed to the avascular necrosis, and he had not discharged that onus considering the trial judge's findings.

The House of Lords affirmed the rule, albeit only by a bare majority, in *Gregg v Scott*.[120] As a result of the defendant doctor's negligent failure to refer the claimant to the hospital for examination, the claimant's cancer was discovered nine months later than it would otherwise have been, allowing it to spread to other organs. It was found that the defendant's negligence reduced the claimant's chance of surviving for more than ten years from 42 to 25 percent. The House of Lords, by a bare majority, upheld the rejection of the claim for negligence. The majority refused to conceptualise the claimant's loss as the lost chance of a favourable outcome, and insisted that factual causation had to be established by proving on the balance of probabilities that the claimant would have survived for more than ten years had he been referred to the hospital earlier.

Hotson and *Gregg* involved a claim in negligence (as opposed to contract), and the negligence occurred in the course of medical treatment. However, neither factor limits the scope of the rule laid down in those cases. It applies to

---

[116] 890 NE 2d 819 (Mass, 2008).

[117] *Laferrière v Lawson* [1991] 1 SCR 541. This was an appeal from Quebec, but the rule has been followed in common law provinces; see *Cottrelle v Gerrard* (2003) 67 OR (3d) 737.

[118] *Tabet v Gett* [2010] HCA 12, (2010) 240 CLR 537.

[119] [1987] AC 750.

[120] [2005] UKHL 2, [2005] 2 AC 176.

personal injury beyond medical negligence,[121] and it should apply to claims in contract unless the contract provides otherwise.[122]

In *Hotson* and *Gregg*, the uncertain event was a natural event, namely developments within the claimant's body. The same approach applies to human conduct. Uncertainty as to whether an employee who suffered a work injury would have worn protective equipment had it been provided by the employer is resolved on the balance of probabilities.[123] This may seem unremarkable as the balance-of-probability approach applies to hypothetical conduct of the claimant even in cases of pure economic loss. Crucially, where it is uncertain whether personal injury would have been suffered, the balance-of-probability approach also applies to hypothetical conduct of a third party.[124] Three decisions of the Court of Appeal illustrate this.

In *Wright v Cambridge Medical Group*,[125] the Court of Appeal resolved on the balance of probabilities the uncertainty as to the treatment a hospital would have chosen to administer to the claimant if the defendant general practitioner had referred the claimant to that hospital.[126] The Court observed that while the decision by the House of Lords in *Gregg* did not strictly exclude a loss of chance approach in the circumstances present in *Wright*, it was for the Supreme Court to expand the loss of chance doctrine into the realm of clinical negligence.[127] In *Vaile v London Borough of Havering*,[128] where the claimant

---

121 *Gregg v Scott* [2005] UKHL 2, [2005] 2 AC 176 [177] (Lord Phillips), [192] (Baroness Hale) ('personal injury').

122 Andrew Burrows, 'Comparing Compensatory Damages in Tort and Contract: Some Problematic Issues' in Simone Degeling, James Edelman and James Goudcamp (eds), *Torts in Commercial Law* (LBC 2011) 383; Clare McKay, 'Concurrent Liability in Claims for Loss of Chance of a Better Medical Outcome' (2012) 20 Torts LJ 29, 48–59

123 *McWilliams v Sir William Arrol & Co Ltd* [1962] 1 WLR 295, 306–07, 309; *Allied Maples Group Ltd v Simmons & Simmons* [1995] 1 WLR 1602, 1610 (Stuart-Smith LJ); *Gregg v Scott* [2005] UKHL 2, [2005] 2 AC 176 [11] (Lord Hoffmann); *Sanderson v Hull* [2008] EWCA Civ 1211, [2009] PIQR P7 [56]–[62].

124 It also seems to apply to hypothetical lawful conduct of the defendant; see *Barnett v Chelsea and Kensington Hospital Management Committee* [1969] 1 QB 428, 439; *Phethean-Hubble v Coles* [2012] EWCA Civ 349, [2012] RTR 31 [47]–[50].

125 [2011] EWCA Civ 669, [2013] QB 312 [82]-[84], [91], [129].

126 The defendant contended that the hospital would have negligently treated the claimant. Lord Neuberger MR rejected this plea on the ground that a wrongdoer cannot rely on the hypothetical wrong of a third party: ibid [56]–[57].

127 ibid [82]–[84], [93]. See also *Barnett v Chelsea and Kensington Hospital Management Committee* [1969] 1 QB 428, 439.

128 [2011] EWCA Civ 246, [2011] ELR 274 [32], [39].

teacher was assaulted by an autistic pupil and it was not certain that protective measures taken by the defendant school would have prevented the assault, the Court of Appeal held the school liable for the entire loss on the ground that it was probable that protective measures would have prevented the assault. In *Cunningham v Rochdale MBC*,[129] where a teacher sued his employer for negligently failing to protect him against a second assault by the same pupil, the Court of Appeal rejected the claim on the ground that the teacher had failed to prove on the balance of probabilities that the measures the school ought to have taken after the first assault would have prevented the student from committing the second assault.

The unavailability of substantial damages for the loss of a less-than-even chance of avoiding personal injury has attracted criticism.[130] The minority judges in *Gregg v Scott* argued that the law fails to provide a remedy for a breach of duty.[131] But this does not explain why the law ought to provide a remedy where it is more likely than not that the defendant's breach of duty made no difference. Furthermore, if the degree-of-probability approach applied to uncertainty as to whether personal injury would have been sustained, it would apply to more-than-even chances as well as less-than-even chances.[132] It is rarely certain that personal injury would have been avoided, and many claimants who currently recover their entire loss would suffer a deduction. The rule laid down in *Hotson* and *Gregg* does conflict with the rule that a material increase in risk may establish factual causation even if one of the alternative causes is a non-wrongful event. However, as explained in Chapter 3, this last rule is difficult to justify in any event.

Others have argued that the distinction between personal injury and pure economic loss is not justifiable.[133] Indeed, in cases of delayed diagnosis of a medical condition, there are often statistics available as to the progress of the

---

129 [2021] EWCA Civ 1719, [2022] ELR 217 [42].

130 eg, Liang Shi Wei and Jeremy Low Kee Yang, 'Recognising Lost Chances in Tort' [2014] Sing J Leg Stud 98; Chen Meng Lam, 'Revisiting Loss of Chance in Medical Negligence: Employing Public Policy Positively as Justification' (2020) 36 Prof Negl 105.

131 [2005] UKHL 2, [2005] 2 AC 176 [4], [25] (Lord Nicholls), [106] (Lord Hope).

132 *Hotson v East Berkshire Health Authority* [1987] AC 750, 783, 793; *Gregg v Scott* [2005] UKHL 2, [2005] 2 AC 176 [221]–[225] (Baroness Hale).

133 James Norton, 'Treating Chance Consistently: Recasting the Approach to Causation and Damage in Negligence' (2019) 42 MULR 954; James O'Hara, 'Loss of Chance as Damage in Negligence' (2020) 26 TLJ 73. For a discussion of arguments pro and con, see James Edelman, 'Loss of a Chance' (2013) 21 TLJ 1.

condition and the survival rate, as was the case in *Gregg v Scott*.[134] While those statistics cannot show whether the individual claimant would have conformed to a trend or been an exception to it, they are often the best indicator of the diminution of the claimant's prospects of recovery.[135] Such statistics do not exist for human conduct, which is usually the uncertain event in cases of pure economic loss.

The distinction between personal injury and pure economic loss has been defended on two grounds. First, Lord Hoffmann in *Gregg v Scott* argued that the chance in cases of financial loss can be characterised as an item of property, like a lottery ticket.[136] This is not convincing. Usually, the chance is personal to the claimant and not transferable. You may be able to sell a lottery ticket, but you cannot sell, for example, the chance that a particular third party enters into a contract with you.

Secondly, Helen Reece seeks to justify the distinction between personal injury and pure economic loss by referencing the difference between deterministic and indeterministic cases. The loss of chance concept only applies to indeterministic situations. The uncertain event in cases of pure economic loss is human conduct, which is indeterministic. By contrast, personal injury cases are deterministic. They involve a past event. For example, whether the plaintiff in *Hotson* would have avoided avascular necrosis if he had been treated immediately depended upon the number of blood vessels left intact by the fall.[137] This theory cannot explain why uncertainty as to what the claimant has done is always resolved on the balance of probabilities, or why uncertainty regarding any human conduct is resolved on the balance of probabilities where it is uncertain whether personal injury would have been sustained without the wrong.

The distinction made by English law is not one between deterministic and indeterministic cases, or between human conduct and natural events, but between damage (in the sense of an interference with the claimant's interest) and loss (in the sense of an adverse consequence of an interference with the

---

134 See also *Schembri v Marshall* [2020] EWCA Civ 358, [2020] PIQR P16.

135 *Gregg v Scott* [2005] UKHL 2, [2005] 2 AC 176 [27]–[33] (Lord Nicholls).

136 [2005] UKHL 2, [2005] 2 AC 176 [83]. See also Andrew Burrows, 'Comparing Compensatory Damages in Tort and Contract: Some Problematic Issues' in Simone Degeling, James Edelman and James Goudkamp (eds), *Torts in Commercial Law* (LBC 2011) 384.

137 Helen Reece, 'Losses of Chances in the Law' (1996) 59 Mod LR 188, approvingly cited in *Gregg v Scott* [2005] UKHL 2, [2005] 2 AC 176 [79] (Lord Hoffmann). For a similar distinction between objective chances and illusory epistemic chances, see James Norton, 'Treating Chance Consistently: Recasting the Approach to Causation and Damage in Negligence' (2019) 42 MULR 954.

claimant's interest).[138] Uncertainty as to damage is resolved on the balance of probabilities whereas chances are evaluated when loss is uncertain. In personal injury cases, different approaches apply to the questions of whether personal injury (ie, damage) would have been suffered and whether consequential loss would have been suffered. In cases of pure economic loss, damage and loss collapse into each other. The loss is the damage. Chances are evaluated even where it is uncertain whether any loss would have been suffered without the wrong.

The distinction between damage and loss can be justified. Loss, even of the non-pecuniary variety, needs to be expressed in money terms in the process of calculating damages. It lends itself to an evaluation of chances. But the interference with the claimant's interest, which may or may not generate loss, is a different matter. It lends itself to a binary approach.[139]

Hypothetical Lawful Conduct of the Defendant

Sometimes, if the defendant had not committed the wrong, it would have been open to the defendant to take a particular action (not being wrongful) that would have led to the claimant suffering the same loss as that resulting from the wrong.[140] But it may be uncertain whether the defendant would in fact have taken this action.

Before examining the law's approaches concerning such uncertainty, it is important to note that the defendant's hypothetical opportunity to inflict the same loss in a non-wrongful manner does not negate the existence of a wrong where proof of loss is not required for actionability, thus permitting an award of at least nominal damages at common law. A breach of contract or fiduciary duty is present even though the wrongdoer could have inflicted the resulting loss in a non-wrongful manner. The same applies to torts actionable per se, as demonstrated by *R (Lumba) v Secretary of State for the Home Department*.[141]

---

[138] This distinction was alluded to in *Gregg v Scott* [2005] UKHL 2, [2005] 2 AC 176 [220] (Baroness Hale).

[139] For a similar argument, see Andrew Burrows, 'Uncertainty about Uncertainty: Damages for Loss of a Chance' [2008] J Pers Inj L 31, 42.

[140] For a discussion of the scenario where there were two possible non-wrongful actions by the defendant and only one of them would have led to the same loss, see Maytal Gilboa, 'Multiple Reasonable Behaviours Cases: The Problem of Causal Underdetermination in Tort Law' (2019) 25 Legal Theory 77.

[141] [2011] UKSC 12, [2012] 1 AC 245. The rules laid down in that case were adopted, on similar facts, in *Lewis v Australian Capital Territory* [2020] HCA 26, (2020) 271 CLR 192. For criticism, see Eric Descheemaeker, 'Against Normative Damages' (2023) 20 Curr Leg Prob 1, 33–35.

On release from prison in England, the claimant immigrants were detained by the Home Office, pending deportation. There was a published policy concerning the circumstances in which immigrants were detained. However, the Home Office applied an unpublished policy of a near blanket ban on release pending deportation. The trial judge and the Court of Appeal dismissed the claim for false imprisonment on the ground that the claimants would have been detained even under the published policy. Before the Supreme Court, it was conceded that the application of the unpublished policy to the claimants had been unlawful. The Supreme Court held that the action for false imprisonment was not precluded by the fact that the claimants could have been detained lawfully.

However, a majority in the Supreme Court held that the claimants were only entitled to nominal damages as they had suffered no loss.[142] This demonstrates that hypothetical lawful conduct of the defendant, while not negating the existence of a wrong actionable per se, does affect the assessment of substantial damages.[143] An example from contract law is *Golden Strait Corporation v Nippon Yusen Kubishika Kaisha (The 'Golden Victory')*.[144] In breach of contract, the charterer of a ship redelivered it in December 2001. The owner claimed damages in the amount of the difference between the contractual hire rate and the market rate between that date and December 2005, which was the earliest date for contractual redelivery. However, if the charterer had not repudiated the contract, it could and would have terminated the contract on the outbreak of the second Gulf War in March 2003, which the charterer would have been entitled to do under a war clause in the contract. A majority in the House of Lords held that the owner could not recover the loss of the contract hire after March 2003.

A defendant's hypothetical opportunity to inflict particular loss in a non-wrongful manner may affect the claimant's recovery for that loss in three different ways. First, it may be irrebuttably presumed that the defendant would have taken the non-wrongful action had the wrongful action not been taken,

---

142 The majority also rejected an award of 'vindicatory damages'; this will be discussed in Ch 8. Exemplary damages were available in principle, but the prerequisites for their award were not satisfied by the facts.

143 Thus, damages for nuisance by way of dust and noise must reflect only the dust and noise above the permissible limit: *Andreae v Selfridge & Co Ltd* [1938] Ch 1, 10–11.

144 [2007] UKHL 12, [2007] 2 AC 353. The decision was affirmed in *Bunge SA v Nidera BV* [2015] UKSC 43, [2015] 3 All ER 1082. For criticism, see Michael Mustill, 'The Golden Victory – Some Reflections' (2008) 124 LQR 569.

thus excluding recovery in all cases.[145] Secondly, it may be required that the defendant would in fact have taken the non-wrongful action, and uncertainty in that respect may be resolved on the balance of probabilities (all or nothing).[146] Finally, the court could award an amount of damages that is proportionate to the degree of probability that the defendant would have taken the non-wrongful action.[147]

In both *Lumba* and *The Golden Victory*, it was unnecessary to choose among the three approaches, as it was certain that the defendant would have taken the non-wrongful action had it not taken the wrongful action. Such certainty was not present in many other cases, and each of the three approaches has found judicial support.

In some cases, it was simply assumed that the defendant would have taken the course of action most detrimental to the claimant.[148] A facet of that principle is the 'least burdensome' rule in contract law:

> The principle is that where a contract-breaker has a choice of methods of performance, damages will be assessed on the basis of the contract-breaker's minimum legal obligation – the method which would have been least onerous to the contract-breaker in the sense that non-compliance with it attracts the lowest measure of damages.[149]

The rule has been applied in many cases.[150] The English Court of Appeal has expressed differing views on whether the assessment of damages for wrongful dismissal should take account of bonuses which the employee would have been expected to receive had the employment continued but which the employer

---

145 eg, *Withers v General Theatre Corp Ltd* [1933] 2 KB 536, 548–51 (Scrutton LJ).

146 eg, ibid 553 (Greer LJ).

147 eg, ibid 556 (Romer LJ).

148 eg, *Hamilton v Open Window Bakery Ltd* [2004] SCC 9, [2004] 1 SCR 303; *Paper Reclaim Ltd v Aotearoa International Ltd* [2007] NZSC 26, [2007] 3 NZLR 169 [25].

149 *Gumland Property Holdings Pty Ltd v Duffy Bros Fruit Market (Campbelltown) Pty Ltd* [2008] HCA 10, (2008) 234 CLR 237 [89] (Gleeson CJ, Kirby, Heydon, Crennan and Kiefel JJ). The rule goes back to *Cockburn v Alexander* (1848) 6 CB 791, 814 (Maule J): 'where there are several ways in which the contract might be performed, that mode is adopted which is the least profitable to the plaintiff, and the least burthensome to the defendant'.

150 eg, *Re Thornett & Fehr* [1921] 1 KB 219; 229–30; *Spiliada Maritime Corp v Louis Dreyfus Corp* [1983] Com LR 268; *Johnson Matthey Bankers Ltd v State Trading Corporation of India Ltd* [1984] 1 Lloyd's Rep 427.

would not have been obliged to pay. In *Lavarack v Woods of Colchester Ltd*,[151] the Court (Lord Denning MR dissenting) applied the 'least burdensome' rule, which amounts to an irrebuttable presumption that the bonuses would not have been paid. In *Horkulak v Cantor Fitzgerald International*,[152] the Court held that the prospect of bonuses should be reflected in the amount of damages. Most recently, in *Mackenzie v AA Ltd*,[153] the Court reaffirmed the applicability of the 'least burdensome' rule.

In a second line of cases, the court determined what the defendant would in fact have done in the absence of the wrong, and resolved uncertainty in that respect on the balance of probabilities.[154] This approach has been taken particularly in cases in which the defendant had a discretion as to the manner of performance.[155] Three cases illustrate this. In *Abrahams v Herbert Reiach Ltd*,[156] a firm of publishers promised to publish certain articles as a book. They had discretion as to the form and price of the book and the number of copies printed. They failed to publish the book at all. The Court of Appeal held that damages were to be calculated by reference to the likely number of copies that would have been printed and not the smallest number that could be described as a publication.[157]

In *Lion Nathan Ltd v CC Bottlers Ltd*,[158] the seller of a company was in breach of a warranty to make a proper forecast of the company's profits. The trial judge calculated damages by reference to the highest figure that a reasonable forecast could have produced. Rejecting that approach, the Privy Council said that 'the only rational course open to a court is to choose the figure which it considers that a forecast made with reasonable care was most likely to have

151 [1967] 1 QB 278.

152 [2004] EWCA Civ 1287, [2005] ICR 402.

153 [2022] EWCA Civ 901, [2022] ICR 1362.

154 eg, *Horkulak v Cantor Fitzgerald International* [2004] EWCA Civ 1287, [2005] ICR 402 [51]; *Barnett v Chelsea and Kensington Hospital Management Committee* [1969] 1 QB 428, 439. A prominent Australian case is *Commonwealth v Amann Aviation Pty Ltd* (1991) 174 CLR 64, where there was a 20% chance that the defendant would have lawfully terminated the contract if it had not repudiated it. Three judges in the High Court favoured a deduction in the damages to reflect the possibility of lawful termination. The other four judges rejected a deduction, determining the matter on the balance of probabilities.

155 It may also apply where a trustee failed to make prudent investments; see *Nestle v National Westminster Bank plc* [1993] 1 WLR 1260, 1280.

156 [1922] 1 KB 477.

157 ibid 480–81 (Bankes LJ), 483–84 (Atkin LJ). Scrutton LJ (at 482) favoured an application of the 'least burdensome' rule but agreed with the amount of damages.

158 [1996] 1 WLR 1438.

produced'.[159] In *Durham Tees Valley Airport Ltd v bmibaby Ltd*,[160] the defendant airline promised to base two aircraft at the claimant airport for ten years but did not promise any particular number of flights or passengers. The operation from the airport was unprofitable for the defendant and was discontinued after a few months. The Court of Appeal rejected an application of the 'least burdensome' rule and stated that the Court 'has to conduct a factual inquiry as to how the contract would have been performed had it not been repudiated'.[161]

In a third line of cases, the court determined which hypothetical course of action was the most probable, and assessed loss by reference to the degree of probability.[162] In *Chaplin v Hicks*,[163] the defendant, in breach of contract, failed to see the plaintiff to decide whether, in his opinion, she was one of the 12 most beautiful women out of a group of 50 women, those 12 obtaining employment in a chorus line. The English Court of Appeal upheld a jury award of substantial damages. Only nominal damages could have been awarded had it been irrebuttably assumed that the defendant, had he seen the plaintiff, would not have selected her. Furthermore, only nominal damages could have been awarded had the plaintiff's loss been determined on the balance of probabilities, as her chance of being selected was only about 25 percent.

The cases are difficult to reconcile. In *Durham Tees Valley Airport Ltd v bmibaby Ltd*,[164] the Court of Appeal observed that the 'least burdensome' rule applies where the defendant promisor had a choice between two or more ways of performing the contract, whereas a factual inquiry into how the defendant would have performed is necessary where the defendant had a discretion as to the manner of performance. This may be the state of the law, but there is no justification for the different treatment of the two categories.

It may be defensible to have a presumption that the defendant would have taken the lawful action most detrimental to the claimant, as this is often the most likely hypothetical scenario.[165] But any such presumption ought to be

---

159 ibid 1447 (Lord Hoffmann speaking for the Privy Council). The same approach was taken in *South Australia Asset Management Corp v York Montague Ltd* [1997] AC 191, 221–22.

160 [2010] EWCA Civ 485, [2011] 1 All ER (Comm) 731.

161 ibid [79] (Patten LJ, with whom Toulson LJ and Mummery LJ agreed).

162 eg, *Lavarack v Woods of Colchester Ltd* [1967] 1 QB 278, 289 (Lord Denning MR, dissenting); *Port Macquarie-Hastings Council v Diveva Pty Ltd* [2017] NSWCA 97 [88].

163 [1911] 2 KB 786.

164 [2010] EWCA Civ 485, [2011] 1 All ER (Comm) 731 [64]–[79].

165 Andrew Burrows, *Remedies for Torts, Breach of Contract, and Equitable Wrongs* (4th edn, OUP 2019) 72.

rebuttable.[166] Where it is clear that the defendant would not have taken the action most detrimental to the claimant, the loss ought to be calculated on that basis. It would not be convincing to deny liability for the loss exceeding minimum performance on the ground that it is outside the scope of the defendant's promise. As Michael Pratt has explained, a claimant obtains damages for the foreseeable loss of profits even though the defendant did not promise that the claimant would make those profits.[167]

Where the court conducts an inquiry into what the defendant would in fact have done in the absence of the wrong, the question arises whether uncertainty ought to be resolved on the balance of probabilities or whether chances ought to be evaluated. The balance-of-probabilities approach is applied to hypothetical conduct of the claimant, which has been justified on the ground that claimants should be able to provide evidence as to their own hypothetical conduct. The same rationale would apply to defendants. While the rationale is not entirely convincing, the same approach should apply to hypothetical conduct of the claimant and hypothetical conduct of the defendant.

TEMPORAL CONSIDERATIONS

Damages Are Assessed Once and For All and in a Lump Sum

At common law, damages for a civil wrong are assessed once and for all.[168] The court assesses not only losses already suffered by the time of the trial but also losses that are likely to be suffered in the future. The matter is final (*res judicata*). The claimant cannot come back and claim additional damages even if unexpected losses arise after judgment. The rule was laid down in *Fitter v Veal*.[169] The plaintiff recovered damages for assault, battery, and wounding. Subsequently, he suffered further injury as a result of the trespass. It was held that the judgment in the first action barred any further action for the same injury.

---

[166] ibid 72–73.

[167] Michael G Pratt, 'Damages for Breach of Contract with Alternative Performance' in Jeff Berryman and Rick Bigwood (eds), *The Law of Remedies: New Directions in the Common Law* (Irwin Law 2010) 116–17. See also *Andrew Burrows, Remedies for Torts, Breach of Contract, and Equitable Wrongs* (4th edn, OUP 2019) 72-73; David McLauchlan, 'An Unsound Rule for the Assessment of Contract Damages' (2022) 53 VUWLR 63; David Pearce, 'Of Ceilings and Flaws: An Analytical Approach to the Minimum Performance Rule in Contract Damages' (2016) 36 OJLS 781.

[168] eg, *Cartledge v E Jopling & Sons Ltd* [1963] AC 758, 780.

[169] (1706) 12 Mod 542; 88 ER 1506.

The 'once and for all' rule applies only within the same cause of action. In *Brunsden v Humphrey*,[170] a road collision injured the plaintiff and damaged his vehicle. He recovered damages for the property damage. Subsequently, he brought an action for the personal injury. The Court of Appeal (Lord Coleridge CJ dissenting) allowed the action on the ground that damage to property and injury to the person are infringements of different rights and give rise to distinct causes of action. However, this is subject to the rule in *Henderson v Henderson*,[171] under which a claim is precluded where it could have been raised in previous proceedings. The continued relevance of *Brunsden v Humphrey* (where *Henderson v Henderson* was not cited) is therefore doubtful.[172]

A continuing wrong may give rise to multiple causes of action. In *Holmes v Wilson*,[173] the defendant wrongfully erected buttresses on the plaintiff's land. The plaintiff brought an action for trespass and received damages. The defendant still refused to remove the buttresses, and the plaintiff brought another action for trespass. It was held that the new action was not barred by the previous action. In *Jalla v Shell International Trading and Shipping Co Ltd*,[174] the Supreme Court observed that a nuisance is continuing only where, outside the claimant's land and usually on the defendant's land, there is a repeated activity by the defendant or an ongoing state of affairs which causes continuing interference with the use and enjoyment of the claimant's land, examples being smoke, noise, smells, vibrations, and overlooking.[175] In that case, an oil spill off the Nigerian coast led to the claimants' properties being contaminated with oil. The Supreme Court held that this was a one-off event and not a continuing nuisance.[176]

A continuing breach of contract exists, for example, where the defendant carries on a business of a certain kind in breach of a promise not to do so; but the failure to pay one instalment is a separate cause of action from the failure to pay another instalment under the same contract.[177]

---

170 (1884) 14 QBD 141.

171 (1843) 3 Hare 100; 67 ER 313. The rule 'is not a true case of res judicata but rather is founded on the principle of public policy in preventing multiplicity of action': *Talbot v Berkshire County Council* [1994] QB 290, 296 (Stuart-Smith LJ).

172 See *Buckland v Palmer* [1984] 1 WLR 1109, 1115–16 (Griffiths LJ); *Talbot v Berkshire County Council* [1994] QB 290, 296, 301.

173 (1839) 10 A & E 503; 113 ER 190.

174 [2023] UKSC 16, [2024] AC 595.

175 ibid [26]. An example is *Shadwell v Hutchinson* (1831) 2 B & A 97; 109 ER 1079 (obstruction of ancient lights).

176 [2023] UKSC 16, [2024] AC 595 [37].

177 *National Coal Board v Galley* [1958] 1 WLR 16, 26.

In cases of personal injury where there is a chance that at some point in the future the injured person will suffer some serious disease or serious deterioration in his physical or mental condition as a result of the same wrong, legislation permits the court to make an award of provisional damages.[178] This means that the court assesses damages on the assumption that the injured person will not suffer the disease or deterioration, but if the injured person does then suffer the disease or deterioration, the court may make another award of damages for the additional loss.[179]

At common law, damages are awarded in the form of a lump sum; the court cannot order the defendant to make periodical payments. This can be problematic where a person suffering personal injury will continue to suffer loss (such as loss of earnings and medical costs) for the rest of her life. The court needs to estimate the injured person's remaining lifespan, and if the actual lifespan transpires to differ significantly from the estimate, the amount of damages will be too high or too low. Addressing this problem, section 2 of the Damages Act 1996 provides that a court awarding damages in respect of personal injury may order that the damages are wholly or partly to take the form of periodical payments; the consent of the parties is required unless the damages are for future pecuniary loss.[180]

The Date of Assessment

Since the value of property, services, and money changes over time, the court needs to assess damages by reference to a particular point in time (the date of assessment). This may be the date of the wrong, the date of the judgment (or trial), or a date in between.

The date of the judgment (or trial) is always used for the assessment of non-pecuniary loss,[181] future pecuniary loss,[182] and equitable compensation.[183]

---

178 Senior Courts Act 1981, s 32A; County Courts Act 1984, s 51. For the procedural details, see Civil Procedure Rules 1999, rules 41.2, 41.3, Practice Direction 41A.

179 For cases of subsequent death, see Damages Act 1996, s 3.

180 For the procedural details, see Civil Procedure Rules 1999, rules 41.4–41.10, Practice Direction 41B.

181 *Wright v British Railways Board* [1983] 2 AC 773, 782; *Walker v John McLean & Sons Ltd* [1979] 1 WLR 760, 765.

182 *Cookson v Knowles* [1979] AC 556, 575; *Walker v John McLean & Sons Ltd* [1979] 1 WLR 760, 765.

183 *Target Holdings Ltd v Redferns* [1996] AC 421, 438–39; *AIB Group (UK) plc v Mark Redler & Co Solicitors* [2014] UKSC 58, [2015] AC 1503 [135].

Where a contracting party repudiates the contract or fails to supply goods or services, and there is an available market in which the innocent party can arrange a substitute transaction, damages are usually assessed as at the date of the breach or a date shortly thereafter. This is because damages are assessed on the assumption that the innocent party immediately went into the market and arranged a substitute transaction; the avoidable loss rule (discussed in Chapter 3) excludes recovery for extra loss caused by a failure to do so.[184] However, an innocent party who does not have the means to arrange a substitute transaction should be entitled to wait for the receipt of compensation, and damages should be assessed as at the date of the trial.[185]

In actions for conversion, the basic measure of damages is the value of the goods at the time of the conversion, but subsequent changes in the value of the goods are sometimes taken into account. This is discussed in Chapter 5.

In all other cases, the default rule is that damages are assessed as at the time of the damage.[186] It is only a default rule, and courts may depart from it where another date more accurately gives effect to the compensatory principle.[187] For example, where the cost of repair work has increased significantly since the date of the damage, the current cost may be awarded where the claimant has not had the money to carry out repair or the defendant firmly denied liability.[188] The avoidable loss rule is again relevant. The cost of repair is assessed as at the time when it was reasonable to begin repair.[189] Similarly, where a

[184] eg, *South Australia Asset Management Corp v York Montague Ltd* [1997] AC 191, 221; *Golden Strait Corporation v Nippon Yusen Kubishika Kaisha (The 'Golden Victory')* [2007] UKHL 12, [2007] 2 AC 353 [10] (Lord Bingham); *Kaines (UK) Ltd v Oesterreichische Warenhandelsgesellschaft Austrowaren GmbH* [1993] 2 Lloyd's Rep 1; *Koch Marine Inc v d'Amica Societa di Navigazione arl (The Elena d'Amico)* [1980] 1 Lloyd's Rep 75; Sale of Goods Act 1979, ss 50(3), 51(3).

[185] James Edelman, *McGregor on Damages* (21st edn, Sweet & Maxwell 2021) [9-044], [20-004].

[186] eg, *Smith New Court Securities Ltd v Citibank NA* [1997] AC 254, 265–6; *Golden Strait Corporation v Nippon Yusen Kubishika Kaisha (The 'Golden Victory')* [2007] UKHL 12, [2007] 2 AC 353 [11] (Lord Bingham); *County Personnel (Employment Agency) Ltd v Alan R Pulver & Co* [1987] 1 WLR 916, 925–26; *Wapshott v Davis Donovan & Co* [1996] PNLR 361.

[187] eg, *Johnson v Agnew* [1980] AC 367, 400–01; *Smith New Court Securities Ltd v Citibank NA* [1997] AC 254, 265–66; *County Personnel (Employment Agency) Ltd v Alan R Pulver & Co* [1987] 1 WLR 916, 925–26.

[188] *Dodd Properties Ltd v Canterbury City Council* [1980] 1 WLR 433; *Alcoa Minerals of Jamaica Inc v Broderick* [2002] 1 AC 371 (PC).

[189] *Dodd Properties Ltd v Canterbury City Council* [1980] 1 WLR 433, 444 (Cantley J).

purchaser of land has repudiated the contract and the vendor has resold the land in a falling market, damages are assessed as at the date of resale as it is impossible to find an alternative purchaser of land immediately.[190]

In determining the existence and extent of loss, the trial judge considers all events up to the time of trial, even if damages are assessed as at an earlier date.[191] The court does not speculate when it knows.[192] But the Court of Appeal or the Supreme Court will not consider evidence that was not before the lower court unless the Court orders otherwise.[193]

The Present Value of Future Pecuniary Loss

A claimant who is awarded damages for future pecuniary loss in a lump sum receives the damages award at an earlier time than the occurrence of the loss, sometimes many years earlier. While the value of the money usually falls due to inflation, this is usually more than outweighed by the interest that the claimant can earn by investing the damages award. It follows that the amount of damages for future pecuniary loss should usually be lower than the amount of the loss. A discount must be made.

In *Wells v Wells*,[194] a case of personal injury, the House of Lords held that the discount rate should be set on the assumption that the plaintiff would invest the damages for future pecuniary loss in index-linked government securities. While such an investment yielded a lower return than a mixed portfolio, it was a risk-free method of investment which fully protected against inflation. The House of Lords adopted a discount rate of 3 percent.

The rates of inflation and interest fluctuate. Section A1 of the Damages Act 1996 empowers the Lord Chancellor to prescribe from time to time a rate of return to be applied to damages for future pecuniary loss in personal injury cases.[195] A court must use that rate unless any party shows that a different

---

190 *Hooper v Oates* [2013] EWCA Civ 91, [2014] Ch 287 [38].

191 *Bwllfa and Merthyr Dare Steam Collieries (1891) Ltd v Pontypridd Waterworks Co* [1903] AC 426, 429, 431, 432–33; *Golden Strait Corporation v Nippon Yusen Kubishika Kaisha (The 'Golden Victory')* [2007] UKHL 12, [2007] 2 AC 353 [36], [65]–[66], [78].

192 *Jobling v Associated Dairies Ltd* [1982] AC 794, 802, 807, 813, 819; *Gray v Thames Trains Ltd* [2009] UKHL 33, [2009] 1 AC 1339 [75], [95].

193 Civil Procedure Rules 1999, rule 52.21(2)(b). Evidence of events since trial was admitted, eg, in *Lim Poh Choo v Camden and Islington Area Health Authority* [1980] AC 174.

194 [1999] 1 AC 345.

195 The details of how to determine the rate are set out in Schedule A1 of the Act.

rate is more appropriate in the case in question. At the time of writing, the prescribed rate is 0.5 percent.[196]

Interest on Compensation

In theory, claimants should obtain compensation for their loss as soon as the loss has occurred. By receiving compensation at a later date (often years later), claimants lose the opportunity to invest the money and earn interest in the meantime. This constitutes an additional loss.

Awards of pre-judgment interest have always been available in equity,[197] at least as simple interest. Compound interest can be awarded where money has been obtained by fraud or has been withheld or misapplied by a trustee or other fiduciary.[198] At common law, by contrast, the courts traditionally refused to award pre-judgment interest, simple or compound.[199]

A statutory power to award pre-judgment interest on any debt or damages was introduced in 1934.[200] An expanded power is now contained in section 35A of the Senior Courts Act 1981. Section 35A(1) provides that a court may award simple interest, at a rate chosen by the court, for the period from the date when the cause of action arose until either the date of the judgment or the date when a damages-reducing payment was made before judgment. Section 35A(2) provides that in cases of personal injury, pre-judgment interest shall be awarded unless there are special reasons to the contrary. Courts have chosen different rates of interest in different circumstances; the picture is very complex.[201]

Section 35A only permits the award of simple interest. If the claimant had received compensation immediately after suffering the loss, the compensation could have been placed in a bank account and attracted compound interest. An award of simple interest still does not give full effect to the compensatory principle. The Law Commission for England and Wales has recommended

---

196 Damages (Personal Injury) Order 2024.

197 eg, *Re Pigott and the Great Western Railway Co* (1881) 18 Ch D 146. The Admiralty Court has also awarded interest in cases involving the collision of ships; see, eg, *The Amalia* (1864) 5 New Rep 164n.

198 *President of India v La Pintada Compania Navigacion SA* [1985] AC 104, 116.

199 *London, Chatham and Dover Railway Co v South Eastern Railway Co* [1893] AC 429.

200 Law Reform (Miscellaneous Provisions) Act 1934, s 3(1).

201 See James Edelman, *McGregor on Damages* (21st edn, Sweet & Maxwell 2021) [19-104]–[19-134].

that a statutory power to award compound interest be introduced.[202] This has not been implemented, but it is now obsolete because of a major change in the common law.

In *Sempra Metals Ltd v Inland Revenue Commissioners*,[203] the House of Lords recognised the problem and held that it is always open to a victim of a breach of contract or tort to plead and prove interest losses, which may involve compound interest, and that such loss is recoverable subject to remoteness and the failure to mitigate. Thus, the court can award compound interest, but the claimant must prove that the non-receipt of compensation at the time of the basic loss has caused interest loss, ie, that the claimant would have invested the money and earned interest or that the claimant was required to borrow money and pay interest on that loan. The rate of interest will thus reflect the circumstances of the individual claimant. Interest loss is usually absent in cases of personal injury.

Every judgment debt carries simple interest until the debt is satisfied.[204] The rate is prescribed by statutory instrument. It has been 8 percent since 1993.[205]

---

202 Law Commission, *Pre-Judgment Interest on Debts and Damages* (Law Com No 287, 2004).

203 [2007] UKHL 34, [2008] 1 AC 561. A majority in the House of Lords also held that compound interest may be recovered as restitution for unjust enrichment. That aspect of *Sempra Metals* was overruled in *Prudential Assurance Co Ltd v Revenue and Customs Commissioners* [2018] UKSC 39, [2019] AC 929.

204 Judgments Act 1838, s 17.

205 Judgment Debts (Rate of Interest) Order 1993.

3. Attribution of responsibility: general principles

INTRODUCTION

Substantial damages for a particular loss cannot be awarded unless the loss can be attributed to the defendant's wrong. This requires the wrong to be a cause of the loss. 'Causation is an expression of the relationship that must be found to exist between the tortious act of the wrongdoer and the injury to the victim in order to justify compensation of the latter out of the pocket of the former'.[1] Causation for legal purposes is concerned with the attribution of responsibility for a given occurrence; it is thus different from causation for philosophical or scientific purposes which seeks to explain phenomena by reference to the relationship between conditions and occurrences.[2] However, there is no agreement as to what inquiries are captured by the notion of causation for legal purposes.

The determination of whether a wrongdoer bears legal responsibility for a particular loss always involves the first two, and sometimes also the third, of the following inquiries:[3]

(1) a largely scientific inquiry into whether the wrong was historically connected with the loss (which will always be the case where the loss would not have occurred but for the wrong, but may also be the case in some other circumstances);
(2) a normative inquiry into whether the loss should be attributed solely to a particular event other than the wrong, ie particular conduct of the claimant or a third party, or a particular natural event;
(3) a normative inquiry into whether the wrongdoer's responsibility for the loss should be denied (particularly on the ground that the loss was not

1 *Snell v Farrell* [1990] 2 SCR 311, 326 (Sopinka J speaking for the Court).

2 *March v E & MH Stramare Pty Ltd* (1991) 171 CLR 506, 509 (Mason CJ); quoted in *Chester v Afshar* [2004] UKHL 41, [2005] 1 AC 134 [75] (Lord Hope).

3 See Christian Witting, *Street on Torts* (16th edn, OUP 2021) 164.

foreseeable) without the loss being attributed to a particular event other than the wrong.

It is contested whether the concept of causation includes all three inquiries,[4] or only the first two inquiries,[5] or only the first inquiry.[6]

It is widespread practice to denote the first inquiry as 'factual causation'.[7] The normative inquiries are often denoted as scope of liability[8] or, in the United States, as proximate cause.[9] The distinction between factual causation and scope of liability or proximate cause has been advocated by leading causation scholars,[10] and has been adopted by the UK Supreme Court,[11] Australian legislators,[12] Canadian courts,[13] and the American Law Institute's

---

4 *Nykredit Mortgage Bank plc v Edward Erdman Group Ltd* [1997] 1 WLR 1627, 1638 (Lord Hoffmann); Simon Deakin and Zoe Adams, *Markesinis and Deakin's Tort Law* (8th edn, OUP 2019) 202–03; Carolyn Sappideen et al, *Fleming's The Law of Torts* (11th edn, Lawbook Co 2024) [9.40].

5 *Humber Oil Terminal Trustee Ltd v Owners of the Ship 'Sivand'* [1998] CLC 751, 762 (Evans LJ); Niranjan Venkatesan, 'The Contract Remoteness Rule: Exclusion, Not Assumption of Responsibility' in Andrew Dyson, James Goudkamp and Frederick Wilmot-Smith (eds), *Defences in Contract* (Hart 2017) 189–92.

6 Jane Stapleton, 'Choosing What We Mean by "Causation" in the Law' (2008) 73 Missouri L Rev 433; *Ediger v Johnston* [2013] SCC 18, [2013] 2 SCR 98 [28]–[29].

7 eg, *Manchester Building Society v Grant Thornton UK LLP* [2021] UKSC 20, [2022] AC 783 [6]; *Meadows v Khan* [2021] UKSC 21, [2022] AC 852 [28].

8 eg, *Kuwait Airways Corp v Iraqi Airways Co (Nos 4 and 5)* [2002] UKHL 19, [2002] 2 AC 883 [69]–[70]; *Harding v Wealands* [2006] UKHL 32, [2007] 2 AC 1 [24] (Lord Hoffmann).

9 eg, *Lexmark International, Inc v Static Control Components*, Inc, 572 US 118, 132 (2014); For criticism of the term, see American Law Institute, *Restatement (Third) of Torts: Physical and Emotional Harm* (2010), comments on §29.

10 Jane Stapleton, 'Choosing What We Mean by "Causation" in the Law' (2008) 73 Missouri L Rev 433, 455, 458; Richard W Wright, 'The Grounds and Extent of Legal Responsibility' (2003) 40 San Diego L Rev 1425, 1448–50.

11 eg, *Manchester Building Society v Grant Thornton UK LLP* [2021] UKSC 20, [2022] AC 783 [6]; *Meadows v Khan* [2021] UKSC 21, [2022] AC 852 [28], [44].

12 eg, Civil Liability Act 2002 (NSW), s 5D(1)(a), (b).

13 eg, *Hussack v Chilliwack School District No 33* [2011] BCCA 258, (2011) 19 BCLR (5th) 257 [54]; *Borgfjord v Boizard* [2016] BCCA 317, (2016) 403 DLR (4th) 745 [54]–[56].

Third Restatement of Torts.[14] This chapter will also use the terms factual causation and scope of liability.

The term 'legal causation' has also been used, but not with a uniform meaning. It has been used to denote the normative inquiries mentioned above,[15] but it has also been used as a short form for causation for legal purposes.[16]

While the claimant bears the legal burden of proving factual causation, the defendant bears the legal burden of pleading and proving a reason why liability should be denied on normative grounds.[17]

This chapter includes a discussion of circumstances where the claimant contributed to the loss and where there are multiple wrongdoers.

FACTUAL CAUSATION

The 'But For' Test

In the vast majority of cases, the inquiry into factual causation can be conducted by asking whether the loss would have occurred but for the defendant's wrong.[18] A negative answer establishes that the wrong was a factual cause of the loss. A positive answer establishes that the wrong was not a factual cause of the loss.[19]

In order to determine what would have happened but for the defendant's wrong, the court needs to construct a hypothetical world. The court needs to refer to the time just before the wrongful conduct, remove the wrongful conduct, and then determine how things would have played out.[20] The relevance of

---

14 American Law Institute, *Restatement (Third) of Torts: Liability for Physical and Emotional Harm* (2010) §26, §29.

15 eg, *Armstead v Royal & Sun Alliance Insurance Co Ltd* [2024] UKSC 6, [2025] AC 406 [56].

16 eg, Carolyn Sappideen et al, *Fleming's The Law of Torts* (11th edn, LBC 2024) [9.40].

17 *Armstead v Royal & Sun Alliance Insurance Co Ltd* [2024] UKSC 6, [2025] AC 406 [60]–[63].

18 eg, *Kuwait Airways Corp v Iraqi Airways Co (Nos 4 and 5)* [2002] UKHL 19, [2002] 2 AC 883 [72].

19 eg, *Barnett v Chelsea and Kensington Hospital Management Committee* [1969] 1 QB 428; *Brown v Lewisham and North Southwark HA* [1999] Lloyd's Rep Med 110; *Bank of Credit and Commerce International SA v Ali (No 2)* [2002] EWCA Civ 82, [2002] 3 All ER 750; *Clough v First Choice Holidays and Flights Ltd* [2006] EWCA Civ 15, [2006] PIQR P22.

20 David Hamer, '"Factual Causation" and "Scope of Liability": What's the Difference?' (2014) 77 Mod LR 155, 163; David W Robertson, 'The Common Sense of Cause in Fact' (1997) 75 Texas L Rev 1765, 1770–71.

actual or hypothetical events that were independently sufficient to bring about the loss in question will be considered later in this chapter.

Where the wrongful conduct is an omission, the court needs to construct the hypothetical world with the required action of the defendant. Where the wrongful conduct is an action, the court needs to construct the hypothetical world by either removing the action or replacing it with a non-wrongful action. In most cases, there is only one alternative to the actual action of the defendant. For example, where the defendant stabbed the claimant, the hypothetical world is one in which the defendant did not stab the claimant.

Sometimes, there are two alternatives to the actual action of the defendant. It has been said that the defendant's conduct is altered to the minimum extent necessary to make it conform to the law.[21] Thus, where the defendant was driving too fast when colliding with the claimant, the hypothetical world is one in which the defendant was still driving at the place and time where and when the collision occurred but was driving at a reasonable speed.[22] It would be a larger departure from the real world to construct a world in which the defendant was not driving at all or had been driving at a lower speed for some time, thus arriving at the place of the collision at a later time.[23]

Sometimes, it is not easy to decide which alternative conduct is the most minimal departure from the real world. A famous scenario is the following. The defendant hands a loaded gun to the nine-year-old claimant, who drops the gun, injuring her foot.[24] Is the hypothetical world one in which the defendant gave the claimant an unloaded gun or no gun at all? It is difficult to decide this question by reference to the principle of minimal departure. Instead, it should be decided by reference to the wrongful aspect principle,[25] which requires 'that the causal relation be shown to exist between *that aspect of the defendant's conduct which is wrongful* and the injury'.[26] What makes the defendant's

---

[21] Robertson, ibid 1770; Jane Stapleton, 'Choosing What We Mean by "Causation" in the Law' (2008) 73 Missouri L Rev 433, 451.

[22] Stapleton, ibid.

[23] Later arrival was, however, considered in *Phethean-Hubble v Coles* [2012] EWCA Civ 349, [2012] RTR 31 [64].

[24] See American Law Institute, *Restatement (Third) of Torts: Liability for Physical and Emotional Harm* (2010) §29, Illustration 3.

[25] Richard W Wright, 'Causation in Tort Law' (1985) 73 Cal L Rev 1735, 1771; Richard W Wright, 'The Grounds and Extent of Legal Responsibility' (2003) 40 San Diego L Rev 1425, 1498–9; Jane Stapleton, 'Choosing What We Mean by "Causation" in the Law' (2008) 73 Missouri L Rev 433, 449 fn 36.

[26] Fleming James and Roger F Perry, 'Legal Cause' (1951) 60 Yale LJ 761, 789 (emphasis in original). See also HLA Hart and Tony Honoré, *Causation in the Law* (2nd edn, Clarendon Press 1985) lviii–lx, 114–22; Tony Honoré, 'Necessary

conduct in the example wrongful is the fact that the gun was loaded (because the claimant could have accidentally discharged it), not the fact that he gave her an object that she might drop on her foot.

Thus, it would be wrong to suggest that the inquiry into factual causation can and should be free from any normative considerations.[27] Conversely, even though normative considerations may be involved in determining whether the wrong was necessary for the occurrence of the harm, the inquiry is still essentially factual,[28] and the phrase 'factual causation' is appropriate.

Causal Overdetermination (Multiple Sufficient Causes)

Sometimes, the defendant's wrong and another event, which may be a wrong committed by a third party or a non-wrongful event, was each sufficient to bring about the claimant's harm, or would each have been sufficient if the other event had not occurred. This situation has been described as one of causal overdetermination,[29] or as involving multiple sufficient causes.[30]

Two categories of overdetermination must be distinguished.[31] One is where each event duplicates or reinforces the effects of the other event (duplicative causation). For example, suppose that D and T independently start separate fires, each of which would have been sufficient to destroy C's house. The fires converge and together burn down the house. The other category of overdetermination is where one event pre-empts the effects of the other event (pre-emptive causation). The pre-empted condition may be an actual event or a hypothetical event (it would have occurred in the absence of the defendant's

---

and Sufficient Conditions in Tort Law' in David G Owen (ed), *Philosophical Foundations of Tort Law* (Clarendon Press 1995) 367–74; *Hughes-Holland v BPE Solicitors* [2017] UKSC 21, [2018] AC 599 [38].

27 Nor should the Australian statutes that distinguish between factual causation and scope of liability be interpreted as excluding all normative considerations at the factual causation stage; see *Paul v Cooke* [2013] NSWCA 311, (2013) 85 NSWLR 167 [11] (Basten JA). Cf *Wallace v Kam* [2013] HCA 19, (2013) 250 CLR 375 [14].

28 Richard W Wright, 'Causation in Tort Law' (1985) 73 Cal L Rev 1735, 1759. Cf David Hamer, '"Factual Causation" and "Scope of Liability": What's the Difference?' (2014) 77 Mod LR 155, 165.

29 Richard W Wright, 'Causation in Tort Law' (1985) 73 Cal L Rev 1735, 1740; Samuel Ferey and Pierre Dehez, 'Overdetermined Causation Cases, Contribution and the Shapley Value' (2016) 91 Chi-Kent L Rev 637.

30 American Law Institute, *Restatement (Third) of Torts: Liability for Physical and Emotional Harm* (2010) §27.

31 The terminology and the examples are taken from Richard W Wright, 'Causation in Tort Law' (1985) 73 Cal L Rev 1735, 1775–76, 1795–96.

wrong). An example of an actual pre-empted condition is where C drinks a cup of tea poisoned by T, but before the poison takes effect, D shoots and kills C instantly. An example of a hypothetical pre-empted condition is where D shoots and kills C just as C was about to drink a cup of tea poisoned by T.

Under the 'but for' test, D's conduct in those examples would not be a cause of C's loss as the loss would have occurred in any event.[32] It is commonly accepted that this would be an absurd outcome, and that the 'but for' test is therefore inappropriate here.[33]

In order to solve the problem, Richard Wright has developed the NESS (Necessary Element of a Sufficient Set) test, under which a factual cause of harm is every element necessary for the sufficiency of a set of conditions that are jointly sufficient to bring about the harm.[34] Wright gives the following example.[35] Five units of pollution were necessary and sufficient for certain environmental damage to occur. Each of seven wrongdoers, acting independently of each other, discharged one unit of pollution. Each wrongdoer can say that its own unit of pollution was neither necessary nor sufficient to inflict the damage. But under the NESS test, each wrongdoer's unit of pollution is a factual cause of the damage because every set of five units was sufficient to inflict the damage, and in every set of five units, each unit was necessary for

---

32 D's conduct may be a factual cause of the initial harm if sufficiently specified; death by being poisoned can be distinguished from death by being shot. However, the courts do not make this specification for the resulting loss.

33 eg, *Rahman v Arearose Ltd* [2001] QB 351 [17]–[18]; *Financial Conduct Authority v Arch Insurance (UK) Ltd* [2021] UKSC 1, [2021] AC 649 [182]; *Meadows v Khan* [2021] UKSC 21, [2022] AC 852 [46].

34 Richard W Wright, 'Causation in Tort Law' (1985) 73 Cal L Rev 1735, 1788–1803; Richard W Wright, 'The NESS Account of Natural Causation: A Response to Criticisms' in Richard Goldberg (ed), *Perspectives on Causation* (Hart 2011) 285. See also *Nader v Urban Transit Authority of New South Wales* (1985) 2 NSWLR 501, 531 (McHugh JA): 'every necessary member of the group of conditions jointly sufficient to produce the injury or damage is a cause of that injury or damage'.

35 Richard W Wright, 'Causation in Tort Law' (1985) 73 Cal L Rev 1735, 1793. See also *Thorpe v Brumfitt* (1873) LR 8 Ch App 650, 656–57 (James LJ): 'Suppose one person leaves a wheelbarrow standing on a way, that may cause no appreciable inconvenience, but if a hundred do so, that may cause a serious inconvenience, which a person entitled to the use of the way has a right to prevent, and it is no defence to any one person among the hundred to say that what he does causes of itself no damage to the complainant.' Assuming that 99 wheelbarrows would still have created serious inconvenience, the contribution of the one wheelbarrow does not satisfy the 'but for' test, but does satisfy the NESS test: Jane Stapleton, 'Unnecessary Causes' (2013) 129 LQR 39, 44.

the sufficiency of that set of units. The UK Supreme Court has stated that factual causation is established in such circumstances.[36]

Duplicative causation

A case of duplicative causation is present where both the defendant's wrong and another event (for which the defendant is not responsible) are each sufficient to bring about the harm suffered by the plaintiff, and each event duplicates or reinforced the effects of the other. The attribution of responsibility in those circumstances depends upon whether the event 'competing' with the defendant's wrong is a wrong committed by a third party or a non-wrongful event.

Where the event 'competing' with the defendant's wrong is a wrong committed by a third party, each wrong is regarded as a factual cause of the harm. For example, suppose that A and B, acting independently of each other, simultaneously shoot at and hit C, each bullet alone being sufficient to kill C instantly. It is commonly accepted that it would be absurd if A and B were exonerated on the ground that the conduct of neither satisfies the 'but for' test; both A's wrong and B's wrong must be regarded as a factual cause of C's harm. The courts explain this outcome by making an exception to the 'but for' test,[37] although there has been the occasional reference to the NESS test mentioned above.[38]

Where the event 'competing' with the defendant's wrong is not a wrong, the defendant escapes liability.[39] This follows from the rule (discussed later in this chapter) that the person responsible for a pre-empting condition is not liable where the pre-empted condition is not a wrong. If a non-wrongful event exonerates the defendant even though its effects were pre-empted by the defendant's wrong, it must do the same if it duplicated or reinforced the effects of the defendant's wrong. However, the exoneration of the defendant should be seen as a matter relating to the scope of liability. The defendant's wrong should be regarded as a factual cause of the harm even if the 'competing' event is non-wrongful.[40] We argue that the concept of material contribution to harm

---

[36] *Financial Conduct Authority v Arch Insurance (UK) Ltd* [2021] UKSC 1, [2021] AC 649 [184]–[185].

[37] eg, *March v E & MH Stramare Pty Ltd* (1991) 171 CLR 506, 516, 524; *Kuwait Airways Corp v Iraqi Airways Co (Nos 4 and 5)* [2002] UKHL 19, [2002] 2 AC 883 [73]-[74]; *Financial Conduct Authority v Arch Insurance (UK) Ltd* [2021] UKSC 1, [2021] AC 649 [182].

[38] *Amaca Pty Ltd v Booth* [2011] HCA 53, (2011) 246 CLR 36 [48] (French CJ).

[39] Glanville Williams, 'Causation in the Law' [1961] Camb LJ 62, 75–77; Jane Stapleton, 'Unnecessary Causes' (2013) 129 LQR 39, 55.

[40] Richard W Wright, 'Causation in Tort Law' (1985) 73 Cal L Rev 1735, 1775–76, 1798; American Law Institute, *Restatement (Third) of Torts: Liability*

discussed later in this chapter does not affect these propositions but merely places upon the defendant the onus of proving that a non-wrongful event would have inflicted the harm in the absence of the defendant's wrong.

So far, it has been assumed that the conduct of the defendant and any third party is a positive action. It is controversial whether the same rules apply to a case of dependent double omissions.[41] These circumstances arise where each of two persons (acting independently of each other) fails to perform a certain act, and harm ensues because the harm could have been prevented only by both persons performing the required act.[42] Under the 'but for' test, neither omission is a factual cause of the harm because the other omission would have inflicted the harm in any event.

For example, suppose that an employer acquires a tool and gives it to an employee to use. The manufacturer of the tool fails to include a warning against a certain use of the tool on the warning sheet, and the employer fails to read that sheet before handing the tool to the employee. The employee is injured by using the tool in the manner against which the manufacturer failed to warn. In those circumstances, the 'but for' test is not satisfied for either the manufacturer's omission (the employee would still have been injured because the employer would not have read the warning) or the employer's omission (the employee would still have been injured because the particular warning was not on the sheet).

There seems to be wide agreement that where one of the double dependent omissions was non-wrongful, the harm is attributed solely to that omission.[43] Thus, an employer who failed to provide an employee with safety equipment is not liable for the employee's injury resulting from the failure to use the equipment if the employee would not have used the equipment had it been provided.[44] This position is consistent with the rules governing multiple sufficient

---

for Physical and Emotional Harm (2010) §27 cmt (d).

41 The terminology is taken from Jane Stapleton, 'Choosing What We Mean by "Causation" in the Law' (2008) 73 Missouri L Rev 433, 477.

42 If performance by either one of the parties alone would have been sufficient to avoid the harm, the 'but for' test is satisfied for both omissions; see *East Metropolitan Health Service v Popovic* [2019] WASCA 18, (2019) 54 WAR 40 [200]. See also *Henville v Walker* [2001] HCA 52, (2001) 206 CLR 459 [57]-[60] (Gaudron J).

43 Jane Stapleton, 'An "Extended But-For" Test for the Causal Relation in the Law of Obligations' (2015) 35 OJLS 697, 715–20; Richard W Wright, 'Causation (Contribution) and the "No Worse Off" Limitation on Liability' (2022) 49 UWALR 5, 30, 53.

44 *McWilliams v Sir William Arrol & Co Ltd* [1962] SC (HL) 70; *Wigley v British Vinegars Ltd* [1964] AC 307, 325–26; *Taylor v Chief Constable of Hampshire*

positive actions and, like there, should be seen as a matter of the scope of liability rather than factual causation. Where both double dependent omissions were wrongful, in particular where (as usual) the omissions did not occur at the same time, the position is controversial.[45] There is much to be said for the view that each omission should be regarded as a factual cause of the harm,[46] again aligning the position with that governing multiple sufficient positive actions.[47]

Pre-emptive causation

A case of pre-emptive causation exists where each of two factors was sufficient to bring about certain harm (or would have been sufficient if the other factor had not been present), but one factor pre-empts the effects of the other factor. The pre-empted factor may be an actual event or an event that would have occurred in the absence of the pre-empting factor.

The pre-empted factor is not a factual cause of the harm, whether or not the pre-empting factor is a wrong.[48] A factor is not a factual cause of harm only because it would have brought about the harm had things been different. Thus, where the claimant has been involved in two accidents for which two different wrongdoers are responsible, the wrongdoer responsible for the second accident is not liable for loss already inflicted by the first accident, even though the second accident would have inflicted that loss had the first accident

---

Police [2013] EWCA Civ 496, [2013] ICR 1150 [19].

[45] For a discussion, reviewing the various positions advanced in the literature, see Yuval Abrams, 'Omissive Overdetermination: Why the Act-Omission Distinction Makes a Difference for Causal Analysis' (2022) 49 UWALR 57.

[46] *Elayoubi v Zipser* [2008] NSWCA 335 [57]. This view was expressed by Jane Stapleton, 'Choosing What We Mean by "Causation" in the Law' (2008) 73 Missouri L Rev 433, 477–9. But she now takes the view that regarding either omission as a factual cause would be exceptional: Jane Stapleton, 'An "Extended But-For" Test for the Causal Relation in the Law of Obligations' (2015) 35 OJLS 697, 715–24.

[47] For a different view, see Yuval Abrams, 'Omissive Overdetermination: Why the Act-Omission Distinction Makes a Difference for Causal Analysis' (2022) 49 UWALR 57.

[48] *Baker v Willoughby* [1970] AC 467, 495; *Dimond v Lovell* [2002] 1 AC 384, 406 (Lord Hobhouse); *Davies v Bridgend County Borough Council* [2024] UKSC 15, [2025] AC 434 [83] (Lord Burrows JSC).

not occurred.[49] The principle applies even where the pre-empting factor is the conduct of the claimant[50] or a natural event.[51]

The principle also applies where the pre-empting event is a non-wrongful omission by the defendant, as demonstrated by *Davies v Bridgend County Borough Council*.[52] The claimant brought an action in nuisance in respect of Japanese knotweed which had encroached onto his land from the defendant's land. It was found that the encroachment had occurred well before 2004 (when the claimant bought his land) but that the defendant had only been in breach of its duty in private nuisance between 2013 (when the defendant first knew, or ought to have known, of the risk of damage by knotweed) and 2018 (when the defendant took action to treat the knotweed). In 2012, mortgage lenders started to limit or refuse to provide mortgages where Japanese knotweed was within seven metres of the property's boundary. The UK Supreme Court rejected the claimant's claim for diminution in value of his land. Lord Stephens JSC explained that 'the diminution in value had occurred long before any breach by the defendant of the relevant duty in private nuisance first occurred in 2013. Accordingly, the application of the "but for" test in this case eliminates the defendant's subsequent breach of duty as a causative factor'.[53]

Where both factors are wrongs (committed by different persons acting independently of each other), the pre-empting factor has been regarded as a factual cause of the harm.[54] By contrast, where the pre-empted factor is not a wrong, the person responsible for the pre-empting factor has not been held liable for

---

[49] *The Haversham Grange* [1905] P 307, 317; *Performance Cars Ltd v Abraham* [1962] 1 QB 33; *Steel v Joy* [2004] EWCA Civ 576, [2004] 1 WLR 3002 [55]–[70].

[50] *Performance Cars Ltd v Abraham* [1962] 1 QB 33, 39 (Lord Evershed MR); *Davies v Bridgend County Borough Council* [2024] UKSC 15, [2025] AC 434 [83] (Lord Burrows JSC).

[51] *Davies v Bridgend County Borough Council* [2024] UKSC 15, [2025] AC 434 [83]–[84] (Lord Burrows JSC), citing *Kerry v England* [1898] AC 742 (PC), where a druggist's negligent supply of poison to a fatally sick patient did not to any appreciable extent accelerate an already imminent death.

[52] [2024] UKSC 15, [2025] AC 434.

[53] ibid [70]. Lord Reed PSC, Lord Lloyd-Jones and Lady Smiler JJSC agreed with Lord Stephens JSC. Lord Burrows JSC delivered a concurring judgment.

[54] *Baker v Willoughby* [1970] AC 467; *Wynn v New South Wales Insurance Ministerial Corporation* (1995) 184 CLR 485, 498–99; *Halsey v Milton Keynes General NHS Trust* [2004] EWCA Civ 576, [2004] 1 WLR 3002 [56]–[70].

the harm.[55] It is not always clear whether the courts deny factual causation[56] or make a value judgement that the harm is outside the scope of liability. On principle, it should be the latter.[57] The pre-empting factor satisfies the NESS test mentioned above and should be regarded as a factual cause of the harm even if the pre-empted factor is not a wrong. The relevant cases are therefore discussed later in this chapter under the scope of liability.

Evidential Problems

Inference of causation

The claimant bears the onus of proving factual causation.[58] Where the claimant is unable to provide evidence directly proving this, the court sometimes draws an inference from the available evidence.[59] It is an inference drawn in the absence of evidence to the contrary but does not involve the shifting of an evidential onus of proof to the defendant.[60]

An example is *Drake v Harbour*.[61] A fire broke out in the claimant's house during a period in which the defendant electrician was rewiring the house and the claimant was not living there. The fire started one night in the loft where the defendant had been working using a festoon cable with light sockets and bulbs, which had been left plugged in overnight. The trial judge found that the cable was old and that the defendant had been negligent in failing to check that the insulation had not been damaged. The judge also found that the negligence was a cause of the fire, even though the defendant pointed to other possible

---

55 *Jobling v Associated Dairies Ltd* [1982] AC 794; *Tate & Lyle Industries Ltd v Greater London Council* [1983] 2 AC 509, 542–43; *Kuwait Airways Corp v Iraqi Airways Co (Nos 4 and 5)* [2002] UKHL 19, [2002] 2 AC 883 [83] (liability for conversion does not extend to loss that the owner would have equally suffered had he retained possession of the goods).

56 *Kuwait Airways Corp v Iraqi Airways Co (Nos 4 and 5)* [2002] UKHL 19, [2002] 2 AC 883 [83].

57 Richard W Wright, 'Causation in Tort Law' (1985) 73 Cal L Rev 1735, 1775–76, 1798; Richard W Wright, 'Causation (Contribution) and the "No Worse Off" Limitation' (2022) 49 UWALR 5, 32. Cf Christian Witting, *Street on Torts* (16th edn, OUP 2021) 179.

58 *Davies v Bridgend County Borough Council* [2024] UKSC 15, [2025] AC 434 [56].

59 For an in-depth discussion of the inference of causation in English, French, and German law, see Sandy Steel, *Proof of Causation in Tort Law* (CUP 2015) 66–101.

60 *Snell v Farrell* [1990] 2 SCR 311, 329–30; approvingly quoted in *Drake v Harbour* [2008] EWCA Civ 25, (2008) 121 Con LR 18 [26].

61 [2008] EWCA Civ 25, (2008) 121 Con LR 18.

causes such as an undetectable defect in the cable, loose light sockets, or moisture in them. The Court of Appeal upheld the trial judge's decision.

In cases of toxic torts, in particular exposure to asbestos dust, a party may seek to rely on epidemiological evidence, ie, the statistical correlation between a particular medical condition and exposure to a particular agent.[62] In *Sienkiewicz v Greif (UK) Ltd*,[63] the House of Lords rejected the argument that factual causation can be established simply by proving that the defendant's wrongful conduct doubled the risk that the claimant would suffer the particular injury. Lord Dyson JSC observed:

> [E]pidemiology is based on the study of populations, not individuals. It seeks to establish associations between alleged causes and effects. With proper scientific interpretation, these correlations lend great weight to an inference of causation. However, in an individual case, epidemiology alone cannot *conclusively* prove causation. At best, it can establish only a certain probability that a randomly selected case of disease was one that would not have occurred absent exposure.[64]

Beyond permitting an inference of factual causation from the evidence, the English courts have developed two distinct concepts that permit a finding of factual causation even though this cannot be established in the orthodox manner. These two concepts will be discussed now.

Material contribution to the harm

It is recognised that a wrong that made a material contribution to the claimant's damage constitutes a factual cause of the damage even if it cannot be established that the damage would not have occurred but for the wrong. However, the precise contours of this rule are not settled.[65]

The rule comes from *Bonnington Castings Ltd v Wardlaw*.[66] The employer of a steel dresser exposed him to silica dust from two sources: the pneumatic hammer at which he worked and the swing grinders. There was no known method of protecting him against the dust emanating from the hammer

---

62 For a discussion, see Per Laleng and Charles Feeny, 'Law and Epidemiological Evidence: Double, Toil and Trouble' (2022) 49 UWALR 159.

63 [2011] UKSC 10, [2011] 2 AC 229. The case is discussed later in this chapter.

64 ibid [218] (emphasis in original).

65 For excellent analyses of the cases, see Sandy Steel, 'Material Contribution to Damage, Again' (2022) 138 LQR 540; SH Bailey, '"Material Contribution" after *Williams v The Bermuda Hospitals Board*' (2018) 38 LS 411; Michael Rawlinson and Charley Turton, 'The Two Cultures: How Disease and Clinical Negligence Practitioners Approach the Application of Material Contribution to Causation in Law' [2022] J Pers Inj L 193.

66 [1956] AC 613.

('innocent dust'). Measures were available to protect him against the dust emanating from the swing grinders ('guilty dust'), but the employer failed to take those measures, which was negligent and in breach of statutory duty. The steel dresser developed pneumoconiosis in the course of his employment and claimed damages from his employer. The employer argued that it had not been proved that the guilty dust was a cause of the pneumoconiosis.

The House of Lords rejected the argument that the employer bore the onus of proof in relation to factual causation. But it held that the steel dresser had discharged his onus. Medical evidence established that pneumoconiosis is caused by the gradual accumulation in the lungs of minute particles of silica over a period of years. Their Lordships said that while the majority of particles in the air that the steelworker had breathed came from the hammer, a non-negligible part came from the swing grinders, and the defendant's breach of duty had therefore materially contributed to the pneumoconiosis.

Their Lordships' reasoning is unclear in two important respects. First, pneumoconiosis is a divisible disease, which is present where the severity of the disease increases with the amount of the claimant's exposure to the noxious substance. In those circumstances, the court should do the best it can to ascertain the share of the damage for which the defendant is responsible and hold the defendant liable for that share and no more. But the House of Lords in *Wardlaw* held the defendant liable for the entire damage. Their Lordships were aware that pneumoconiosis is a divisible disease but, without explanation, treated the case as if it involved an indivisible disease. Perhaps their Lordships regarded it as impossible to ascertain the proportions of the innocent dust and the guilty dust and resolved that uncertainty against the defendant.

Secondly, the House of Lords in *Wardlaw* made no reference to whether the innocent dust alone was sufficient to bring about the pneumoconiosis (at the time at which it was suffered) or whether this fact was unclear. This gives rise to two possible interpretations of the decision, which are relevant only for indivisible diseases. *Wardlaw* may be authority for the proposition that a person who made a wrongful contribution is liable even if it is established that the non-wrongful contribution alone was sufficient to bring about the damage. Alternatively, *Wardlaw* may be authority only for the proposition that where it is unclear whether the non-wrongful contribution alone was sufficient to bring about the damage, the uncertainty will be resolved against the defendant.[67]

There are thus three possible interpretations of the decision in *Wardlaw*:

---

[67] *Loftus-Brigham v London Borough of Ealing* [2003] EWCA Civ 1490, (2003) 103 Con LR 102 is another case in which the defendant's wrong combined with a non-wrongful event, and factual causation was found without investigating whether the non-wrongful event would have been sufficient to bring about the harm.

(1) *Wardlaw* is relevant only for divisible diseases and established that a person who made a wrongful contribution to the disease may be liable for the entire damage where the share in the damage for which that person is responsible cannot be ascertained.
(2) *Wardlaw* is relevant only for indivisible diseases and established that a person who made a wrongful contribution to the disease is liable even if the evidence shows that a non-wrongful contribution alone was sufficient to bring about the damage.
(3) *Wardlaw* is relevant only for indivisible diseases and established that where it is unclear whether a non-wrongful contribution alone was sufficient to bring about the damage, the uncertainty will be resolved against the defendant.

Each of those three interpretations has found support in the English Court of Appeal. In *Bailey v Ministry of Defence*,[68] the claimant, a patient in the defendant's hospital, aspirated her vomit which led to a cardiac arrest that caused her to suffer brain damage. It was found that the physical cause of the aspiration was the claimant's weakness, which was partly due to her recovering from an operation and partly due to lack of care on the defendant's part. The Court of Appeal held the defendant liable. The Court stated that 'where medical science cannot establish the probability that "but for" an act of negligence the injury would not have happened but can establish that the contribution of the negligent cause was more than negligible, the "but for" test is modified, and the claimant will succeed'.[69] Crucially, the Court added this: 'If the evidence demonstrates on the balance of probabilities that the injury would have occurred as a result of the non-tortious cause or causes in any event, the claimant will have failed to established that the tortious cause contributed.'[70] The same Court approvingly quoted those statements in *Reaney v University Hospital of North Staffordshire NHS Trust*.[71] These cases thus subscribed to the third interpretation of *Wardlaw* set out above.

The Court of Appeal seems to have endorsed the second interpretation in *Heneghan v Manchester Dry Docks Ltd*.[72] Lord Dyson MR, with whom Tomlinson LJ and Sales LJ agreed, stated, citing *Wardlaw*, that 'where the disease is caused by the cumulative effect of an agency part of which is attributable to breach of duty on the part of the defendant and part of which involves

---

68 [2008] EWCA Civ 883, [2009] 1 WLR 1052.
69 ibid [46] (Waller LJ speaking for the Court).
70 ibid.
71 [2015] EWCA Civ 1119, [2016] PIQR Q3 [35].
72 [2016] EWCA Civ 86, [2016] 1 WLR 2036.

no breach of duty, the defendant will be liable on the ground that his breach of duty made a "material contribution" to the disease'.[73]

In *Ministry of Defence v AB*,[74] which involved cancer, the Court of Appeal stated that the *Wardlaw* rule does not apply to an indivisible disease; it applies only where the disease is divisible and it is not possible to apportion the harm between the various contributions.[75] Thus, the Court adopted the first interpretation of *Wardlaw* set out above.

Subsequently, in *Holmes v Poeton Holdings Ltd*,[76] the Court of Appeal rejected what had been said in *AB*.[77] The Court said that it was bound by *Bailey* to find that the *Wardlaw* rule applies to indivisible diseases.[78] With regard to divisible diseases, the Court[79] referred to its previous decision in *Holtby v Brigham & Cowan (Hull) Ltd*,[80] which involved asbestosis (a divisible disease) and in which the Court held that where the disease is divisible, the defendant is liable only for its share of the damage. In *Holmes*, the Court also made clear that where the *Wardlaw* rule applies, the claimant does not have to show that the injury would not have occurred but for the defendant's wrong.[81] The Court[82] rejected a statement by the Privy Council suggesting that the 'but for' test had been satisfied in *Bailey*.[83]

The interpretation of *Wardlaw* adopted in *Bailey* and *Reaney* ought to prevail. Where the disease is divisible, the defendant ought to be liable only for its share in the damage.[84] Where it is difficult to determine the impact of each contribution, the court should take a broad-brush approach, being generous to the claimant.

Where the disease is indivisible, the *Wardlaw* rule makes an exception to the 'but for' test.[85] Gemma Turton has argued that factual causation is established

---

73 ibid [23].

74 [2010] EWCA Civ 1317, (2011) 117 BMLR 101.

75 ibid [134].

76 [2023] EWCA Civ 1377, [2024] KB 521.

77 ibid [64]–[65].

78 ibid [63].

79 ibid [60].

80 [2000] 3 All ER 421, approving *Thompson v Smiths Shiprepairers (North Shields) Ltd* [1984] QB 405.

81 [2023] EWCA Civ 1377, [2024] KB 521 [63].

82 ibid [67].

83 *Williams v Bermuda Hospitals Board* [2016] UKPC 4, [2016] AC 888 [47].

84 *Sienkiewicz v Greif (UK) Ltd* [2011] UKSC 10, [2011] 2 AC 229 [17] (Lord Phillips PSC); approvingly quoted in *Allianz Australia Insurance Ltd v Pomfret* [2015] NSWCA 4, (2015) 88 NSWLR 192 [49].

85 For a different view, see Neil Foster, 'Material Contribution in *Bonnington*: Not an Exception to "But For" Causation' (2022) 49 UWALR 404. In any event,

under the NESS test because the defendant's contribution is necessary for the sufficiency of a set that contains the defendant's contribution and only so much of the other contributions that is necessary to make the set sufficient; the disaggregation of the other contributions should be permitted.[86] Disaggregation of the non-wrongful contribution may be possible in the *Wardlaw* scenario as it involves a multitude of silica particles.[87] By contrast, it is difficult to see how the claimant's natural post-operative weakness in *Bailey* can be divided into component parts.[88]

The non-negligible contribution to an indivisible disease ought to be regarded as a factual cause of the disease, either under the NESS test or a modification of the 'but for' test. There remains the question of whether the defendant's responsibility for the harm should be denied (at the scope of liability stage) where there was a non-wrongful contribution which alone was sufficient to bring about the indivisible disease. As explained earlier in this chapter, responsibility is denied where the defendant's wrong pre-empted a non-wrongful event from bringing about the loss. This rule could be criticised, but it is too entrenched to be abolished. For consistency, responsibility should also be denied where the defendant's wrong coincided with a non-wrongful event which alone was sufficient to bring about the loss.[89] However, evidential uncertainty as to whether the non-wrongful event was sufficient ought to be resolved against the defendant.

Material increase in risk

The concept of material increase in risk has been developed in relation to the following circumstances. Each of two or more events, which include the

---

the 'but for' test is satisfied insofar as the defendant's wrong accelerated the onset of the disease.

[86] Gemma Turton, 'Using NESS to Overcome the Confusion Created by the "Material Contribution to the Harm" Test for Causation in Negligence' (2014) 30 Prof Negl 50.

[87] A possible objection is that it might not have been possible for the pneumatic hammer to emanate only that amount of silica dust which was required in combination with the silica dust emanating from the swing grinders to have just enough silica dust to bring about the pneumoconiosis; see Mark Kelman, 'The Necessary Myth of Objective Causation Judgments in Liberal Political Theory' (1987) 63 Chi-Kent L Rev 579, 604 (discussing Wright's pollution example set out earlier in this chapter).

[88] For the argument that drunkenness and the willingness to kill cannot be disaggregated, see Ben Gifford, 'State v Brelo and the Problem of Actual Causation' (2017) 44 Am J Crim L 157, 184.

[89] The defendant is, however, liable for any acceleration in the onset of the harm.

defendant's wrong and may include non-wrongful events, is capable of having caused the claimant's indivisible harm. It is clear from the evidence that only one of those events caused the harm. But it is unclear which one it was. The notorious example is that of two hunters who, independently of each other, shoot in the direction of the claimant, who is hit by one bullet; it cannot be established which of the two hunters fired that bullet.[90] The claimant cannot discharge the usual onus of proving factual causation.

Where the inability to prove factual causation is due to limits of scientific knowledge,[91] the English courts have developed a rule assisting the claimant, essentially starting with *Fairchild v Glenhaven Funeral Services Ltd*.[92] The claimants developed mesothelioma after having been wrongfully exposed to asbestos dust during their employment. However, each claimant was exposed to asbestos dust by two or more separate employers. According to the medical evidence presented in that case, mesothelioma may be caused by a single asbestos fibre and the condition once caused is not aggravated by further exposure to asbestos fibres.[93] Thus, only one employer of each claimant caused the mesothelioma, but it could not be established which one. The House of Lords unanimously held that all employers were liable.

The House of Lords clarified the *Fairchild* principle in *Barker v Corus (UK) Ltd*,[94] which involved the same facts as *Fairchild* except that one claimant had an additional period of exposure to asbestos dust while he was self-employed. The House of Lords pronounced three rules.[95] First, the *Fairchild* principle does not require that every possible cause of the harm was due to a wrong. Secondly, the *Fairchild* principle does require that all potential causative agents operated in the same way. Thus, it would not apply where it cannot be established whether the plaintiff's lung cancer was caused by smoking or by exposure to asbestos. Thirdly, and most importantly, a defendant who is liable under the *Fairchild* principle is liable only for a proportion of the

---

90 These were the facts of *Summers v Tice*, 33 Cal 2d 80 (1948) and *Cook v Lewis* [1951] SCR 830. In each case, the claimant succeeded against both hunters.

91 A lack of evidence or of factual findings made by the trial judge is not sufficient to render the *Fairchild* principle applicable; see *Sanderson v Hull* [2008] EWCA Civ 1211, [2009] PIQR P7 [54]–[63].

92 [2002] UKHL 22, [2003] 1 AC 32. The House of Lords relied on its previous decision in *McGhee v National Coal Board* [1973] 1 WLR 1, but that decision has been interpreted in different ways. *McGhee* had been applied in *Fitzgerald v Lane* [1987] QB 781.

93 The single fibre theory has since been discredited; see *Sienkiewicz v Greif (UK) Ltd* [2011] UKSC 10, [2011] 2 AC 229 [102] (Lord Phillips PSC).

94 [2006] UKHL 20, [2006] 2 AC 572.

95 Lord Rodger dissented in relation to the third rule.

the chain of causation where it was the result of mental illness caused by the wrong,[163] or where the duty breached by the defendant aimed to prevent the victim's suicide.[164] Otherwise, suicide may break the chain of causation.[165] The same rules apply to a failed suicide attempt.[166] Furthermore, where the claimant experiences an unintended pregnancy because of the defendant's negligent performance of a sterilisation operation, the claimant's decision not to terminate the pregnancy and not to give the child up for adoption does not break the chain of causation.[167] It has been said that such a decision is not so unreasonable as to eclipse the defendant's wrongdoing.[168] It may be better to say that the claimant does not have a truly free choice as the decision to terminate a pregnancy or to give the child up for adoption may have a detrimental impact on the claimant (and her partner).

The final category is where the claimant engaged in unreasonable conduct which, in conjunction with the defendant's wrong, led to the loss in question. In *McKew v Holland & Hannen & Cubitts (Scotland) Ltd*,[169] the respondent's negligence caused the appellant an injury as a result of which he occasionally, but without warning, lost control of his left leg. Shortly after the accident, the appellant, accompanied by his family, went to inspect a first-floor flat with a view to renting it. On leaving the flat, he went down the steep stairs which had no handrail. Suddenly, his left leg gave way and, in order to save himself from falling, the appellant jumped some ten steps and fractured his ankle. The House of Lords held that the respondent was not liable for the fractured ankle because the appellant's decision to descend steep stairs without a handrail and without adult assistance had been unreasonable and had broken the chain of causation.

---

163 *Corr v IBC Vehicles Ltd* [2008] UKHL 13, [2008] 1 AC 884; *Pigney v Pointer's Transport Services Ltd* [1957] 1 WLR 1121.

164 *Reeves v Commissioner of Police of the Metropolis* [2000] 1 AC 360 (where the suicide was, however, held to constitute contributory negligence).

165 *Corr v IBC Vehicles Ltd* [2008] UKHL 13, [2008] 1 AC 884 [15], approving *Wright Estate v Davidson* (1992) 88 DLR (4th) 698, 705.

166 *Corr v IBC Vehicles Ltd* [2008] UKHL 13, [2008] 1 AC 884 [26].

167 *McFarlane v Tayside Health Board* [2000] 2 AC 59, 74, 81, 97, 105, 112–13. A claimant's decision to have sexual intercourse in the knowledge that she is not sterile does break the chain of causation: *Sabri-Tabrizi v Lothian Health Board* 1998 SC 373.

168 *Emeh v Kensington and Chelsea and Westminster Area Health Authority* [1985] QB 1012, 1019, 1024, 1027.

169 1970 SC (HL) 20. Cf *Wieland v Cyril Lord Carpets Ltd* [1969] 3 All ER 1006, which had similar facts, but the defendant was held liable as the plaintiff had taken sufficient regard for her own safety.

It may be said that the appellant's conduct in *McKew* was not just unreasonable but grossly unreasonable. Indeed, it is established that the claimant's conduct must reach a high degree of unreasonableness in order to break the chain of causation;[170] 'it must constitute an event of such impact that it obliterates the wrongdoing of the defendant'.[171] This is demonstrated by *Spencer v Wincanton Holdings Ltd*.[172] As a result of the defendant's negligence, the claimant's knee had to be amputated. Eight months after the amputation, the claimant filled his car at a petrol station without asking for help or using sticks or his prosthesis. He tripped and fell, sustaining further injury which confined him to a wheelchair permanently. The Court of Appeal held that the defendant was liable for the further injury. While the claimant's conduct was unreasonable (and thus constituted contributory negligence),[173] it did not reach the degree of unreasonableness required for a break in the chain of causation. The Court refused to lay down a definition of the required degree such as recklessness.[174]

In *Clay v TUI UK Ltd*,[175] the Court of Appeal observed that whether the conduct of the claimant breaks the chain of causation depends upon the extent to which the conduct was reasonably foreseeable, the degree of unreasonableness of the conduct, and the extent to which it was voluntary and independent conduct.

Conduct of the claimant does not break the chain of causation where the claimant was incapable of appreciating the danger because of youth[176] or mental disability,[177] or where the claimant needed to make a quick decision in an emergency created by the defendant.[178]

Unreasonable conduct of the claimant may affect the defendant's liability for resulting loss also through the avoidable loss rule and the doctrine of contributory negligence. The relationship of these two doctrines to each other and

---

170 eg, *Emeh v Kensington and Chelsea and Westminster Area Health Authority* [1985] QB 1012, 1019. For a discussion in the context of contract law, see Wayne Courtney, 'Contract Damages and the Promisee's Role in Its Own Loss' (2019) 42 MULR 406, 422, 435–36.

171 *Stephen v Peters* 2005 SCLR 513 [36] (Lord Menzies).

172 [2009] EWCA Civ 1404, [2010] PIQR P8.

173 Contributory negligence is discussed later in this chapter.

174 [2009] EWCA Civ 1404, [2010] PIQR P8 [19], [43].

175 [2018] EWCA Civ 1177, [2018] 4 All ER 672 [28].

176 *Lynch v Nurdin* (1841) 1 QB 29, 38 (Lord Denman CJ); *Latham v R Johnson & Nephew Ltd* [1913] 1 KB 398, 413; *Glasgow Corporation v Taylor* [1922] 1 AC 44; *Yachuk v Oliver Blais Co Ltd* [1949] AC 386 (PC).

177 *Atchison, Topeka & Santa Fe Railway Co v Parry*, 73 Pac 105 (Kan, 1903).

178 *Jones v Boyce* (1816) 1 Starkie 493; 171 ER 540; *Latham v R Johnson & Nephew Ltd* [1913] 1 KB 398, 413.

to the doctrine of *novus actus interveniens* (as applied to the conduct of the claimant) will be discussed later in this chapter.

Basic loss: independent subsequent event

In this section and the next section, we consider the situation where both the defendant's wrong and a subsequent event were each sufficient to bring about the loss in respect of which compensation is claimed. This section is concerned with a subsequent event that has the following three features. First, the defendant's wrong is not a factual cause of the subsequent event. Second, the defendant is not responsible for the subsequent event.[179] Finally, the defendant's wrong pre-empted the effects of the subsequent event. It is thus a case of pre-emptive causation mentioned earlier in this chapter.

The subsequent event may be wrongful or non-wrongful, and it may be actual (it did occur) or hypothetical (it would have occurred had the defendant's wrong not occurred). There are thus four categories of case.

An actual wrongful event does not remove the loss from the scope of the defendant's liability. As an illustration, Lord Hobhouse has stated that if a car is negligently damaged by one tortfeasor and destroyed by fire the next day by the negligence of another, the first tortfeasor remains liable for the cost of repairing the damage he caused.[180] The leading case for the rule is *Baker v Willoughby*.[181] The plaintiff's left leg was injured in 1964 when he was knocked down by a car negligently driven by the defendant. The ankle became stiff, and the plaintiff suffered pain, loss of those amenities of life as dependent on the ability to move freely, and some loss of earning capacity. In 1967, the plaintiff was shot in the same leg during an armed robbery, and the leg had to be amputated above the knee.

The House of Lords held that the amputation did not obliterate the effect of the defendant's negligence and that he remained liable, beyond 1967, for the loss caused by the plaintiff's left leg hypothetically being stiff rather than healthy. Lord Pearson explained that the robber would be liable only for the loss of a stiff leg, not a healthy leg; thus, if the second tort obliterated the effect of the first tort, the plaintiff would not receive full compensation.[182] His Lordship made this argument particularly in relation to the loss of earning capacity. Lord Reid made clear that if the result of the amputation was that the plaintiff could no longer suffer pain in the left leg, he could not claim for pain

---

179 A defendant who is responsible for both the wrong and the subsequent event is liable for a loss that either event on its own was sufficient to inflict: *Cambridge v Anastasopoulos* [2012] NSWCA 405 [49]–[50].

180 *Dimond v Lovell* [2002] 1 AC 384, 406.

181 [1970] AC 467.

182 ibid 495.

after the amputation; however, the facts on this were not clear, and the sum for pain was probably only a small part of the damages award.[183]

An actual non-wrongful event does remove the loss from the scope of the defendant's liability. For example, the owner of a negligently damaged vessel has no claim for the loss of profit during the time of repair where the repair was done during a period in which the ship was in any event detained by ice or an embargo.[184] The leading case for the rule is *Jobling v Associated Dairies Ltd*.[185] In 1973, the plaintiff suffered a work injury as a result of the negligence of his employer, the defendant. He was left with continuing back pain, which reduced his earning capacity by 50 percent. In 1976, the plaintiff was found to be suffering from a condition (spondylotic myelopathy) which was not connected with the work injury and which rendered him totally unfit to work by the end of 1976. The House of Lords held that the plaintiff was not entitled to damages for loss of earning capacity from the end of 1976. *Baker v Willoughby* was distinguished on the ground that the supervening event there had been wrongful whereas the supervening event in *Jobling* was non-wrongful. Lord Edmund-Davies made clear that it was not relevant whether the illness developed after the wrong or was already present, but dormant, at the time of the wrong.[186]

Hypothetical subsequent events are treated in the same way as actual ones. Thus, a hypothetical wrongful event does not remove the loss from the scope of the defendant's liability. A defendant's responsibility is not diminished by the likelihood that, had the defendant not wronged the claimant, someone else would have done so.[187]

---

183 ibid 494.

184 *Carslogie Steamship Co Ltd v Royal Norwegian Government* [1952] AC 292, 300, citing *The York* [1929] P 178, 185–86. In *The York*, damage negligently caused by the defendant to the plaintiff's vessel was repaired while the vessel was in dry dock for inspection by a prospective buyer. The claim for loss of profit during the time of repair was rejected.

185 [1982] AC 794.

186 ibid 807–08. For a discussion of *Baker v Willoughby* and *Jobling*, see Eoin Quill, 'Successive Causes and the Measurement of Damages' (2002) 37 Ir Jur 91.

187 *Kuwait Airways Corp v Iraqi Airways Co (Nos 4 and 5)* [2002] UKHL 19, [2002] 2 AC 883 [82] (Lord Nicholls); *AIB Group (UK) plc v Mark Redler & Co Solicitors* [2014] UKSC 58, [2015] AC 1503 [58] (Lord Toulson JSC). Nor can a defendant escape liability by saying that if he had not breached this duty, he would have breached some other duty and caused the same damage: *Bolitho v City and Hackney Health Authority* [1998] AC 232, 240. Lord Neuberger MR endorsed both propositions in *Wright v Cambridge Medical Group* [2011] EWCA Civ 669, [2013] QB 312 [56]–[61].

A hypothetical non-wrongful event does affect the defendant's liability. It excludes liability completely where it is certain that the event would have inflicted the same loss had the defendant's wrong not occurred.[188] Often, such certainty does not exist. Uncertainty may be resolved on the balance of probabilities (all or nothing) or by making a proportionate damages award. The relevant principles are discussed in Chapter 2.

Hypothetical conduct of the claimant, which is always determined on the balance of probabilities, was present in *Calvert v William Hill Credit Ltd.*[189] The defendant bookmaker offered the claimant, whom the bookmaker knew to be a compulsive gambler, the choice of a self-exclusion agreement whereby, at the request of the claimant, the defendant would not accept telephone bets from him for six months. The claimant made such a request, but due to an oversight by the defendant's employees, the defendant continued to accept bets from the claimant, who lost £2m in the following six months. An action by the claimant in negligence was rejected on the ground that, had the defendant refused to accept bets from the claimant in those six months, the claimant would probably have lost the same amount of money by placing bets with other bookmakers.[190]

Basic loss: dependent subsequent event

This section, like the previous one, is concerned with the situation where both the defendant's wrong and a subsequent event were each sufficient to bring about the loss in respect of which compensation is claimed. We now consider a subsequent event that would not have occurred but for the defendant's wrong. Where the subsequent event falls within the scope of the defendant's liability, the defendant is undoubtedly liable for the loss in question. Liability for the loss has been denied where the subsequent event falls outside the scope of the defendant's liability. Three cases illustrate this rule.

---

188 eg, *Golden Strait Corporation v Nippon Yusen Kubishika Kaisha (The 'Golden Victory')* [2007] UKHL 12, [2007] 2 AC 353; *R (Lumba) v Secretary of State for the Home Department* [2011] UKSC 12, [2012] 1 AC 245. These cases are discussed in Ch 2.

189 [2008] EWCA Civ 1427, [2009] Ch 330.

190 Stiggelbout, who supports the exclusion of liability by virtue of a hypothetical non-wrongful event, criticises the decision in *Calvert* on the ground that the hypothetical wagers with other bookmakers cannot be regarded as loss as they would have been voluntary transactions for consideration: Mark Stiggelbout, 'The Case of "Losses in Any Event": A Question of Duty, Cause or Damages?' (2010) 30 LS 558, 577–80.

The first is *Carslogie Steamship Co Ltd v Royal Norwegian Government*,[191] the facts of which were set out earlier in this chapter. The plaintiff's vessel remained in dry dock for 50 days, during which period the collision damage, the heavy weather damage, and some other, unrelated damage were repaired. It was agreed that repairing only the collision damage would have taken 10 days, and that repairing only the heavy weather damage would have taken 30 days. While the plaintiff's claim for the cost of the collision repairs succeeded, the House of Lords rejected the claim for the loss of chartered hire for 10 days. Viscount Jowitt, acknowledging that this claim would have succeeded if the heavy weather damage had not occurred,[192] explained:

> If there had been no collision [the plaintiff's vessel] would have been detained in dock for 30 days to repair [the heavy weather] damage. I cannot see that her owners sustained any damages in the nature of demurrage by reason of the fact that for 10 days out of the 30 days she was also undergoing repairs in respect of the collision.[193]

This explanation can only be accepted if it is assumed that the vessel would have experienced the same heavy weather if, instead of sailing from Scotland to New York at a particular time, it had sailed from Scotland to West Africa at a different time. But such an assumption cannot be made and was not made by the House of Lords.[194]

Carslogie was applied in *Beoco Ltd v Alfa Laval Co Ltd*.[195] In 1987, the first defendant installed a heat exchanger in the plaintiff's seed-oil plant. In August 1988, a crack was discovered, and the second defendant purported to repair it. Subsequently, a hydraulic pressure test was conducted. Even though it failed, the plaintiff's engineers put the system in operation again. In October 1988, the heat exchanger exploded, causing significant damage to equipment and loss of profit. Both defendants were liable for breach of contract, but the action of the plaintiff's engineers was held to be reckless and a *novus actus interveniens*. The plaintiff argued that the first defendant was still liable for the cost of repairing the heat exchanger (including loss of profit during the time

---

191 [1952] AC 292.

192 ibid 302.

193 ibid 301.

194 The decision has been explained by saying that the defendant was not liable for the heavy weather damage because it was coincidental damage: James Edelman, *McGregor on Damages* (21st edn, Sweet & Maxwell 2021) [8-056]. True, the denial of responsibility on the defendant's part for *additional* damage inflicted by the heavy weather was justified. But it does not follow that responsibility must also be denied for the loss of use of the vessel for 10 days, which loss would have occurred even without the heavy weather and was not coincidental.

195 [1995] QB 137.

of repair) which would have been incurred but for the explosion. The Court of Appeal held that the first defendant was liable only for the cost of replacing the defective casing of the heat exchanger and loss of profit during the period of the second defendant's repair work. The Court relied on both *Carslogie* and *Jobling v Associated Dairies Ltd*,[196] and made no distinction between dependent and independent subsequent events.

The final case is *Gray v Thames Trains Ltd*,[197] the facts of which were set out earlier in this chapter. The claimant argued that if he had not committed the manslaughter (and thus had not been detained in a mental hospital), he would still have suffered loss of earnings because of the PTSD caused by the defendant's negligence. The House of Lords rejected the claim for such loss of earnings. Lord Hoffmann expressed the view that the claim was precluded by the *Jobling* principle.[198] Similarly, Lord Rodger observed that 'it would be highly artificial to ignore the fact that, by committing manslaughter, the claimant had created a new set of circumstances which actually made it impossible for him to work and to earn after that date'.[199] Lord Brown observed that the *Jobling* principle did not apply because the subsequent event in *Jobling* (myelopathy) was unconnected with the defendant's negligence whereas in *Gray* the manslaughter and detention would not have occurred but for the defendant's negligence.[200] But his Lordship thought that the claim was nonetheless precluded by the same principle of consistency that excluded the claim for the consequences of a criminal sanction.[201] This is unconvincing. The claim for loss of earnings was solely based on the PTSD and not on any criminality.

Apart from Lord Brown's reasoning in *Gray*, the courts in the three cases gave a dependent non-wrongful event the same effect as an independent non-wrongful event, namely the removal of the loss from the scope of the defendant's liability. It means that the defendant is exculpated by an event that would not have occurred but for the defendant's wrong. It is difficult to find a justification for this rule.

Remoteness of Loss

Remoteness of loss is a term that has been used with various meanings. In its widest meaning, it captures any loss outside the scope of the defendant's

---

196 [1982] AC 794, discussed earlier in this chapter.
197 [2009] UKHL 33, [2009] 1 AC 1339.
198 ibid [49].
199 ibid [75].
200 ibid [96].
201 ibid [99]–[101], relying on *State Rail Authority of NSW v Wiegold* (1991) 25 NSWLR 500.

liability. A narrower meaning comprises intervening acts and unforeseeable loss. In its most limited meaning, which we use in this book, it is only concerned with unforeseeable loss. Depending on what one understands by causation and remoteness, the doctrine of remoteness may be part of the causal inquiry or may be a doctrine that limits liability separately from the causal inquiry. In any event, remoteness must not be understood in a physical or temporal sense. 'Ultimately remoteness is a value judgment about the scope of liability for consequences.'[202] The defendant bears the legal burden of pleading and proving that a particular item of loss is too remote.[203]

Damage factually caused by the defendant's wrong may be too remote (in its narrowest sense) if the defendant did not intend to inflict that damage and if a reasonable person in the defendant's position was unable to foresee the type of damage at a certain date with a certain degree of probability. This applies particularly to breaches of contract and negligence. However, the remoteness rules for contract and negligence differ with regard to the date at which, and the degree of probability with which, the type of damage needs to have been foreseeable. Liability for some other wrongs, in particular intentional torts, extends to unforeseeable loss. The relevant rules are discussed for the various types of wrong in Chapters 4–6.

Purpose of the Duty Breached

Sometimes, the courts have denied liability for a particular loss on the grounds that the duty breached by the defendant does not aim to prevent this type of loss. Thus, even though the defendant's wrong was a factual cause of the loss, the loss is not attributed to the defendant for policy reasons.[204] The principle finds its main field of application in the tort of negligence, but it should also apply to breach of contract.[205]

---

[202] Janet O'Sullivan, 'Negligent Damage to Bailed Property and Foreseeable Financial Loss' (2024) 83 Camb LJ 218, 221.

[203] *Armstead v Royal & Sun Alliance Insurance Co Ltd* [2024] UKSC 6, [2025] AC 406 [62].

[204] In the tort of negligence, the duty of care may be limited to a particular class of persons. For example, an auditor's duty to exercise reasonable care in auditing a company's accounts is owed to the company's existing shareholders but not to prospective shareholders: *Caparo Industries plc v Dickman* [1990] 2 AC 605.

[205] Andrew Burrows, 'Comparing Compensatory Damages in Tort and Contract: Some Problematic Issues' in Simone Degeling, James Edelman and James Goudkamp (eds), *Torts in Commercial Law* (LBC 2011), 373–74.

A prominent case is *South Australia Asset Management Corporation v York Montague Ltd*,[206] which combined cases with the following facts. A lender engaged a valuer to value a property on the security of which the lender was considering advancing money on mortgage. The valuer considerably overvalued the property, which constituted a breach of contract and negligence. The loan was made, which it would not have done had the lender known the true value of the property. The borrower subsequently defaulted. In the meantime, the property market had fallen substantially, and the proceeds of the sale of the property fell far short of the outstanding loan. The lender claimed damages (for negligence and breach of contract) in the amount of this shortfall. The House of Lords held that the valuer could not be liable for more than the difference between the incorrectly reported value and the actual value of the property at the time of the valuation. The valuer's duty to exercise care in the valuation does not aim to protect the lender from a fall in the property market.

Lord Hoffmann, who gave the only reasoned speech, stated that '[n]ormally the law limits liability to those consequences which are attributable to that which made the act wrongful. In the case of liability for negligence for providing inaccurate information, this would mean liability for the consequences of the information being inaccurate'.[207] His Lordship provided the following example:

> A mountaineer about to undertake a difficult climb is concerned about the fitness of his knee. He goes to a doctor who negligently makes a superficial examination and pronounces the knee fit. The climber goes on the expedition, which he would not have undertaken if the doctor had told him the true state of his knee. He suffers an injury which is an entirely foreseeable consequence of mountaineering but has nothing to do with his knee … The injury has not been caused by the doctor's bad advice because it would have occurred even if the advice had been correct.[208]

---

206 [1997] AC 191 ('*SAAMCO*').

207 ibid 213.

208 ibid.

The decision has been controversial,[209] and was not followed by the High Court of Australia.[210] But the UK Supreme Court confirmed the 'purpose of the duty' principle, and extended it to all professional advisers and beyond pure economic loss, in two cases decided on the same day, although the principle was seen as defining the scope of the duty of care rather than negating causation.[211] In *Manchester Building Society v Grant Thornton UK LLP*,[212] which involved negligent advice by an auditor, Lord Hodge DPSC and Lord Sales JSC, with whom Lord Reed PSC, Lord Kitchin JSC and Lady Black agreed, stated:

> [T]he scope of the duty of care assumed by a professional adviser is governed by the purpose of the duty, judged on an objective basis by reference to the reason why the advice is being given … [I]n the case of negligent advice given by a professional adviser one looks to see what risk the duty was supposed to guard against and then looks to see whether the loss suffered represented the fruition of that risk. This is the point of the mountaineer's knee example given by Lord Hoffmann in *SAAMCO*.[213]

In *Meadows v Khan*,[214] the claimant consulted the defendant general practitioner to establish whether she was a carrier of the haemophilia gene. The defendant negligently advised her that she was not, when in fact she was. Subsequently, the claimant gave birth to a son who suffered from haemophilia as well as autism, which was unrelated to the haemophilia. If the claimant had known that she was a carrier of the haemophilia gene, she would have undergone foetal testing, would have discovered that the foetus was affected, and would have terminated the pregnancy. She sought damages for the addi-

---

209 Some commentators take the view that the valuer should be liable for the entire loss; eg, David M McLauchlan, 'A Damages Dilemma' (1997) 12 JCL 114. Others have suggested a different way of limiting the valuer's liability; eg, Alexander Loke, 'The Valuer's Liability for Negligent Valuation – Toward a More Principled Allocation of the Risk of Market Decline' (1999) 19 LS 47. In *Platform Home Loans Ltd v Oyston Shipways Ltd* [2002] 2 AC 190, it was held that a deduction for contributory negligence must be made before applying the *SAAMCO* limit.

210 *Kenny & Good Pty Ltd v MGICA (1992) Ltd* [1999] HCA 25, (1999) 199 CLR 413. For a discussion of that case, see Stanley W Drummond, 'Liability of Valuers and Other Professionals: *Kenny & Good v MGICA*' (1999) 7 Torts LJ 217.

211 The principle so re-conceptualised was applied to negligence on the part of solicitors in *Hughes-Holland v BPE Solicitors* [2017] UKSC 21, [2018] AC 599.

212 [2021] UKSC 20, [2022] AC 783.

213 ibid [13], [17]. Their Lordships (at [18]–[22]) added that there was no distinction between 'advice' and 'information', which had been made in *SAAMCO*.

214 [2021] UKSC 21, [2022] AC 852.

tional cost of raising her son.[215] The Supreme Court held that the claimant could recover the additional cost associated with the child's haemophilia but not the cost associated with his autism. This was because the defendant had been under a duty to give accurate advice in respect of haemophilia but not in respect of an unrelated risk which might arise in any pregnancy.[216]

THE CLAIMANT'S CONTRIBUTION TO THE LOSS

Sometimes, a claimant behaved unreasonably either before or after the defendant's wrong, and a particular item of loss factually caused by the defendant's wrong would have been avoided had the claimant behaved reasonably. Some civil law systems have a general rule (for contract and tort) that the court may, in those circumstances, exclude or reduce the defendant's liability for the relevant loss, having regard to the conduct of each party.[217] Common law systems do not have such a general rule. Instead, the effect of unreasonable conduct of the claimant on the defendant's liability is addressed by several doctrines which differ in their effect and in relation to the types of wrong to which they apply. This section discusses those doctrines.

Overview of the Relevant Doctrines

Common law systems have developed two doctrines specifically for the purpose of addressing the effect of unreasonable conduct of the claimant on the defendant's liability: the avoidable loss rule (as part of the doctrine of mitigation), which originated in contract and has spread to tort,[218] and the doctrine of contributory negligence,[219] which originated in the tort of negligence and

---

[215] In English law, the parents of an unintended child cannot recover the ordinary cost of raising a child but only the special cost associated with rearing a child with a serious disability: *Parkinson v St James and Seacroft University Hospital NHS Trust* [2001] EWCA Civ 530, [2002] QB 266.

[216] [2021] UKSC 21, [2022] AC 852 [67]–[68].

[217] Eg §254 of the German Civil Code.

[218] *Admiralty Commissioners v Owners of Steamship Chekiang* [1926] AC 637, 646 (Lord Sumner); *The Liverpool (No 2)* [1963] P 64, 77–78.

[219] In US legal terminology, the phrase 'contributory negligence' denotes the complete exoneration of the defendant at common law, while the phrase 'comparative negligence' denotes the apportionment of liability either at common law (in maritime cases) or under legislation. In other common law jurisdictions, the phrase 'contributory negligence' denotes both the complete bar and the apportionment regime. This book adopts the terminology prevalent in England and the British Commonwealth.

has spread to some other torts and some breaches of contract. In addition, as mentioned before in this chapter, certain post-wrong conduct of the claimant may constitute a *novus actus interveniens* removing the relevant loss from the scope of the defendant's liability. This applies to contract and tort. In some cases involving breach of contract, recovery for loss resulting from the unreasonable conduct of the claimant has been denied on the ground that the loss was too remote.[220] The defendant bears the legal burden of invoking any of those doctrines.[221]

The two specific doctrines differ in their effect and in relation to the types of wrong to which they apply. The avoidable loss rule applies in contract and tort and completely bars recovery for any loss that the claimant could have avoided. By contrast, the doctrine of contributory negligence applies only to some torts and some breaches of contract and leads to an apportionment of the loss to which the claimant contributed. It is, therefore, important to determine the circumstances in which each doctrine applies.

Many commentators suggest that the doctrine of contributory negligence applies to conduct of the claimant before the defendant's wrong and the avoidable loss rule to conduct thereafter.[222] It is indeed established that the avoidable loss rule applies only to conduct of the claimant after the claimant became aware of the wrong.[223] This is appropriate, as the harsh consequence of the avoidable loss rule (complete exclusion of recovery for the relevant head of loss rather than apportionment) can be justified only where the claimant knew at least the facts disclosing the wrong.[224] It does not follow that the avoidable loss rule must apply to every such conduct. The legislation that provides for an

---

220 *Baxendale v London, Chatham and Dover Railway Co* (1874) LR 10 Ex 35; *Berryman v London Borough of Hounslow* [1997] PIQR P83; *Burns v MAN Automotive (Aust) Pty Ltd* (1986) 161 CLR 653, 668–69. The concept of remoteness is explained earlier in this chapter.

221 *Armstead v Royal & Sun Alliance Insurance Co Ltd* [2024] UKSC 6, [2025] AC 406 [60]-[63].

222 eg, Peter Cane, *Atiyah's Accidents, Compensation and the Law* (8th edn, CUP 2013) 50 fn 36; James Edelman, *McGregor on Damages* (21st edn, Sweet & Maxwell 2021) [6-018]; James Goudkamp, 'Rethinking Contributory Negligence' in Stephen GA Pitel, Jason W Neyers and Erika Chamberlain (eds), *Tort Law: Challenging Orthodoxy* (Hart 2013) 309, 330–31; David Rolph, Jason NE Varuhas, Penelope Crossley and Michael Douglas, *Balkin & Davis: Law of Torts* (6th edn, LexisNexis 2021) [27.27].

223 *Smith New Court Securities Ltd v Citibank NA* [1997] AC 254, 266 (Lord Browne-Wilkinson); *Standard Chartered Bank v Pakistan National Shipping Corp* [1999] 1 Lloyd's Rep 747, 760.

224 See Wayne Courtney, 'Contract Damages and the Promisee's Role in Its Own Loss' (2019) 42 MULR 406, 430–31. Contra Andrew Burrows, 'Contributory

apportionment of liability by virtue of contributory negligence – such as the Law Reform (Contributory Negligence) Act 1945 (UK) – contains no temporal limitation and has, in some cases been applied to conduct of the claimant after the claimant became aware of the wrong.[225]

We suggest that there are two different concepts of unreasonableness at work here. Where the conduct is unreasonable because the claimant failed to take a particular action in response to the defendant's wrong (or took an inappropriate action), the avoidable loss rule applies.[226] Where the conduct is not unreasonable in that sense, but would be unreasonable even for a person who is not the victim of a wrong, the conduct constitutes contributory negligence (if the doctrine applies to the type of wrong in question) or, if there is a particularly high degree of unreasonableness, a *novus actus interveniens*.[227]

The point is illustrated by *McKew v Holland & Hannen & Cubitts (Scotland) Ltd*[228] and *Spencer v Wincanton Holdings Ltd*,[229] both of which were discussed earlier in this chapter and both of which involved unreasonable conduct of the claimant after the claimant became aware of the wrong. In neither case was the claimant's conduct (descending the staircase in *McKew* and filling the tank of the car in *Spencer*) a response, or a failure to respond, to the defendant's wrong. It was therefore appropriate that the avoidable loss rule was not mentioned in either case. But the conduct of each claimant would have been unreasonable even for a person that had the claimant's disability but not as a result of a wrong. The conduct therefore constituted contributory negligence (as found in *Spencer*) or a *novus actus interveniens* (as found in *McKew* where contributory negligence does not seem to have been pleaded).

Negligence in Contract: Ammunition for the Law Commission' (1993) 109 LQR 175, 176.

225 *Corr v IBC Vehicles Ltd* [2008] UKHL 13, [2008] 1 AC 884 [30]–[32], [47], [58]; *The Calliope* [1970] P 172; *Commonwealth v McLean* (1996) 41 NSWLR 389, 398.

226 See *Sainsbury's Supermarkets Ltd v Visa Europe Services LLC* [2020] UKSC 24, [2020] 4 All ER 807 [214] (Lord Reed P, Lord Hodge, Lord Lloyd-Jones, Lord Sales, Lord Hamblen): 'failure of a claimant to act reasonably in its response to its loss'.

227 For further discussion, see Sirko Harder, 'The Demarcation Line Between Contributory Negligence and the Avoidable Loss Rule' in Russell L Weaver and Duncan Fairgrieve (eds), *Damages, Injunctive Relief and Other Remedies in Tort and Free Speech Cases* (Cambridge Scholars Publishing 2023) 93.

228 1970 SC (HL) 20. Cf *Wieland v Cyril Lord Carpets Ltd* [1969] 3 All ER 1006, which had similar facts, but the defendant was held liable as the plaintiff had taken sufficient regard for her own safety.

229 [2009] EWCA Civ 1404, [2010] PIQR P8.

The Avoidable Loss Rule and Its Corollary

The avoidable loss rule is part of the doctrine of mitigation, which applies to all common law wrongs[230] and is an aspect of the concept of causation.[231] The doctrine of mitigation comprises three rules.[232] First, a claimant who behaved unreasonably in awareness of the defendant's wrong cannot recover for loss that reasonable conduct would have avoided. Secondly, the claimant can recover the cost of reasonable steps taken to mitigate loss, even if those steps in the event increase the loss. Thirdly, the claimant cannot recover for avoided loss, even if the loss is avoided by an action that the claimant was not required to take under the first rule (ie, not taking the action would have been reasonable). The third rule is discussed in Chapter 2.

The first rule of mitigation—the avoidable loss rule—'imposes on a plaintiff the duty of taking all reasonable steps to mitigate the loss consequent on the breach, and debars him from claiming any part of the damage which is due to his neglect to take such steps'.[233] The rule can be justified on grounds of fairness between the parties, economic efficiency, and autonomy concerns.[234] It is for the defendant to plead and prove that the claimant has failed to take reasonable steps to mitigate the loss.[235] Conduct that may be unreasonable, depending upon the individual circumstances, includes the refusal of the victim of a breach of contract to enter into a new contract with the defaulting party,[236] the

---

230 *Lagden v O'Connor* [2003] UKHL 64, [2004] 1 AC 1067 [51] (Lord Hope); *Armstead v Royal & Sun Alliance Insurance Co Ltd* [2024] UKSC 6, [2025] AC 406 [60].

231 *Lagden v O'Connor* [2003] UKHL 64, [2004] 1 AC 1067 [99]–[100] (Lord Scott), citing *Koch Marine Inc v d'Amica Societa di Navigazione arl (The Elena d'Amico)* [1980] 1 Lloyd's Rep 75, 88.

232 *Sharp Corp Ltd v Viterra BV* [2024] UKSC 14, [2024] Bus LR 871 [85], citing *Koch Marine Inc v d'Amica Societa di Navigazione arl (The Elena d'Amico)* [1980] 1 Lloyd's Rep 75, 88 and James Edelman, *McGregor on Damages* (21st edn, Sweet & Maxwell 2021) [9.002]–[9.007].

233 *British Westinghouse Electric and Manufacturing Co Ltd v Underground Electric Railways Company of London Ltd* [1912] AC 673, 689 (Viscount Haldane LC).

234 Katy Barnett, 'Substitutive Damages and Mitigation in Contract Law' (2016) 28 Sing Ac LJ 795, 806–07.

235 eg, *Armstead v Royal & Sun Alliance Insurance Co Ltd* [2024] UKSC 6, [2025] AC 406 [60]; *Samuels v Benning* [2002] EWCA Civ 858 [26]; *LE Jones (Insurance Brokers) Ltd v Portsmouth City Council* [2002] EWCA Civ 1723, [2003] 1 WLR 427 [26]; *Geest plc v Lansiquot* [2002] UKPC 48, [2002] 1 WLR 3111.

236 *Brace v Calder* [1895] 2 QB 253; *Payzu Ltd v Saunders* [1919] 2 KB 581.

repair of a car at a cost exceeding the market value of the car,[237] and the refusal of a personal injury victim to undergo free medical treatment.[238] But the law is not too demanding of a claimant, particularly in a case of emergency.[239] A claimant is not obliged to pursue complicated litigation against a third party,[240] or to take steps that the claimant cannot afford.[241]

The second rule of mitigation is a corollary of the first. Since the claimant is penalised for not taking reasonable steps to mitigate loss, the claimant must be permitted to claim the cost of taking such steps.[242] Reasonable costs may include, for example, the cost of having damaged property repaired,[243] the cost of hiring a substitute chattel,[244] and the cost of purchasing a replacement for a destroyed chattel.[245] The reasonable cost of medical treatment would also fall into this category, but this is usually compensated simply as a loss caused by the personal injury without invoking the doctrine of mitigation.[246] Where the steps taken by the claimant in order to mitigate loss in fact increased the loss, the cost of taking the steps and the additional loss caused by them can still be recovered if the steps were reasonable judged as at the time of taking them.[247]

---

237 *Darbishire v Warren* [1963] 1 WLR 1067.

238 *Lagden v O'Connor* [2003] UKHL 64, [2004] 1 AC 1067 [99]-[100] (Lord Scott), citing *McAuley v London Transport Executive* [1957] 2 Lloyd's Rep 500; *Geest plc v Lansiquot* [2002] UKPC 48, [2002] 1 WLR 3111.

239 *Banco de Portugal v Waterlow and Sons Ltd* [1932] AC 452, 506 (Lord Macmillan).

240 *Armstead v Royal & Sun Alliance Insurance Co Ltd* [2024] UKSC 6, [2025] AC 406 [54], citing *Pilkington v Wood* [1953] Ch 770, 777.

241 *Lagden v O'Connor* [2003] UKHL 64, [2004] 1 AC 1067; *Alcoa Minerals of Jamaica Inc v Broderick* [2002] 1 AC 371 (PC).

242 For the recoverability of the cost of mitigating steps taken prior to the wrong, see Donal Nolan, 'Preventive Damages' (2016) 132 LQR 68.

243 eg, *Alcoa Minerals of Jamaica Inc v Broderick* [2002] 1 AC 371 (PC).

244 eg, *Lagden v O'Connor* [2003] UKHL 64, [2004] 1 AC 1067. The cost cannot be recovered where the claimant does not have to pay the hiring fee because the contract between the claimant and the lessor is unenforceable: *Dimond v Lovell* [2002] 1 AC 384.

245 eg, *Moore v DER Ltd* [1971] 1 WLR 1476.

246 James Edelman, *McGregor on Damages* (21st edn, Sweet & Maxwell 2021) [9-102].

247 eg, *The World Beauty* [1970] P 144, 156 (Winn LJ); *Esso Petroleum Co Ltd v Mardon* [1976] QB 801, 829, 833; *Gebruder Metelmann GmbH & Co KG v NBR (London) Ltd* [1984] 1 Lloyd's Rep 614, 634 (Browne-Wilkinson LJ); *Kuwait Airways Corp v Iraqi Airways Co (Nos 4 and 5)* [2002] 2 AC 883, 1059 (CA).

Contributory Negligence

Contributory negligence denotes unreasonable conduct of the claimant that contributed to the occurrence of the defendant's wrong or the ensuing loss. As mentioned earlier in this chapter, the doctrine of contributory negligence is often applied to pre-wrong conduct of the claimant but has occasionally been applied to post-wrong conduct. The defendant bears the legal burden of pleading and proving contributory negligence.[248]

The doctrine originated in tort where, at common law, it was a complete defence to an action in negligence or certain other torts. The Law Reform (Contributory Negligence) Act 1945 replaced the complete defence with an apportionment of liability according to each party's responsibility for the loss in question. The complete defence at common law did not generally apply to breach of contract, but the statutory apportionment regime applies to certain breaches. Neither the common law defence nor the statutory apportionment regime applies in equity, which has not developed a concept comparable to contributory negligence. The rules on contributory negligence are discussed separately for each type of wrong in Chapters 4–6.[249]

MULTIPLE WRONGDOERS

Introduction

A claimant may suffer harm as a result of conduct of two or more wrongdoers. Where separate aspects of the harm can be attributed to the conduct of separate wrongdoers, each wrongdoer is liable only for the part for which he or she is responsible.[250] Where the harm is indivisible, a legal system has the choice between two regimes. One regime is proportionate liability, under which each wrongdoer is liable only for a proportion of the harm according to each wrongdoer's relative contribution to the harm. Every wrongdoer needs to be solvent and be sued by the claimant (where damages are not paid voluntarily) for the claimant to obtain full compensation. The other regime is solidary liability

---

248 *Owners of SS Heranger v Owners of SS Diamond* [1939] AC 94, 104; *Armstead v Royal & Sun Alliance Insurance Co Ltd* [2024] UKSC 6, [2025] AC 406 [60].

249 For a detailed discussion of contributory negligence, see James Goudkamp and Donal Nolan, *Contributory Negligence* (2nd edn, OUP 2023). The same authors undertook an empirical study of UK cases from 2000 to 2016 in relation to contributory negligence: James Goudkamp and Donal Nolan, *Contributory Negligence in the Twenty-First Century* (OUP 2019).

250 *Rahman v Arearose Ltd* [2001] QB 351.

(called joint and several liability in common law systems), under which the claimant may claim full compensation from each wrongdoer but cannot obtain more than full compensation in total. Thus, the claimant will obtain full compensation as long as at least one wrongdoer is solvent. The wrongdoer who pays compensation to the claimant should generally be able to obtain contribution from the other wrongdoer(s) according to each wrongdoer's relative contributions to the harm.

The merits of the two regimes are mixed.[251] Proportionate liability can be criticised on the ground that it is unjust that a claimant is unable to obtain full compensation from wrongdoer X (whose conduct was sufficient to bring about the harm) only because wrongdoer Y also contributed to the harm, even where X and Y acted independently of each other. Joint and several liability can be criticised on the ground that it is unjust that a wrongdoer who made only a minor contribution to the harm may have to pay full compensation to the claimant and bear the burden of seeking contribution from the other wrongdoer(s) who may be insolvent.

The common law originally opted for solidary liability, but the law has changed in some jurisdictions by virtue of either legislation or the development of the common law. In the US, only a minority of states still adhere to solidary liability in all cases; the majority of states have a mix of proportionate and solidary liability, depending upon the circumstances (which vary from state to state).[252] In Australia, the common law still adheres to solidary liability, but legislation provides for proportionate liability in some circumstances involving property damage or pure economic loss.[253] In Canada, proportionate liability exists only in some limited circumstances; solidary liability remains the rule.[254] In England, which is the focus of the rest of this section, proportionate liability exists only in the exceptional circumstances covered by *Barker v Corus (UK) Ltd*[255] and *International Energy Group Ltd v Zurich Insurance*

[251] For a discussion, see Kit Barker and Jenny Steele, 'Drifting Towards Proportionate Liability: Ethics and Pragmatics' (2015) 74 Camb LJ 49.
[252] See American Law Institute, *Restatement (Third) of Torts (Apportionment of Liability)* (2000).
[253] See Katy Barnett and Sirko Harder, *Remedies in Australian Private Law* (3rd edn, CUP 2024) [4.30]–[4.45].
[254] See Kit Barker and Jenny Steele, 'Drifting Towards Proportionate Liability: Ethics and Pragmatics' (2015) 74 Camb LJ 49, 55–57.
[255] [2006] UKHL 20, [2006] 2 AC 572.

plc UK Branch,[256] and not governed by section 3 of the Compensation Act 2006.[257]

The Position at Common Law

At least in relation to tortious liability, the common law distinguishes between joint tortfeasors and several concurrent tortfeasors in the way solidary liability works. There are three categories of joint tortfeasors: where one person is responsible for the tort of another (because of authorisation, vicarious liability, or the presence of a non-delegable duty of care); where there is the breach of a joint duty (for example, several occupiers of the same property); and where the tortfeasors act in concert or in pursuance of a common design.[258] The last category concerns parties who cooperate with interrelated intentions that each understands the other(s) to share; it requires communication between the parties, although this may be non-verbal.[259] Several concurrent tortfeasors are those who, acting independently of each other, contribute to the same indivisible harm and are not joint tortfeasors.

In the case of joint tortfeasors, the common law position is that there is only one cause of action against all tortfeasors. Judgment against one tortfeasor thus bars an action against any of the others, even if the judgment remains unsatisfied.[260] Similarly, the release of one of the tortfeasors from liability releases all of them,[261] although an agreement not to sue does not have the same effect.[262] Another consequence is that the sum of exemplary damages is the lowest sum that could be awarded against any of the tortfeasors.[263] In the case of several concurrent tortfeasors, the fact that the claimant has obtained judgment against

---

256 [2015] UKSC 33, [2016] AC 509.

257 ie, cases that do not involve mesothelioma but have similar features; see the discussion earlier in this chapter.

258 *The Koursk* [1924] P 140, 155 (Scrutton LJ); Simon Deakin and Zoe Adams, *Markesinis and Deakin's Tort Law* (8th edn, OUP 2019) 878.

259 *Lifestyle Equities CV v Ahmed* [2024] UKSC 17, [2025] AC 1 [118], citing *Fish & Fish Ltd v Sea Shepherd UK* [2015] UKSC 10, [2015] AC 1229 [44] (Lord Sumption JSC) and *Unilever plc v Gillette (UK) Ltd* [1989] RPC 583, 609.

260 *Brinsmead v Harrison* (1872) LR 7 CP 547; *Wah Tat Bank Ltd v Chan Cheng Kum* [1975] AC 507, 515 (PC).

261 *Thurman v Wild* (1840) 11 A & E 453; 113 ER 487; *Re EWA, a debtor* [1901] 2 KB 642, 648.

262 *Apley Estates Co Ltd v De Bernales* [1947] Ch 217.

263 *Cassell & Co Ltd v Broome* [1972] AC 1027, 1063, 1090; *Kuddus v Chief Constable of Leicestershire Constabulary* [2001] UKHL 29, [2002] 2 AC 122 [127]–[128] (Lord Scott).

one tortfeasor does not prevent the claimant from suing another tortfeasor,[264] although the total recovery must not exceed the claimant's loss.[265]

A wrongdoer (whether joint or several concurrent) who pays full compensation to the claimant will want to obtain contribution from the other wrongdoer(s). The common law generally denies an entitlement to contribution in the case of concurrent tortfeasors,[266] but both the common law and equity recognise it in the case of joint contractors.[267] A contribution claim lies in equity also between trustees under a common liability for breach of trust and between company directors under a common liability for breach of an equitable duty towards the company.[268]

The Position Under the Civil Liability (Contribution) Act 1978

The common law rules have been changed by legislation throughout the common law world. In England, the relevant statute today is the Civil Liability (Contribution) Act 1978. Section 3 of the Act provides that a judgment recovered against any person liable for any debt or damage is no bar to an action against any other person who is jointly liable for the same debt or damage. Therefore, a claimant who has obtained an unsatisfied judgment against a joint wrongdoer can still sue another joint wrongdoer, without double recovery. However, once the judgment against one tortfeasor is satisfied, the claimant can no longer sue another (joint or several) tortfeasor liable for the same damage.[269] It has been held that section 3 does not apply to a release by agreement,[270] but the (convincing) opposite view has been taken for the corresponding provisions in

264 *The Koursk* [1924] P 140.

265 *Personal Representatives of Tang Man Sit v Capacious Investments Ltd* [1996] AC 514, 522.

266 *Merryweather v Nixan* (1799) 8 Term Rep 186; 101 ER 1337. In that respect, equity follows the law: James Watson, 'From Contribution to Apportioned Contribution to Proportionate Liability' (2004) 78 Aust LJ 126, 129.

267 *Davitt v Titcumb* [1990] Ch 110, 117; *Lumley v Robinson* [2002] EWCA Civ 94 [12].

268 See *Soldiers, Sailors, Airmen and Families Association v Allgemeines Krankenhaus Viersen GmbH* [2022] UKSC 29, [2023] AC 597 [47].

269 *Jameson v Central Electricity Generating Board* [2000] 1 AC 455. The same applies to a satisfied compromise that represents the full value of the claim (*Heaton v AXA Equity and Law Life Assurance Society plc* [2002] UKHL 15, [2002] 2 AC 329 [3]–[4]) and to a satisfied consent order: *Vanden Recycling Ltd v Kras Recycling BV* [2017] EWCA Civ 354.

270 *Gladman Commercial Properties v Fisher Hargreaves Proctor* [2013] EWCA Civ 1466 [22], [84]–[85]. The release of one of joint wrongdoers releases all of them (unless the right to sue the others is reserved) even if the release takes

the Australian jurisdictions.[271] Section 3 is subject to the rule in *Henderson v Henderson*,[272] under which a claim is precluded if it could have been brought in previous proceedings.[273] In addition, section 4 of the Act provides that the claimant is not entitled to costs in a second or subsequent action unless the court is of the opinion that there was a reasonable ground for bringing the action.

Section 1(1) provides that 'any person liable in respect of any damage suffered by another person may recover contribution from any other person liable in respect of the same damage (whether jointly with him or otherwise)'. This applies whatever the legal basis of liability, whether tort, breach of contract, breach of trust, or otherwise: section 6(1).[274] Thus, even a tortfeasor can now claim contribution from another tortfeasor liable for the same damage. The right under section 1(1) overrides any right (other than an express contractual right) to contribution (as opposed to an indemnity) otherwise than under the Act: section 7(3).[275] The maximum amount of contribution payable by a wrongdoer under section 1(1) is the amount the claimant could have claimed from that wrongdoer: section 2(3). This is important because one of the wrongdoers may enjoy a limit of liability (because, for example, of an agreement between that wrongdoer and the claimant) not enjoyed by another wrongdoer.

The Court of Appeal has held that multiple wrongdoers are liable for the 'same damage' whenever payment by one of them to the claimant relieves all other wrongdoers from their liability towards the claimant.[276] In *Royal*

the form of a consent judgment: *Morris v Wentworth-Stanley* [1999] QB 1004, 1012–16.

271 *Thompson v Australian Capital Television Pty Ltd* (1996) 186 CLR 574, 583–85, 592, 612–15; *Baxter v Obacelo Pty Ltd* [2001] HCA 66, (2001) 205 CLR 635 [49], [69], [91]. Section 3(3)(a) of the Wrongs Act 1954 (Tas) expressly provides that the release of one person does not discharge another person unless the release so provides.

272 (1843) 3 Hare 100; 67 ER 313.

273 *Morris v Wentworth-Stanley* [1999] QB 1004, 1016–17.

274 It includes a claim for knowing receipt of trust property: *Charter plc v City Index Ltd* [2007] EWCA Civ 1382, [2008] Ch 313.

275 Thus, it overrides (among others) the equitable right to contribution between trustees under a common liability for breach of trust and between company directors under a common liability for breach of an equitable duty towards the company: *Soldiers, Sailors, Airmen and Families Association v Allgemeines Krankenhaus Viersen GmbH* [2022] UKSC 29, [2023] AC 597 [47].

276 *Eastgate Group Ltd v Lindsey Morden Group Inc* [2001] EWCA Civ 1446, [2002] 1 WLR 642 [19]; *Hurstwood Developments Ltd v Motor & General & Andersley & Co Insurance Services Ltd* [2001] EWCA Civ 1785, [2002] PNLR 250 [23]–[25].

Brompton Hospital NHS Trust v Hammond,[277] the House of Lords appears to have rejected that test without formulating an alternative test. We suggest that the mutual discharge test should apply, but that a full indemnity (as opposed to contribution) lies where the nature and rationale of each wrongdoer's liability towards the claimant indicate that, as between the wrongdoers, one of them should ultimately be liable for the entire damage.[278]

The right to claim contribution is subject to a limitation period of two years from the date on which that right arose.[279] Furthermore, contribution cannot be claimed where the liability of the wrongdoer who is seeking it cannot be established because an action by the claimant against him is statute-barred.[280] But where the claimant sued a wrongdoer before the limitation period against that wrongdoer expired, contribution is not excluded only because that period has expired by the time contribution is sought: section 1(2). Nor is contribution excluded by the fact that an action by the claimant against the wrongdoer from whom contribution is sought would now be statute-barred unless the statute extinguishes the claim (which is not generally the case): section 1(3). A wrongdoer who has paid compensation to the claimant as part of a bona fide settlement or compromise can claim contribution without having to establish that he was in fact liable, provided that he would have been liable if the factual basis of the claim against him could be established: section 1(4).

Section 2(1) provides that 'the amount of the contribution recoverable from any person shall be such as may be found by the court to be just and equitable having regard to the extent of that person's responsibility for the damage in question'. As in the context of contributory negligence (discussed in Chapter 5), the court considers the causal potency and the blameworthiness of each wrongdoer's conduct.[281] Where the claimant was contributorily negligent, the court must first apportion the damage between the claimant and the wrongdoers as a group and must then apportion the wrongdoers' share among them.[282]

Section 2(2) permits the court to assign shares of nil and 100 percent among the wrongdoers. This is important because, as mentioned earlier, the nature and rationale of each wrongdoer's liability towards the claimant may indicate

---

277 [2002] UKHL 14, [2002] 1 WLR 1397.

278 For a detailed discussion, see Sirko Harder, 'Several Concurrent Wrongdoers and the Civil Liability (Contribution) Act 1978' (2017) 25 RLR 208.

279 Limitation Act 1980, s 10.

280 See s 1(6): 'References in this section to a person's liability in respect of any damage are references to any such liability which has been or could be established . . . .'

281 eg, *Purrunsing v A'Court & Co* [2016] EWHC 789 (Ch), [2016] 4 WLR 81 [62]; *Horn v Knott* [2023] EWHC 1351 (Comm), [2024] 1 All ER (Comm) 528 [17].

282 *Fitzgerald v Lane* [1989] AC 328, 339–40.

that, as between the wrongdoers, one of them should ultimately bear responsibility for the entire damage. Furthermore, the Act does not affect a right to an indemnity: section 7(3). The House of Lords has held that an employer who is vicariously liable for a tort of an employee is entitled to an indemnity from the employee.[283] However, the employer's liability towards the claimant is usually satisfied by an insurer (who is subrogated to the employer's claim against the employee), and the insurance companies in the UK do not pursue indemnity claims against an employee unless the loss resulted from criminal, dishonest, or intentional conduct of the employee.[284]

283 *Lister v Romford Ice and Cold Storage Co Ltd* [1957] AC 555. The employer's claim for an indemnity is generally abolished in New South Wales; see Employees Liability Act 1991 (NSW), ss 3–5.

284 See *Pemberton Greenish LLP v Henry* [2017] EWHC 246 (QB).

4. Compensation in contract

INTRODUCTION

A contracting party may fail to perform one or more of its obligations under the contract by performing defectively, later than required by the contract, or not at all. Such a party is in breach of contract, provided that the contract is valid and enforceable and that the failure to perform in accordance with the contract is not excused by such performance having become impossible, illegal, or something radically different from what the parties envisaged when the contract was made.[1] Unlike some civil law jurisdictions, the common law does not require fault for the existence of a breach of contract.[2]

A breach of contract gives the innocent party (the claimant) a right to damages. There are two mutually exclusive types of damages at common law: nominal damages and substantial damages.[3] Where substantial damages are not available (because the breach of contract has caused no loss and no other type of substantial damages is available), a nominal sum (such as £10) will be awarded to mark the presence of a breach of contract.[4] Nominal damages are discussed in Chapter 8.

At common law, substantial damages for breach of contract usually compensate for the loss caused by the breach. A claimant who can prove that recoverable loss has been caused by a breach of contract is entitled to an award of substantial damages in the amount of the loss. The court has no discretion. Some types of breach give the innocent party the right to terminate the

---

[1] See *Fibrosa Spolka Akcyjna v Fairbairn Lawson Combe Barbour Ltd* [1943] AC 32, 50, 55, 82.

[2] See, eg, *Barclays Bank plc v Fairclough Building Ltd* [1995] QB 214. Sometimes, a party is only under an obligation to take care; see, eg, *Greaves & Co (Contractors) Ltd v Baynham Meikle & Partners* [1975] 1 WLR 1095, 1100 (Lord Denning MR). Such an obligation can be breached only by a failure to take care.

[3] Alternatively, damages may be available under Lord Cairns' Act discussed in Ch 7. In Canada and the US, exemplary (or punitive) damages are available for some breaches of contract. This is not the case in other common law jurisdictions.

[4] eg, *Bunge SA v Nidera BV* [2015] UKSC 43, [2015] 3 All ER 1082 [36], where US$5 was awarded.

contract,[5] which absolves both parties from their future primary obligations under the contract.[6] An innocent party who has validly terminated the contract can (in addition to rights already accrued at the time of termination) claim damages for the loss of the contract-breaker's outstanding performance, sometimes called 'loss of bargain damages'.[7] Such damages are subject to the same rules as other damages for breach of contract. These are the rules discussed in Chapters 2 and 3 and the rules specific to contract discussed in this chapter.

As mentioned in Chapter 1, some scholars identify two types of substantial damages for breach of contract: damages that substitute for performance or for the right to performance (substitutionary damages) and damages for consequential loss. Substitutionary damages are not concerned with the compensation of loss and are therefore not subject to the rules relating to remoteness, mitigation and (where relevant) contributory negligence. The scholars differ in relation to the calculation of substitutionary damages. For Stephen Smith[8] and David Winterton,[9] it is generally the cost of substitute performance; for Robert Stevens,[10] it is the difference in value between the performance contracted for and that provided.

As also mentioned in Chapter 1, Edelman J in the High Court of Australia has expressed support for the distinction between substitutionary damages and damages for consequential loss. In *Moore v Scenic Tours Pty Ltd*,[11] his Honour distinguished between two kinds of contractual damages: compensation directly for the performance interest and compensation for consequential losses.[12] Compensation for the performance interest aims 'to provide the promisee with the difference between the value of what was promised and the value of what was received', and 'is not concerned with loss in any real or

---

5 Namely the breach of a condition, a serious breach of an intermediate term, and a repudiation of the contract; see, eg, *Bell v Peter Browne & Co* [1990] 2 QB 495, 511–12 (Mustill LJ).

6 eg, *General Billposting Co Ltd v Atkinson* [1909] AC 118.

7 eg, *Geys v Société Générale, London Branch* [2012] UKSC 63, [2013] 1 AC 523 [113] (Lord Sumption JSC).

8 Stephen A Smith, *Contract Theory* (OUP 2004) 420–23; Stephen A Smith, 'Substitutionary Damages' in Charles EF Rickett (ed), *Justifying Private Law Remedies* (Hart 2008) 100–05.

9 David Winterton, 'Money Awards Substituting for Performance' [2012] LMCLQ 446, 450–51; David Winterton, *Money Awards in Contract Law* (Hart 2015).

10 Robert Stevens, 'Damages and the Right to Performance: A *Golden Victory* or Not?' in Jason W Neyers, Richard Bronaugh and Stephen GA Pitel (eds), *Exploring Contract Law* (Hart 2009) 171–74.

11 [2020] HCA 17, (2020) 268 CLR 326.

12 ibid [63].

factual sense'.[13] The second component is concerned with true consequential losses. These are financial losses that 'go beyond the value of the promised performance and are within the boundaries of legal responsibility' as well as some non-pecuniary losses.[14] The rules about legal responsibility (in particular remoteness of loss and mitigation) apply only to the second component.

Otherwise, however, courts in common law jurisdictions have not expressly supported the concept of substantial damages for breach of contract that are not concerned with the compensation of loss (or based on the gain made by the defendant).[15] On the contrary, Lord Sumption JSC in the UK Supreme Court has stated that compensatory damages for breach of contract 'are concerned with the price of the goods or services which would have been delivered under the contract. They are not concerned with the value of the contract as an article of commerce in itself'.[16] In cases in which it was difficult to accept that the breach has caused loss, the courts still identified a loss to justify the award of substantial damages.[17] Moreover, the theories of substitutionary damages have faced strong criticism. Robert Stevens's theory in particular has been said to conflict with the conventional understanding of damages and the law on mitigation and cannot account for nominal damages.[18]

This chapter adopts the courts' conceptualisation of damages awards. However, the theories of substitutionary damages will be mentioned in contexts where they have particular relevance.

---

13 ibid [64].

14 ibid [66].

15 For the exceptional availability of an account of profits for breach of contract recognised in *Attorney-General v Blake* [2001] 1 AC 268, see Ch 9. Negotiating damages calculated by reference to a hypothetical licence fee, which we discuss in Ch 8, are now conceptualised as compensatory: *One Step (Support) Pty Ltd v Morris-Garner* [2018] UKSC 20, [2019] AC 649.

16 *Bunge SA v Nidera BV* [2015] UKSC 43, [2015] 3 All ER 1082 [21]. Lord Sumption was expressing support for the majority decision in *The Golden Victory* [2007] UKHL 12, [2007] 2 AC 353, mentioned in Ch 2. Kramer has argued that these two cases conflict with the substitutionary damages theories of Stevens and Winterton: Adam Kramer, 'Contract Damages' in William Day and Sarah Worthington (eds), *Challenging Private Law: Lord Sumption on the Supreme Court* (Hart 2020) 80–83.

17 A prominent example is *Clark v Macourt* [2013] HCA 56, (2013) 253 CLR 1, discussed in Katy Barnett and Sirko Harder, *Remedies in Australian Private Law* (3rd edn, CUP 2024) [5.12]–[5.16].

18 Andrew Burrows, 'Are "Damages on the *Wrotham Park* Basis" Compensatory, Restitutionary or Neither?' in Djakhongir Saidov and Ralph Cunnington (eds), *Contract Damages: Domestic and International Perspectives* (Hart 2008) 181–85.

THE INTERESTS OF THE CLAIMANT AND THEIR HIERARCHY

The Primacy of the Expectation Interest

An outline of the common law's approach to compensating loss caused by a breach of contract must start with a reference to a two-part article published by US scholars Fuller and Perdue in 1936–37.[19] Fuller and Perdue provided a clear exposition of the interests of a party aggrieved by a breach of contract, and the terminology they introduced has been generally adopted even though their substantive claim has not.

Fuller and Perdue distinguished three interests of a party aggrieved by a breach of contract: the expectation interest, the reliance interest and the restitution interest. The expectation interest is protected when the claimant obtains specific performance or the money value of the defendant's performance. The object is to put the claimant in as good a position as if the defendant had performed in accordance with the contract. The reliance interest is protected when the court awards damages to undo the harm the claimant has suffered by changing his position in reliance on the defendant's promise. The object is to put the claimant in as good a position as he was in before the promise was made. The restitution interest is protected when the court orders the defendant to disgorge any value the claimant has conferred on the defendant in reliance on the latter's promise. Fuller and Perdue observed that the defendant may be left with a gain not taken from the claimant or not obtained as a result of the claimant's reliance on the defendant's promise, but usually the gain results from such reliance, and the restitution interest is then a special case of the reliance interest.[20]

The three interests may be illustrated by a simple example. Assume that C and D enter into a contract for the sale of D's land to C for £100,000. C immediately pays £10,000 to D as a deposit. C also instructs solicitors to prepare the documents for the completion of the contract (ie, payment of the balance by C to D and conveyance of the title to the land from D to C) and for the subsequent registration of C's title in the land register. The solicitor's fee is £1,000. Before completion, D repudiates the contract and C accepts the repudiation.[21]

---

[19] LL Fuller and William R Perdue, 'Reliance Interest in Contract Damages: 1' (1936) 46 Yale LJ 52; LL Fuller and William R Perdue, 'Reliance Interest in Contract Damages: 2' (1937) 46 Yale LJ 373.

[20] LL Fuller and William R Perdue, 'Reliance Interest in Contract Damages: 1' (1936) 46 Yale LJ 52, 53–55.

[21] It means that C terminates the contract. Alternatively, C would be likely to obtain specific performance; see Ch 7.

C intended to erect a building on the land (for a cost of £200,000) and has evidence to demonstrate that the land with that building could be sold for £400,000. C's expectation interest is £100,000, which is the expected gross revenue of £400,000 minus the necessary expenses of £300,000 (£100,000 for the land and £200,000 for the building). C's reliance interest is £11,000. C's restitution interest is £10,000.

Fuller and Perdue argued that the restitution interest has the strongest claim to judicial protection and the expectation interest the weakest. The restitution interest presents twice as strong a claim to judicial intervention as the reliance interest because the defendant not only caused the claimant to lose one unit but appropriated that unit to himself. Furthermore, a claimant who has actually relied on the defendant's promise, even though he did not thereby enrich the defendant, presents a more pressing case for relief than a claimant who merely demands satisfaction for his disappointment in not getting what was promised. While the protection of the restitution interest constitutes corrective justice, the protection of the expectation interest constitutes distributive justice.[22]

The terminology coined by Fuller and Perdue has been generally adopted. It is now common to refer to 'expectation loss', 'expectation damages', 'reliance loss' and 'reliance damages'.[23] However, Fuller and Perdue's key argument—that the restitution interest has the strongest claim to judicial protection and the expectation interest the weakest—has not been adopted. The restitution interest is protected through an action in restitution (or unjust enrichment) where the contract has been validly terminated. However, the key or even sole objective of an award of compensatory damages for breach of contract is to protect the expectation interest. English courts still apply the rule expressed by Parke B in *Robinson v Harman*:

> [W]here a party sustains a loss by reason of a breach of contract, he is, so far as money can do it, to be placed in the same situation, with respect to damages, as if the contract had been performed.[24]

---

22 LL Fuller and William R Perdue, 'Reliance Interest in Contract Damages: 1' (1936) 46 Yale LJ 52, 56. For the difference between corrective justice and distributive justice in general, see Ernest J Weinrib, *Corrective Justice* (OUP 2012) 15ff.

23 The term restitution is used not only in the sense used by Fuller and Perdue (reversal of a transfer from the claimant to the defendant) but also for the disgorgement by the defendant of a gain not obtained from the claimant, and sometimes for the compensation of loss.

24 (1848) 1 Ex 850, 855; 154 ER 363, 365.

A claimant who can prove the amount of (recoverable) expectation loss will obtain an award of damages in that amount. This award incidentally protects the reliance interest. There can be no award of reliance damages in excess of the amount of expectation loss. The expectation interest is paramount. It does not follow that the reliance interest has no role to play. This will be discussed next.

The Role of the Reliance Interest

Reliance loss is the loss suffered by the claimant as a result of changing her position in reliance on the defendant's promise to perform the contract. In their seminal article, Fuller and Perdue distinguished between two kinds of reliance.[25] Essential reliance is the price of the benefits of the contract for the claimant, in particular, the performance of the claimant's own obligations. Incidental reliance is other reliance, for example, expenses incurred in preparing to receive the defendant's performance and putting it to profitable use, the expenses being wasted as a result of the defendant's failure to perform. The role of wasted expenses in the calculation of contractual damages is the focus of the following discussion.

It is often necessary for a claimant to incur expenses in order to make a profit out of using the defendant's performance. The net profit is the difference between the gross revenue obtained from using the defendant's performance and the amount of expenditure necessary to obtain that revenue. An expenditure incurred before the claimant became aware of the defendant's breach may be wasted as a result of the breach where it cannot be used for another purpose.[26] On the other hand, knowledge of the defendant's breach may prompt the claimant not to incur an expenditure that would have been necessary to make a profit out of the defendant's performance (saved expenses).[27]

The amount of damages may be calculated in two ways, both of which produce the same result: lost gross revenue minus saved expenses; alternatively, lost net profit plus wasted expenses.[28]

---

[25] LL Fuller and William R Perdue, 'Reliance Interest in Contract Damages: 1' (1936) 46 Yale LJ 52, 78.

[26] Other profits that can be made by using the expenditure must be taken into account in assessing damages.

[27] The avoidable loss rule (discussed in Ch 3) bars recovery for futile expenses incurred after knowledge of the defendant's breach.

[28] *Omak Maritime Ltd v Mamola Challenger Shipping Co Ltd* [2010] EWHC 2026 (Comm), [2011] 2 All ER (Comm) 155 [15]. See also *Cullinane v British 'Rema' Manufacturing Co Ltd* [1954] 1 QB 292, 315 (Morris LJ); *TC Industrial Plant Pty Ltd v Robert's Queensland Pty Ltd* (1963) 180 CLR 130, 141.

A simple example illustrates this. Suppose that C, a concert organiser, enters into a contract with singer D, under which D promises to give a concert at a particular venue on a particular day and C promises to pay D £10,000 on that day. C spends £2,000 on advertising the concert and quickly sells all available tickets for a total of £20,000. D then repudiates the contract,[29] and C is forced to refund all tickets. The expected gross revenue is £20,000. The necessary expenses are £12,000, resulting in an expected net profit of £8,000. The expenditure of £2,000 is wasted; the expenditure of £10,000 is saved.[30]

There are two ways of calculating damages in this example. One way is to deduct saved expenses (£10,000) from the lost gross revenue (£20,000). The other way is to add wasted expenses (£2,000) to the lost net profit (£8,000). Either way, the amount of damages is £10,000.

Adopting the formula of adding wasted expenses to lost net profit, the US Supreme Court in *United States v Behan* stated that these are two distinct heads of damage and that damages may be awarded for wasted expenses even where no damages can be awarded for lost net profit because its amount cannot be proved.[31] Strictly, this would allow wasted expenses to be compensated even where it is clear that the claimant entered into a losing contract and would not have recouped the expenses from the gross revenue. This would place the claimant in a better position than if the defendant had performed. In *L Albert & Son v Armstrong Rubber Co*, the US Court of Appeals for the Second Circuit recognised this, stating that wasted expenses can be compensated only up to the value of the defendant's performance but that it is for the defendant to show that the value of the performance is less than the wasted expenditure.[32] Thus, as an alternative to expectation damages, the claimant may seek reliance damages less any loss that the defendant can prove would have been suffered had the contract been performed.[33]

By contrast, while the High Court of Australia has used wasted expenditure as an evidential tool in determining the amount of expectation loss,[34] it

---

29 C will not obtain specific performance (see Ch 7) and is thus forced to accept the repudiation.

30 C's termination of the contract absolves C from the obligation to pay the £10,000; see *General Billposting Co Ltd v Atkinson* [1909] AC 118.

31 110 US 338, 344–45 (1884).

32 178 F 2d 182, 189 (1949).

33 American Law Institute, *Restatement (Second) of Contracts* (1981), §349. See also LL Fuller and William R Perdue, 'Reliance Interest in Contract Damages: 1' (1936) 46 Yale LJ 52, 75–80, suggesting that recovery for essential (as opposed to incidental) reliance should generally be limited to the contract price.

34 *McRae v Commonwealth Disposals Commission* (1951) 84 CLR 377; *Commonwealth v Amann Aviation Pty Ltd* (1991) 174 CLR 64, 82; *Cessnock City*

has rejected the notion of reliance loss constituting a separate item of loss. In *Commonwealth v Amann Aviation Pty Ltd*, Mason CJ and Dawson J observed that 'the expressions "expectation damages", "damages for loss of profits", "reliance damages" and "damages for wasted expenditure" are simply manifestations of the central principle enunciated in *Robinson v Harman* rather than discrete and truly alternative measures of damages which a party not in breach may elect to claim'.[35] In *Cessnock City Council v 123 259 932 Pty Ltd*, Edelman, Steward, Gleeson, and Beech-Jones JJ observed that where the defendant's breach has made it difficult to determine the amount of expectation loss, the law facilitates proof of expectation loss by giving the claimant an evidential benefit of any relevant doubt that reasonable expenditure incurred would have been recouped had the defendant performed; the strength of that benefit depends upon the extent of the uncertainty created by the defendant's breach.[36] Reliance loss is therefore a proxy for, or a species of, expectation loss.[37]

The position in England is somewhere between the position in the US and the position in Australia. In *Anglia Television Ltd v Reed*,[38] the defendant actor contracted with the plaintiff to play the leading man's part in a television play the plaintiff was producing. A few days afterwards, the defendant repudiated the contract. The plaintiff could not get a substitute for the defendant and abandoned the production. The plaintiff claimed damages for their wasted expenditure, including expenditure incurred before the contract was concluded. The Court of Appeal held that the plaintiff was entitled to such damages. Lord Denning MR, speaking for the Court, said that a party aggrieved by a breach of contract can either claim for loss of profit or for wasted expenditure but not both,[39] and that expenditure incurred before the contract was concluded can be recovered where such expenditure was reasonably in the parties' contemplation as likely to be wasted if the contract was broken (which was the case on the facts).[40]

Council v 123 259 932 Pty Ltd [2024] HCA 17, (2024) 418 ALR 304.

[35] (1991) 174 CLR 64, 82, approvingly quoted in *Cessnock City Council v 123 259 932 Pty Ltd* [2024] HCA 17, (2024) 418 ALR 304 [31] (Gageler CJ), [51] (Gordon J).

[36] [2024] HCA 17, (2024) 418 ALR 304 [139].

[37] ibid [119]. See Katy Barnett, *Damages for Breach of Contract* (2nd edn, Sweet & Maxwell 2022) [3–007].

[38] [1972] 1 QB 60.

[39] ibid 63–64. This had already been recognised in *Cullinane v British 'Rema' Manufacturing Co Ltd* [1954] 1 QB 292.

[40] [1972] 1 QB 60, 64. His Lordship was applying the remoteness test discussed later in this chapter.

In *C & P Haulage v Middleton*,[41] the Court of Appeal held that an award of reliance damages must not place the claimant in a better financial position than if the contract had been performed properly. The defendant was wrongfully ejected from premises he had leased from the plaintiff for his vehicle repair business. He claimed damages for the expenditure he had incurred in making the plaintiff's premises suitable for his business. The Court of Appeal rejected the claim because the contract provided that any fixtures installed by the defendant were to be left on the premises after the end of the lease. Fox LJ stated that 'while it is true that the expenditure could in a sense be said to be wasted in consequence of the breach of contract, it was equally likely to be wasted if there had been no breach ... the waste resulted from what was, on the defendant's side, a very unsatisfactory and dangerous bargain'.[42]

In *CCC Films (London) Ltd v Impact Quadrant Films Ltd*,[43] Hutchison J stated that it is for the defendant to prove that the contract was a losing one for the claimant. His Honour also stated that the claimant can recover reliance damages irrespective of whether it is impossible to prove expectation loss.[44] In *Grange v Quinn*,[45] the Court of Appeal affirmed the first but doubted the second of these propositions. Thus, where the defendant's breach has made it impossible to determine the amount of lost profit, the claimant will obtain damages for wasted expenses, as the defendant will by definition be unable to prove that the expenses would not have been recouped out of the profit. There is a presumption of profitability as parties do not generally enter into a contract and incur expenditure unless they expect to at least break even.[46] The principle applies also where the benefit from the contract was non-financial, as it can be presumed that the value of the defendant's performance to the claimant was at least the amount of expenditure incurred.[47] It has also been said that an award

---

41 [1983] 1 WLR 1461, 1467–68.

42 ibid 1468–69. Reliance loss is also diminished by benefits the claimant has received as a result of the breach: *Omak Maritime Ltd v Mamola Challenger Shipping Co Ltd* [2010] EWHC 2026 (Comm), [2011] 2 All ER (Comm) 155; *Soteria Insurance Ltd v IBM United Kingdom Ltd* [2022] EWCA Civ 440, [2022] 2 All ER (Comm) 1082 [39].

43 [1985] QB 16, 38–40.

44 ibid 32.

45 [2013] EWCA Civ 24, [2013] 1 P & CR 18 [64]–[65]. The second proposition was rejected in *Liu Shu Ming v Koh Chew Chee* [2023] SGHC(A) 15, [2023] 1 SLR 1477 [217].

46 *Soteria Insurance Ltd v IBM United Kingdom Ltd* [2022] EWCA Civ 440, [2022] 2 All ER (Comm) 1082 [190].

47 *Royal Devon and Exeter NHS Foundation Trust v ATOS IT Services UK Ltd* [2017] EWHC 2197 (TCC), [2017] BLR 533 [61]–[63] (software supplied to NHS Trust was defective).

of reliance damages gives effect to the compensatory principle laid down in *Robinson v Harman*.[48]

In *Soteria Insurance Ltd v IBM United Kingdom Ltd*,[49] the Court of Appeal observed that reliance loss is not a separate head of loss. However, the actual decision on the facts demonstrates that the English position may not be the same as the Australian position. An exclusion clause in a contract provided that 'neither party shall be liable to the other or any third party for any Losses arising under and/or in connection with this Agreement … which are indirect or consequential losses, or for loss of profit, revenue [or] savings …'. The Court of Appeal held that this clause did not exclude a claim for wasted expenditure. The Court stated that a claimant can either claim its loss of profits or, alternatively, its wasted expenditure.[50] Despite the presumption that expenditure would have been recouped out of profits, wasted expenditure is not a method of assessing or claiming lost profits; these are different types of claim.[51]

ASSESSMENT OF EXPECTATION LOSS IN SPECIFIC CONTEXTS

Sale of Goods

Where a buyer of goods fails to pay the purchase price in accordance with the terms of the contract, the seller is entitled to damages even if the seller is not entitled to sue for the price.[52] Where the buyer wrongfully refuses to accept and pay for the goods, the seller may bring an action for damages for non-acceptance.[53] Section 50(2) of the Sale of Goods Act 1979 provides that the measure of damages for non-acceptance is 'the estimated loss directly and

---

48 *Omak Maritime Ltd v Mamola Challenger Shipping Co Ltd* [2010] EWHC 2026 (Comm), [2011] 2 All ER (Comm) 155 [55], [59]; *Yam Seng Pte Ltd v International Trade Corporation Ltd* [2013] EWHC 111 (QB), [2013] 1 All ER (Comm) 1321 [186].

49 [2022] EWCA Civ 440, [2022] 2 All ER (Comm) 1082 [41].

50 ibid [40].

51 ibid [83]–[85]. See also *Royal Devon and Exeter NHS Foundation Trust v ATOS IT Services UK Ltd* [2017] EWHC 2197 (TCC), [2017] BLR 533 [60]–[69]: a clause excluding liability for loss of profit does not bar damages for the loss of a functioning software system, these being assessed by reference to wasted expenditure.

52 Michael Bridge (ed), *Benjamin's Sale of Goods* (12th edn, Sweet & Maxwell 2023) [16-029]. For the action for the price, see Sale of Goods Act 1979, s 49(1), (2).

53 Sale of Goods Act 1979, s 50(1).

naturally resulting, in the ordinary course of events, from the buyer's breach of contract'. This reflects the first limb of *Hadley v Baxendale*,[54] discussed later in this chapter. Section 50(3) provides: 'Where there is an available market for the goods in question the measure of damages is prima facie to be ascertained by the difference between the contract price and the market or current price at the time or times when the goods ought to have been accepted or (if no time was fixed for acceptance) at the time of the refusal to accept.' This rule too reflects the position at common law.[55]

Where there is a market for the goods and the seller does not immediately resell them, any subsequent market fluctuation is on the seller's account.[56] Where the seller resells the goods immediately, the seller will generally be awarded the difference between the contract price and the (lower) market price at that time. The amount will not generally be increased where the seller sells below the market price,[57] as it must be assumed that a reasonable seller would have obtained the market price,[58] and recovery of the extra loss is thus barred by the avoidable loss rule discussed in Chapter 3. The Court of Appeal has held that a sale above the market price will also be ignored and will not reduce the amount of damages.[59] This conflicts with the avoided loss rule discussed in Chapter 2.

Where there is no available market for the goods, section 50(2) applies. The amount of damages is generally the difference between the contract price and the value of the goods to the seller at the time and place of the buyer's breach.[60] The price achieved on a resale of the goods may be evidence of that value. Even though section 50(2) contains only the first limb of *Hadley v Baxendale* (loss arising in the ordinary course of events), loss covered by the second limb (loss arising from special circumstances which was in the parties' contemplation)

---

[54] (1854) 9 Ex 341, 156 ER 145.

[55] Eg, *Dampskibsselskabet 'Norden' A/S v Andre & CIE SA* [2003] EWHC 84 (Comm), [2003] 1 Lloyd's Rep 287 [41].

[56] See *Jamal v Moolla Dawood, Sons & Co* [1916] 1 AC 175 (PC) (sale of shares).

[57] *Aercap Partners 1 Ltd v Avia Asset Management AB* [2010] EWHC 2431 (Comm), [2010] 2 CLC 578 [108].

[58] Michael Bridge (ed), *Benjamin's Sale of Goods* (12th edn, Sweet & Maxwell 2023) [16-077].

[59] *Campbell Mostyn (Provisions) Ltd v Barnett Trading Co* [1954] 1 Lloyd's Rep 65. See also *Aercap Partners 1 Ltd v Avia Asset Management AB* [2010] EWHC 2431 (Comm), [2010] 2 CLC 578 [108].

[60] *Harlow & Jones Ltd v Panex (International) Ltd* [1967] 2 Lloyd's Rep 509, 530.

must also be recoverable, as section 54 provides that the Act does not affect the right to recover 'special damages' where they are recoverable by law.[61]

With regard to a breach by the seller, English law distinguishes between consumer contracts (where the seller acts in the course of a business and the consumer does not) and other contracts. Sections 19 to 26 of the Consumer Rights Act 2015 provide for the buyer's remedies under a consumer contract, including damages. The complex details are beyond the scope of this book.[62] Sections 51, 53, and 54 of the Sale of Goods Act 1979 provide for the buyer's right to claim damages under a contract other than a consumer contract covered by the 2015 Act. Section 51 addresses non-delivery. It also applies where the seller delivers defective goods and the buyer is entitled to and does reject the goods.[63] Section 53 makes provision for damages where the buyer is not entitled to, or chooses not to, reject defective goods. The Sale of Goods Act contains no provision for delayed delivery, but it is accepted that rules analogous to those in sections 51, 53, and 54 apply.

Sections 51(2) and 53(2) provide that the measure of damages is the loss arising in the ordinary course of events from the seller's breach. This reflects the first limb of *Hadley v Baxendale*. However, loss covered by the second limb must also be recoverable, as section 54 preserves the right to recover 'special damages'.[64] For example, loss of profit under a resale of the goods is recoverable where the seller could foresee the resale,[65] which will be the case where the buyer is a merchant.[66]

Section 51(3) provides that where there is an available market, the measure of damages for non-delivery is prima facie the difference between the contract price and the market or current price of the goods at the time when they ought to have been delivered or (if no time was fixed) at the time of the refusal to deliver.[67] Section 53(3) provides that the ordinary loss resulting from the lack of satisfactory quality is prima facie the difference between the value of the goods at the time of delivery to the buyer and the value they would have had without the defect. Section 53 must also apply to defects other than lack of

---

61 Michael Bridge (ed), *Benjamin's Sale of Goods* (12th edn, Sweet & Maxwell 2023) [16-048].

62 For a discussion, see ibid [14-111]–[14-125].

63 Goods are defective when they do not correspond to a description or a sample, or when they are not of satisfactory quality or fit for a particular purpose; see ss 13–15.

64 *Bostock & Co Ltd v Nicholson & Sons Ltd* [1904] 1 KB 725, 735–36.

65 *Molling & Co v Dean & Son Ltd* (1901) 18 TLR 217.

66 *Kwei Tek Chao v British Traders and Shippers Ltd* [1954] 2 QB 459, 489.

67 The provision assumes that the buyer has not yet paid the price. If he has paid already, damages must include the price as well.

satisfactory quality.[68] In the case of delay, the measure of damages is prima facie the difference between the value of the goods at the time when they ought to have been delivered and their value at the time of actual delivery.[69] These rules reflect the fact that the buyer can obtain substitute goods in the market. If the buyer delays the purchase of substitute goods, any fluctuation in the market price (in either direction) is on the buyer's account.

Where the buyer resold the goods prior to the seller's breach, the question arises whether the buyer's loss is assessed by reference to the market value of the goods or the price to be paid by the sub-buyer. In cases in which the seller did not deliver the goods at all and the buyer had resold them at a lower price than their market value at the time of breach, the difference between the market value and the contract price was taken as the amount of damages.[70] This was explained on the ground that the resale contract is not the seller's concern and that the market value is relevant whether it is higher or lower than the resale price.[71] This rationale was undermined by *Re R and H Hall Ltd v WH Pim Jnr & Co's Arbitration*,[72] where the buyer resold at above the market price and the House of Lords awarded damages in the difference between the resale price and the contract price, the loss of profit having been foreseeable. The true rationale of ignoring a resale at a lower than the market value is that the buyer needs to buy substitute goods in the market to fulfil the resale contract, and the buyer's loss is therefore the difference between the contract price and the cost of substitute goods.

The same applies in cases of defective goods and delay if the buyer is required to buy substitute goods to fulfil the resale contract. But the buyer may be able to fulfil the resale contract with the goods delivered by the seller even though they are defective or delivered late (because the sub-buyer accepts the goods regardless). It is controversial whether this fact should be taken into account (to the effect that the buyer has suffered no loss) or be ignored (to the effect that the buyer obtains damages assessed by reference to the market value of the goods).

---

68 *Deutsche Bank AG v Total Global Steel Ltd* [2012] EWHC 1201 (Comm), [2012] Env LR D7 [129] (fitness for a particular purpose).

69 *Koufos v C Czarnikow Ltd* [1969] 1 AC 350, 417–18 (Lord Pearce), citing *Elbinger Actien-Gesellschaft v Armstrong* (1874) LR 9 QB 473, 477.

70 *Rodocanachi, Sons & Co v Milburn Brothers* (1886) 18 QBD 67; *Williams Brothers v ED T Agius Ltd* [1914] AC 510.

71 *Rodocanachi, Sons & Co v Milburn Brothers* (1886) 18 QBD 67; *Williams Brothers v ED T Agius Ltd* [1914] AC 510, 522–23.

72 (1928) Lloyd's Law Rep 159.

In *Wertheim v Chicoutimi Pulp Co*,[73] which involved delayed delivery, the Privy Council held that the resale contract must be taken into account. Lord Atkinson, speaking for the Privy Council, stated that the value of the goods to the buyer is presumed to be their market value at the time of actual delivery, but if the buyer manages to sell them at a higher price, the presumption is rebutted and the buyer's loss must be assessed by reference to the price obtained; otherwise, the buyer would 'be compensated for a loss he never suffered'.[74] It has been objected that the buyer was not obliged to fulfil the resale contract with the goods bought from the seller; if the buyer had fulfilled the sub-contract with substitute goods bought on the market, he would have been left with goods delivered at a time when the market value was lower than the resale price.[75] This is correct. But the buyer did fulfil the resale contract with the goods bought from the seller, and this cannot be ignored if the loss is determined by reference to the actual position of the buyer.[76]

The Court of Appeal has made conflicting decisions in two cases involving defective goods. In *Slater v Hoyle & Smith Ltd*,[77] the buyer bought cloth of a particular specification from the seller in order to fulfil a contract which (unbeknown to the seller) the buyer had already made with a sub-buyer. The seller delivered cloth that was not of the contractual specification. However, the buyer was able to fulfil the contract with the sub-buyer with the defective cloth and received the full price from the sub-buyer. The seller argued that the buyer had suffered no loss. The Court of Appeal held that the buyer was entitled to damages for diminution in value. Scrutton LJ said:

> If the buyer is lucky enough, for reasons with which the seller has nothing to do, to get his goods through on the sub-contract without a claim against him, this on principle cannot affect his claim against the seller any more than the fact that he had to pay very large damages on his sub-contract would affect his original seller.[78]

In *Bence Graphics International Ltd v Fasson UK Ltd*,[79] the seller manufactured vinyl film and sold it to the buyer, who printed identification marks on it and sold it on to customers for use in labelling bulk containers. It was a contractual condition that the film would stay in good condition for five years,

---

73 [1911] AC 301.
74 ibid 308.
75 *Slater v Hoyle & Smith Ltd* [1920] 2 KB 11, 23–24 (Scrutton LJ).
76 Robert Stevens, 'Damages and the Right to Performance: A Golden Victory or Not?' in Jason W Neyers, Richard Bronaugh and Stephen GA Pitel (eds), *Exploring Contract Law* (Hart 2009) 179.
77 [1920] 2 KB 11.
78 ibid 23.
79 [1998] QB 87.

but a defect caused it to degrade so that the marks became illegible. Some end users complained. The Court of Appeal held that the buyer could recover damages only for its liability towards its customers. The prima facie measure under section 53(3) (diminution in value) is displaced and cannot be elected by the buyer where it was in the parties' contemplation at the time of the contract that the goods sold would be used in making a product which would be sold on. In those circumstances, the measure of damages is not diminution in value but the buyer's liability to the users of the product. This applies whether the buyer's liability towards the users is higher or lower than the prima facie measure under section 53(3). Auld LJ stated that *Slater* ought to be reconsidered.[80]

Slater and *Bence Graphics* illustrate the difference between an abstract determination of the buyer's loss by reference to the market value of the goods (ignoring the position of the individual buyer) and a concrete determination of the buyer's loss by reference to the position of the individual buyer.[81] Each approach can be defended. The abstract determination can be defended on the grounds that it makes the assessment of damages easier as there is no need to look into any resale arrangements made by the buyer (the fate of which may not be clear when the buyer claims damages from the seller).[82] The concrete determination of loss can be defended on the grounds that it is more in line with the general rule in *Robinson v Harman* (that the innocent party is to be placed in the position as if the contract had been performed) as it avoids both over- and under-compensation.

The case of defective goods raises particular issues. Section 53(1)(a) provides that the buyer may 'set up against the seller the breach of warranty in diminution or extinction of the price'. It is a defence against the seller's action for the price and not the set-off of a cross-action for damages.[83] The amount of the price reduction is the difference between the actual value of the goods delivered and the value they ought to have had.[84] Thus, the buyer who has not paid yet may deduct from the price the loss determined in an abstract

---

80 ibid 102. For criticism of the case, see GH Treitel, 'Damages for Breach of Warranty of Quality' (1997) 113 LQR 188.

81 A concrete determination was also undertaken in *Euro-Asian Oil SA v Credit Suisse AG* [2018] EWCA Civ 1720, [2019] 1 All ER (Comm) 706 [72]–[73].

82 Michael Bridge, 'Markets and Damages in Sale of Goods Cases' (2016) 132 LQR 405, 418.

83 *Gilbert-Ash (Northern) Ltd v Modern Engineering (Bristol) Ltd* [1974] AC 689, 717 (Lord Diplock), citing *Mondel v Steel* (1841) 8 M & W 858, 872; 151 ER 1288, 1294.

84 ibid.

manner. But the manner in which the loss is determined should not depend upon whether the buyer has already paid.[85]

On the other hand, as mentioned before, it has been held that the buyer can recover the loss of profit under a resale where the resale was foreseeable.[86] This is consistent only with a concrete determination of the loss. The flipside of this approach is that there is no loss where the buyer has been able to fulfil the resale contract with the defective goods delivered by the seller. Since the seller has rendered some performance, there is no total failure of consideration,[87] which would allow the buyer to reclaim the price paid.[88] This outcome is not just.

Some civil law systems and transnational instruments address the issue by granting the buyer the right to a reduction in the price in the proportion in which the value of the goods delivered falls short of the value they would have had without the defect; a buyer who has already paid is entitled to a partial refund.[89] With regard to consumer contracts, section 24 of the Consumer Rights Act 2015 grants the buyer the right to a price reduction 'by an appropriate amount' (which may be the total price) in certain circumstances. Price reduction is a remedy separate from compensation for loss and does not require the presence of loss.

Robert Stevens has argued that damages in the amount of the objective value of the contractual right infringed are available irrespective of whether the breach has caused loss. In cases of non-delivery, the objective value is the difference between the market value of the goods and the contract price. In cases of defective goods, it is the difference between the value of the goods delivered and the value they would have had without the defect. In cases of delay, it is the difference between what was promised and what was delivered at the time of breach.[90] This theory can explain the outcome (but not the reasoning) in *Slater* and in the cases involving non-delivery, but it cannot explain the outcome in *Wertheim* or *Bence Graphics*. Stevens' theory of substitutive

---

85 Michael Bridge, 'Markets and Damages in Sale of Goods Cases' (2016) 132 LQR 405, 420.

86 *Molling & Co v Dean & Son Ltd* (1901) 18 TLR 217.

87 For the suggestion that it might, see Michael Bridge, 'Markets and Damages in Sale of Goods Cases' (2016) 132 LQR 405, 420.

88 See *Rowland v Divall* [1923] 2 KB 500; Sale of Goods Act 1979, s 54(1).

89 eg, German Civil Code (BGB), §441; United Nations Convention on Contracts for the International Sale of Goods (1980), Art 50; Principles of European Contract Law, Art 9.401.

90 Robert Stevens, 'Damages and the Right to Performance: A Golden Victory or Not?' in Jason W Neyers, Richard Bronaugh and Stephen GA Pitel (eds), *Exploring Contract Law* (Hart 2009) 172–83.

damages extends beyond the sale of goods and beyond contract law, and it is discussed more generally (together with other theories of substitutive damages) in Chapter 1.

Contract for Building Work

Where building work is not done in accordance with the contractual specifications or not done at all, there are two possible measures of the customer's loss. One measure is the cost of cure, which is the cost of employing a third party to rectify the defect or carry out the work that the defendant failed to perform. It places the customer in the same physical situation as if the defendant had performed properly. The other measure of the customer's loss is diminution in value, which is the difference between the actual value of the property and the value it would have had if the defendant had performed properly. It places the customer in the same financial situation as if the defendant had performed properly. Some general remarks about those two measures and their conceptualisations by various scholars are made in Chapter 2. The question now is which measure applies in the present context.

Where diminution in value exceeds the cost of cure, only the latter will be awarded if repair work can restore the property to the value it would have without the defendant's breach. If even the best repair work is incapable of achieving this, the remaining diminution in value may be recovered in addition to the cost of cure.[91] Where, as usual, the cost of cure exceeds diminution in value, the law is more complex.

A claimant who employed the defendant to carry out particular building work did so in order to obtain a particular physical state of affairs, not just to improve her financial position. Indeed, the work in question may have no impact on the value of the property at all. It is therefore recognised that diminution in value is not the default measure of damages in the present context. As Oliver J said in *Radford v De Froberville*, the words 'the same situation, with respect to damages, as if the contract had been performed' in *Robinson v Harman* do not mean 'as good a *financial* position as if the contract had been performed'.[92]

Cost of cure is the default measure of damages where a promise to do building work or maintain a building has been breached. However, it will not be awarded where it would be unreasonable to carry out repair work.[93] This is the

---

[91] *Strange v Westbury Homes (Holdings) Ltd* [2009] EWCA Civ 1247, (2009) 128 Con LR 26.

[92] [1977] 1 WLR 1262, 1273 (emphasis added).

[93] Eg, *East Ham Corporation v Bernard Sunley & Sons Ltd* [1966] AC 406, 434–35 (Lord Cohen); *Ruxley Electronics and Construction Ltd v Forsyth* [1996]

case where no reasonable person would obtain any benefit from it. For example, where a builder undertook to use second-hand bricks but used new bricks of first quality, it would be unreasonable to demolish the house and re-erect it using second-hand bricks.[94]

Reinstatement is not unreasonable only because the claimant's interest in it is purely aesthetic or even eccentric.[95] As Oliver J said in *Radford v De Froberville*, 'it may be that, viewed objectively, it is not to the plaintiff's financial advantage to be supplied with the article or service which he has stipulated... But that, surely, must be for the plaintiff to judge. Pacta sunt servanda'.[96] Cost-of-cure damages may thus be awarded to a claimant who contracted for the construction of a folly on his land even if it reduces the value of the land.[97]

In *Ruxley Electronics and Construction Ltd v Forsyth*,[98] the House of Lords held that reinstatement is unreasonable where its cost is out of proportion to the benefit to be obtained from it. Ruxley Electronics and Construction Ltd ('Ruxley') undertook to construct a swimming pool on Mr Forsyth's property to a depth of seven feet six inches, for a fee of £17,797.40. The pool constructed was only six feet nine inches deep, although it was still suitable for diving. Mr Forsyth claimed damages in the amount of the cost of rebuilding the pool to the contractual depth (£21,560). The House of Lords rejected the claim on the ground that rebuilding the pool would be unreasonable as the cost of rebuilding was out of all proportion to the benefit to be obtained from it. Lord Bridge explained that no reasonable claimant would think of incurring disproportionate costs.[99] The House of Lords did not disturb the trial judge's award of £2,500 for loss of amenity, ie non-pecuniary loss.[100] Lord Lloyd explained that the instant case fell within one of the exceptions to the general proscription of

---

AC 344, 368. For criticism, see Charlie Webb, 'Performance and Compensation: An Analysis of Contract Damages and Contractual Obligation' (2006) 26 OJLS 41, 63–64.

[94] Example given in *Bellgrove v Eldridge* (1954) 90 CLR 613, 618.

[95] *Tito v Waddell (No 2)* [1977] Ch 106, 332.

[96] [1977] 1 WLR 1262, 1270.

[97] Example given in *Ruxley Electronics and Construction Ltd v Forsyth* [1996] AC 344, 358, 370–71.

[98] [1996] AC 344. Reliance was placed on *Jacob & Youngs Inc v Kent*, 129 NE 889, 891 (NY, 1921) where Cardozo J stated: 'The owner is entitled to the money which will permit him to complete, unless the cost of completion is grossly and unfairly out of proportion to the good to be attained'.

[99] [1996] AC 344, 353.

[100] Ruxley did not attack that award. Indeed, for tactical reasons, Mr Forsyth attacked it as part of his argument that the denial of cost-of-cure damages would leave him with only nominal damages. For a criticism of the award, see Katy

contractual damages for non-pecuniary loss, namely where a major object of the contract was to provide enjoyment, pleasure or the like.[101]

Forsyth can be contrasted with the Australian case *Tabcorp Holdings Ltd v Bowen Investments Pty Ltd*,[102] where the tenant of an office building undertook not to alter the premises without the landlord's consent. The landlord had installed a new foyer made of expensive materials. The tenant made significant changes to the foyer without the landlord's consent. The value of the property was unaffected, except for the loss of some lettable space on the ground floor. The cost of restoring that space was AU$33,820. The cost of restoring the foyer to its original condition was AU$1.38m, consisting of AU$580,000 as the cost of the work and AU$800,000 as the loss of rental income while the work was being carried out. The High Court of Australia held that the landlord was entitled to an award of AU$1.38m. While the Court confirmed that cost-of-cure damages cannot be awarded where remedial work is unreasonable,[103] it also stated that the test of unreasonableness is satisfied only in 'fairly exceptional circumstances', namely where, in the words of Oliver J in *Radford v De Froberville*,[104] the plaintiff is 'merely using a technical breach to secure an uncovenanted profit'.[105] The Court said that the facts of *Forsyth* were 'plainly distinguishable',[106] but failed to explain why. It is difficult to regard the award of AU$1.38m as being proportionate to a purely aesthetic benefit of rectification.[107]

On principle, the requirement of proportionality may be defended with the argument that it prevents economic waste.[108] On the other hand, the requirement involves a significant degree of uncertainty since reasonable minds (including those of judges) may differ on whether the cost of cure is disproportionate in particular circumstances. This may discourage claimants from

---

Barnett, *Accounting for Profit for Breach of Contract: Theory and Practice* (Hart 2012) 173.

101 [1996] AC 344, 473. The general rule and its exceptions are discussed later in this chapter.

102 [2009] HCA 8, (2009) 236 CLR 272.

103 ibid [17], citing *Bellgrove v Eldridge* (1954) 90 CLR 613, 618.

104 [1977] 1 WLR 1262, 1270.

105 [2009] HCA 8, (2009) 236 CLR 272 [17] (French CJ, Gummow, Heydon, Crennan and Kiefel JJ).

106 ibid [18] (French CJ, Gummow, Heydon, Crennan and Kiefel JJ).

107 Cf *Stone v Chappel* [2017] SASCFC 72, (2017) 128 SASR 165 [441] (Hinton J).

108 Arthur Linton Corbin, *Corbin on Contracts: A Comprehensive Treatise on the Working Rules of Contract Law* (West 1963) §1089.

seeking cost-of-cure damages and in turn reduce the incentive of contractors to comply with contractual specifications.[109]

Another controversial question is whether an award of cost-of-cure damages should be conditional on the work actually being carried out (where it has not been done already). For Stephen Smith, such a requirement follows from his conceptualisation of cost-of-cure damages as substitute specific performance.[110] Charlie Webb has argued that an award of the cost of repair work ought to be conditional on the claimant giving an undertaking to use the award for that purpose; an award not so restricted gives effect to neither the performance interest nor the compensation interest, and cannot be justified.[111]

We suggest that two categories of cases should be distinguished. The first category is where it is impossible for the claimant to have repair work carried out because the property has been destroyed, the claimant has sold it unrepaired, or there is some other external factor such as the lack of planning permission. There is some authority for the unavailability of cost-of-cure damages in those circumstances.[112] This is convincing. Where it is impossible for the claimant to have repair work carried out, it cannot be said that the claimant has suffered a loss in the amount of the cost of the work.

The second category is where the claimant is still in possession of the property and thus able to have repair work carried out. In those circumstances, it is not settled whether an intention to have repair work carried out is a prerequisite for an award of cost-of-cure damages. In some cases, it has been said that such an intention is a prerequisite.[113] In other cases, it has been said that it is

---

[109] Janet O'Sullivan, 'Loss and Gain at Greater Depth: The Implications of the *Ruxley* Decision' in Francis Rose (ed), *Failure of Contracts: Contractual, Restitutionary and Proprietary Consequences* (Hart 1997) 11.

[110] Stephen A Smith, *Contract Theory* (OUP 2004) 422.

[111] Charlie Webb, 'Performance and Compensation: An Analysis of Contract Damages and Contractual Obligation' (2006) 26 OJLS 41, 63.

[112] *Eldon Weiss Home Construction Ltd v Clark* (1982) 39 OR (2d) 129. In *A Meredith Jones & Co Ltd v Vangemar Shipping Co Ltd (The Apostolis) (No 2)* [2000] 2 Lloyd's Rep 337, 348, where the owner of a damaged ship sold it unrepaired, the availability of cost-of-cure damages was not challenged on that ground, but they were denied in any event because they were disproportionate.

[113] *Tito v Waddell (No 2)* [1977] Ch 106, 332–33; *Radford v De Froberville* [1977] 1 WLR 1262, 1283–84; *Birse Construction Ltd v Eastern Telegraph Co Ltd* [2004] EWHC 2512 (TCC), (2004) 47 EG 164 (CS) at [48]; *London Fire and Emergency Planning Authority v Halcrow Gilbert Associates Ltd* [2007] EWHC 2546 (TCC), (2008) 24 Const LJ 103 [672]; *St James Oncology SPC Ltd v Lendlease Construction (Europe) Ltd* [2022] EWHC 2504 (TCC) [347]–[348] (intention found on the facts).

not a prerequisite.[114] Remarkably, none of the statements on either side mentions the existence of judicial statements to the contrary.

The House of Lords was not required to decide the issue in *Forsyth* as the cost of cure was disproportionate and therefore irrecoverable in any event. Two law lords nonetheless commented on the issue. Lord Jauncey stated that intention is relevant to the reasonableness of reinstatement, but a court has no concern with the use to which a claimant puts an award of damages.[115] It is difficult to see how the reasonableness of reinstatement, if it were to be carried out, can depend upon whether the claimant intends to have it carried out. Lord Lloyd stated that intention is relevant to the reasonableness of awarding cost-of-cure damages.[116] It is thus the award that needs to be reasonable and not just the reinstatement.

It might be argued that if cost-of-cure damages are denied where external factors prevent the claimant from having repair work carried out, cost-of-cure damages must also be denied where the claimant has no intention to have repair work carried out. The claimant will not incur the cost of the work in either scenario. However, if the availability of cost-of-cure damages depends on the claimant's intention, the court must either make a finding on that issue, which involves the risk of the claimant giving self-serving testimony, or require the claimant to give an undertaking and in effect supervise the claimant after judgment. It may therefore be more practicable not to make the availability of cost-of-cure damages dependent upon the claimant's intentions.[117]

---

[114] *Dean v Ainley* [1987] 1 WLR 1729, 1737–38 (Kerr LJ); *Darlington Borough Council v Wiltshier Northern Ltd* [1995] 1 WLR 68, 80 (Steyn LJ); *Giedo van der Garde BV v Force India Formula One Team Ltd* [2010] EWHC 2373 (QB) [457]-[485]; *De Beers UK Ltd v Atos Origin IT Services UK Ltd* [2010] EWHC 3276 (TCC), [2011] BLR 274 [345].

[115] [1996] AC 344, 359.

[116] ibid 373; approvingly quoted in *Alfred McAlpine Construction Ltd v Panatown Ltd* [2001] 1 AC 518, 556 (Lord Goff). See also *Endurance Corporate Capital Ltd v Sartex Quilts & Textiles Ltd* [2020] EWCA Civ 308, [2020] 2 All ER (Comm) 1050 [63]–[64].

[117] For similar arguments, see John Ren, 'Measure of Damages for Defective Building Work' (2014) 32 J Cont L 69, 90–91; Solène Rowan, 'Cost of Cure Damages and the Relevance of the Injured Promisee's Intention to Cure' (2017) 76 Camb LJ 616, 638–40. Cf Kwan Ho Lau, 'Recovering Cost of Cure Damages: The Necessity of Showing an Intention to Cure' (2024) 140 LQR 342.

SPECIAL TYPES OF LOSS

Transferred Loss

Introduction

Suppose that C and D make a contract, D breaches the contract, and T, who is not a party to the contract, suffers loss. At common law, T has no contractual claim against D (doctrine of privity).[118] However, the Contracts (Rights of Third Parties) Act 1999 gives T the right to enforce the contract if C and D intended this.[119] Alternatively, T may have a claim against D in tort or under statute, or T may have a claim (in contract or otherwise) against C, who can then claim an indemnity from D. Difficulties arise where T has no claim against either C or D, and C, who would have a claim against D, has not—on the face of it—suffered loss.

Under the view taken by some scholars that any breach of contract entitles the innocent party to an award of damages as a substitute for performance, the award not being concerned with the compensation of loss, C can recover damages from T; there is no unanimity as to the measure of such damages.[120]

The courts have not adopted the concept of substitutionary damages and require proof of loss for an award of substantial damages. The general rule is that a party can recover damages only for its own loss.[121] However, there are considerable exceptions.

One exception is where one member of a family books a holiday or meal for the whole family and loss is suffered (also) by other members of the family. It is recognised that the family member who entered into the contract may recover damages for the loss suffered by all members. Thus, in *Jackson v*

118 *Dunlop Pneumatic Tyre Co Ltd v Selfridge and Co Ltd* [1915] AC 847.

119 For a discussion of the 1999 Act, which is beyond the scope of this book, see Andrew Burrows, 'The Contracts (Rights of Third Parties) Act 1999 and Its Implications for Commercial Contracts' [2000] LMCLQ 540; Robert Stevens, 'The Contracts (Rights of Third Parties) Act 1999' (2004) 120 LQR 292. Parties generally contract out of the Act: Katy Barnett, *Damages for Breach of Contract* (2nd edn, Sweet & Maxwell 2022) [2–053].

120 See Robert Stevens, 'Damages and the Right to Performance: A Golden Victory or Not?' in Jason W Neyers, Richard Bronaugh and Stephen GA Pitel (eds), *Exploring Contract Law* (Hart 2009) 189–90 (difference in value between the performance promised and the performance delivered); David Winterton, *Money Awards in Contract Law* (Hart 2015) 163–64 (the cost of substitute performance or, where this is unquantifiable, a hypothetical release fee).

121 *Beswick v Beswick* [1968] AC 58, 72–73 (Lord Reid); *Woodar Investment Development Ltd v Wimpey Construction (UK) Ltd* [1980] 1 WLR 277.

Horizon Holidays Ltd,[122] the plaintiff bought a four-week holiday in a hotel for himself, his wife and his children. The hotel did not have the facilities described in the brochure. The Court of Appeal upheld the trial judge's award of £1,100. Lord Denning MR stated that the award would have been excessive as compensation for the plaintiff's loss alone but was an acceptable amount for the total loss suffered by the whole family, which the plaintiff was entitled to recover.[123] Lord Denning MR pronounced a general rule that where a contract is made for the benefit of a third party, the promisee can sue on the contract for the third party's benefit.[124] In *Woodar Investment Development Ltd v Wimpey Construction (UK) Ltd*,[125] the House of Lords rejected this wide rule but did not disapprove the decision on the facts of *Jackson*. Lord Wilberforce stated that there is a type of contract that calls for special treatment, for example contracting for a family holiday, ordering meals in a restaurant for a party, and hiring a taxi for a group.[126]

Another exception to the rule that a party can only claim for its own loss is that of transferred loss. The paradigm scenario is where a seller of goods enters into a contract for the carriage of the goods to the buyer and the goods are damaged after the property in the goods (or at least the risk) has passed to the buyer. The buyer, who remains obliged to pay the purchase price, has no claim against the carrier,[127] and the seller may be said to have suffered no loss. However, it has long been recognised that the seller has a claim against the carrier, which is for the loss suffered by the buyer. In *The Albazero*,[128] the House of Lords affirmed this rule and also made clear that the seller is accountable to the buyer for any damages recovered from the carrier.[129] Where the goods are carried by sea, the claim lies with the holder of the bill of lading.[130] The

122 [1975] 1 WLR 1468. An earlier example is *Hobbs v London and South Western Railway Co* (1875) LR 10 QB 111 (discussed later in this chapter), where the plaintiff recovered damages for the inconvenience suffered by himself, his wife and his children.

123 [1975] 1 WLR 1468, 1473.

124 ibid, relying on *Lloyd's v Harper* (1880) 16 Ch D 290, 321 (Lush LJ).

125 [1980] 1 WLR 277.

126 ibid 283.

127 Unless, where the goods are carried by sea, the buyer becomes the holder of the bill of lading: Carriage of Goods by Sea Act 1992, s 2(1).

128 [1977] AC 774.

129 ibid 844.

130 Carriage of Goods by Sea Act 1992, s 2(4).

justification for this rule is to avoid a 'black hole' where the person who has a claim has suffered no loss and the person who has suffered loss has no claim.[131]

The rule has been extended to building contracts, first in *Linden Gardens Trust Ltd v Lenesta Sludge Disposals Ltd*.[132] The key facts of the two combined cases were as follows. C engaged D to carry out work on C's property. At the time of the contract, it was clear to D that C was likely to transfer the property to another person. C did transfer the property to T. D breached the contract with C by performing the work defectively. C purported to assign its rights against D to T, but the transfer was ineffective as it was excluded by the contract between C and D. The House of Lords held that C had a claim against D. Two different bases featured in the judgment. They are commonly known as the 'broader ground', to be discussed further below, and the 'narrow ground'.

The 'narrow ground'

The narrow ground was developed in *Linden Gardens* by Lord Browne-Wilkinson, with whom Lord Keith, Lord Bridge, and Lord Ackner agreed. Lord Browne-Wilkinson stated that the instant case fell within the rationale of the *Albazero* rule. Both parties knew that the property was going to be occupied, and possibly purchased by third parties. It was therefore foreseeable that a breach by the contractor would cause loss to a later owner and not just the contracting party. But later owners would have no rights against the contractor. Therefore, the parties were to be treated as having entered into the contract on the footing that the employer would be entitled to enforce contractual rights for the benefit of those who suffered from defective performance but had no claim against the contractor.[133]

In *Linden Gardens*, C was the owner of the property when contracting with D. In *Darlington Borough Council v Wiltshier Northern Ltd*,[134] the narrow ground developed in *Linden Gardens* was applied in circumstances where C was never the owner of the property. A contractor had contracted with Morgan Grenfell, a finance company, to construct a recreational centre on land owned by the local authority.[135] The contractor was aware that the centre was built for the authority. Morgan Grenfell assigned all its rights under the contract to the local authority. The local authority sued the contractor for alleged defects. Since it was enforcing a right assigned to it by Morgan Grenfell, the authority

[131] *Alfred McAlpine Construction Ltd v Panatown Ltd* [2001] 1 AC 518, 529 (Lord Clyde).

[132] [1994] 1 AC 85 ('*Linden Gardens*').

[133] ibid 114–15.

[134] [1995] 1 WLR 68.

[135] The local authority did not contract with the contractor because of restrictions on local authority borrowing.

could recover substantial damages only if Morgan Grenfell could have recovered them had the assignment not taken place. Relying on Lord Browne-Wilkinson's speech in *Linden Gardens*, the Court of Appeal held that Morgan Grenfell could have recovered substantial damages; the fact that it had no proprietary interest was no obstacle. Dillon LJ, with whom Waite LJ agreed on this point,[136] added that if Morgan Grenfell had recovered substantial damages from the contractor, it would have held them on trust for the local authority.[137]

In *Alfred McAlpine Construction Ltd v Panatown Ltd*,[138] the House of Lords held that the narrow ground developed in *Linden Gardens* did not apply where the third party has a direct claim against the contractor. Panatown Ltd ('Panatown') employed Alfred McAlpine Construction Ltd ('McAlpine') to build an office block and a multi-storey car park on land owned by UIPL. Panatown and UIPL were associated companies, and the purpose of the scheme was the (lawful) avoidance of tax. McAlpine entered into a separate Duty of Care Deed with UIPL, which gave successive owners of the site remedies for breach of a duty of care. The building was found to be defective, and Panatown claimed damages for the loss suffered by UIPL. The House of Lords (Lord Goff and Lord Millett dissenting) held that Panatown was entitled to nominal damages only. The narrow ground developed in *Linden Gardens* did not apply. Its purpose was to provide a remedy where there would be none otherwise. Even though UIPL's rights under the Duty of Care Deed were not identical to Panatown's rights under the building contract (which also imposed strict obligations), the fact that UIPL was entitled to substantial damages took the case out of the scope of the narrow ground laid down in *Linden Gardens*.[139]

Lord Sumption JSC in *Swynson Ltd v Lowick Rose LLP* summarised the narrow ground in this way:

> It applies where the known object of a transaction is to benefit a third party or a class of persons to which the third party belongs, and the anticipated effect of a breach of duty will be to cause loss to the third party. It has hitherto been recognised only in cases where the third party suffers loss as the intended transferee of the property affected by the breach.[140]

Lord Sumption JSC added that it is an essential feature of the principle that the recognition of C's right to recover T's loss is necessary to avoid a 'legal black hole' where the party entitled to recover is different from the party suffering

---

[136] ibid 81.
[137] ibid 75, citing *Lloyd's v Harper* (1880) 16 Ch D 290.
[138] [2001] 1 AC 518 ('*McAlpine*').
[139] ibid 531–32 (Lord Clyde), 568 (Lord Jauncey), 576–77 (Lord Browne-Wilkinson).
[140] [2017] UKSC 32, [2018] AC 313 [14].

loss. The principle is not available where T has a direct right of action against D on whatever basis.[141]

The 'broader ground'

The broader ground was advanced by Lord Griffiths in *Linden Gardens*.[142] His Lordship stated that in contracts for work it is irrelevant whether the promisee has any proprietary interest in the property. If the work done is defective, the promisee can recover the cost of repair work in order to obtain the benefit of the bargain the builder promised to deliver. Lord Griffiths gave the example of a husband who employs a builder to place a new roof on the matrimonial home. The work done is defective, and the husband has to pay another builder to complete the work. The husband can claim the cost of repair because he has not received the bargain for which he contracted with the first builder. It is immaterial whether the husband or his wife was the owner of the property at the time of the contract or the time of the breach.

The key difference between the narrow ground and the broader ground is that under the narrow ground, the promisee can claim damages for the loss suffered by the third party (which have to be passed on to the third party), whereas the broader ground identifies the cost of repair as the promisee's own loss, and the promisee is not obliged to pass the damages on to the third party.[143] However, the promisee may be obliged to use the damages to procure the rectification of the defect.[144]

In *Linden Gardens*, Lord Keith and Lord Bridge expressed sympathy for Lord Griffith's broader ground but did not make it the basis of their decision.[145] Lord Browne-Wilkinson observed that the point required academic consideration.[146] Steyn LJ endorsed the broader ground in *Darlington Borough Council v Wiltshier Northern Ltd*.[147]

In *McAlpine*, the dissentient law lords (Lord Goff and Lord Millett) used the broader ground as the basis of their view that Panatown had a claim against

---

141 ibid [16]. See also Andrew Burrows, *A Restatement of the English Law of Contract* (2nd edn, OUP 2020) 242 (rule 46(4)).

142 [1994] 1 AC 85, 96–97.

143 The distinction was explained in *McAlpine* [2001] 1 AC 518, 532 (Lord Clyde), 573 (Lord Jauncey).

144 This was Lord Goff's view in *McAlpine* [2001] 1 AC 518, 559–60.

145 ibid 95 (Lord Keith), 95 (Lord Bridge).

146 ibid 112.

147 [1995] 1 WLR 68, 80–81 (stating that the promisee may recover cost-of-cure damages irrespective of whether repair has been or will be carried out). Dillon LJ (at 75) refused to endorse the broader ground. Waite LJ (at 81) stated that he based his decision on the narrow ground.

McAlpine even though UIPL had a direct claim against McAlpine under the Duty of Care Deed.[148] Lord Browne-Wilkinson mentioned that in *Linden Gardens* he had called for academic consideration of the issue and that this had happened without serious difficulties being disclosed.[149] However, his Lordship did not expressly endorse the broader ground, merely assuming its soundness.[150] He also confined it to cases where T has no direct claim against D; if C recovers damages from D, D cannot also be liable to T, yet C is not liable to account to T for the damages.[151] His Lordship stated that Panatown had suffered no damage to its performance interest as UIPL had a direct claim against McAlpine.[152]

Lord Clyde rejected the broader ground. Instead of constructing a theoretical loss on C's part, he said, a more realistic and practical solution is to permit C to recover damages for the loss that C and T have suffered; it is for Parliament to introduce a more radical approach.[153] Lord Jauncey also rejected the broader ground, regarding it as problematic if C could claim the cost of repair without spending the money on repair.[154] Both Lord Clyde and Lord Jauncey also pointed out that where T has no claim against D, there is no recovery for consequential loss under the broader ground.[155] In Lord Griffiths' example of the husband engaging a contractor, neither the husband nor the wife could recover the loss of rent suffered by the wife.[156]

It has been held that the broader ground can apply only if C and D intended to benefit T. In *Swynson Ltd v Lowick Rose LLP*,[157] considered in Chapter 2, the claimant was not permitted to recover the loss suffered by Mr Hunt. Lord Sumption JSC pointed out that since Mr Hunt did not suffer his loss in his capacity as the owner of property, only the broader principle of transferred loss could be relevant; however, it was no part of the object of retaining the defendant accountants to benefit Mr Hunt.[158]

---

148 [2001] 1 AC 518, 545–48 (Lord Goff), 587–91 (Lord Millett).
149 ibid 577.
150 ibid.
151 ibid 577–78. The argument is unconvincing because exactly the same thing will happen where T has no claim against D.
152 ibid.
153 ibid 535.
154 ibid 571.
155 ibid 534 (Lord Clyde), 573 (Lord Jauncey).
156 ibid 534 (Lord Clyde).
157 [2017] UKSC 32, [2018] AC 313.
158 ibid [17]. See also the comments by Lord Neuberger PSC ibid [107]–[108].

In *BV Nederlandse Industrie van Eiprodukten v Rembrandt Enterprises Inc*,[159] there was a contract for the supply of egg white powder. After shipments began, the seller informed the buyer that some of the powder was to be supplied by the seller's sister company. Subsequently, the buyer repudiated the contract, and the seller claimed damages for loss of profit, including profit from supplies made by its sister company. The Court of Appeal held that the seller could not recover damages for the loss of profit from supplies made by its sister company. Coulson LJ, with whom Longmore LJ and Peter Jackson LJ agreed on this issue, stated that the broader ground requires that, at the time of the contract, it was the common intention or a known object of the contracting parties to benefit the third party or a class of persons to which the third party belonged.[160] Otherwise, a main contractor could always claim against the employer the loss suffered by a subcontractor even if the employer had no knowledge of the subcontractor; it would turn transferred loss, which is supposed to be a narrow exception to the rule that a party can only claim for its own loss, into a commonplace route of recovery.[161] The buyer in the instant case had not been aware of the third party's existence at the time of the contract.[162]

There is some uncertainty as to the scope of the broader ground. Lord Griffiths in *Linden Gardens* saw it as a claim for the cost of repair available only if repair has been or is likely to be carried out.[163] Lord Goff and Lord Millett in *McAlpine* went further, saying that the broader ground reflects C's performance interest and includes cases of delay; the claim is not necessarily for the cost of repair.[164] The broader ground may cover cases such as *Jackson v Horizon Holidays Ltd*.[165] But it is uncertain whether the broader ground permits C to recover damages for consequential loss.[166]

Another uncertainty relates to whether C can claim under the broader ground where T has a claim against D. In *McAlpine*, Lord Browne-Wilkinson gave a negative answer.[167] Lord Goff and Lord Millett took the opposite view.

---

159 [2019] EWCA Civ 596, [2020] QB 551.

160 ibid [73].

161 ibid [75].

162 ibid [74]. See also *SmithKline Beecham plc v Apotex Europe Ltd* [2006] EWCA Civ 658, [2007] Ch 71 [94]–[95].

163 [1994] 1 AC 85, 96–97.

164 [2001] 1 AC 518, 554–56 (Lord Goff), 591–92 (Lord Millett).

165 ibid 552 (Lord Goff), 588 (Lord Millett).

166 See Katy Barnett, *Damages for Breach of Contract* (2nd edn, Sweet & Maxwell 2022) [2–049].

167 ibid 577–78.

However, Lord Millett stated that C's loss cannot exceed T's loss,[168] and Lord Goff observed that where C recovers damages for the cost of repair, C is obliged to spend them on repair or pass them to T.[169]

The relationship between the broader ground and the narrow ground is also somewhat unclear. Every case that falls within the scope of the narrow ground also falls within the scope of the broader ground. But C cannot invoke both grounds. C cannot recover damages for its own loss under the broader ground as well as damages for T's loss under the narrow ground. It has been suggested that the broader ground should not be available where the narrow ground applies.[170]

The area of transferred loss would benefit from clarification by the Supreme Court.

Non-Pecuniary Loss

Non-pecuniary loss such as mental distress is not generally recoverable in contract.[171] The rule is said to stem from *Addis v Gramophone Co Ltd*,[172] where the House of Lords held that damages cannot be recovered for distress caused by the manner of dismissal from employment.[173] The general rule is now firmly established.[174]

In *Watts v Morrow*,[175] Bingham LJ observed that the general rule is founded on considerations of policy. But he did not explain what policy considerations they are. Different rationales have been suggested.[176] Staughton LJ in *Hayes v James & Charles Dodd* referred to the risk of large US-style awards being

---

168 ibid 594–96.

169 ibid 558–60.

170 Adam Kramer, *The Law of Contract Damages* (3rd edn, Hart 2022) [21–53].

171 Some general remarks about non-pecuniary loss are made in Ch 2.

172 [1909] AC 488. For an argument that such a general rule was not laid down in the case, see Nelson Enonchong, 'Breach of Contract and Damages for Mental Distress' (1996) 16 OJLS 617, 620–25.

173 Even financial loss resulting from the manner of dismissal cannot be recovered at common law as the remedies are exclusively set out in legislation: *Johnson v Unisys Ltd* [2001] UKHL 13, [2003] 1 AC 518; *Edwards v Chesterfield Royal Hospital NHS Foundation Trust* [2011] UKSC 58, [2012] 2 AC 22.

174 *Groom v Crocker* [1939] 1 KB 194, 224; *Bliss v South East Thames Regional Health Authority* [1987] ICR 700, 717–18; *Watts v Morrow* [1991] 1 WLR 1421, 1445; *Johnson v Unisys Ltd* [2001] UKHL 13, [2003] 1 AC 518 [69] (Lord Millett); *Farley v Skinner* [2001] UKHL 49, [2002] 2 AC 732 [16].

175 [1991] 1 WLR 1421, 1445.

176 For a discussion, see Sirko Harder, *Measuring Damages in the Law of Obligations: The Search for Harmonised Principles* (Hart 2010) 104–14.

made.[177] This fear is unfounded as the awards made by English courts in tort actions demonstrate. Staughton LJ added that he 'would not view with enthusiasm the prospect that every shipowner in the Commercial Court, having successfully claimed for unpaid freight or demurrage, would be able to add a claim for mental distress suffered while he was waiting for his money'.[178] This floodgate argument is unconvincing, not least because many parties to commercial contracts (and in particular shipowners) are corporations, which cannot suffer distress.

It has been said that in ordinary commercial contracts, non-pecuniary loss such as mental suffering consequent on breach is not within the contemplation of the parties and thus too remote; conversely, the ordinary feelings of anxiety, frustration, and disappointment caused by any breach of contract are so common that the parties must be regarded as having agreed to take the risk of their occurrence.[179] This argument has force, but instead of supporting the general rule, it demonstrates that there is no need for a special rule proscribing contractual damages for non-pecuniary loss. The matter can be left to the general rules of contract law, in particular the rules relating to remoteness of loss.

The general rule is subject to considerable exceptions, although damages will be modest.[180] There are at least three, and possibly four, exceptions.

First, where a breach of contract causes personal injury, damages may be awarded for the resulting non-pecuniary loss (pain and suffering and loss of amenities of life)[181] unless the injury was unforeseeable.[182] Damages for non-pecuniary loss have been awarded, for example, where defective goods caused the buyer to become ill,[183] and where tenants suffered injury because their

---

177 [1990] 2 All ER 815, 823.

178 ibid.

179 *Johnson v Unisys Ltd* [2001] UKHL 13, [2003] 1 AC 518 [70] (Lord Millett); *Fidler v Sun Life Assurance Co of Canada* [2006] SCC 30, [2006] 2 SCR 3 [45].

180 *Ruxley Electronics and Construction Ltd v Forsyth* [1996] AC 344, 374 (Lord Lloyd); *Farley v Skinner* [2001] UKHL 49, [2002] 2 AC 732 [28] (Lord Steyn); *Watts v Morrow* [1991] 1 WLR 1421, 1445.

181 *Wood v TUI Travel plc* [2017] EWCA Civ 11, [2018] QB 927 [1]. In most contract cases, the types of non-pecuniary losses resulting from personal injury were not specified.

182 *Hobbs v London and South Western Railway Co* (1875) LR 10 QB 111 (cold suffered as a result of a train going to the wrong station); *Cook v Swinfen* [1967] 1 WLR 457, 461–62 (nervous breakdown suffered as a result of a solicitor's negligence in divorce proceedings); *Berryman v Hounslow London Borough Council* [1997] PIQR P83 (slipped disc suffered as a result of a lift not working).

183 *Wren v Holt* [1903] 1 KB 610; *Grant v Australian Knitting Mills Ltd* [1936] AC 85 (PC); *Godley v Perry* [1960] 1 WLR 9; *Wood v TUI Travel plc* [2017] EWCA Civ 11, [2018] QB 927.

landlord had failed to repair defects in the property.[184] In cases in which there is concurrent liability in contract and tort (such as in employment relationships), the action is often brought solely in tort.[185]

Secondly, contractual damages for distress may be awarded where the distress is consequent on physical inconvenience or discomfort caused by the breach and was foreseeable.[186] This exception stems from *Hobbs v London and South Western Railway Co*,[187] where the plaintiff and his family were taken to the wrong station by the railway company, requiring them to walk for four to five miles on a drizzling night. The Divisional Court upheld a jury award for inconvenience. More recent cases falling into this category involved a landlord or surveyor being liable in respect of defective dwellings, and the claimant suffering physical inconvenience because of the defects[188] or because of repair work being carried out.[189]

The physical discomfort in these cases was an unpleasant sensory experience such as a bad smell, noise, or (in *Hobbs*) being cold. In *Farley v Skinner*,[190] Lord Scott explained that the category of physical inconvenience is confined to a sensory experience (sight, touch, hearing, smell, etc.) and does not include physical inconvenience suffered because of anxiety or worry about the consequences of the breach, even if the anxiety or worry leads to a mental breakdown. Adam Kramer suggests that where a breach of contract has the potential to cause physical inconvenience, physical convenience must have been a major object of the contract or not too remote a consequence.[191]

Thirdly, contractual damages for non-pecuniary loss may be recovered where a major object of the contract was to provide pleasure, relaxation or the like.[192] The Court of Appeal established this category in cases in which holidays fell short of the promised standard, depriving the holidaymakers of

---

184 *Griffin v Pillett* [1926] 1 KB 17; *Porter v Jones* [1942] 2 All ER 570; *Summers v Salford Corporation* [1943] AC 283; *McCoy & Co v Clark* (1984) 13 HLR 87.

185 eg, *Barber v Somerset County Council* [2004] UKHL 13, [2004] 1 WLR 1089.

186 *Watts v Morrow* [1991] 1 WLR 1421, 1445.

187 (1875) LR 10 QB 111. Cf *Hamlin v Great Northern Railway Co* (1856) 1 H & N 408; 156 ER 1261.

188 eg, *Perry v Sidney Phillips & Son* [1982] 1 WLR 1297, 1302–03; *Wallace v Manchester City Council* (1998) 30 HLR 1111; *Farley v Skinner* [2001] UKHL 49, [2002] 2 AC 732 [30], [37], [58]–[60], [101].

189 *Watts v Morrow* [1991] 1 WLR 1421, 1441, 1445.

190 [2001] UKHL 49, [2002] 2 AC 732 [85].

191 Adam Kramer, *The Law of Contract Damages* (3rd edn, Hart 2022) [19-79].

192 For a brief overview of the development of this exception, see *Yearworth v North Bristol NHS Trust* [2009] EWCA Civ 37, [2010] QB 1 [56].

the expected relaxation.[193] This exception to the *Addis* rule has been applied in a large variety of contexts, including where a surveyor failed to disclose aircraft noise, which he had been expressly asked to investigate,[194] where a solicitor failed to secure an injunction for non-molestation against the client's former partner,[195] and where an accountant's negligence led to the client being bankrupt for longer than necessary.[196] The loss of a pleasurable amenity, as occurred in *Ruxley Electronics and Construction Ltd v Forsyth*[197] also falls into this category,[198] but not ordinary commercial contracts.[199]

It has been argued that the 'object of the contract' category is not an exception to the *Addis* rule but falls outside its rationale, as the non-pecuniary loss is the direct result of the breach and not the manner of the breach.[200] This cannot explain the cases in which damages for non-pecuniary loss have been denied even though that loss was the result of the breach and not the manner of the breach. For example, damages for mental distress have been denied where a bank made phantom deductions from the customer's bank account,[201] where a Rolls Royce car was not properly repaired,[202] and where a brand-new dwelling had defective foundations.[203]

It has been argued that an award of damages for non-pecuniary loss in this category reflects the 'consumer surplus' by which the consumer's valuation of goods or services exceeds their financial or objective valuation.[204] However, consumers enter into many contracts with the object of obtaining a benefit beyond the financial benefit. For example, consumers enter into contracts for

193 *Jarvis v Swans Tours Ltd* [1973] QB 233; *Jackson v Horizon Holidays Ltd* [1975] 1 WLR 1468. *Jackson* was discussed in a different context earlier in this chapter.

194 *Farley v Skinner* [2001] UKHL 49, [2002] 2 AC 732.

195 *Heywood v Wellers* [1976] QB 446, 458–59, 461, 463–64.

196 *Demarco v Bulley Davey (a firm)* [2006] EWCA Civ 188, [2006] PNLR 27 [76]–[77].

197 [1996] AC 344. The case was discussed in a different context earlier in this chapter.

198 *Farley v Skinner* [2001] UKHL 49, [2002] 2 AC 732 [21] (Lord Steyn).

199 *Hayes v James & Charles Dodd* [1990] 2 All ER 815, 818, 823–24; *Regus (UK) Ltd v Epcot Solutions Ltd* [2007] EWHC 938 (Comm), [2007] 2 All ER (Comm) 766 [48].

200 *Johnson v Unisys Ltd* [2001] UKHL 13, [2003] 1 AC 518 [70] (Lord Millett).

201 *McConville v Barclays Bank plc* [1993] 2 Bank LR 211.

202 *Alexander v Rolls Royce Motor Cars Ltd* [1996] RTR 95.

203 *Harrison v Shepherd Homes Ltd* [2011] EWHC 1811 (TCC), (2011) 27 Const LJ 709 [324].

204 Donald Harris, Anthony Ogus and Jennifer Phillips, 'Contract Remedies and the Consumer Surplus' (1979) 95 LQR 581, 595–96.

a current bank account or a credit card in order to have the peace of mind of knowing that they can pay cashless, which is necessary for online purchases and now also required by some shops. If the notion of the consumer surplus is taken seriously, most consumer contracts ought to fall into the 'object of the contract' category. But this is not the case, as demonstrated by the examples given in the previous paragraph. The boundaries of the exception are unclear.

The Supreme Court of Canada has made a distinction between normal commercial contracts, where the likelihood of a breach causing mental distress is not ordinarily within the reasonable contemplation of the parties, and a contract an object of which is to secure a psychological benefit. In the latter category, damages for mental distress are recoverable where the distress was in the reasonable contemplation of the parties when the contract was made; this is simply an application of the rule in *Hadley v Baxendale* (discussed later in this chapter).[205]

A potential fourth exception to the *Addis* rule involves loss of reputation. Bank customers have recovered damages for loss of financial reputation where the bank wrongfully dishonoured a cheque,[206] or negligently caused the customer to become bankrupt.[207] Damages for loss of publicity have been awarded to actors and singers when their employer breached a promise to let them give a public performance,[208] and to writers when they were not permitted to publish or write a particular article or book.[209]

However, the damages awarded in these cases may be seen as compensating not non-pecuniary loss but pecuniary loss that could not be proven.[210] When explaining that it is not only traders who can claim damages for loss of credit when a bank wrongfully dishonours a cheque, Evans LJ in *Kpohraror*

---

205 *Fidler v Sun Life Assurance Co of Canada* [2006] SCC 30, [2006] 2 SCR 3 [44]–[49].

206 *Larios v Bonany y Gurety* (1873) LR 5 PC 346; *Kpohraror v Woolwich Building Society* [1996] 4 All ER 119. Lord Atkinson referred to this rule in *Addis v Gramophone Co Ltd* [1909] AC 488, 495.

207 *Wilson v United Counties Bank Ltd* [1920] AC 102.

208 *Bunning v Lyric Theatre* (1894) 71 LT 396; *Marbe v George Edwardes (Daly's Theatre) Ltd* [1928] 1 KB 269; *Herbert Clayton and Jack Waller Ltd v Oliver* [1930] AC 209. For the discussion of a duty to provide an entertainer with an opportunity to perform, in English and US law, see Neil A Shanzer, 'The Loss of Publicity as an Element of Damages for Breach of Contract to Employ an Entertainer' (1973) 27 U Miami L Rev 465.

209 *Joseph v National Magazine Co Ltd* [1959] Ch 14; *Sadler v Reynolds* [2005] EWHC 309 (QB).

210 See Andrew Burrows, *A Restatement of the English Law of Contract* (2nd edn, OUP 2020) 132–33 (rule 20(8)(d)); Adam Kramer, *The Law of Contract Damages* (3rd edn, Hart 2022) [8-40], [8-43].

v Woolwich Building Society stated that individuals may also be affected, for example in relation to their mortgages, hire-purchases, and banking facilities.[211] He added: 'Damages for loss of reputation simpliciter are excluded, whether in contract or for torts other than defamation.'[212] It implies that the award for loss of credit is for unspecified pecuniary detriments. Similarly, the awards for loss of publicity recovered by actors and singers may be seen as compensating the loss of unspecified profit from future engagements.[213]

Insofar as the cases involving loss of reputation do involve non-pecuniary loss, it seems that most of them can be placed in the 'object of the contract' exception. A major object of a bank's promise to honour cheques when there are sufficient funds must be the preservation of the customer's credit standing, and a major object of the promise of a public performance made to an actor or singer may well be the enhancement of the performer's reputation. There is certainly no reason why loss of reputation should be excluded from the 'object of the contract' exception. As Ralph Gibson LJ stated in *Cambridge Nutrition Ltd v British Broadcasting Corporation*:

> I do not think that the decision in *Addis v Gramophone Co Ltd* is a bar to the recovery of damages for injury to reputation in an action for breach of contract, where the contractual provision proved to have been broken had as its purpose, or one of its purposes, the protection of the claimant against the sort of damage suffered.[214]

Adam Kramer has suggested that the *Addis* rule and its exceptions are superfluous as the same results could generally be achieved by applying the contractual remoteness test; where recovery for non-pecuniary loss is denied, this is because the loss was unforeseeable or the defendant did not assume responsibility for it.[215] Kramer regards the concept of assumption of responsibility as being more firmly recognised than it actually is. Nevertheless, there is much to be said for the view that the contractual remoteness test ought to replace the *Addis* rule and its exceptions,[216] as there is no justification to treat non-pecuniary loss (that is not *de minimis*) differently from pecuniary loss.

---

211 [1996] 4 All ER 119, 124.

212 ibid 125, citing in support *Joyce v Sengupta* [1993] 1 WLR 337.

213 This is assumed, without discussion, by Neil A Shanzer, 'The Loss of Publicity as an Element of Damages for Breach of Contract to Employ an Entertainer' (1973) 27 U Miami L Rev 465.

214 [1990] 3 All ER 523, 540.

215 Adam Kramer, *The Law of Contract Damages* (3rd edn, Hart 2022) [9-36].

216 Nelson Enonchong, 'Breach of Contract and Damages for Mental Distress' (1996) 16 OJLS 617; Andrew Phang, 'The Crumbling Edifice? The Award of Contractual Damages for Mental Distress' [2003] JBL 341, 388.

SCOPE OF LIABILITY

Chapter 3 discusses the general rules on the attribution of responsibility that apply to contract-breakers and some other wrongdoers. This section discusses the remoteness test that applies in actions for breach of contract and the effect of contributory negligence in such actions.

Remoteness of Loss

The general rule

The general rule for the extent of contractual liability was laid down by Alderson B in *Hadley v Baxendale*:

> Where two parties have made a contract which one of them has broken, the damages which the other party ought to receive in respect of such breach of contract should be such as may fairly and reasonably be considered either arising naturally, i.e., according to the usual course of things, from such breach of contract itself, or such as may reasonably be supposed to have been in the contemplation of both parties, at the time they made the contract, as the probable result of the breach of it.[217]

In that case, the crankshaft in the plaintiff's mill broke, rendering the mill unworkable. The plaintiff contracted with the defendant for the delivery by the defendant of the broken crankshaft to engineers to be used as a model for a new crankshaft, and the delivery of the new crankshaft to the plaintiff. In breach of contract, the defendant delayed the transport, as a result of which the mill was at a standstill for five days more than necessary. The court denied the plaintiff's claim for loss of profit on the ground that such loss did not arise in the usual course of things from a delay in the delivery of a crankshaft, and the loss had not been in the contemplation of the parties as the defendant was unaware that the mill was unworkable without a new shaft.

Alderson B set out two categories of loss: (1) loss arising in the usual course of things from such breach as occurred; and (2) loss that may be supposed to have been in the parties' contemplation, when they made the contract, as the probable result of breach. These are often called the two 'limbs' of *Hadley v Baxendale*, the first limb covering usual loss and the second limb covering unusual loss that was in the parties' contemplation.[218] However, the first limb

---

217 (1854) 9 Ex 341, 354; 156 ER 145, 151.

218 eg, *Transfield Shipping Inc v Mercator Shipping Inc (The Achilleas)* [2008] UKHL 48, [2009] 1 AC 61 [58]–[59] (Lord Rodger); *Attorney General of the Virgin Islands v Global Water Associates Ltd* [2020] UKPC 18, [2021] AC 23 [21].

is a subset of the second limb.[219] The contemplation of the parties is the contemplation of a reasonable person in each party's position,[220] and the reasonable person knows the ordinary course of things.[221]

Furthermore, the reference in the *Hadley v Baxendale* test to the *parties'* contemplation is really a reference to the *defendant's* contemplation. 'No case has been found in which recovery was denied because the injured party did not foresee the loss.'[222] Whether a particular loss is too remote thus depends upon what the defendant, at the time of the contract, knew about the claimant's circumstances. As Lord Reid stated in *The Heron II*:

> The crucial question is whether, on the information available to the defendant when the contract was made, he should, or the reasonable man in his position would, have realised that such loss was sufficiently likely to result from the breach of contract to make it proper to hold that the loss flowed naturally from the breach or that loss of that kind should have been within his contemplation.[223]

The language of 'contemplation' rather than 'foreseeability', which is used in negligence, might be thought to imply that the parties, at the time of the contract, must have turned their minds to the possibility and consequences of breach. But this is not the case: 'The court has to assume, though it be contrary to the fact, that the parties had in mind the breach that has occurred.'[224] What is required is that the parties *could* have contemplated the loss suffered had they turned their minds to the possibility of breach.[225] Indeed, the *Hadley v Baxendale* test has often been expressed as one of 'foreseeability'.[226]

---

219 *Jackson v Royal Bank of Scotland plc* [2005] UKHL 3, [2005] 1 WLR 377 [25], [47]–[49].

220 *Koufos v C Czarnikow Ltd (The Heron II)* [1969] 1 AC 350, 385 (Lord Reid), 424 (Lord Upjohn); *Christopher Hill Ltd v Ashington Piggeries Ltd* [1969] 3 All ER 1496, 1524.

221 *Victoria Laundry (Windsor) Ltd v Newman Industries Ltd* [1949] 2 KB 528, 539; Melvin Aron Eisenberg, 'The Principle of Hadley v Baxendale' (1992) 80 Cal L Rev 563, 565–66.

222 Arthur G Murphey, 'Consequential Damages in Contracts for the International Sale of Goods and the Legacy of Hadley' (1989) 23 GWJILE 415, 435.

223 *Koufos v C Czarnikow Ltd (The Heron II)* [1969] 1 AC 350, 385.

224 *Parsons (Livestock) Ltd v Uttley Ingham & Co Ltd* [1978] QB 791, 807 (Scarman LJ).

225 *Victoria Laundry (Windsor) Ltd v Newman Industries Ltd* [1949] 2 KB 528, 540.

226 ibid 539.

It might be thought that the *Hadley v Baxendale* test is identical to the foreseeability test applying in negligence and some other torts, discussed in Chapter 5. But there are two differences. The first relates to the time at which the loss needs to be foreseeable. In negligence, this is the time when the duty is breached,[227] whereas in contract, it is the time at which the contract is made.[228] The second difference between the tests relates to the degree of likelihood with which the loss must be foreseeable. In negligence, as explained in Chapter 5, it is sufficient that a reasonable person would not brush the risk aside as far-fetched. In *The Heron II*,[229] the House of Lords held that a higher degree of likelihood is required in contract, although it may be less than 50 percent. Unfortunately, each law lord used a slightly different formula to express the degree of likelihood required in contract. The courts have since used synonymously[230] the formulae 'not unlikely'[231] and 'serious possibility'.[232]

Contractual liability for unusual loss has been considered unfair on the ground that the defendant, had he been aware of the claimant's special susceptibility at the time of the contract, might have charged a higher price, or negotiated for an exclusion clause, or refused to contract at all; the defendant must not be deprived of that opportunity.[233] It has also been argued that disclosure of the plaintiff's special susceptibility at the time of the contract fosters economic efficiency by enabling the defendant to take optimal precautions

---

227 eg, *Doughty v Turner Manufacturing Co Ltd* [1964] 1 QB 518, 528 (Harman LJ). The case is considered in Ch 5.

228 eg, *Hydraulic Engineering Co Ltd v McHaffie, Goslett & Co* (1878) 4 QBD 670, 676 (Brett LJ).

229 *Koufos C Czarnikow Ltd (The Heron II)* [1969] 1 AC 350.

230 eg, *Wellesley Partners LLP v Withers LLP* [2015] EWCA Civ 1146, [2016] Ch 529 [146], [168] (Roth J).

231 eg, *Bence Graphics International Ltd v Fasson UK Ltd* [1998] QB 87, 97 (Otton LJ); *Berryman v Hounslow London Borough Council* [1997] PIQR P83, P88.

232 eg, *SC Confectia SA v Miss Mania Wholesale Ltd* [2014] EWCA Civ 1484 [4]; *Attorney General of the Virgin Islands v Global Water Associates Ltd* [2020] UKPC 18, [2021] AC 23 [32].

233 *Hadley v Baxendale* (1854) 9 Ex 341, 355; 156 ER 145, 151; *Seven Seas Properties Ltd v Al-Essa (No 2)* [1993] 1 WLR 1083, 1088; *Jackson v Royal Bank of Scotland plc* [2005] UKHL 3, [2005] 1 WLR 377 [36] (Lord Hope).

against breach.[234] However, the economic argument has been challenged.[235] Furthermore, the argument that the *Hadley v Baxendale* rule leads contracting parties to disclose a special susceptibility to their contract partner assumes that contracting parties know the law in that detail, and this assumption is wrong in many instances.[236]

The remoteness tests in contract and negligence have two things in common. First, both tests are subject to the rule that a wrongdoer must take his victim as he finds him.[237] Second, it is only the type of loss, and not its extent, which needs to be foreseeable. This is illustrated, in the contractual context, by *Parsons (Livestock) Ltd v Uttley Ingham & Co Ltd*.[238] The plaintiff, a pig farmer, bought a bulk food storage hopper from the defendant in which to store pignuts for his pigs. When installing the hopper, the defendant forgot to unseal the ventilator, with the result that the nuts dispensed by the hopper were mouldy. This caused the outbreak of an intestinal infection caused by the bacterium *Escherichia coli*, killing 254 pigs. The defendant, having breached a contractual warranty that the hopper would be reasonably fit for the purpose of storing pignuts in a condition suitable for feeding to the plaintiff's pigs, was held liable for the death of the pigs even though it had not been foreseeable as a serious possibility that the improper installation of the hopper could cause

---

234 Ian Ayres and Robert Gertner, 'Filling Gaps in Incomplete Contracts: An Economic Theory of Default Rules' (1989) 99 Yale LJ 87, 101–04; Lucian Ayre Bebchuk and Steven Shavell, 'Information and the Scope of Liability for Breach of Contract: The Rule of *Hadley v Baxendale*' (1991) 7 JLEO 284, 285 ff; Richard A Posner, *Economic Analysis of Law* (9th edn, Aspen 2014) §4.11; Peter Cane, *Tort Law and Economic Interests* (2nd edn, Clarendon Press 1996) 145; Roger Halson, 'Remoteness' in Donald Harris, David Campbell and Roger Halson, *Remedies in Contract and Tort* (2nd edn, CUP 2005) 91–93.

235 See Melvin Aron Eisenberg, 'The Principle of *Hadley v Baxendale*' (1992) 80 Cal L Rev 563, 592–96; Jason S Johnston, 'Strategic Bargaining and the Economic Theory of Contract Default Rules' (1990) 100 Yale LJ 615, 627–36; Andrew Tettenborn, '*Hadley v Baxendale* Foreseeability: A Principle Beyond Its Sell-By Date?' (2007) 23 J Cont L 120, 132–33; Louis E Wolcher, 'Price Discrimination and Inefficient Risk Allocation under the Rule of *Hadley v Baxendale*' (1989) 12 Res in Law and Econ 9, 19–20.

236 For further discussion, see Sirko Harder, *Measuring Damages in the Law of Obligations: The Search for Harmonised Principles* (Hart 2010) 57–68.

237 See *Vacwell Engineering Co Ltd v BDH Chemicals Ltd* [1971] 1 QB 88; *Total Transport Corporation v Arcadia Petroleum Ltd* [1998] CLC 90, 103. *Vacwell* and the 'thin skull' rule are discussed in Ch 5.

238 [1978] QB 791. See also *Brown v KMR Services Ltd* [1995] 4 All ER 598, 620–21 (Stuart-Smith LJ).

an outbreak of *E. coli*. The majority in the English Court of Appeal held that it was necessary to foresee some illness in the pigs, but not specifically *E. coli*.[239]

The basic remoteness test in contract has been summarised as follows:

> The general rule is that loss is too remote if that type of loss could not reasonably have been contemplated by the defendant as a serious possibility at the time the contract was made assuming that, at that time, the defendant had thought about the breach.[240]

This is expressed as the 'general rule' because liability for foreseeable loss could potentially be denied on the ground that the defendant did not assume responsibility for it. This will be discussed next.

Assumption of responsibility as the ultimate criterion

The use of an assumption of responsibility as the ultimate criterion of contractual liability has been suggested by a number of scholars,[241] and it has gained impetus from *The Achilleas*.[242] A bulk carrier was chartered with a specified date for redelivery. Prior to that date, the owner of the vessel fixed a follow-on charter with a different company, commencing almost immediately after the redelivery date under the first charter. The vessel was not returned on the date agreed, and the owner had to renegotiate the second charter and accept a lower rate of hire. As damages for breach of contract, the owner claimed the difference between the rate originally agreed in the follow-on charter and the

239 [1978] QB 791, 805 (Orr LJ), 810–13 (Scarman LJ). Lord Denning MR (at 802–04) opined that the *Wagon Mound* test, which was satisfied on the facts, applied to liability in contract as well as negligence in respect of injury to the person or property (as opposed to pure economic loss). This view has found no support in any other case.

240 Andrew Burrows, *A Restatement of the English Law of Contract* (2 edn, OUP 2020) 134 (rule 21(2)); approvingly quoted in *Attorney General of the Virgin Islands v Global Water Associates Ltd* [2020] UKPC 18, [2021] AC 23 [29].

241 Roger Halson, 'Remoteness' in Donald Harris, David Campbell and Roger Halson, *Remedies in Contract and Tort* (2nd edn, CUP 2005) 97; Adam Kramer, 'An Agreement-Centred Approach to Remoteness and Contract Damages' in Nili Cohen and Ewan McKendrick (eds), *Comparative Remedies for Breach of Contract* (Hart 2005) 269–70; D McLauchlan, 'Remoteness Re-Invented?' (2009) 9 OUCLJ 109, 113; Andrew Tettenborn, '*Hadley v Baxendale* Foreseeability: A Principle Beyond Its Sell-By Date?' (2007) 23 J Cont L 120, 144–45; John Wightman, 'Negligent Valuations and a Drop in the Property Market: The Limits of the Expectation Loss Principle' (1998) 61 Mod LR 68, 76.

242 *Transfield Shipping Inc v Mercator Shipping Inc (The Achilleas)* [2008] UKHL 48, [2009] 1 AC 61.

reduced rate agreed in the renegotiated follow-on charter, for the duration of that charter. The House of Lords held that the owner was entitled only to the difference between the market rate and the rate under the breached charter, for the nine days between the contractual date of redelivery and the actual date of redelivery.

Lord Hoffmann and Lord Hope held that the charterer had not assumed responsibility for the loss of hire under a follow-on charter, considering the general understanding in the relevant market.[243] It was therefore immaterial whether the loss had been foreseeable. The *Hadley v Baxendale* rule was said to involve a prima facie assumption about what the parties intended but could be rebutted by showing that the contract-breaker assumed no responsibility for the loss in question.[244] Lord Rodger expressed no view on the relevance of an assumption of responsibility,[245] and rejected the charterer's liability on the ground that the owner's loss had been unforeseeable.[246] Lord Walker's judgment is unclear, not least because he expressed agreement with Lord Hoffmann, Lord Hope, and Lord Rodger.[247] Baroness Hale expressed doubts as to whether the charterer's liability should be limited, but added that if it was, she preferred Lord Rodger's reasons.[248]

Even though only two law lords in *The Achilleas* endorsed the concept of assumption of responsibility, the case has had an impact on the contractual remoteness test in English law. The English Court of Appeal has since stated that the *Hadley v Baxendale* rule reflects the risks that a contracting party assumes in the ordinary case; but the circumstances of an individual case may demonstrate that a party assumed responsibility for an unforeseeable loss[249] or, conversely, did not assume responsibility for a forseeable loss.[250]

The concept of the assumption of responsibility as the ultimate criterion of contractual liability has not been adopted in other common law jurisdictions

---

243 ibid [11]–[26] (Lord Hoffmann), [30]–[36] (Lord Hope).

244 ibid [9] (Lord Hoffmann), [32] (Lord Hope).

245 ibid [63].

246 ibid [60]. For criticism, see Adam Kramer, 'The New Test of Remoteness in Contract' (2009) 125 LQR 408, 409; David McLauchlan, 'Remoteness Re-Invented?' (2009) 9 OUCLJ 109, 123.

247 [2008] UKHL 48, [2009] 1 AC 61 [87].

248 ibid [93].

249 *Siemens Building Technologies FE Ltd v Supershield Ltd* [2010] EWCA Civ 7, [2010] 2 All ER (Comm) 1185 [43].

250 ibid; *John Grimes Partnership Ltd v Gubbins* [2013] EWCA Civ 37, [2013] BLR 126 [24].

and has been rejected by Singapore's Court of Appeal.[251] Andrew Robertson has criticised the agreement-centred approach to remoteness on the basis that contracting parties rarely think about the allocation of loss in the event of breach, providing the court with little material from which to infer the parties' intentions.[252] Lord Hoffmann, writing extra-judicially, has objected that this argument pays insufficient attention to the objective approach to contract interpretation, under which the understanding of a reasonable person is relevant; the reasonable person may infer a certain allocation of risk from the circumstances in which the contract was made, even if the parties themselves are unaware.[253] However, there will be cases in which an allocation of risk by the parties cannot be ascertained, even objectively. The *Hadley v Baxendale* test fills that gap. But where clear evidence as to the parties' intention does exist, the allocation of risk by the parties ought to override the *Hadley v Baxendale* test or inform its application to the facts.

Contributory Negligence

Contributory negligence is unreasonable conduct of the claimant that contributes to the loss or the event causing the loss. The doctrine is mainly concerned with the conduct of the claimant before the claimant became aware of the wrong, but it has sometimes been applied to later conduct. The relationship of this doctrine to the avoidable loss rule and the doctrine of *novus actus interveniens* is discussed in Chapter 3.

At common law, contributory negligence generally constituted a complete defence to liability in negligence and some other torts.[254] But it was no defence to liability in contract except where a contractual duty of care co-extensive

---

251 *MFM Restaurants Pte Ltd v Fish & Co Restaurants Pte Ltd* [2010] SGCA 36, [2011] 1 SLR 150 [112]; *Out of the Box Pte Ltd v Wanin Industries Pte Ltd* [2013] SGCA 15, [2013] 2 SLR 363 [24]–[47].

252 Andrew Robertson, 'The Basis of the Remoteness Rule in Contract' (2008) 28 LS 172. The argument has been adopted by Max Harris, 'Fairness and Remoteness of Damage in Contract Law: A Lexical Ordering Approach' (2011) 28 J Cont L 122, 133; Mark Stiggelbout, 'Contractual Remoteness, "Scope of Duty" and Intention' [2012] LMCLQ 97, 118–20; Paul CK Wee, 'Contractual Interpretation and Remoteness' [2010] LMCLQ 150, 167–69; Alice Zheng, 'The Achilleas Heel of Contractual Damages: What Does the "Assumption of Risk" Principle Add to the Law of Remoteness' (2011) 24 CLQ 11, 15–16.

253 Lord Hoffmann, 'The *Achilleas*: Custom and Practice or Foreseeability?' (2010) 14 Edin LR 47, 60–61.

254 See Ch 5.

with a tortious duty of care was breached.[255] The position in tort was changed by the Law Reform (Contributory Negligence) Act 1945, which provides for an apportionment of the loss between the parties. The details of how the 1945 Act operates are discussed in Chapter 5 in the context of tort law.

The 1945 Act was enacted in order to change the effect of contributory negligence in tort law. It makes no reference to liability in contract. However, where a defendant is concurrently liable for the breach of a contractual duty of care and a tortious duty of care, which is usually the case for the liability of employers and often for the liability of professionals, the reduction of the tortious liability under the 1945 Act would be futile if the contractual liability remained unaffected by the claimant's contributory negligence. The courts have recognised this and have interpreted the 1945 Act as applying to contractual liability in those circumstances.[256] The same position obtains in Australia by virtue of legislative intervention,[257] after the High Court of Australia (Callinan J dissenting) had held that the original version of the Australian statutes (which was similar to the 1945 Act) did not apply to any contractual liability.[258] The apportionment statutes in the other major Commonwealth jurisdictions have been interpreted in the same way as the 1945 Act.[259]

The 1945 Act does not apply to the breach of a contractual duty of care that is not concurrent with a tortious duty of care[260] and, crucially, does not

---

[255] For a detailed discussion of the common law position before 1945, see *Primeo Fund v Bank of Bermuda (Cayman) Ltd* [2023] UKPC 40, [2024] AC 727 [337]–[348].

[256] *Forsikringsaktieselskapet Vesta v Butcher* [1989] AC 852, 860–67, 875, 879; *Barclays Bank plc v Fairclough Building Ltd* [1995] QB 214, 228–29, 233; *Trebor Bassett Holdings Ltd v ADT Fire and Security plc* [2012] EWCA Civ 1158, [2012] BLR 441 [11], [13]; *Primeo Fund v Bank of Bermuda (Cayman) Ltd* [2023] UKPC 40, [2024] AC 727 [353].

[257] Civil Law (Wrongs) Act 2002 (ACT), s 101; Law Reform (Miscellaneous Provisions) Act 1965 (NSW), s 8; Law Reform (Miscellaneous Provisions) Act 1956 (NT), s 15(1); Law Reform Act 1995 (Qld), s 5; Law Reform (Contributory Negligence and Apportionment of Liability) Act 2001 (SA), s 4(1)(b); Wrongs Act 1954 (Tas), s 2; Wrongs Act 1958 (Vic), s 25; Law Reform (Contributory Negligence and Tortfeasors' Contribution) Act 1947 (WA), s 3A. The South Australian statute also applies to the breach of a contractual duty of care that is not co-extensive with a tortious duty of care.

[258] *Astley v Austrust Ltd* [1999] HCA 6, (1999) 197 CLR 1.

[259] See the review of cases from Canada, New Zealand, and Singapore in *Primeo Fund v Bank of Bermuda (Cayman) Ltd* [2023] UKPC 40, [2024] AC 727 [309]–[311], [322]–[323].

[260] *Den Danske Bank A/S v Skipton Building Society* [1998] 1 EGLR 155, 185. These circumstances are rare, although the undertaking of a contractual duty of

apply to strict contractual liability (ie, liability not dependent upon fault),[261] which is the usual type of contractual liability. Therefore, where the defendant's conduct constitutes both a breach of contract and the tort of negligence, it is important to determine whether the contractual obligation breached is strict. This depends upon whether the defendant promised to achieve a particular outcome or standard or merely promised to take reasonable care in a particular task.

Two decisions by the English Court of Appeal illustrate this. In *Barclays Bank plc v Fairclough Building Ltd*,[262] the Court held that the defendant's obligation to clean and treat the asbestos cement sheets on the roofs of the plaintiff's warehouses was an obligation to attain a particular standard of workmanship and not merely to exercise reasonable care; therefore, the plaintiff's contributory negligence did not affect the defendant's liability in contract. In *Trebor Bassett Holdings Ltd v ADT Fire & Security plc*,[263] the Court held that the defendant's obligation to provide a tailor-made fire suppression system was not analogous to the strict obligation of a seller of goods to supply goods that are of satisfactory quality and fit for purpose, as the system had no inherent characteristics that could be independently assessed; it was merely an obligation to take reasonable care in the design of the system, and the defendant's liability in contract (as well as tort) was reduced by virtue of the claimant's contributory negligence.

The unavailability of apportionment by virtue of contributory negligence in cases of strict contractual liability is not in line with international standards. For example, Article 7.4.7 of the UNIDROIT Principles of International Commercial Contracts 2016 provides for an apportionment of liability in all cases of contractual liability.[264] The position in England (and other common

---

care does not necessarily entail the assumption of a tortious duty of care: *Robinson v PE Jones (Contractors) Ltd* [2011] EWCA Civ 9, [2012] QB 44 [81], [94].

261 *Bank of Nova Scotia v Hellenic Mutual War Risks Association (Bermuda) Ltd (The Good Luck)* [1990] 1 QB 818, 904; *Barclays Bank plc v Fairclough Building Ltd* [1995] QB 214, 228–30, 233; *Trebor Bassett Holdings Ltd v ADT Fire and Security plc* [2012] EWCA Civ 1158, [2012] BLR 441 [11], [13].

262 [1995] QB 214, 223.

263 [2012] EWCA Civ 1158, [2012] BLR 441 [42]–[59].

264 The same is true for Art 9.504 of the *Principles of European Contract Law* and Art 167(3) of the European Code of Contract, published as a special issue of the *Edinburgh Law Review 2004*. The United Nations Convention on Contracts for the International Sale of Goods does not address contributory negligence in general but contains the avoidable loss rule (Art 77) and excludes liability where one party causes the other party to breach (Art 80).

law jurisdictions) has been defended with the argument (among others)[265] that the availability of apportionment in cases of strict liability would bring the claimant under a duty to supervise the defendant's performance, which would undermine the strictness of the defendant's obligation.[266] This fear is unfounded, as apportionment would be available only where the claimant acted unreasonably, and it is usually reasonable for a contracting party to rely on the other party.

Moreover, the exclusion of apportionment with a view to protecting the claimant may have the opposite effect by forcing a complete exoneration of the defendant on the ground of causation or remoteness. In particular, post-wrong conduct of the claimant may be characterised as an intervening act breaking the chain of causation.[267] An illustration is *Quinn v Burch Brothers (Builders) Ltd*.[268] When the defendant, in breach of contract, failed to supply the plaintiff with a stepladder, the plaintiff made do with a folded trestle that was not footed. He fell to the ground and was injured. Paull J considered the use of the trestle unreasonable. He stated that he would have apportioned liability if apportionment had been available.[269] Since it was a case of strict contractual liability, apportionment was unavailable, and Paull J classified the plaintiff's conduct as a *novus actus interveniens*.[270]

---

265 For a discussion of various arguments, see Sirko Harder, *Measuring Damages in the Law of Obligations: The Search for Harmonised Principles* (Hart 2010) 162–67.

266 Law Commission, 'Contributory Negligence as a Defence in Contract' (Law Com No 219, 1993) [4.2]–[4.4]; PA Chandler, 'Contributory Negligence and Contract: Some Underlying Disparities' (1989) 40 NILQ 152, 172.

267 See Ch 3.

268 [1966] 2 QB 370.

269 ibid 375.

270 ibid 378.

5. Compensation in tort

INTRODUCTION

Some torts are actionable only when loss has been caused. Other torts are actionable per se; where no loss has been caused, nominal damages (discussed in Chapter 8) will be awarded. Either way, the claimant is entitled to damages for the loss caused by a tort.

As mentioned in Chapter 1, Robert Stevens makes a distinction between 'substitutive damages', which are assessed objectively as at the time of the infringement and are available even if there is no loss to the claimant, and damages for consequential loss, which are assessed subjectively as at the time of the judgment and are subject to limitations that do not apply to the substitutive award, such as remoteness of loss.[1]

Similarly, in *Lewis v Australian Capital Territory*,[2] Edelman J in the High Court of Australia distinguished between compensation to rectify a wrongful act and compensation for the consequences of a wrong. The amount of compensation to rectify a wrongful act is either the monetary equivalent of the action that would rectify the wrongful act (eg, the value of the chattel taken in actions for detinue),[3] or the amount that would have made the defendant's act lawful, in particular a reasonable licence fee awarded in cases of conversion, trespass to land, or the infringement of an intellectual property right.[4] Compensation to rectify a wrongful act is available even if no actual loss has been suffered.[5]

English courts have not made such a distinction, at least not expressly. Leaving aside aggravated, exemplary, gain-based, and nominal damages, damages for a tort are characterised as compensation for loss. We adopt the

---

1 Robert Stevens, *Torts and Rights* (OUP 2007) 60. He now prefers the labels of 'general' and 'special' damages: Robert Stevens, *The Laws of Restitution* (OUP 2023) 295–97.

2 [2020] HCA 26, (2020) 271 CLR 192 [140]–[150].

3 ibid [143].

4 ibid [144].

5 ibid [145].

orthodox understanding, but we will mention the new concepts in contexts where they are relevant.

Below, we will first discuss the assessment of compensation in tort and then the rules of remoteness of loss and the effect of contributory negligence in negligence and some other torts.

ASSESSMENT OF COMPENSATION

In a passage approvingly quoted by the House of Lords and the UK Supreme Court on many occasions,[6] Lord Blackburn in *Livingstone v Rawyards Coal Co* stated that compensation for loss caused by a tort aims to place the victim 'in the same position as he would have been in if he had not sustained the wrong'.[7] A corollary is that the claimant cannot recover more than the loss suffered.[8]

The courts rarely apply Lord Blackburn's general principle directly to the facts of an individual case. They have developed concrete rules in a variety of contexts. Most of these rules constitute a refinement of the general principle to fit the circumstances in question, but some rules deviate from the general principle. The rules developed in certain contexts will now be discussed. This discussion is structured according to particular conduct or events. It is not directly structured according to torts, although particular factual circumstances may be linked to one or more torts. Nor is this section directly structured according to types of protected interests, since the same interest can be violated in different ways, attracting different measures of compensation. Limitations of space prevent the consideration of defamation and personal injury.

---

6 eg, *Lim Poh Choo v Camden and Islington Area Health Authority* [1980] AC 174, 187; *Sainsbury's Supermarkets Ltd v Visa Europe Services LLC* [2020] UKSC 24, [2020] 4 All ER 807 [194].

7 (1880) 5 App Cas 25, 39.

8 'The court in applying the compensatory principle is charged with avoiding under-compensation and also over-compensation. Justice is not achieved if a claimant receives less or more than its actual loss': *Sainsbury's Supermarkets Ltd v Visa Europe Services LLC* [2020] UKSC 24, [2020] 4 All ER 807 [217]. However, over-compensation is accepted where the only alternative on the facts is under-compensation: *Swift v Carpenter* [2020] EWCA Civ 1295, [2021] QB 339 [206]. See generally David McLauchlan, 'Some Damages Dilemmas in Private Law' (2021) 52 VUWLR 875.

Damage to Land or Fixtures

Where land has been damaged or fixtures on the land have been damaged or destroyed,[9] there are three different ways of measuring the claimant's financial loss. The first is the cost of employing someone to repair the damage (cost of cure), assuming it can be repaired. The second is the difference between the value of the property after the tort and the value it would have had without the tort (diminution in value).[10] The third is the cost of purchasing a property that is equivalent to the subject property (without the damage) less the value of the subject property in its damaged state (replacement cost). There is often not a huge difference between diminution in value and replacement cost since a property that is equivalent to the subject property (without the damage) must by definition be of the same or similar value as the subject property.[11] Cost of cure and diminution in value are not always mutually exclusive as the necessity or extent of future remedial work may be uncertain,[12] or some diminution in value may remain even after repair work has been carried out.[13]

Some general remarks about cost of cure and diminution in value are made in Chapter 2. In deciding which measure to use in the present context, it has been said that the damages must be reasonable as between the claimant and the

---

9 The discussion focusses on actions for negligence or trespass to land. The rules discussed in that context generally also apply to liability under the Defective Premises Act 1972; see *Bole v Huntsbuild Ltd* [2009] EWCA Civ 1146, (2009) 127 Con LR 154. In actions for nuisance, damages may be awarded for the cost of abating the nuisance, for any remaining diminution in value, and for non-pecuniary loss such as annoyance and distress; see, eg, *Bunclark v Hertfordshire CC* (1977) 243 EG 455.

10 The hypothetical value may reflect development potential destroyed by the tort: *Farmer Giles Ltd v Wessex Water Authority* [1990] 1 EGLR 177, 179.

11 In *Dominion Mosaics and Tile Co Ltd v Trafalgar Trucking Co Ltd* [1990] 2 All ER 246, where business premises with a pre-tort value of £85,000 were destroyed, the plaintiff acquired new premises for £390,000 (to rebuild the original building would have cost £570,000). The court (at 251–52) held that the plaintiff had acted reasonably and that the replacement cost could be recovered without any betterment discount. The betterment discount is discussed in Ch 2.

12 See *Harrison v Shepherd Homes Ltd* [2012] EWCA Civ 904, (2012) 143 Con LR 69 [17]–[22].

13 *Bunclark v Hertfordshire CC* (1977) 243 EG 455.

defendant.[14] It is irrelevant whether the claimant has received the cost of cure from an insurer who is subrogated to the claim.[15]

In the present context, two broad principles were enunciated by Donaldson LJ in *Dodd Properties Ltd v Canterbury City Council*:

> If [the claimant] reasonably intends to sell the property in its damaged state, clearly the diminution in capital value is the true measure of damage. If he reasonably intends to continue to occupy it and to repair the damage, clearly the cost of repairs is the true measure.[16]

Donaldson LJ's first proposition is borne out by the cases. In actions for tortious damage to land or fixtures, English courts have refused to award cost-of-cure damages where the claimant had no intention of having the damage repaired.[17] The same applies where reinstatement is impossible, for example because it is prohibited by planning law.[18]

Donaldson LJ's second proposition is not borne out by the cases. While it is no longer the law that the cost of cure can never be awarded,[19] it has not been awarded in every case in which cure was intended. The picture is more complex.

Cost-of-cure damages will be awarded where the property is unique or of special significance to the claimant. The prime example is a historic building.[20] Other properties may also be unique. In *Hollebone v Midhurst and Fernhurst Builders*, where the plaintiff's house was negligently damaged, the judge awarded the cost of repair because 'by reason of its size, its position, its features, its seclusion and the area in which it is located the property is

---

14 *CR Taylor (Wholesale) Ltd v Hepworths Ltd* [1977] 1 WLR 659, 667; *Farmer Giles Ltd v Wessex Water Authority* [1990] 1 EGLR 177, 179.

15 *CR Taylor (Wholesale) Ltd v Hepworths Ltd* [1977] 1 WLR 659, 669; *Coles v Hetherton* [2013] EWCA Civ 1704, [2015] 1 WLR 160 [34]–[35].

16 [1980] 1 WLR 433, 456–57.

17 *Hole & Sons (Sayers Common) Ltd v Harrisons of Thurnscoe Ltd* [1973] 1 Lloyd's Rep 345; *CR Taylor (Wholesale) Ltd v Hepworths Ltd* [1977] 1 WLR 659, 669–70.

18 *Ward v Cannock Chase District Council* [1986] Ch 546, 577–78.

19 Authority for the old position is *Jones v Gooday* (1841) 8 M & W 146, 151 ER 985.

20 The example was given in *Moss v Christchurch Rural District Council* [1925] 2 KB 750, 752. Cost-of-cure damages were awarded in *Duke of Newcastle v Hundred of Broxtowe* (1832) 4 B & Ad 273, 282; 110 ER 458, 461–62, where Nottingham Castle was partially destroyed.

properly termed unique or of a nature that comparable properties are few and far between'.[21]

Where the claimant's property was not unique, the courts have awarded cost-of-cure damages in some cases,[22] and refused to award them in others.[23] It has been said that diminution in value is the 'primary measure' of damages,[24] and that, following the position in contract (discussed in Chapter 4), cost of cure cannot be awarded where it is out of all proportion to the benefit to be obtained from cure.[25] The matter is 'highly fact sensitive'.[26]

The appropriate measure of damages for the destruction of business premises may depend upon reasonable actions taken by the claimant in order to mitigate ongoing loss of profit.[27] Depending upon the circumstances, this may be the cost of quickly acquiring new premises,[28] or the cost of rebuilding the original site.[29]

Where cost-of-cure damages are in principle available, it is only the cost of reasonable work that can be recovered. This is not necessarily the cost of restoring the building or fixture to exactly the same state as before the tort.[30]

---

21 [1968] 1 Lloyd's Rep 38, 39 (Norman Richards QC). See also *Ward v Cannock Chase District Council* [1986] Ch 546, 574 (Scott J: 'a land holding of special and particular value to the plaintiff').

22 eg, *Jones v Stroud District Council* [1986] 1 WLR 1141, 1150. The entitlement to damages for the cost of reasonable repairs was common ground in *Dodd Properties Ltd v Canterbury City Council* [1980] 1 WLR 433, 439.

23 eg, *Moss v Christchurch Rural District Council* [1925] 2 KB 750.

24 *Ward v Cannock Chase District Council* [1986] Ch 546, 582 (Scott J).

25 *Lea Valley Developments Ltd v Derbyshire* [2017] EWHC 1353 (TCC), [2017] 4 WLR 120 [38].

26 ibid [37] (Adrian Williamson QC).

27 The avoidable loss rule is discussed in Ch 3.

28 *Dominion Mosaics and Tile Co Ltd v Trafalgar Trucking Co Ltd* [1990] 2 All ER 246, 251–52.

29 *Harbutt's 'Plasticine' Ltd v Wayne Tank and Pump Co Ltd* [1970] 1 QB 447. The case involved breach of contract but has been regarded as authority for tort actions too; see, eg, *Dominion Mosaics and Tile Co Ltd v Trafalgar Trucking Co Ltd* [1990] 2 All ER 246, 249–50.

30 *Lodge Holes Colliery Co Ltd v Wednesbury Corporation* [1908] AC 323 (unreasonable to raise road to previous level instead of building an equally commodious road); *Dodd Properties Ltd v Canterbury City Council* [1980] 1 WLR 433, 441; *British Coal Corp v Gwent County Council* (1996) 71 P & CR 482, (cheaper to build new school than repairing the damaged school); *Bryant v Macklin* [2005] EWCA Civ 762 (damaged mature trees to be replaced with young trees).

In addition to cost of cure or diminution in value, damages may be awarded for consequential loss such as the cost of moving home,[31] loss of profit,[32] and loss of amenity.[33] In actions for negligence or nuisance, this requires that the loss was foreseeable, as discussed later in this chapter. Where the claimant has neither lost profit nor rented a substitute property, damages for the loss of use of the property should be available, the valuation of which should be the same as in the case of chattels (except that land does not depreciate).[34] In actions for trespass to land, aggravated and/or exemplary damages may be awarded;[35] these types of damages are discussed in Chapter 8.

Other Wrongful Interference with Land

Wrongful interference with land can occur without physical damage to the land or fixtures. The defendant may wrongfully evict the claimant, withhold possession of the land from the claimant, otherwise use the claimant's land, or interfere with the claimant's enjoyment of the property. The relevant causes of action are nuisance, trespass to land, and an action for the recovery of possession of land ('action of ejectment').

The normal measure of damages for wrongful occupation of land that has come to an end is the market rent for the property during the period of the trespass ('mesne profits').[36] The normal measure of damages for wrongful use (without occupation) of land that has come to an end is the usual reasonable charge for the use during the period of the trespass ('wayleave').[37] It is irrelevant whether the claimant would have used or let the property during

[31] *Ward v Cannock Chase District Council* [1986] Ch 546, 579–80.

[32] *Network Rail Infrastructure Ltd v Conarken Group Ltd* [2011] EWCA Civ 644, [2012] 1 All ER (Comm) 692.

[33] *Scutt v Lomax* (2000) 79 P & CR D31, D33; *Bryant v Macklin* [2005] EWCA Civ 762 [27].

[34] In *Bella Casa Ltd v Vinestone Ltd* [2005] EWHC 2807 (TCC), [2006] BLR 72, damages for the loss of use of a leased flat in London were awarded, calculated by reference to the wasted cost of maintenance (such as service charges and utility bills), but interest on the rent paid was rejected. The position in relation to chattels is discussed later in this chapter.

[35] *Scutt v Lomax* (2000) 79 P & CR D31, D32.

[36] *Inverugie Investments Ltd v Hackett* [1995] 1 WLR 713 (PC); *Earlrose Golf and Leisure Ltd v Fair Acre Investments Ltd* [2009] EWCA Civ 1295.

[37] *Whitwham v Westminster Brymbo Coal and Coke Company* [1896] 2 Ch 538; *Penarth Dock Engineering Co v Pounds* [1963] 1 Lloyd's Rep 359; *Swordheath Properties Ltd v Tabet* [1979] 1 WLR 285.

that period.[38] Where the wrongful occupation or use continues into the future (because an injunction is denied on discretionary grounds[39]), the measure of damages is a reasonable price that would be payable for the acquisition of the right in question.[40] These measures reflect the 'user principle'.[41] It used to be unclear whether such user damages are gain-based, loss-based or rights-based,[42] but the UK Supreme Court in *One Step (Support) Ltd v Morris-Garner* pronounced that they compensate loss.[43] We discuss them in Chapter 8.

The wrongful occupation or use of part of the claimant's land may affect the remaining part. Damages may be recovered for the resulting loss, such as the diminution in value of the land,[44] lost rent,[45] or lost profit.[46] Non-pecuniary loss such as anxiety and mental stress, may also be compensated in actions for trespass to land.[47] In appropriate circumstances, aggravated and/or exemplary damages may be awarded; these types of damages are discussed in Chapter 8.

In actions for nuisance not entailing physical damage,[48] a person with an interest in the land affected can recover damages for the cost of abating the nuisance,[49] and for any diminution in value of the interest, which may be

---

[38] *Penarth Dock Engineering Co v Pounds* [1963] 1 Lloyd's Rep 359; *Swordheath Properties Ltd v Tabet* [1979] 1 WLR 285; *Inverugie Investments Ltd v Hackett* [1995] 1 WLR 713 (PC).

[39] Injunctions are discussed in Ch 7.

[40] *Bracewell v Appleby* [1975] Ch 408; *Jones v Ruth* [2011] EWCA Civ 804, [2012] 1 WLR 1495 [39]; *Enfield LBC v Outdoor Plus Ltd* [2012] EWCA Civ 608, [2012] CP Rep 35.

[41] *Stoke-on-Trent City Council v W & J Wass Ltd* [1988] 1 WLR 1406, 1416 (Nicholls LJ).

[42] See Andrew Burrows, 'Are "Damages on the *Wrotham Park* Basis" Compensatory, Restitutionary, or Neither?' in Djakhongir Saidov and Ralph Cunnington (eds), *Contract Damages: Domestic and International Perspectives* (Hart 2008) 165.

[43] [2018] UKSC 20, [2019] AC 649 [95].

[44] *Whitwham v Westminster Brymbo Coal and Coke Company* [1896] 2 Ch 538.

[45] *Barclays Bank Ltd v Jones* [1955] JPL 822.

[46] *Ramzan v Brookwide Ltd* [2011] EWCA Civ 985, [2012] 1 All ER 903 [59]–[60].

[47] *Smith v Khan* [2018] EWCA Civ 1137, [2018] HLR 31 [45].

[48] For nuisance entailing physical damage, see *Bunclark v Hertfordshire CC* (1977) 243 EG 455.

[49] *Wandsworth LBC v Railtrack plc* [2001] 1 WLR 368, 385 (public nuisance); *Dobson v Thames Water Utilities Ltd* [2011] EWHC 3253 (TCC) [1016].

reflected in the diminution of capital value or rental value.[50] Consequential financial loss, such as loss of profit or damage to chattels on the land, can also be compensated if it was foreseeable.[51] Since nuisance protects proprietary rights in land, no separate award can be made for annoyance, distress, or personal discomfort; those matters are reflected in the award for the loss of the use value of the property.[52]

Damage to Goods

Where goods have been damaged or destroyed,[53] there are, as in the case of land, three different ways of measuring the claimant's financial loss.[54] The first is the cost of employing someone to repair the damage (cost of cure), assuming it can be repaired. The second is the difference between the value of the goods after the tort and the value they would have had without the tort (diminution in value). The third is the cost of purchasing goods that are equivalent to the subject goods (without the damage) less the value of the subject goods in their damaged state (replacement cost).[55] Where there is a market for the types of goods, it is usually possible for the claimant to buy goods that are equivalent in terms of age and specifications to the subject goods without the damage,[56] and diminution in value and replacement cost are the same or similar.[57]

---

50 *Hunter v Canary Wharf Ltd* [1997] AC 655, 724 (Lord Hope); *Dobson v Thames Water Utilities Ltd* [2011] EWHC 3253 (TCC) [1027].

51 *Midwood & Co Ltd v Manchester Corporation* [1905] 2 KB 597; *Hunter v Canary Wharf Ltd* [1997] AC 655, 706 (Lord Hoffmann), 719 (Lord Cooke).

52 *Hunter v Canary Wharf Ltd* [1997] AC 655, 706 (Lord Hoffmann), 724 (Lord Hope); *Dobson v Thames Water Utilities Ltd* [2009] EWCA Civ 28, [2009] 3 All ER 319 [31]–[35]; *Raymond v Young* [2015] EWCA Civ 456, [2015] HLR 41 [27]–[28].

53 The most relevant torts are negligence and trespass to goods.

54 This section concerns a claimant who is the owner of the goods. A defendant who has negligently damaged a car hired by the claimant is liable to compensate the claimant for the latter's contractual liability towards the car hire company resulting from the damage: *Armstead v Royal & Sun Alliance Insurance Co Ltd* [2024] UKSC 6, [2025] AC 406.

55 See *Thatcher v Littlejohn* [1978] RTR 369, 370.

56 For example, in the case of a (modern) car, it is usually possible to find a car of the same make, model, age, etc, on the market.

57 A significant difference existed in *Southampton Container Terminals Ltd v Schiffahrtsgesellschaft 'Hansa Australia' mbH & Co (The Maersk Colombo)* [2001] EWCA Civ 717, [2001] 2 Lloyd's Rep 275, where damages were limited to diminution in value on the grounds that the replacement cost was out of proportion to the benefit of replacement and that replacement was not intended.

Some general remarks about cost of cure and diminution in value are made in Chapter 2. In the present context, it has sometimes been said that the cost of repair is the prima facie measure of diminution in value.[58] However, this is often not the case. Even the best repair may not be able to restore the goods to their pre-tort value, in which case damages may be recovered for the cost of repairs and the remaining diminution in value.[59] Conversely, the cost of repair often exceeds diminution in value, in which case the cost of repair may be recovered only when it is reasonable to repair the goods.

In *Darbishire v Warran*,[60] the owner of a damaged car had it repaired at a cost of £192. Equivalent cars could be bought for £80 to £100. The Court of Appeal held that the owner had acted unreasonably vis-à-vis the defendant and could not recover the cost of repair but only the lower market value of the damaged car.

By contrast, in *Aerospace Publishing Ltd v Thames Water Utilities Ltd*,[61] the claimant had an archive of historical material, including photographs and artwork, relating to aviation. The claimant used materials from the archive in publishing partworks and journals about aviation. The archive was damaged by water escaping from the defendant's water main. The Court of Appeal held that the claimant was entitled to recover about £2.7m as the cost of reinstating the archive and was not limited to diminution in value, which was £300,000. This was because the value of the archive to the claimant was greater than the sum that could be obtained by selling it.[62] The Court made clear that the reinstatement cost could not have been recovered if the claimant had been about to go out of business, if there had been no prospect of future publications for which the archive would have a use, or if the claimant had been able to make the same sort of income without the archive.[63]

Aerospace Publishing suggests that cost-of-cure damages cannot be awarded where there is no prospect of repair work being carried out. However, the weight of authority supports the contrary position. In cases involving damage to a ship, cost-of-cure damages were awarded even though the ship was sold unrepaired,[64] or the ship struck a mine and sank before repairs were carried

58 *The London Corporation* [1935] P 70, 77; *Payton v Brooks* [1974] RTR 169, 176 (Roskill LJ); *Sainsbury's Supermarkets Ltd v Visa Europe Services LLC* [2020] UKSC 24, [2020] 4 All ER 807 [200].

59 *The Georgiana v The Anglican* (1873) 21 WR 280; *Payton v Brooks* [1974] RTR 169.

60 [1963] 1 WLR 1067.

61 [2007] EWCA Civ 3, [2007] Bus LR 726.

62 ibid [52].

63 ibid [53].

64 *The London Corporation* [1935] P 70, 78.

out.[65] In *Dimond v Lovell*,[66] Lord Hobhouse approved these latter cases and stated that where a car is negligently damaged by X and the next day is negligently destroyed by Y, X remains liable for the cost of repair.

In addition to cost of cure or diminution in value, the claimant can recover damages for consequential financial loss, subject to remoteness and mitigation. For example, in *Aerospace Publishing*, the claimant recovered (in addition to the cost of reinstating the archive) the loss of profit until such time as the archive was restored[67] and the cost of staff time dealing with the aftermath of the water damage.[68]

Where repair is reasonable and the claimant needs to hire a substitute during the period of repair,[69] the cost of hiring a substitute can be recovered. This is particularly relevant for cars. Where the damaged car is a luxury car, the claimant is generally entitled to recover the cost of hiring an equivalent substitute car rather than the lower cost of hiring a more modest car that fulfils the same function as the damaged car (for example, a Ford instead of a Rolls Royce).[70] Where the damaged car was used for business purposes and the cost of hiring a substitute car during the period of repair significantly exceeds the loss of profit in that period, only the loss of profit can be recovered unless it was reasonable to hire a substitute car.[71]

Special considerations arise where the claimant uses a credit car hire company. These companies allow the hirer credit on the charges until the hirer's claim for damages (which is conducted by the company) is concluded and, for this reason, have substantially higher charges than ordinary car hire companies. In *Dimond v Lovell*,[72] the contract between the claimant and the credit car hire company was unenforceable because it did not comply with the form requirements under section 61 of the Consumer Credit Act 1974. The House of Lords held that the claimant could not recover the hire charges (which the claimant did not have to pay) from the defendant. A majority further stated that if the car hire agreement had been enforceable, the claimant could have recovered from the defendant only the lower hire charges charged by ordinary car hire companies since the use of a credit car hire company involves benefits not

---

65 *The Glenfinlas* [1918] P 363n; approved in *The York* [1929] P 178, 184–85.

66 [2002] 1 AC 384, 406.

67 [2007] EWCA Civ 3, [2007] Bus LR 726 [68].

68 ibid [86]–[87].

69 The need was absent in *Singh v Yaqubi* [2013] EWCA Civ 23, [2013] RTR 15.

70 *HL Motorworks (Willesden) Ltd v Alwahbi* [1977] RTR 276; *Daily Office Cleaning Contractors Ltd v Shefford* [1977] RTR 361; *Brain v Yorkshire Rider Ltd* [2007] Lloyd's Rep IR 564. Cf *Watson Norie v Shaw* [1967] 1 Lloyd's Rep 515.

71 *Hussain v EUI Ltd* [2019] EWHC 2647 (QB), [2020] RTR 7.

72 [2002] 1 AC 384.

recoverable from the defendant. However, in *Lagden v O'Connor*,[73] the House of Lords (by majority) held that the higher charges of a credit car hire company can be recovered by a claimant who, because of a lack of financial means, was compelled to use a credit car hire company.

A claimant who has neither lost profit nor hired a substitute may obtain damages for the loss of use of the chattel. This principle was first laid down in cases in which a ship employed for public use was damaged,[74] and has been extended to other non-profit-earning chattels.[75] Three different methods, which may be cumulated,[76] have been used to place a money value on such loss of use: interest on the capital value of the chattel during the period of repair,[77] the depreciation of the chattel during the period of repair,[78] and the wasted cost of maintaining the chattel during the period of repair.[79] Two other methods have been rejected: the letting value of the damaged chattel where it would not in fact have been let,[80] and the hypothetical cost of hiring a substitute where none has in fact been hired.[81]

---

73 [2003] UKHL 64, [2004] 1 AC 1067; discussed later in this chapter.

74 *Owners of No 7 Steam Sand Pump Dredger v Owners of SS 'Greta Holme' (The Greta Holme)* [1897] AC 596; *Owners of the Steamship 'Mediana' v Owners, Master and Crew of the Lightship 'Comet' (The Mediana)* [1900] AC 113; *Mersey Docks and Harbour Board v Owners of the SS Marpessa (The Marpessa)* [1907] AC 241; *Commissioners for Executing Office of Lord High Admiral of the UK v Owners of Steamship Chekiang (The Chekiang)* [1926] AC 637; *Commissioners for Executing Office of Lord High Admiral of the UK v Owners of Steamship Susquehanna (The Susquehanna)* [1926] AC 655; *The Hebridean Coast* [1961] AC 545.

75 *Birmingham Corporation v Sowsbery* [1970] RTR 84 (public bus); *Beechwood Birmingham Ltd v Hoyer Group UK Ltd* [2010] EWCA Civ 647, [2011] QB 357 (car owned by motor dealer); *West Midlands Travel Ltd v Aviva Insurance UK Ltd* [2013] EWCA Civ 887, [2014] RTR 10 (public bus).

76 *The Susquehanna* [1926] AC 655, 663–64 (Lord Sumner); *West Midlands Travel Ltd v Aviva Insurance UK Ltd* [2013] EWCA Civ 887, [2014] RTR 10 [33].

77 *The Greta Holme* [1897] AC 596, 605 (Lord Hershell); *The Hebridean Coast* [1961] AC 545; *Beechwood Birmingham Ltd v Hoyer Group UK Ltd* [2010] EWCA Civ 647, [2011] QB 357 [45].

78 *The Marpessa* [1907] AC 241, 244–45; *The Susquehanna* [1926] AC 655, 663–64 (Lord Sumner); *Beechwood Birmingham Ltd v Hoyer Group UK Ltd* [2010] EWCA Civ 647, [2011] QB 357 [52]; *West Midlands Travel Ltd v Aviva Insurance UK Ltd* [2013] EWCA Civ 887, [2014] RTR 10 [33].

79 *The Marpessa* [1907] AC 241, 244–45; *The Susquehanna* [1926] AC 655, 664 (Lord Sumner).

80 *The Susquehanna* [1926] AC 655.

81 *The Marpessa* [1907] AC 241, 244–45; *The Susquehanna* [1926] AC 655; *The Hebridean Coast* [1961] AC 545; *Dimond v Lovell* [2002] 1 AC 384; *Bee v*

Other Wrongful Interference with Goods

A defendant may interfere with a claimant's interest in goods by converting them or withholding possession from the claimant. The cause of action is conversion, previously called trover. Sections 2 and 3 of the Torts (Interference with Goods) Act 1977 abolished the action in detinue but made the remedies for detinue available in actions for conversion.

The normal measure of damages is the market value of the goods at the date of conversion.[82] A subsequent fall in the value is taken into account where the conversion was temporary,[83] but is ignored where the goods have been irreversibly converted and the claimant has lost them.[84] Where the market value has risen since the date of conversion, damages are assessed by reference to the goods' value at the date when the claimant could have brought an action for their return[85] or should have bought replacement goods in the market.[86] This reflects the avoidable loss rule (discussed in Chapter 3), and the value of the goods at the date of judgment may be adopted where it was reasonable for the claimant to delay the purchase of replacement goods until judgment.[87]

Where there is no market for the converted goods, the cost of having replacement goods made may be recovered if that is a reasonable course to adopt.[88]

The measure of damages must reflect any limitations on the claimant's title to the goods.[89] For example, where an unpaid seller converts the goods, the

---

Jenson [2007] EWCA Civ 923, [2007] 4 All ER 791 [21]; *Beechwood Birmingham Ltd v Hoyer Group UK Ltd* [2010] EWCA Civ 647, [2011] QB 357 [46]. For a discussion of the five methods and their role in English law and Australian law, see Sirko Harder, 'Valuing the Inconvenience Resulting from the Temporary Unavailability of One's Property' (2023) 44 Adel L Rev 111.

82 eg, *Henderson & Co v Williams* [1895] 1 QB 521; *Chubb Cash Ltd v John Crilley & Son* [1983] 1 WLR 599.

83 *Brandeis Goldschmidt & Co Ltd v Western Transport Ltd* [1981] QB 864.

84 *Rhodes v Moules* [1895] 1 Ch 236, 254; *Solloway v McLaughlin* [1938] AC 247, 259 (PC); *BBMB Finance (Hong Kong) Ltd v EDA Holdings Ltd* [1990] 1 WLR 409 (PC). For a discussion, see Jamie Glister, 'Breach of Trust and Conversion in a Falling Market' [2014] LMCLQ 511, 512–20.

85 *Sachs v Miklos* [1948] 2 KB 23.

86 *Industria Azucarera Nacional SA v Empresa Exportadora de Azucar* [1982] Com LR 171, 176.

87 *Trafigura Beheer BV v Mediterranean Shipping Co SA* [2007] EWCA Civ 794, [2008] 1 All ER (Comm) 385 [38]–[40].

88 *J & E Hall Ltd v Barclay* [1937] 3 All ER 620; *Wilson v Robertsons (London) Ltd* [2006] EWCA Civ 1088, [2007] CTLC 84 [43]–[44].

89 See Torts (Interference with Goods) Act 1977, s 7.

buyer recovers the value of the goods less the purchase price,[90] and where a hirer-purchaser converts the goods, the owner can recover only the amount remaining unpaid under the hire-purchase agreement.[91]

In addition to the market value of the goods, the claimant may recover damages for consequential financial loss, subject to remoteness and mitigation.[92] This is particularly relevant where the claimant would have used the converted or detained goods in a business. Consequential financial loss that can be compensated (subject to remoteness and mitigation) includes the loss of hire (where the claimant would have let the goods for hire),[93] other loss of profit,[94] and the reasonable cost of hiring substitute goods until the replacement or return of the detained goods.[95]

In *Strand Electric and Engineering Co Ltd v Brisford Entertainments Ltd*,[96] the defendant wrongfully made use of portable switchboards which the claimant owned and hired out in the course of its business. The Court of Appeal held that the claimant could recover the market rate of hire of such switchboards for the period in which the defendant had used them. It was immaterial that the claimant might not have been able to find a customer willing to hire those switchboards during that period. This is an example of 'user damages',[97] which we discuss in Chapter 8.

Non-pecuniary loss resulting from wrongful interference with goods does not seem to be recoverable. Recoverability has been denied for injury to feelings[98] or reputation.[99]

---

90 *Chinery v Viall* (1860) 5 H & N 288, 157 ER 1192.

91 *Belsize Motor Supply Co v Cox* [1914] 1 KB 244, where it was held that the conversion did not deprive the hirer of the right to obtain the title to the goods by paying the remaining amounts under the agreement.

92 The remoteness test in conversion is discussed later in this chapter.

93 *Hillesden Securities Ltd v Ryjack Ltd* [1983] 1 WLR 959.

94 *Kuwait Airways Corporation v Iraqi Airways Co (Nos 4 and 5)* [2002] UKHL 19, [2002] 2 AC 883 [95], [130]; *Cash v Chief Constable of Lancashire* [2008] EWHC 396 (Ch), [2008] Po LR 182 [47]–[51] (lost sale of foals that detained horse would have sired).

95 *Strand Electric and Engineering Co Ltd v Brisford Entertainments Ltd* [1952] 2 QB 246, 252 (Denning LJ); *Kuwait Airways Corporation v Iraqi Airways Co (Nos 4 and 5)* [2002] UKHL 19, [2002] 2 AC 883 [95], [130].

96 [1952] 2 QB 246.

97 *One Step (Support) Pty Ltd v Morris-Garner* [2018] UKSC 20, [2019] AC 649 [95].

98 *Cash v Chief Constable of Lancashire* [2008] EWHC 396 (Ch), [2008] Po LR 182 [57].

99 *Dixon v Calcraft* [1892] 1 QB 458, 464 (Lord Esher MR); *Lonrho plc v Fayed (No 5)* [1993] 1 WLR 1489, 1495–96, 1504.

Exemplary damages may be awarded where the conditions for their award are satisfied.[100] Exemplary damages are discussed in Chapter 8.

Misrepresentation

A false statement of fact by the defendant may induce the claimant (who believes the statement to be true) to make a financial decision, in particular to enter into a contract with the defendant or a third party. The claimant may be able to recover damages from the defendant if the financial decision proves disadvantageous to the claimant.[101] The defendant may be liable in the tort of deceit (where the defendant made the false statement fraudulently),[102] or in the tort of negligence (where the defendant made the false statement in breach of a duty of care owed to the claimant),[103] or under section 2(1) of the Misrepresentation Act 1967 (where the statement induced the claimant to enter into a contract with the defendant who cannot prove that he had reasonable grounds to believe and did believe in the truth of the statement).[104] The causes of action differ in relation to the remoteness test and the availability of apportionment by virtue of contributory negligence, both of which are discussed later in this chapter. Otherwise, the measure of damages is largely the same.[105]

The aim of damages for misrepresentation is to place the claimant in the position as if the statement (and thus the claimant's financial decision) had not

---

[100] They are expressly authorised, in a specific context, by s 13(2) of the Reserve and Auxiliary Forces (Protection of Civil Interests) Act 1951.

[101] It is not required that the claimant has made a loss. It is sufficient to show that without the misrepresentation, the claimant would have entered into a more profitable transaction: *Clef Aquitaine SARL v Laporte Materials (Barrow) Ltd* [2001] QB 488.

[102] Fraud is present where 'a false representation has been made: (1) knowingly, or (2) without belief in its truth, or (3) recklessly, careless whether it be true or false': *Derry v Peek* (1889) 14 App Cas 337, 374 (Lord Herschell).

[103] The duty of care was recognised in *Hedley Byrne & Co Ltd v Heller & Partners Ltd* [1964] AC 465.

[104] Pursuant to s 2(4) of the 1967 Act, damages under s 2(1) cannot be claimed by a person who has a right to redress under Pt 4A of the Consumer Protection from Unfair Trading Regulations 2008 in respect of the conduct constituting the misrepresentation.

[105] The controversial decision in *Smith Kline & French Laboratories Ltd v Long* [1989] 1 WLR 1, where damages exceeding the loss were awarded, has been said to involve a special rule for deceit that does not apply to negligent misstatements: *Inter Export LLC v Townley* [2018] EWCA Civ 2068 [66].

been made;[106] not in the position as if the statement had been true. Shortly, the claimant recovers reliance loss, not expectation loss.[107] For example, damages have been awarded for the loss suffered as a result of being induced to make a payment that was not due,[108] the loss of earnings from a job that the claimant was induced to leave,[109] and the loss of profit that the claimant would have made from transactions that the defendant's statement induced the claimant not to enter into.[110]

Where, as is often the case, the defendant's representation induced the claimant to enter into a transaction with the defendant or a third party, the basic measure of damages is the difference in value between the assets the claimant gave away in that transaction and the assets the claimant received in the transaction.[111] In the simple case of the claimant being induced to buy an asset at overvalue, the basic measure of damages is the difference between the price paid by the claimant and the actual value of the asset bought.[112] This measure assumes that the claimant would not have bought the asset if the false statement had not been made. Where, in the absence of the false statement, the claimant would still have bought the asset, albeit at a lower price, the measure of damages is the difference between the actual price paid and the hypothetical lower price.[113]

The date at which the relevant values are ascertained is generally the date of the impugned transaction.[114] However, in *Smith New Court Securities Ltd v Citibank NA*,[115] the House of Lords held that this rule is not inflexible and

---

106 The relevant hypothetical world is one in which the false statement was not made at all, not one in which the truth was told: *SK Shipping Europe Ltd v Capital VLCC 3 Corp* [2022] EWCA Civ 231, [2022] 2 All ER (Comm) 784 [61].

107 eg, *Doyle v Olby (Ironmongers) Ltd* [1969] 2 QB 158 (deceit); *Downs v Chappell* [1997] 1 WLR 426, 433–34 (negligence); *Royscot Trust Ltd v Rogerson* [1991] 2 QB 297, 304–05 (s 2(1) of the 1967 Act).

108 *Standard Chartered Bank v Pakistan National Shipping Corp* [2001] EWCA Civ 55, [2001] 1 All ER (Comm) 822.

109 *McNally v Welltrade International Ltd* [1978] IRLR 497, 499.

110 *Parabola Investments Ltd v Browallia Cal Ltd* [2010] EWCA Civ 486, [2011] QB 477.

111 However, some benefits may be ignored. Benefits resulting from a wrong are discussed in Ch 2.

112 eg, *Peek v Derry* (1887) 37 Ch D 541; *Heinemann v Cooper* (1987) 19 HLR 262, 265; *CEMP Properties (UK) Ltd v Dentsply Research & Development Corp* [1991] 2 EGLR 197, 200, 201–02; *Smith New Court Securities Ltd v Citibank NA* [1997] AC 254, 261, 269, 284.

113 *MDW Holdings v Norvill* [2022] EWCA Civ 883, [2023] 4 WLR 33 [78].

114 eg, *Platt v Platt* [2001] 1 BCLC 698, 705, 710.

115 [1997] AC 254.

that the court may choose a later date where this is necessary to give effect to the compensatory principle. This is particularly the case where the misrepresentation continued to operate so as to induce the claimant to retain the asset or where, by reason of the misrepresentation, the claimant was locked into the property. In those circumstances, the court may use the lower value of the asset at the date the claimant sold it rather than its higher value at the date of the impugned transaction.[116]

In addition to the basic measure of damages, the claimant may recover damages for consequential loss,[117] subject to mitigation and, in negligence, foreseeability. For example, a claimant who was induced to purchase a business may recover damages for money invested in the business (less profit made if any).[118]

Where, had the claimant not entered into the impugned transaction, she would have entered into an alternative transaction and made a profit from it, this lost profit can be recovered as part of the claimant's reliance loss.[119] More precisely, the claimant's loss (subject to mitigation and remoteness) is calculated as follows:[120]

- money spent in the impugned transaction;

plus

- revenue that would have been obtained from the alternative transaction;

minus

- revenue obtained from the impugned transaction;

minus

- money that would have been spent in the alternative transaction.

---

116 An illustration is *Naughton v O'Callaghan* [1990] 3 All ER 191, where the claimant was induced to buy a racehorse, whose value fell dramatically when it failed to win races. The claimant recovered the difference between the purchase price and the value of the horse at the time of the trial.

117 eg, *CEMP Properties (UK) Ltd v Dentsply Research & Development Corp* [1991] 2 EGLR 197, 200, 201–02; *Downs v Chappell* [1997] 1 WLR 426, 439.

118 eg, *Doyle v Olby (Ironmongers) Ltd* [1969] 2 QB 158; *Esso Petroleum Co Ltd v Mardon* [1976] QB 801.

119 *East v Maurer* [1991] 1 WLR 461, 467, 468. By the same token, it should be open to a defendant to show that the claimant would have made a loss under the alternative transaction; see *Yam Seng Pte Ltd v International Trade Corp Ltd* [2013] EWHC 111 (QB), [2013] 1 All ER (Comm) 1321 [217].

120 See *East v Maurer* [1991] 1 WLR 461, 468 (Mustill LJ).

Distress and inconvenience resulting from a misrepresentation have been compensated in actions for deceit,[121] for negligence,[122] and under section 2(1) of the 1967 Act.[123]

Aggravated and exemplary damages are available in deceit in appropriate circumstances. They are discussed in Chapter 8.

REMOTENESS OF LOSS

We now consider remoteness of loss (in its narrowest sense, ie, concerned only with the foreseeability of loss)[124] as one of the concepts used to limit the scope of liability in tort as a matter of policy.[125] There is no such limitation where the defendant intended to inflict the loss for which compensation is claimed. 'The intention to injure the plaintiff negatives all excuses and disposes of any question of remoteness of damage.'[126] In addition, for some torts, such as defamation and breach of statutory duty, the question of remoteness of loss does not arise as the requirements of the tort are so stringent that there is no need to have a remoteness test to avoid excessive liability. Other torts do have a remoteness test, but the test is not the same for all those torts. In particular, reasonable foreseeability of the loss is generally required in negligence and some other torts but not in deceit. Broadly, it may be said that the extent of liability increases with the degree of culpability required for liability. The main remoteness tests used in tort are now examined, followed by a discussion of the 'thin skull' rule, which applies irrespective of the remoteness test otherwise applying.

---

121 *Mafo v Adams* [1970] 1 QB 548; *Shelley v Paddock* [1979] QB 120, 131; *Archer v Brown* [1985] QB 401, 428; *Saunders v Edwards* [1987] 1 WLR 1116, 1128–29; *East v Maurer* [1991] 1 WLR 461, 464; *Kinch v Rosling* [2009] EWHC 286 (QB) [19].

122 *McNally v Welltrade International Ltd* [1978] IRLR 497, 499.

123 ibid; *Chesneau v Interhome Ltd* [1983] CLY 988.

124 The different meanings of remoteness are explained in Ch 3.

125 The difference between factual causation and scope of liability is explained in Ch 3.

126 *Quinn v Leathem* [1901] AC 495, 537 (Lord Lindley). See also Glanville L Williams, *Joint Torts and Contributory Negligence* (Stevens & Sons 1951) 201.

The Wagon Mound Test of Reasonable Foreseeability

The relevant torts

Reasonable foreseeability of the loss is required for liability in negligence,[127] as well as for liability under the rule in *Rylands v Fletcher*[128] or in nuisance.[129] It is also generally required in conversion (which does not require fault),[130] as the Court of Appeal has denied liability for consequential loss above the market value of the goods, which resulted from special circumstances of the claimant that were unknown to the defendant.[131] However, in *Kuwait Airways Corporation v Iraqi Airways Co (Nos 4 and 5)*,[132] Lord Nicholls stated in obiter dicta that liability in conversion should require reasonable foreseeability of the loss only where the defendant acted in good faith, whereas a person who has knowingly converted another's goods should—like a fraudster—be liable for all direct and natural consequences of the tort. The other law lords expressed general agreement with Lord Nicholls' reasons, Lord Hope adding that he wished, in particular, to associate himself with Lord Nicholls' distinction between honest and dishonest conversions in relation to liability for consequential loss beyond the market value of the goods.[133]

Three concepts of foreseeability in negligence

In the tort of negligence, the concept of reasonable foreseeability also informs the determination of whether there was a duty of care and whether that duty was breached.[134] But the duty, breach, and remoteness inquiries employ three

---

127 *Overseas Tankship (UK) Ltd v Morts Dock & Engineering Co Ltd (The Wagon Mound (No 1))* [1961] AC 388. Sometimes, the contractual remoteness test applies, as explained later in this chapter.

128 (1868) LR 3 HL 330.

129 *Overseas Tankship (UK) Ltd v Miller Steamship Co Pty Ltd (The Wagon Mound (No 2))* [1967] AC 617, 636–40; *Cambridge Water Co v Eastern Counties Leather plc* [1994] 2 AC 264.

130 *Kuwait Airways Corporation v Iraqi Airways Co (Nos 4 and 5)* [2002] UKHL 19, [2002] 2 AC 883 [103].

131 *The Arpad* [1934] P 189; *Saleslease Ltd v Davis* [1999] 1 WLR 1664. Liability in conversion for unforeseeable items of loss was also denied in *Trafigura Beheer BV v Mediterranean Shipping Co SA* [2007] EWHC 944 (Comm), [2007] 2 All ER (Comm) 149. The requirement of foreseeability was common ground in *Sandeman Comprimar SA v Transitos v Transportes Integrales SL* [2003] EWCA Civ 113, [2003] QB 1270; see at [26]–[27].

132 [2002] UKHL 19, [2002] 2 AC 883 [99]–[104].

133 ibid [169].

134 See, eg, *Pratley v Surrey County Council* [2003] EWCA Civ 1067, [2004] ICR 159 [46]–[48] (Ward LJ).

different concepts of reasonable foreseeability. While our interest is in the remoteness stage, some comments on the role of reasonable foreseeability at the duty and breach stages are warranted.

For a defendant to be under a duty of care towards a claimant, it is required (among other things) that it is reasonably foreseeable as a possibility that careless conduct of any kind on the defendant's part may result in damage of some kind to a class of persons including the claimant.[135]

Whether the defendant breached the duty of care depends upon what a reasonable person would have done.[136] There can be no breach unless it was foreseeable that the defendant's conduct involved a risk of injury to the claimant or a class of persons including the claimant; a risk was foreseeable if it was not far-fetched or fantastic.[137] Other factors to be considered in determining what a reasonable person would have done are the probability and likely seriousness of the harm, the burden of taking precautions to avoid the risk, and the social utility of the activity that created the risk.[138] The foreseeability of a risk of harm is part of a 'calculus of risk'.[139]

Damage suffered by the claimant will be too remote unless it was foreseeable that the kind of damage was a possible outcome of the defendant's conduct.[140] It should be noted that the foreseeability requirement becomes progressively more stringent from the duty stage to the remoteness stage. Where the foreseeability requirement at the remoteness stage is satisfied, so must the foreseeability requirements at the duty stage and the breach stage. This raises the question of why the duty and breach stages still have a foreseeability requirement at all. James Plunkett suggests for the duty stage that the courts are reluctant to discard well-established authority and that there is a persistent

---

[135] eg, *Donoghue v Stevenson* [1932] AC 562, 580, 620; *Bourhill v Young* [1943] AC 92; *Home Office v Dorset Yacht Co Ltd* [1970] AC 1004.

[136] *Blyth v Birmingham Waterworks* (1856) 11 Ex 781, 784; 156 ER 1047, 1049 (Alderson B); *Glasgow Corporation v Muir* [1943] AC 448.

[137] *Overseas Tankship (UK) Ltd v Miller Steamship Co Pty Ltd (The Wagon Mound (No 2))* [1967] AC 617, 641–42; *Jolley v Sutton London Borough Council* [2000] 1 WLR 1082, 1092.

[138] *Overseas Tankship (UK) Ltd v Miller Steamship Co Pty Ltd (The Wagon Mound (No 2))* [1967] AC 617, 642–44; *Tomlinson v Congleton Borough Council* [2003] UKHL 47, [2004] 1 AC 46 [34]. Legislation also requires a consideration of the social utility of the activity: Compensation Act 2006, s 1; Social Action, Responsibility and Heroism Act 2015, s 2.

[139] *Phee v Gordon* [2013] CSIH 18, 2013 SC 379 [26].

[140] *Overseas Tankship (UK) Ltd v Morts Dock & Engineering Co Ltd (The Wagon Mound (No 1))* [1961] AC 388.

belief that the duty stage must have a foreseeability requirement to prevent the imposition of a duty of care to avoid causing unforeseeable harm.[141]

The courts have not always clearly distinguished between the foreseeability requirements at the three different stages of determining liability in negligence. A prominent example is the Scottish case *Hughes v Lord Advocate*,[142] where the defendant's workmen temporarily left a manhole unguarded but surrounded by paraffin lamps. An eight-year-old boy knocked or lowered one of the lamps into the hole. An explosion occurred, the boy fell into the hole and suffered severe burns. It was common ground that while damage through direct contact with the flame had been foreseeable, the explosion had not. The House of Lords held the defendant liable, stating that the precise sequence of events leading to the damage need not be foreseeable. Lord Reid and Lord Pearce saw it as a remoteness issue.[143] Lord Jenkins and Lord Morris saw it as a duty issue.[144] Lord Guest saw it as a breach issue.[145]

The foreseeability test at the remoteness stage

For some time, the courts vacillated between two tests for the remoteness of damage in negligence. One test required the foreseeability of the loss for which compensation was claimed.[146] The other test is the one still applied to 'intentional torts' and required only that the loss be a direct consequence of the careless conduct.[147] Even under the second test, liability in negligence required the foreseeability of some loss, but the foreseeable loss did not have to be the loss for which compensation was claimed. A prominent illustration is *Re Polemis v Furness, Withy & Co Ltd*.[148] Stevedores carelessly allowed a board to fall into the hold of a ship, causing a spark, which ignited petrol vapour and produced a fire that destroyed the ship. Even though the generation of a spark by a falling board had not been foreseeable, the Court of Appeal held the stevedores' employer liable in negligence on the ground that some other damage from a falling board had been foreseeable.

---

141 James Plunkett, *The Duty of Care in Negligence* (Hart 2018) 106–07.

142 [1963] AC 837.

143 ibid 846–47 (Lord Reid), 857–58 (Lord Pearce).

144 ibid 850–51 (Lord Jenkins), 853 (Lord Morris).

145 ibid 857. The Lord Ordinary and the Inner House of the Court of Session also saw it as a breach issue: 1961 SC 310.

146 *Rigby v Hewitt* (1850) 5 Ex 240, 243 (Pollock CB); *Greenland v Chaplin* (1850) 5 Ex 243, 248.

147 *Smith v London & South Western Railway Co* (1870) LR 6 CP 14; *Weld-Blundell v Stephens* [1920] AC 956, 983–84 (Lord Sumner); *Thurogood v Van Den Berghs & Jurgens Ltd* [1951] 2 KB 537.

148 [1921] 3 KB 560.

The test of foreseeability prevailed in *The Wagon Mound (No 1)*.[149] Employees of the defendant, who had chartered the ship *Wagon Mound*, carelessly allowed a large quantity of furnace oil to spill into Sydney Harbour. The oil spread to the plaintiff's wharf, where welding work was being carried out. Pieces of molten metal from the welding fell into the water onto a piece of cotton waste, and the oil ignited and caused a fire, resulting in damage to the wharf and to two ships lying there. The trial judge found that it had been unforeseeable that the oil could be set alight when spread on water.[150] Nevertheless, applying *Re Polemis*, he held the defendant liable in negligence on the ground that pollution damage had been foreseeable.[151] The Privy Council overturned the decision. Viscount Simonds, who delivered the judgment, disapproved *Re Polemis* by stating that:

> it does not seem consonant with current ideas of justice or morality that for an act of negligence, however slight or venial, which results in some trivial foreseeable damage the actor should be liable for all consequences however unforeseeable and however grave, so long as they can be said to be 'direct'.[152]

The English courts have since applied the foreseeability test in many actions for negligence.[153] The probability with which the harm needs to be foreseeable is as low as it is at the breach stage: a risk is foreseeable unless it can be brushed aside as far-fetched.[154]

It is important to note that the sole function of the foreseeability requirement at the remoteness stage is to exclude liability for unforeseeable loss. It does not follow that liability in negligence (or in another tort in which the foreseeability requirement applies) always extends to all foreseeable loss. The concept of remoteness (in its narrowest sense) is only one of several concepts used to limit the scope of liability. As explained in Chapter 3, responsibility even for foreseeable loss may be denied because of an intervening event or because the loss is not of a type that the duty breached aims to prevent.

---

149 *Overseas Tankship (UK) Ltd v Morts Dock & Engineering Co Ltd (The Wagon Mound (No 1))* [1961] AC 388.

150 *Overseas Tankship (UK) Ltd v Morts Dock & Engineering Co Ltd* [1958] 1 Lloyd's Rep 575, 582.

151 ibid 584–85, aff'd [1959] 2 Lloyd's Rep 697.

152 [1961] AC 388, 422.

153 eg, *Doughty v Turner Manufacturing Co Ltd* [1964] 1 QB 518; *Sandeman Comprimar SA v Transitos v Transportes Integrales SL* [2003] EWCA Civ 113, [2003] QB 1270 [25]–[31].

154 *Koufos v C Czarnikow Ltd* [1969] 1 AC 350, 422 (Lord Upjohn); *Attia v British Gas plc* [1988] QB 304, 313 (Dillon LJ).

Moreover, it is only the kind of damage, not its extent, which needs to be foreseeable. This was expressed in the *Wagon Mound* cases,[155] and applied in subsequent cases.[156] An example is *Muirhead v Industrial Tank Specialities Ltd*,[157] where an English fish merchant lost his entire stock of lobsters because the oxygenation pumps failed. This was because the motors of the pumps had been manufactured in France and were not suited to the UK range of voltages. The trial judge denied the liability of the manufacturer of the motors on the ground that the killing of the entire stock of lobsters had not been foreseeable. The Court of Appeal held the manufacturer liable on the ground that the type of damage (physical harm to fish) had been foreseeable and that it was of no relevance that, by reason of the full stocking of the tank, the fish died more quickly or in greater quantities.[158]

The remoteness test requires the court to decide whether the loss suffered is of the same type as the loss that was foreseeable. There is no general list of types of loss that applies in all cases. The denial of liability on the ground of remoteness is based on policy considerations, which are fact-sensitive. Losses that are regarded as being of the same type in one context may not be so regarded in another.[159] This is particularly true for personal injury, as demonstrated by two cases.

In *Doughty v Turner Manufacturing Co Ltd*,[160] the asbestos cement cover of a cauldron containing molten liquid in the defendant's factory was inadvertently knocked into the cauldron by one of the defendant's employees. The cover slid beneath the molten liquid, causing it to erupt and injure the plaintiff. According to the knowledge at the time, it was foreseeable that the knocking of the cover into the molten liquid could cause a splash, but not that the immersion of the cover could cause an explosion. The Court of Appeal held that the defendant was not liable because the damage resulting from the explosion was not damage of a kind that could reasonably have been foreseen and was altogether different from a foreseeable splash of the liquid in the cauldron.

---

155 *Overseas Tankship (UK) Ltd v Morts Dock & Engineering Co Ltd (The Wagon Mound (No 1))* [1961] AC 388, 426; *Overseas Tankship (UK) Ltd v Miller Steamship Co Pty Ltd (The Wagon Mound (No 2))* [1967] AC 617, 636.

156 eg, *Armstead v Royal & Sun Alliance Insurance Co Ltd* [2024] UKSC 6, [2025] AC 406.

157 [1986] QB 507.

158 ibid 532–33.

159 Personal injury and property damage should always constitute different types of damage; see James Edelman, *McGregor on Damages* (21st edn, Sweet & Maxwell 2021) [8-082].

160 [1964] 1 QB 518.

In *Jolley v Sutton London Borough Council*,[161] a rotten boat was left abandoned on land owned by the defendant council, and the council was aware of this. Two boys, aged 13 and 14, propped up the boat in order to repair it. The boat fell on the plaintiff, crushing him. The plaintiff suffered spinal injuries resulting in paraplegia. The Court of Appeal held the defendant not liable on the grounds that while it had been foreseeable that children would play on the boat and be injured, it had not been foreseeable that they would prop up the boat and be injured by it falling off the prop. The House of Lords allowed the appeal, holding that since the risk of children being injured by falling through the rotten planks had been foreseeable, the wider risk of more serious injury, which could have been eliminated without additional expense, also fell within the scope of the defendant's duty of care.

In both *Doughty* and *Jolley*, personal injury caused in a particular way was foreseeable, and personal injury caused in a different way was suffered. The defendant was held liable in *Jolley* but not in *Doughty*. This does not necessarily mean that the two cases are irreconcilable, as different policy considerations may have been at play. Unfortunately, the House of Lords in *Jolley* did not explain the difference between the two cases.

Where a claimant has suffered psychiatric illness resulting from shock, English law distinguishes between primary victims and secondary victims. Primary victims are those who suffer shock out of fear for their own safety; where the defendant was under a duty of care to avoid causing personal injury, liability does not require that psychiatric illness was foreseeable.[162] Secondary victims are those who suffer psychiatric illness because another person has been wrongfully injured or killed; for the person causing that injury or death to be liable for the secondary victim's psychiatric illness, it is necessary (but by no means sufficient) that psychiatric illness in a person of ordinary fortitude was foreseeable.[163] This is a matter of whether there is a duty of care to avoid causing psychiatric illness, not a matter of remoteness of damage, and will not be further explored here.[164]

---

161 [2000] 1 WLR 1082.

162 *Page v Smith* [1996] AC 155. See also *Corr v IBC Vehicles Ltd* [2008] UKHL 13, [2008] 1 AC 884.

163 *Alcock v Chief Constable of South Yorkshire Police* [1992] 1 AC 310; *Taylor v A Novo (UK) Ltd* [2013] EWCA Civ 194, [2014] QB 150.

164 For an overview of the law on this matter in the main common law jurisdictions as well as Scotland and South Africa, see Peter Handford, *Tort Liability for Mental Harm* (3rd edn, Lawbook Co 2017) chs 2 and 3. For English law, see also *Paul v Royal Wolverhampton NHS Trust* [2024] UKSC 1, [2025] AC 459.

Other Remoteness Tests Used in Tort

The other main remoteness test used in tort is that of direct and natural consequences, which include unforeseeable loss. This test is firmly established for deceit. In *Doyle v Olby (Ironmongers) Ltd*,[165] false statements fraudulently made by the defendant induced the plaintiff to purchase the defendant's ironmongers' business. The plaintiff invested £7,000 in the business, but it proved unprofitable, and the plaintiff sold it after three years. The Court of Appeal held that the plaintiff could recover damages for the money he had spent on the business, less any benefits received. The Court stated that a fraudster is liable for all losses directly flowing from the fraud.[166] Lord Denning MR added that 'it does not lie in the mouth of the fraudulent person to say that [the loss] could not reasonably have been foreseen'.[167] The House of Lords confirmed this position in *Smith New Court Securities Ltd v Citibank NA*.[168]

In *Royscot Trust Ltd v Rogerson*,[169] the Court of Appeal held that the test of direct and natural consequences also applies to a claim under section 2(1) of the Misrepresentation Act 1967. This has been criticised on the ground that the claimant-friendly remoteness test applying to a fraudster's liability should not be applied to a defendant who was merely negligent in making a false statement.[170]

As already mentioned, Lord Nicholls in *Kuwait Airways Corporation v Iraqi Airways Co (Nos 4 and 5)* expressed the view that the test of direct and natural consequences should apply to cases of dishonest conversion.[171]

In trespass to the person, foreseeability of the loss is not required,[172] and the remoteness test thus is the same, or at least very similar, to the one in deceit. The test of direct and natural consequences seems to apply generally to torts that require an intention of some sort.[173] In *Palmer Bruyn & Parker Pty Ltd v*

---

165 [1969] 2 QB 158.

166 ibid 167, 168, 171.

167 ibid 167.

168 [1997] AC 254, 266–67, 282.

169 [1991] 2 QB 297.

170 eg, Richard Hooley, 'Damages and the Misrepresentation Act 1967' (1991) 107 LQR 547.

171 [2002] UKHL 19, [2002] 2 AC 883 [99]–[104].

172 *Wainwright v Home Office* [2001] EWCA Civ 2081, [2002] QB 1334 [71] (Buxton LJ); *Breslin v McKenna* [2009] NIQB 50 [272].

173 *Smith New Court Securities Ltd v Citibank NA* [1997] AC 254, 279 (Lord Steyn); James Edelman, *McGregor on Damages* (21st edn, Sweet & Maxwell 2021) [8-062].

Parsons,[174] the High Court of Australia applied it to injurious falsehood and stated that it applies to all intentional torts.[175]

An application of the foreseeability requirement has also been rejected for liability under the Race Relations Act 1976[176] or the Protection from Harassment Act 1997.[177]

An exception to the applicability of the *Wagon Mound* test to liability in negligence for pure economic loss exists where the tortious duty of care is concurrent with a contractual duty of care, which is usually the case for professionals. In those circumstances, the contractual remoteness test applies to liability in negligence as well as contract. This was stated by the Court of Appeal in *Wellesley Partners LLP v Withers LLP*,[178] where solicitors negligently failed to draft a partnership agreement in accordance with the client's instructions. Floyd LJ explained that the rationale of the contractual remoteness test is each party's opportunity to draw the other party's attention to special circumstances, creating a consensus as to the type of damage for which each party would be responsible; the concurrent duty in tort should not upset this consensus, not least because it arises out of the same assumption of responsibility as the contractual duty.[179] The rule has been applied in several cases.[180]

Abnormality of the Claimant or the Claimant's Property

Liability in tort cannot be reduced on the ground that a pre-existing abnormality of the claimant or the claimant's property has rendered the loss resulting from the tort more extensive than it would otherwise have been.[181] As Lord

---

174 [2001] HCA 69, (2001) 208 CLR 388.

175 ibid [13], [66]. For a discussion of the Australian position, see Katy Barnett and Sirko Harder, *Remedies in Australian Private Law* (3rd edn, CUP 2024) [6.62]–[6.65].

176 *Essa v Laing Ltd* [2004] EWCA Civ 2, [2004] ICR 746.

177 ibid [31] (Pill LJ); *Jones v Ruth* [2011] EWCA Civ 804, [2012] 1 WLR 1495.

178 [2015] EWCA Civ 1146, [2016] Ch 529. The facts of the case are set out in Ch 2.

179 ibid [80]. The loss in the instant case was held not to be too remote even under the contractual test.

180 eg, *Wright v Lewis Silkin LLP* [2016] EWCA Civ 1308, [2017] PNLR 16 [60]–[65]; *Radius Housing Association Ltd v JNP Architects* [2018] NIQB 57, [2018] PNLR 31 [66]–[67].

181 However, damages will be reduced to the extent to which the pre-existing condition would have led to the same loss if the wrong had not occurred; see, eg, *Boom v Thomas Hubbuck & Son Ltd* [1967] 1 Lloyd's Rep 491; *Jason v Batten* (1930) Ltd [1969] 1 Lloyd's Rep 281; *Environment Agency v Ellis* [2008] EWCA Civ 1117, [2009] PIQR P5 [36].

Wright stated in *Bourhill v Young*, 'if the wrong is established the wrongdoer must take the victim as he finds him'.[182] The rule is known as the 'eggshell skull' rule or the 'thin skull' rule because of the way it was expressed by Kennedy J in *Dulieu v White & Sons*:

> If a man is negligently run over or otherwise negligently injured in his body, it is no answer to the sufferer's claim for damages that he would have suffered less injury, or no injury at all, if he had not had an unusually thin skull or an unusually weak heart.[183]

Bourhill and *Dulieu* were decided before the test of reasonable foreseeability was firmly established for the tort of negligence in *The Wagon Mound (No 1)*.[184] But the 'thin skull' rule has survived. It was applied only a few months after *The Wagon Mound (No 1)* in *Smith v Leech Brain & Co Ltd*.[185] An employee of the defendant galvanising company was struck on the lower lip by a piece of molten metal, causing a burn. He developed cancer at the site of the burn and died from it. The burn was the promoting agent of cancer in tissues which already had a pre-malignant condition. But for the burn, cancer might never have developed. The defendant was held liable for the death even though it had not been reasonably foreseeable that the burn would cause cancer and death.

Lord Parker CJ explained that it was sufficient that the type of injury (the burn) had been foreseeable; the amount of loss depended upon the characteristics and constitution of the victim.[186] He stated that he would follow *The Wagon Mound (No 1)* (even though decisions by the Judicial Committee of the Privy Council are not binding in English cases),[187] but that the 'thin skull' rule does not conflict with the restriction of negligence liability to foreseeable loss, as it is only the type of damage, not its extent, that needs to be foreseeable:

---

182 [1943] AC 92, 109–10. See also *Clippens Oil Co Ltd v Edinburgh and District Water Trustees* [1907] AC 291, 303 (Lord Collins): 'the wrong-doer must take his victim talem qualem'.

183 [1901] 2 KB 669, 679. See also *Owens v Liverpool Corporation* [1939] 1 KB 394, 400–01 (MacKinnon LJ speaking for the Court of Appeal): 'one who is guilty of negligence to another must put up with idiosyncrasies of his victim that increase the likelihood or extent of damage to him: it is no answer to a claim for a fractured skull that its owner had an unusually fragile one.'

184 [1961] AC 388, discussed earlier in this chapter.

185 [1962] 2 QB 405.

186 ibid 415.

187 ibid 415–16.

> I am quite satisfied that the Judicial Committee in the *Wagon Mound* case did not have what I may call, loosely, the thin skull cases in mind ... The Judicial Committee were not, I think, saying that a man is only liable for the extent of damage which he could anticipate, always assuming the type of injury could have been anticipated.[188]

Lord Parker CJ thus expressed the view that the 'thin skull' rule is not an exception to the *Wagon Mound* test but an application of the distinction between the type and extent of damage. On this view, the sole function of the 'thin skull' rule is to express in a 'catchy' way that the extent of damage does not need to be foreseeable. However, the 'thin skull' rule may inform the determination of whether the damage suffered in a particular case is of the same type as the damage that had been foreseeable in that case, as this is based on policy considerations. A burn and cancer do not immediately appear to be the same type of damage. However, policy considerations, expressed through the 'thin skull' rule, led to the conclusion in *Smith v Leech Brain & Co Ltd* that cancer was merely a more severe form of the same type of damage (namely personal injury) as the burn.[189]

The 'thin skull' rule has mainly been applied in cases of bodily injury,[190] although a case actually involving a thin skull does not seem to have come to court. The rule also applies to psychiatric illness.[191] In *Page v Smith*,[192] a near collision with the defendant caused the plaintiff to suffer a recurrence of chronic fatigue syndrome, which he had suffered 20 years prior to the accident. A majority in the House of Lords held that for the defendant to be liable, it was not required that chronic fatigue syndrome had been foreseeable, provided that some personal injury had been foreseeable. Lord Lloyd stated that there was no difference between an eggshell skull and an eggshell personality.[193]

---

188 ibid 414–15 (footnote omitted).

189 See Andrew Tettenborn (ed), *Clerk & Lindsell on Torts* (24th edn, Sweet & Maxwell 2023) [2-166].

190 eg, *Warren v Scruttons* [1962] 1 Lloyd's Rep 497; *Robinson v Post Office* [1974] 1 WLR 1176.

191 The question arises only where there is a duty of care to avoid causing psychiatric illness; see the comments earlier in this chapter.

192 [1996] AC 155.

193 ibid 189, citing *Malcolm v Broadhurst* [1970] 3 All ER 508, 511. See also *Simmons v British Steel plc* [2004] UKHL 20, 2004 SC (HL) 94; *Essa v Laing Ltd* [2004] EWCA Civ 2, [2004] ICR 746; *Brice v Brown* [1984] 1 All ER 997.

The 'thin skull' rule also applies to property damage.[194] In *Vacwell Engineering Co Ltd v BDH Chemicals Ltd*,[195] the defendant supplied a chemical called boron tribromide to the plaintiff without warning the latter of the danger of explosion when the chemical came in contact with water. When the chemical did come in contact with water in the plaintiff's lab, a violent explosion occurred causing extensive damage to the plaintiff's property. Even though only a minor explosion causing minor damage had been foreseeable, the defendant was held liable (for negligence and breach of contract) on the ground that it was sufficient that an explosion had been foreseeable and it was irrelevant that its magnitude and the extent of damage had not been foreseeable.[196]

Finally, the 'thin skull' rule also applies where the claimant lacks the financial means to take the measures to mitigate loss that a person with sufficient financial means would be required to take lest recovery be denied by the avoidable loss rule discussed in Chapter 2. The House of Lords expressed the opposite rule in *The Liesbosch*,[197] but overruled *The Liesbosch* in *Lagden v O'Connor*.[198] The claimant's car was negligently damaged by the defendant and needed repair. During the period of repair, the claimant needed a replacement car. Due to lack of finances, the claimant was unable to hire a car through an ordinary car hire company and was required to use a credit car hire company which gave credit for the hire charges but, for that reason, was more expensive. A majority in the House of Lords held that the claimant could recover the cost of using a credit car hire company. Lord Hope stated that the rule that a wrongdoer must take his victim as he finds him 'applies to the economic state of the victim in the same way as it applies to his physical and mental vulnerability'.[199]

Australian courts have also applied the 'thin skull' rule to the claimant's family circumstances,[200] and the claimant's cultural and religious beliefs.[201] This has been criticised as being difficult to reconcile with *The Wagon Mound (No 1)*.[202] Furthermore, an application of the 'thin skull' rule to loss resulting from the conduct of the claimant or a third party after the defendant's wrong

---

194 See *The Arpad* [1934] P 189, 202–03, where Scrutton LJ gave the example of injuring the favourite horse for the Derby, preventing the horse from competing.

195 [1971] 1 QB 88.

196 ibid 109–10.

197 *Owners of Dredger Liesbosch v Owners of Steamship Edison* [1933] AC 449.

198 [2003] UKHL 64, [2004] 1 AC 1067.

199 ibid [61].

200 *Nader v Urban Transit Authority of NSW* (1985) 2 NSWLR 501.

201 *Kavanagh v Akhtar* (1998) 45 NSWLR 588, 601.

202 Martin Davies, Ian Malkin and Tania Voon, *Focus: Torts* (10th edn, LexisNexis 2024) [4.61].

may prevent a proper investigation into whether that conduct broke the chain of causation.

The 'thin skull' rule is concerned with an abnormal weakness of the claimant or the claimant's property. Loss resulting from a tort may also be increased because the claimant is exceptionally rich or the claimant's property is of exceptionally high value. Liability does not require that such high values were foreseeable, as long as the type of damage was foreseeable. As Scrutton LJ famously observed in *The Arpad*:

> You negligently run down a shabby-looking man in the street, and he turns out to be a millionaire engaged in a very profitable business which the accident disables him from carrying on; or you negligently and ignorantly injure the favourite for the Derby whereby he cannot run. You have to pay damages resulting from the circumstances of which you have no notice.[203]

CONTRIBUTORY NEGLIGENCE

Contributory negligence is unreasonable conduct of the claimant that contributed to the occurrence of the defendant's wrong or to the loss resulting from it. As explained in Chapter 3, the main field of application of the doctrine is the conduct of the claimant that occurred before the defendant's wrong, but it has sometimes been applied to later conduct of the claimant. The defendant bears the legal burden of pleading and proving contributory negligence.[204]

At common law, contributory negligence operated as a complete defence to an action in negligence or nuisance,[205] unless the defendant had the last opportunity to avoid the damage, in which case the defendant was liable for the entire loss.[206] The Law Reform (Contributory Negligence) Act 1945 replaced the common law position with an apportionment of the loss.[207] Section 1(1) provides:

---

203 [1934] P 189, 202–03.

204 *Owners of SS Heranger v Owners of SS Diamond* [1939] AC 94, 104; *Armstead v Royal & Sun Alliance Insurance Co Ltd* [2024] UKSC 6, [2025] AC 406 [60].

205 *Butterfield v Forrester* (1809) 11 East 60, 103 ER 926; *Davey v London and South Western Railway Co* (1883) 12 QBD 70.

206 *Davies v Mann* (1842) 10 M & W 546, 152 ER 588. A 'constructive last opportunity' existed where earlier negligence on the defendant's part disabled him from avoiding the harm after the claimant's conduct: *British Columbia Electric Railway Co Ltd v Loach* [1916] 1 AC 719 (PC).

207 Different apportionment regimes apply in particular circumstances: Merchant Shipping Act 1995, s 187; Nuclear Installations Act 1965, s 13(7).

> Where any person suffers damage as the result partly of his own fault and partly of the fault of another person or persons, a claim in respect of that damage shall not be defeated by reason of the fault of the person suffering the damage, but the damages recoverable in respect thereof shall be reduced to such extent as the court thinks just and equitable having regard to the claimant's share in the responsibility for the damage …

Section 4 of the Act defines 'fault' as 'negligence, breach of statutory duty or other act or omission which gives rise to a liability in tort or would, apart from this Act, give rise to the defence of contributory negligence'. The first limb of this definition (ending with 'tort') applies to defendants and the second limb to claimants.[208] Thus, the Act applies only where contributory negligence constitutes a complete defence at common law.

The 1945 Act applies to liability in negligence, in nuisance,[209] and for breach of statutory duty.[210] It does not apply to liability in deceit,[211] or trespass to the person.[212] Even though it has been held that the measure of damages under section 2(1) of the Misrepresentation Act 1967 is the same as in the tort of deceit,[213] the 1945 Act has been considered applicable to a claim under section 2(1).[214] In actions for defamation, false imprisonment, or malicious prosecution, the measure of damages may be affected by the conduct, character, and circumstances of the claimant,[215] but this is not done through an application of the 1945 Act.[216]

Legislation imposing strict liability often provides for the applicability of the 1945 Act. For example, section 10 of the Animals Act 1971 provides for

---

208 Glanville L Williams, *Joint Torts and Contributory Negligence* (Stevens & Sons 1951) 318; *Reeves v Commissioner of Police of the Metropolis* [2000] 1 AC 360, 382 (Lord Hope); *Standard Chartered Bank v Pakistan National Shipping Corporation (Nos 2 and 4)* [2002] UKHL 43, [2003] 1 AC 959 [11].

209 *Trevett v Lee* [1955] 1 WLR 113, 122.

210 eg, *National Coal Board v England* [1954] AC 403.

211 *Standard Chartered Bank v Pakistan National Shipping Corporation (Nos 2 and 4)* [2002] UKHL 43, [2003] 1 AC 959.

212 *Pritchard v Co-operative Group Ltd* [2011] EWCA Civ 329, [2012] QB 320 (assault and battery); *R (on the application of Diop) v Secretary of State for the Home Department* [2018] EWHC 3420 (Admin) [74] (false imprisonment).

213 *Royscot Trust Ltd v Rogerson* [1991] 2 QB 297, mentioned earlier in this chapter.

214 *Gran Gelato Ltd v Richcliff (Group) Ltd* [1992] Ch 560, 573–74; *Taberna Europe CDO II plc v Selskabet AF1* [2016] EWCA Civ 1262, [2017] QB 633 [51]-[52].

215 *Alexander v Home Office* [1988] 1 WLR 968, 978.

216 In *Grobbelaar v News Group Newspapers Ltd* [2002] UKHL 40, [2002] 1 WLR 3024 [86], Lord Scott said that the 1945 Act might apply to defamation.

the applicability of the 1945 Act to liability under that Act for damage done by animals, and section 6(4) of the Consumer Protection Act 1987 provides for the applicability of the 1945 Act to strict liability for defective products. By contrast, section 11(1) of the Torts (Interference with Goods) Act 1977 provides: 'Contributory negligence is no defence in proceedings founded on conversion, or on intentional trespass to goods.'[217] This excludes the application of the 1945 Act in those cases. The unavailability of apportionment in cases of unintentional conversion is difficult to justify.[218]

Contributory negligence does not require that the claimant breached a duty of care to the defendant,[219] although it includes such a case (for example, a collision between two vehicles). Contributory negligence means that the claimant did not, in their own interest, take reasonable care of their affairs.[220] It must be asked what a reasonable person in the claimant's circumstances would have done.[221] Depending on the circumstances, a reasonable person guards against the possible negligence of others.[222]

The standard of care applied in the context of contributory negligence is an objective one; the claimant's idiosyncrasies are ignored.[223] However, a child is held to the standard of an ordinary child of the same age.[224] The characteristics of the reasonable person may also take account of the claimant's mental disability[225] or physical disability.[226]

---

[217] For an exception, see Banking Act 1979, s 47.

[218] Andrew Burrows, *Remedies for Torts, Breach of Contract, and Equitable Wrongs* (4th edn, OUP 2019) 138.

[219] *Nance v British Columbia Electric Railway Co Ltd* [1951] AC 601, 611 (PC); *Froom v Butcher* [1976] QB 286, 291.

[220] ibid.

[221] *AC Billings & Sons Ltd v Riden* [1958] AC 240, 255.

[222] *Grant v Sun Shipping Co Ltd* [1948] AC 549, 567 (Lord Du Parcq); *Jones v Livox Quarries Ltd* [1952] 2 QB 608, 615 (Denning LJ).

[223] *Froom v Butcher* [1976] QB 286, 294.

[224] *Gough v Thorne* [1966] 1 WLR 1387; *C v Imperial Design Ltd* [2001] Env LR 33 [39]. See also *Jackson v Murray* [2015] UKSC 5, 2015 SC (UKSC) 105 [55]. Interestingly, a review of cases from this century found no evidence of leniency towards children older than 9: James Goudkamp and Donal Nolan, 'Contributory Negligence in the Twenty-First Century: An Empirical Study of First Instance Decisions' (2016) 79 Mod LR 575, 609.

[225] *Young v Kent County Council* [2005] EWHC 1342 (QB) [32]; *Spearman v Royal United Bath Hospitals NHS Foundation Trust* [2017] EWHC 3027 (QB), [2018] Med LR 244 [73]–[74].

[226] *M'Kibbin v Glasgow Corporation* 1920 SC 590, 597 (Lord Salvesen). However, a reasonable person with a physical disability will take that disability into account in deciding how to respond to risks; see Joachim Dietrich and Iain

It has been said that the standard of care applied in the context of contributory negligence is the same as the standard of care applied when determining whether a defendant was negligent.[227] This is appropriate where the claimant engaged in an activity that created a risk for herself as well as others, such as driving a car. But the equivalence is not appropriate where the claimant created a risk only for her own interests. It is not unreasonable to run a higher risk of damage to one's own property than a reasonable person would run in respect of someone else's property.[228]

The courts have in fact shown some leniency towards claimants. Where the defendant's wrong placed the claimant in an emergency, the claimant may be said to have acted reasonably even though hindsight shows that other options were open to the claimant.[229] A trivial instance of carelessness on the part of an employee injured at work does not constitute contributory negligence.[230] The client of a professional is generally entitled to rely on the professional's advice.[231] More generally, it is recognised that a claimant is not required to be a paragon of circumspection[232] or listen to a counsel of perfection.[233]

Field, 'The "Reasonable Tort Victim": Contributory Negligence, Standard of Care and the "Equivalence Theory"' (2017) 41 MULR 602, 615.

[227] *Casson v Spotmix Ltd* [2017] EWCA Civ 1994 [6]; *Campbell v Advantage Insurance Co Ltd* [2021] EWCA Civ 1698, [2022] QB 354 [36]. Statutes in the Australian states prescribe this equivalence; see, eg, Civil Liability Act 2002 (NSW), s 5R.

[228] Kenneth W Simons, 'Victim Fault and Victim Strict Responsibility in Anglo-American Tort Law' (2015) 8 J Tort L 29; Joachim Dietrich and Iain Field, 'The "Reasonable Tort Victim": Contributory Negligence, Standard of Care and the "Equivalence Theory"' (2017) 41 MULR 602.

[229] *Jones v Boyce* (1816) 1 Starkie 493, 171 ER 540; *Brandon v Osborne Garrett and Co Ltd* [1924] 1 KB 548.

[230] *Caswell v Powell Duffryn Associated Collieries Ltd* [1940] AC 152; *Jones v Staveley Iron and Chemical Co Ltd* [1955] 1 QB 474. However, a review of cases from this century found evidence of leniency towards employees only at the apportionment stage: James Goudkamp and Donal Nolan, 'Contributory Negligence in the Twenty-First Century: An Empirical Study of First Instance Decisions' (2016) 79 MLR 575, 606.

[231] For an empirical study of cases, see James Goudkamp and Donal Nolan, 'Contributory Negligence and Professional Negligence: An Empirical Perspective' in Kit Barker and Ross Grantham (eds), *Apportionment in Private Law* (Hart 2019) 161.

[232] *AC Billings & Sons Ltd v Riden* [1958] AC 240, 255 (Lord Reid).

[233] *Williams v Devon County Council* [2003] EWCA Civ 365, [2003] CP Rep 47 [7].

Contributory negligence will also be denied where the defendant breached a statutory duty to protect the claimant from the risk that materialised.[234]

Intentional self-harm by the claimant may constitute contributory negligence (or—better—contributory fault).[235] In *Reeves v Commissioner of Police of the Metropolis*,[236] a person in police custody committed suicide, which the police had a duty of care to prevent (and which therefore did not constitute a *novus actus interveniens*).[237] The House of Lords applied the 1945 Act to reduce the defendant's liability under the Fatal Accidents Act 1976 to the dependants of the deceased, who had been of sufficiently sound mind. In *Corr v IBC Vehicles Ltd*,[238] an employee of the defendant suffered disfiguring personal injury at work. He became depressed and committed suicide nearly six years after the accident. In his widow's action against the defendant under the Fatal Accidents Act, the House of Lords held that the suicide was not a *novus actus interveniens*. A majority regarded the 1945 Act as applicable in the circumstances.[239]

The claimant's unreasonable conduct must be a cause of the loss for which compensation is claimed.[240] Where the claimant who was injured in a traffic accident was not wearing a seat belt, damages cannot be reduced under the 1945 Act unless it is shown that the injuries would have been less severe if the claimant had worn a seat belt.[241] That the claimant's unreasonable conduct was a factual cause of the loss is necessary for the applicability of the 1945 Act, but it is not sufficient. It is also necessary that the risk that has materialised is the risk that made the claimant's conduct unreasonable. In *Jones v Livox Quarries Ltd*,[242] the plaintiff was standing on a traxcavator and was injured when a dumper crashed into the back of the traxcavator. The Court of Appeal emphasised that the 1945 Act requires that contributory negligence was a legal as well as factual cause of the loss, which the Court held was the case on the facts.

---

234 eg, *Hutchinson v London and North Eastern Railway Co* [1942] 1 KB 481; *Nixon v Chanceoption Developments Ltd* [2002] EWCA Civ 558 [18]; *Toole v Bolton Metropolitan Borough Council* [2002] EWCA Civ 588.

235 For the terminology, see Robert Stevens, 'Should Contributory Fault be Analogue or Digital?' in Andrew Dyson, James Goudkamp and Frederick Wilmot-Smith (eds), *Defences in Tort* (Hart 2015) 257.

236 [2000] 1 AC 360.

237 *Novus actus interveniens* is discussed in Ch 3.

238 [2008] UKHL 13, [2008] 1 AC 884.

239 A deduction was not made as the issue had not been considered in the lower courts.

240 *Caswell v Powell Duffryn Associated Collieries Ltd* [1940] AC 152, 165 (Lord Atkin).

241 *Lertora v Finzi* [1973] RTR 161; *Stanton v Collinson* [2010] EWCA Civ 81, [2010] RTR 26.

242 [1952] 2 QB 608.

The Court further explained that the 1945 Act would not have been applicable if the plaintiff had been shot by a negligent sportsman.[243]

Section 1(1) of the 1945 Act permits an apportionment only of loss to which the claimant's unreasonable conduct contributed.[244] The Court of Appeal emphasised this in *Froom v Butcher*[245] and *O'Connell v Jackson*.[246] In *O'Connell v Jackson*, however, the Court found it impossible to ascertain the proportion of the claimant's total loss to which the claimant had contributed, and reflected the claimant's contribution to his loss by reducing the damages for the total loss by 15 percent.[247]

Where contributory negligence has contributed to the claimant's loss, section 1(1) of the 1945 Act instructs the court to reduce the damages in respect of that loss 'to such an extent as the court thinks just and equitable'.[248] It also provides that the court should have regard to the claimant's share in the responsibility for the damage. This share can only be determined by comparing the claimant's conduct with that of the defendant.[249]

The court considers the parties' relative blameworthiness and the 'causative potency' of their conduct.[250] Thus, where a car has struck a pedestrian, a higher proportion of the pedestrian's loss will usually be allocated to the car

---

243 ibid 616, 618.

244 *O'Connell v Jackson* [1972] 1 QB 270, 277–78.

245 [1976] QB 286, 296. The trial judge had suggested a reduction of the total damages by 20%, which the Court of Appeal applied because the plaintiff had not objected to it.

246 [1972] 1 QB 270, 277–78.

247 ibid 278.

248 An appellate court will not interfere with the apportionment of the loss by the court below unless the latter committed an error of law, failed to consider a relevant matter, or made an apportionment that was not reasonably open to it: *Jackson v Murray* [2015] UKSC 5, 2015 SC (UKSC) 105 [35], [46]. For a review of relevant decisions by the Court of Appeal, see James Goudkamp and Donal Nolan, 'Contributory Negligence in the Court of Appeal: An Empirical Study' (2017) 37 LS 437.

249 *Miraflores (Owners) v George Livanos (Owners)* [1967] 1 AC 826, 846 (Lord Pearce).

250 eg, *Davies v Swan Motor Co (Swansea) Ltd* [1949] 2 KB 291, 326 (Denning LJ); *Stapley v Gypsum Mines Ltd* [1953] AC 663, 682 (Lord Reid); *Froom v Butcher* [1976] QB 286, 296; *Jackson v Murray* [2015] UKSC 5, 2015 SC (UKSC) 105 [40]. For criticism of the causal potency concept, see James Goudkamp and Lewis Klar, 'Apportionment of Damages for Contributory Negligence: The Causal Potency Criterion' (2016) 53 Alta L Rev 849.

driver because of the significantly higher causative potency of driving a car compared to walking.[251]

The court will reduce the damages by a particular percentage.[252] In some cases, damages were reduced to nil.[253] However, the Court of Appeal has held that a reduction to nil cannot be made.[254] This view finds support in the literature.[255] Two arguments are made. First, section 1(1) of the 1945 Act provides that a claim 'shall not be defeated' by reason of contributory negligence.[256] However, considering that the purpose of the 1945 Act was to abolish the common law rule that contributory negligence was a complete defence, the quoted phrase may refer to an automatic defeat of the claim in every case, not to an exceptional defeat of the claim as a result of comparing the claimant's conduct with the defendant's conduct.

Secondly, a finding of 100 percent contributory negligence means that the claimant alone is responsible for the loss, which then is not 'the result' partly of the defendant's fault as required by section 1(1) of the 1945 Act.[257] This is in principle a sound argument, and post-wrong conduct of the claimant will

---

[251] *Lunt v Khelifa* [2002] EWCA Civ 801; *Eagle v Chambers* [2003] EWCA Civ 1107, [2004] RTR 9; *Smith v Chief Constable of Nottinghamshire* [2012] EWCA Civ 161, [2012] RTR 23; *Jackson v Murray* [2015] UKSC 5, 2015 SC (UKSC) 105 [40]–[41].

[252] An empirical study has found that the most popular discounts are fractions used in everyday life, ie, one half, one third, and one quarter: James Goudkamp and Donal Nolan, 'Contributory Negligence in the Twenty-First Century: An Empirical Study of First Instance Decisions' (2016) 79 MLR 575, 599.

[253] eg, *McMullen v National Coal Board* [1982] ICR 148; *Jayes v IMI (Kynoch) Ltd* [1985] ICR 155. The possibility of a reduction to nil was also recognised in obiter dicta in *Imperial Chemical Industries Ltd v Shatwell* [1965] AC 656, 672 (Lord Reid).

[254] *Pitts v Hunt* [1991] 1 QB 24, 48, 51; *Anderson v Newham College of Further Education* [2002] EWCA Civ 505, [2003] ICR 212 [14]–[19]; *Buyukardicli v Hammerson UK Properties plc* [2002] EWCA Civ 683 [7].

[255] eg, James Goudkamp, 'Rethinking Contributory Negligence' in Stephen GA Pitel, Jason W Neyers and Erika Chamberlain (eds), *Tort Law: Challenging Orthodoxy* (Hart 2013) 319, 344–46; Andrew Tettenborn (ed), *Clerk & Lindsell on Torts* (24th edn, Sweet & Maxwell 2023) [26-117]; Paula Giliker, *Tort* (8th edn, Sweet & Maxwell 2023) [16-020].

[256] *Pitts v Hunt* [1991] 1 QB 24, 48 (Beldam LJ); *Anderson v Newham College of Further Education* [2002] EWCA Civ 505, [2003] ICR 212 [14]; *Buyukardicli v Hammerson UK Properties plc* [2002] EWCA Civ 683 [7].

[257] *Pitts v Hunt* [1991] 1 QB 24, 51 (Balcombe LJ); *Anderson v Newham College of Further Education* [2002] EWCA Civ 505, [2003] ICR 212 [19]. See also the authors cited in fn 255.

be regarded as a *novus actus interveniens* where it obliterates the defendant's wrong, as discussed in Chapter 3. However, none of the judges or commentators opposing a reduction to nil has explained which precise legal doctrine can completely exonerate the defendant where the claimant's unreasonable conduct occurred before the defendant's wrong and thus cannot constitute an intervening act. Loss resulting from unreasonable conduct of the claimant may not necessarily be unforeseeable or fall outside the risk that the duty breached by the defendant aims to prevent. Interestingly, statutes in several Australian jurisdictions expressly permit a reduction to nil in certain circumstances,[258] even though in the same circumstances, the same statutes also permit a denial of the defendant's responsibility for the claimant's loss by reference to policy considerations,[259] which should include the claimant's contribution to the loss.[260]

258 eg, Civil Liability Act 2002 (NSW), s 5S.

259 eg, Civil Liability Act 2002 (NSW), s 5D(1), (4).

260 Barbara McDonald, 'The Impact of the Civil Liability Legislation on Fundamental Policies and Principles of the Common Law of Negligence' (2006) 14 Torts LJ 268, 294.

6. Compensation in equity

INTRODUCTION

Common law damages are not available for purely equitable wrongs such as breach of trust or breach of fiduciary duty. Trustees are required to account for their management of the trust fund, and this exercise may be said to contain a compensatory element.[1] Otherwise, a compensatory remedy used to be unavailable for equitable wrongs,[2] but it exists today.

The availability of a compensatory remedy for breach of fiduciary duty was recognised in *Nocton v Lord Ashburton*.[3] Nocton was the solicitor of Lord Ashburton, and the solicitor and business partner of Baring, Lord Ashburton's brother. Baring lent money to the developers of certain property and, acting upon Nocton's advice, Lord Ashburton also lent money to those developers. Both loans were secured by a mortgage over the property to be developed, Lord Ashburton's mortgage having priority over Baring's. Acting upon Nocton's advice, Lord Ashburton released the most valuable part of the property from his mortgage, with the effect that Baring's mortgage, in which Nocton had an interest, became the first charge on that land. When the developers became insolvent, Lord Ashburton claimed compensation for his loss from Nocton. The House of Lords upheld an order of compensation on the ground that Nocton had breached his fiduciary duty towards Lord Ashburton.

Compensatory awards in equity's inherent jurisdiction have since proliferated. The availability of the remedy is recognised for breach of trust,[4] breach of fiduciary duty,[5] dishonest assistance of a breach of trust or breach of fiduciary

---

[1] The accounting principles are outlined later in this chapter.

[2] See *Ex parte Adamson* (1878) 8 Ch D 807, 819.

[3] [1914] AC 932. For a detailed discussion of the case, see James Edelman, 'Nocton v Lord Ashburton (1914)' in Charles Mitchell and Paul Mitchell (eds), *Landmark Cases in Equity* (Hart 2012) 473.

[4] *Target Holdings Ltd v Redferns* [1996] AC 421; *AIB Group (UK) plc v Mark Redler & Co Solicitors* [2014] UKSC 58, [2015] AC 1503. These cases are discussed in this chapter.

[5] *Swindle v Harrison* [1997] 4 All ER 705; *Cia de Seguros Imperio v Heath (REBX) Ltd* [2001] 1 WLR 112; *Gwembe Valley Development Co Ltd v Koshy*

duty,[6] breach of an equitable duty of care,[7] and breach of confidence.[8] The remedy is usually labelled 'equitable compensation'. It has sometimes been labelled 'equitable damages'.[9] We will avoid this term as it might create confusion with damages under Lord Cairns' Act, which are mainly for common law wrongs and are discussed in Chapter 7.

However, the label 'equitable compensation' is used in different contexts with different meanings. It is 'a more flexible concept than common law damages',[10] a 'category of concealed multiple reference',[11] and 'a wide concept capable of more than one application'.[12] The remedy may not always be concerned with the compensation of loss. A particular controversy in that respect exists in relation to the unauthorised disbursement of trust property, which will be discussed in this chapter. Furthermore, the personal remedy relating to a benefit received by a fiduciary in breach of his duty of loyalty to the principal (discussed in Chapter 9) has been described as 'equitable compensation'.[13]

[2003] EWCA Civ 1048, [2004] 1 BCLC 131.

6 *Grupo Torras SA v Al-Sabah* [2001] Lloyd's Rep Bank 36 [123]; *Hurstanger Ltd v Wilson* [2007] EWCA Civ 299, [2007] 1 WLR 2351 [48]; *Hotel Portfolio II UK Ltd v Ruhan* [2023] EWCA Civ 1120, [2024] 2 All ER 903 [71].

7 *Bristol and West Building Society v Mothew* [1998] Ch 1, 17. The principle enunciated in that case is discussed in this chapter.

8 *Force India Formula One Team Ltd v 1 Malaysia Racing Team SDN BHD* [2012] EWHC 616 (Ch), [2012] RPC 29 [393]; *PJSC Uralkali v Rowley* [2020] EWHC 3442 (Ch) [538]; *Ensign House Ltd v Ensign House (FEC) Ltd* [2023] EWHC 1563 (Ch) [798]. The label 'damages' is often used; see, eg, *MVF 3 APS v Bestnet Europe Ltd* [2016] EWCA Civ 541, [2017] FSR 5.

9 eg, *ABCI v Banque Franco-Tunisienne* [2003] EWCA Civ 205, [2003] 2 Lloyd's Rep 146 [16]–[17]; *P & O Nedlloyd BV v Arab Metals Co (No 2)* [2006] EWCA Civ 1717, [2007] 1 WLR 2288 [39]; *Gresport Finance Ltd v Battaglia* [2018] EWCA Civ 540 [25]. For arguments in support of this label, see The Honourable Justice Edelman, 'Equitable Damages' in Ben McFarlane and Steven Elliott (eds), *Equity Today: 150 Years After the Judicature Reforms* (Hart 2023) 147.

10 *Sinclair Investments (UK) Ltd v Versailles Trade Finance Ltd* [2011] EWCA Civ 347, [2012] Ch 453 [47] (Lord Neuberger MR speaking for the Court).

11 JD Heydon, MJ Leeming and PG Turner, *Meagher, Gummow and Lehane's Equity: Doctrines and Remedies* (5th edn, LexisNexis 2015) [23-015].

12 *Auden McKenzie (Pharma Division) Ltd v Patel* [2019] EWCA Civ 2291, [2020] BCC 316 [30] (David Richards LJ). The case is discussed in this chapter.

13 *FHR European Ventures LLP v Cedar Capital Partners LLC* [2014] UKSC 45, [2015] AC 250 [7]–[8] (Lord Neuberger speaking for the Court).

This labelling is confusing as the principal's personal accounting remedy is concerned with the reversal of a gain and not the compensation of loss.[14]

Where equitable compensation is concerned with the compensation of loss, three things should be noted. First, the date at which loss is assessed is generally the date of the judgment.[15] Secondly, where the breach of duty has caused physical damage to property and the cost of repair exceeds diminution in value,[16] it has been said that equity should follow the law and deny a cost-of-cure award where it is out of all proportion to the benefit of repair or where there is no prospect of repair in fact being undertaken.[17]

Finally, non-pecuniary loss is not generally compensated in equity.[18] However, where a breach of confidence affects the claimant's personal or private interests, equitable compensation may be awarded for distress and disappointment.[19] Turner has criticised this development as an undisciplined exercise of discretion that may in consequence lead to awards of aggravated and exemplary damages in equity; if harm to purely personal interests as a result of a breach of confidence is to be compensated at all, that should be achieved by establishing a statutory liability.[20] By contrast, Khun has argued that the jurisdictional basis for ordering equitable compensation to remedy a breach of confidence causing emotional distress (but no pecuniary loss) is the same as in commercial contexts: the compensation remedies the departure from the standards of conduct mandated by equity.[21] On principle, there is no

---

[14] *Aquila Advisory Ltd v Faichney* [2021] UKSC 49, [2021] 1 WLR 5666 [48].

[15] *Target Holdings Ltd v Redferns* [1996] AC 421, 438–39; *AIB Group (UK) plc v Mark Redler & Co Solicitors* [2014] UKSC 58, [2015] AC 1503 [135].

[16] The difference between those measures is explained in Ch 2.

[17] *Brudenell-Bruce v Moore* [2014] EWHC 3679 (Ch), [2015] WTLR 373 [146]–[151]. For criticism, see Paul S Davies, 'Compensatory Remedies for Breach of Trust' in Richard C Nolan, Kelvin FK Low and Tang Hang Wu (eds), *Trusts and Modern Wealth Management* (CUP 2018) 327.

[18] For an exception, see *M(K) v M(H)* [1992] 3 SCR 6 (breach of fiduciary duty involving child sexual abuse).

[19] *Cornelius v De Taranto* [2001] EMLR 329 [66]–[69]; *Archer v Williams* [2003] EWHC 1670 (QB), [2003] EMLR 869; *McKennitt v Ash* [2005] EWHC 3003 (QB), [2006] EMLR 178.

[20] PG Turner, 'Rudiments of the Equitable Remedy of Compensation for Breach of Confidence' in Simone Degeling and Jason NE Varuhas (eds), *Equitable Compensation and Disgorgement of Profit* (Hart 2017) 270–73. See also PG Turner, 'Privacy Remedies Viewed Through an Equitable Lens' in Jason NE Varuhas and NA Moreham (eds), *Remedies for Breach of Privacy* (Hart 2018) 272–74.

[21] William Khun, 'Equity's Wergeld: Monetary Remedies for Emotional Distress by way of the Equitable Obligation of Confidence' (2020) 42 Syd LR 181.

reason why significant non-pecuniary loss resulting from an equitable wrong should not be compensated.[22]

UNAUTHORISED DISBURSEMENT OF TRUST PROPERTY

A trustee's power to disburse trust property is often subject to conditions. A trustee who makes an unauthorised disbursement must reconstitute the trust fund.[23] Sometimes, the trust fund would have been diminished even if the trustee had disbursed the asset in an authorised manner. Whether this fact affects the trustee's obligation to reconstitute the trust fund has been the subject of several cases and a lot of commentary. At the heart of the debate is the question of whether the trustee's obligation to reconstitute the trust fund is a primary obligation and thus independent of what would have happened if the duty had not been breached, or whether it is an obligation to compensate for the loss suffered by the trust fund and thus subject to a causal inquiry.

The discussion starts with a brief outline of the trust accounting principles and then moves to a consideration of modern cases and their evaluation by commentators.

Trust Accounting Principles

Trustees need to account for their management of the trust fund.[24] There is a distinction between an account of administration in common form and an account on the basis of 'wilful default', and between falsification and surcharge.[25]

---

22 Andrew Burrows, *Remedies for Torts, Breach of Contract, and Equitable Wrongs* (4th edn, OUP 2019) 512; Sirko Harder, *Measuring Damages in the Law of Obligations: The Search for Harmonised Principles* (Hart 2010) 125.

23 Section 61 of the Trustee Act 1925 gives the court the power to relieve a trustee wholly or partly from personal liability for breach of trust where the trustee acted honestly and reasonably and ought fairly to be excused for the breach of trust. It is for the trustee to satisfy the court that he acted honestly and reasonably: *Santander UK Plc v RA Legal Solicitors* [2014] EWCA Civ 183, [2014] PNLR 20 [20], [106].

24 The two forms of accounts discussed here must be distinguished from an account of profits, which is a gain-based remedy for various equitable wrongs and is discussed in Ch 9.

25 For an outline of the principles set out in the next two paragraphs, see *Ultraframe (UK) Ltd v Fielding* [2005] EWHC 1638 (Ch), [2006] FSR 17 [1513]; *Libertarian Investments Ltd v Hall* [2013] HKCFA 93, [2014] 1 HKC 368 [168]–[172]. For the historical development of the accounting principles, see Joshua Getzler, 'Fiduciary Principles in English Common Law' in Evan J Criddle, Paul B

An account of administration in common form is only concerned with assets that the trustee has actually received. The beneficiary may request a common account without the need to allege any wrongdoing on the trustee's part. If the account shows that the trustee has made an unauthorised disbursement, the beneficiary has a choice. The beneficiary may adopt the disbursement, and the asset received in the transaction will remain a trust asset; the beneficiary will do this where the transaction was profitable for the trust fund. Alternatively, the beneficiary may falsify the disbursement. The trustee is then required to return the asset *in specie* or, where this is not possible, to pay its present value into the trust fund.[26]

Where the beneficiary complains that the trustee, in breach of duty, failed to obtain an asset for the trust, the beneficiary can 'surcharge' the account by asking for it to be taken on the basis of 'wilful default'. The beneficiary needs to establish a breach of duty on the trustee's part, but conscious wrongdoing is not required. If this is successful, the trustee will be obliged to make good the deficiency of the trust fund by the payment of money. The amount of the surcharge is the difference between what the trustee has obtained (if anything) and what the trustee acting with due care and diligence would have obtained (or possibly the highest intermediate value of what the trustee would have obtained). A causal inquiry is conceptually required. The remedy may therefore be described as compensation for loss.

In the case of the unauthorised disbursement of a trust asset, a causal inquiry is not conceptually required. Where the beneficiary falsifies the transaction, the trustee could be required to pay the present value of the asset into the trust fund regardless of how the trust fund would have developed without the trustee's breach. This was indeed equity's traditional approach in all cases of unauthorised disbursement, as exemplified by *White v Baugh*.[27] A receiver, in breach of trust, gave a third party the right to veto any withdrawals by the receiver from a bank account holding trust money. When the bank went bankrupt, the receiver was held liable to restore to the trust the money held in the bank account, even though it had been proper for the receiver to place the trust money with that bank and even though the money would still have been lost without the third party's veto right. Lord Lyndhurst observed: 'The Court

---

Miller and Robert H Sitkoff (eds), *The Oxford Handbook of Fiduciary Law* (OUP 2019) 471.

[26] For the question of whether the trustee can be ordered to pay the highest value of the lost asset between the date of the wrong and the date of the judgment, see Jamie Glister, 'Breach of Trust and Conversion in a Falling Market' [2014] LMCLQ 511, 529–34.

[27] (1835) 3 Cl & F 44; 6 ER 1354. See also *Salway v Salway* (1831) 2 Russ & M 215, 39 ER 376; *Magnus v Queensland National Bank* (1888) 37 Ch D 466.

says, "You cannot be relieved from your liability unless your conduct has been strictly regular, whether the loss has been occasioned by the irregularity of your conduct or not.'"[28]

The Change to a Compensatory Remedy Requiring a Causal Inquiry

It is no longer the case that a trustee who has disbursed a trust asset in breach of trust must always pay the present value of the asset into the trust fund regardless of what would have happened without the breach. In two modern cases, the beneficiary's remedy for an unauthorised disbursement was described as equitable compensation, and its object was described as the compensation of loss caused by the trustee's breach. However, the new approach may not apply in every case of an unauthorised disbursement. It is necessary to look at the modern cases in detail.

A causal inquiry was first undertaken in *Target Holdings Ltd v Redferns*.[29] A firm of solicitors (Redferns) acted for a prospective purchaser of land (Crowngate) and also for the prospective mortgagee (Target). Target gave Redferns about £1,525,000 to be held on bare trust and be transferred to Crowngate once the property had been purchased and charged to Target. In breach of trust, Redferns paid away £1,490,000 before Crowngate purchased the property. One month later, the property was charged to Target. Subsequently, Crowngate became insolvent, and Target sold the property for £500,000.

Target sued Redferns for about £1m, being the difference between the amount paid away in breach of trust and the amount realised on the sale of the property. Target argued that as soon as Redferns had paid out the money in breach of trust, Redferns had come under an obligation to restore it, and it was irrelevant that Target had eventually received the security required. Rejecting that argument, the House of Lords held that, at least in the case of a bare trust, a common-sense view of causation applies.[30] Lord Browne-Wilkinson, who gave the only reasoned speech, said:

> The breach of trust committed by Redferns left Target in exactly the same position as it would have been if there had been no such breach: Target advanced the same amount of money, obtained the same security and received the same amount on the realisation of that security.[31]

28 (1835) 3 Cl & F 44, 66; 6 ER 1354, 1362.
29 [1996] AC 421.
30 ibid 438–39.
31 ibid 431.

In the wake of *Target Holdings*, some scholars have suggested a distinction between 'reparative compensation' and 'substitutive compensation'. Reparative compensation compensates for loss caused by a breach of trust and is comparable to compensatory damages at common law. Substitutive compensation concerns the value of a trust asset dissipated without authority and is comparable to the specific performance of a contract; concepts concerned with the attribution of loss to a wrongdoer apply to reparative compensation but not to substitutive compensation.[32] The new terminology has been used in some cases,[33] but has also been criticised as confusing the matter.[34]

The UK Supreme Court confirmed the *Target Holdings* approach in *AIB Group (UK) plc v Mark Redler & Co Solicitors*.[35] Borrowers sought to remortgage their property, then valued at £4.25m. The claimant bank advanced £3.3m to the defendant solicitors, who were to first fully discharge the existing mortgage for around £1.5m (held by Barclays), release the remaining sum to the borrowers, and secure a first legal charge over the property in favour of the claimant. Through a combination of a misunderstanding and negligence on their part, the solicitors paid Barclays only around £1.2m (a little under £300,000 less than required to discharge the mortgage) and released the rest of the money to the borrowers. When the error was discovered, Barclays permitted the claimant's charge to be registered as a second charge. The borrowers defaulted and went bankrupt. The value of the property had fallen drastically, and it was sold for £1.2m. Barclays had priority and took the amount still owing to it under the undischarged mortgage (£273,777.42 plus interest), and so the claimant only obtained £867,697.

The claimant sued the defendants for breach of contract, negligence, and breach of trust. For the former two causes of action, the compensation was limited to the loss of £273,777.42 plus interest. However, for breach of trust, the claimant claimed compensation in the full amount of the loan less the amount recovered by it (around £2.5m), arguing that the defendants had had

---

[32] Steven B Elliott, 'Remoteness Criteria in Equity' (2002) 65 Mod LR 588, 590; Steven B Elliott and Charles Mitchell, 'Remedies for Dishonest Assistance' (2004) 67 Mod LR 16, 23–34; James Edelman and Steven B Elliott, 'Money Remedies against Trustees' (2004) 18 TLI 116, 116–25. See also Paul Matthews et al, *Underhill and Hayton: Law Relating to Trusts and Trustees* (20th edn, LexisNexis 2022) [91.11], distinguishing 'substitutive performance claims' and 'reparation claims'.

[33] eg, *Interactive Technology Corp Ltd v Ferster* [2018] EWCA Civ 1594, [2021] WTLR 561 [16]–[20]; *Davies v Ford* [2023] EWCA Civ 167 [125]–[127].

[34] Matthew Conaglen, 'Equitable Compensation for Breach of Trust: Off *Target*' (2016) 40 MULR 126, 151.

[35] [2014] UKSC 58, [2015] AC 1503.

no authority to release any money to the borrowers unless and until they had a redemption statement from Barclays. Applying *Target Holdings*, the Supreme Court held that the claimant was entitled to only £273,777.42 plus interest because even if the defendants had discharged Barclays' mortgage, the claimant would still have suffered loss due to the fall in the value of the property. Only Lord Toulson JSC and Lord Reed JSC gave reasoned speeches.

Lord Toulson JSC noted that *Target Holdings* had been criticised by scholars for confusing substitutive compensation and reparative compensation.[36] Nevertheless, he refused 'to impose or maintain a rule that gives redress to a beneficiary for loss which would have been suffered if the trustee had properly performed its duties'.[37] He said that 'a monetary award which reflected neither loss caused nor profit gained by the wrongdoer would be penal'.[38] The trust in this case was effectively part of a contractual machinery where the role of the trustee was closely defined and limited, and accordingly, it was appropriate that the rules applied should be analogous to contract.[39] He added that this principle applies not only to bare trusts as an incident of a commercial transaction but also to traditional trusts.[40]

Lord Reed JSC reviewed cases from various common law jurisdictions and concluded that 'the model of equitable compensation, where trust property has been misapplied, is to require the trustee to restore the trust fund to the position it would have been in if the trustee had performed his obligation'.[41] He added that the measure of equitable compensation for breach of trust is not the same as the measure of damages for tort or breach of contract since the obligations breached are of a different nature.[42] However, different rules can be justified only insofar as the obligations breached do differ in nature, and not merely because of the historical origin of the relevant rules.[43]

In light of the statements of principle in *Target Holdings* and *AIB Group*, one would expect a causal inquiry to have been undertaken in every subsequent case involving an unauthorised disbursement of trust property. However, the Court of Appeal took the traditional approach in *Main v Giambrone & Law (a firm)*.[44] Investors in a property development in Italy paid deposits to

---

36 ibid [56].
37 ibid [62].
38 ibid [64].
39 ibid [70]. See also Katy Barnett, 'Equitable Compensation and Remoteness: Not So Remote from the Common Law After All' (2014) 38 UWALR 48, 73–78.
40 [2014] UKSC 58, [2015] AC 1503 [70].
41 ibid [134].
42 ibid [136]–[137].
43 ibid [138].
44 [2017] EWCA Civ 1193, [2018] PNLR 2.

a firm of solicitors who practised in England and Italy. The solicitors were to hold the deposits on trust until the property developer provided a guarantee as required by Italian law. Even though only wholly inadequate guarantees were received, the solicitors, in breach of trust, paid the deposits to the property developer. The development was not completed, and the purchasers lost their money. The purchasers sued for the amount of their deposits. It was common ground that the purchasers would have lost their deposits even if guarantees compliant with Italian law had been obtained because such guarantees would not have covered the events leading to the failure of the property development. Thus, the causal inquiry required by *Target Holdings* and *AIB Group* would have led to a denial of an award. But the Court of Appeal awarded the amount of the deposits. It distinguished *Target Holdings* and *AIB Group* on the basis that the solicitors in those cases were required to take positive steps to obtain a particular security, whereas the solicitors in the instant case were under no such duty; their duty was to keep the deposits until the developer produced appropriate guarantees.[45]

It is also useful to consider *Auden McKenzie (Pharma Division) Ltd v Patel*,[46] even though it involved breach of fiduciary duty rather than breach of trust. Mr Patel caused Auden McKenzie, a company he and his sister owned and controlled at the time, to pay £13.7m against sham invoices. The company received no value for the payments. Auden McKenzie was subsequently acquired by another company and sued Mr Patel, seeking equitable compensation for breach of fiduciary duty in the amount of the payments. Mr Patel argued that if the unlawful payments had not been made, he would have caused the company to pay the same amount to him and his sister lawfully as dividends, and that the company therefore suffered no loss as a result of his breach. The trial judge ordered summary judgment against Mr Patel on the ground that he did not have a valid defence. The Court of Appeal set the judgment aside because it was not prepared to say that Mr Patel's defence was unsustainable in law. However, the Court made clear that it did not think that Mr Patel's argument would succeed. David Richards LJ, with whom Newey LJ and Lewison LJ agreed, said about *Target Holdings* and *AIB Group*:

> They are restricted to circumstances where the beneficiary obtained the full benefit for which it bargained or where, if the trustee had fully performed its obligations, the loss would have been less than the amount of the unauthorised payment made by the trustee … In the case of Mr Patel, not only were the hypothetical dividends

---

[45] ibid [60]–[62]. The same outcome on similar facts was reached in *Cocker v Quayle* (1830) 1 Russ & M 535; 39 ER 206.

[46] [2019] EWCA Civ 2291, [2020] BCC 316.

not paid but there was no obligation on the company or its directors to pay any such dividends.[47]

The outcome in *Giambrone* cannot be reconciled with the reasoning employed in *Target Holdings* and *AIB Group*; nor can the outcome in *Auden McKenzie* if it is assumed that the principle laid down in *Target Holdings* and *AIB Group* for breach of trust extends to breach of fiduciary duty. The principle continues to attract criticism,[48] and it is difficult to predict what the English courts will do next in this area.[49] Furthermore, some commentators have argued that the outcomes in *Target Holdings* and *AIB Group* could have been reached through the traditional accounting process.

Lord Millett has argued extra-judicially that the outcome in *Target Holdings* could have been reached under the traditional accounting principles by regarding the eventual acquisition of the mortgage as 'an authorised application of what must be treated as trust money notionally restored to the trust estate'.[50] However, a similar argument by the claimant in *AIB Group* was rejected by Lord Toulson JSC as involving 'fairy tales'.[51] Edelman J, writing extrajudicially, also opposes Lord Millett's analysis but comes to the same outcome reached in *Target Holdings* by arguing that Target evinced an election not to insist on a reconstitution of the trust fund because it held the mortgage as security for more than two years.[52] Penner argues that the claimant in *AIB*

---

47 ibid [49].

48 eg, James Edelman, 'An English Misturning with Equitable Compensation' in Simone Degeling and Jason NE Varuhas (eds), *Equitable Compensation and Disgorgement of Profits* (Hart 2017) 91; James Penner, 'The Beneficiary's Performance Interest in a Trust: *AIB v. Redler* and the March of the Compensatory Principle' in Richard C Nolan, Kelvin FK Low and Tang Hang Wu (eds), *Trusts and Modern Wealth Management* (CUP 2018) 277; Nicholas A Tiverios and Clare McKay, 'Orthodoxy Lost: The (Ir)relevance of Causation in Quantifying Breach of Trust Claims' (2016) 90 Aust LJ 231.

49 Paul Matthews et al, *Underhill and Hayton: Law Relating to Trusts and Trustees* (20th edn, LexisNexis 2022) [91.46].

50 PJ Millett, 'Equity's Place in the Law of Commerce' (1998) 114 LQR 214, 227. Supported by Matthew Conaglen, 'Explaining *Target Holdings v Redferns*' (2010) 4 J Eq 288; Graham Virgo, *The Principles of Equity and Trusts* (5th edn, OUP 2023) 570–71.

51 [2014] UKSC 58, [2015] AC 1503 [69].

52 James Edelman, 'Money Awards of the Cost of Performance' (2010) 4 J Eq 122, 128–30. See also The Honourable Justice Edelman, 'Equitable Damages' in Ben McFarlane and Steven Elliott (eds), *Equity Today: 150 Years After the Judicature Reforms* (Hart 2023) 147, arguing that the outcome in *AIB Group* should have been different if a claim for a common law debt had been made.

Group, by negotiating with Barclays in order to acquire a second charge over the property, adopted the defendants' payment to Barclays as a disbursement on the claimant's behalf.[53]

Ho and Nolan explain the modern cases by reference to the distinction between a trustee's duties and a trustee's discretionary powers.[54] Trustees should not be allowed to assert that they would have used their discretionary powers in a particular way and thereby caused loss to the trust, as this would invite self-serving evidence. But trustees should be allowed to point to their duties to delineate the scope of their liability. The solicitors in *AIB Group* had a duty, and not just a power, to obtain a first charge over the property. They did not obtain a first charge, but they did obtain a second charge. Therefore, the loss to the trust fund was the difference between the hypothetical realisation of a first charge and the actual realisation of the second charge, which was £300,000.[55] Ho and Nolan see a difference between *Target Holdings* and *AIB Group* on the one hand and *Giambrone* on the other in that the fund was partially or wholly restored in the first two cases but not in the last as adequate guarantees were never obtained.[56]

The distinction between duty and power drawn by Ho and Nolan can also explain the outcome in *Auden McKenzie*, as the company had no duty (but only a power) to pay dividends.[57] However, the distinction may not always be easy to draw in practice,[58] and it is not in line with the concern of preventing self-serving testimony. Ho and Nolan are right to say that trustees should not be allowed to diminish their liability for the unauthorised disbursement of trust property by pointing to some random investment which they would have had the power to make with that property and which would have led to a bad outcome for the trust fund. But such an argument was not open to the solicitors in *Giambrone*. They had the power to release the deposits only against particular guarantees; they had no power to do anything else with the deposits.

---

[53] James Penner, 'Falsifying the Trust Account and Compensatory Equitable Compensation' in Simone Degeling and Jason NE Varuhas (eds), *Equitable Compensation and Disgorgement of Profits* (Hart 2017) 145.

[54] Lusina Ho and Richard C Nolan, 'The Performance Interest in the Law of Trusts' (2020) 136 LQR 402, 414. For a similar suggestion of focussing on all of the trustee's obligations, see Sarah Worthington, 'Four Questions on Fiduciaries' (2016) 2 CJCCL 723, 760–63.

[55] Lusina Ho and Richard C Nolan, 'The Performance Interest in the Law of Trusts' (2020) 136 LQR 402, 415.

[56] ibid 416.

[57] Jamie Glister and James Lee, *Hanbury and Martin: Modern Equity* (23rd edn, Sweet & Maxwell 2024) [24-013].

[58] ibid [24-012].

It may be true that the outcome in *Giambrone* is unavoidable if traditional accounting principles are applied, as adequate guarantees were not obtained and the trust fund was thus not reconstituted. But it is difficult to see why a beneficiary should be able to invoke the traditional accounting principles to be placed in a better position than without the trustee's breach. Those principles should be absorbed within the concept of equitable compensation understood as the compensation of loss factually caused by the breach of trust.[59] However, the trustee, who is in possession of the relevant information, ought to bear the burden of proving the lack of a connection between the breach and the loss.[60]

The Scope of Liability

Considering that the liability of a trustee for the unauthorised disbursement of trust property is now regarded as the compensation of loss (at least in some circumstances), the question arises whether the trustee is liable for all loss factually caused by the breach or whether there are principles limiting the scope of the trustee's liability (beyond the principle discussed in the previous section). Since the conceptualisation of the trustee's liability as compensation for loss is relatively recent, principles limiting the scope of liability have rarely been considered. Lord Reed JSC in *AIB Group* made the following observations on this issue:

> The foreseeability of loss is generally irrelevant, but the loss must be caused by the breach of trust, in the sense that it must flow directly from it. Losses resulting from unreasonable behaviour on the part of the claimant will be adjudged to flow from that behaviour, and not from the breach. The requirement that the loss should flow directly from the breach is also the key to determining whether causation has been interrupted by the acts of third parties.[61]

Thus, while the foreseeability of loss is irrelevant, loss resulting from particular conduct of the claimant or a third party will be outside the scope of the trustee's liability. If Lord Reed JSC meant to suggest that every unreasonable action of the claimant breaks the chain of causation, then this would be a more stringent rule than the one applied at common law where the claimant's

---

[59] See Andrew Burrows, *Remedies for Torts, Breach of Contract, and Equitable Wrongs* (4th edn, OUP 2019) 516–17; Sarah Worthington, 'Four Questions on Fiduciaries' (2016) 2 CJCCL 723, 760–63.

[60] Lusina Ho, 'An Account of Accounts' (2016) 28 SAcLJ 849, 872. Turner speaks of a defence of want of causation: PG Turner, 'Want of Causation as a Defence to Liability for Misapplication of Trust Assets' in Paul S Davies, Simon Douglas, and James Goudkamp (eds), *Defences in Equity* (Hart 2018) 155.

[61] [2014] UKSC 58, [2015] AC 1503 [135].

conduct must reach a particularly high threshold of unreasonableness to have this effect.[62] With regard to the conduct of third parties, Lord Reed JSC approved two cases,[63] and it is useful to consider those cases.

In *Caffrey v Darby*,[64] a property (a pub) was placed with trustees with the instruction that one Peter Priest should be entitled to have possession of the property as long as he paid into the trust £100 per year and £800 in total. The trustees gave possession of the property to Priest, who paid only £250 into the trust in eight years and then went bankrupt. In a dispute between the trustees and the assignee of Priest's bankrupt estate over the rights to the property, the court wrongly decided that the trustees had no right to the property. The property was sold, but the trustees received nothing of the proceeds. In the beneficiaries' claim against the trustees, the latter argued that the cause of the loss was the incorrect judgment. However, Lord Eldon MR held that the trustees were liable because the loss would not have occurred if the trustees had enforced Priest's liability to pay £100 per year as soon as he was in arrears; they could not rely on subsequent events.[65]

In *Canson Enterprises Ltd v Boughton & Co*,[66] the defendant solicitor acted for the plaintiffs in the purchase of land for development. In breach of his fiduciary duty towards the plaintiffs, the defendant failed to disclose to them that an intermediate company (in which he had an interest) had bought the land and resold it to the plaintiffs at a substantially higher price. They proceeded with the development of the land but suffered substantial losses when piles supporting a constructed warehouse began to sink. The plaintiffs obtained judgment against the soil engineers and pile-driving company they had retained, but these defendants were insolvent. The plaintiffs then sued the solicitor for breach of fiduciary duty, alleging that they would not have purchased the land had they known about the involvement of the intermediate company. The Supreme Court of Canada denied compensation for the loss resulting from the negligence of the soil engineers and pile-driving company, on the ground that this negligence constituted an intervening act.

Commenting on *Canson Enterprises*, Lord Reed JSC in *AIB Group* observed that the wrongful conduct of the third parties occurred after the plaintiffs had taken control of the property and was unrelated to the defendant's earlier breach of fiduciary duty.[67] However, the difference between the two cases can be explained better by reference to the purpose of the duty breached. The duty

---

62 See Ch 3.
63 [2014] UKSC 58, [2015] AC 1503 [135].
64 (1801) 6 Ves 488; 31 ER 1159.
65 (1801) 6 Ves 478, 496; 31 ER 1159, 1162.
66 [1991] 3 SCR 534.
67 [2014] UKSC 58, [2015] AC 1503 [135].

to collect debts without delay aims to protect the creditor from the debtor's insolvency, and it may be said that this includes protection from disputes with the assignee in bankruptcy. By contrast, a fiduciary's duty to disclose a personal interest in a transaction to be entered into by the principal does not aim to protect the principal from all of the consequences of that transaction.

BREACH OF FIDUCIARY DUTY

Hypothetical Consent by the Principal

Equitable compensation for breach of fiduciary duty is concerned with the compensation of loss. A requirement of factual causation applies; 'a court of equity will apply a "but for" test of causation, thus precluding recovery for loss that would have occurred even if the breach of duty had not taken place'.[68] The loss is identified by comparing the principal's actual financial position (the real world) with the financial position the principal would have been in without the fiduciary's breach (the hypothetical world).

Since the principal may always authorise what would otherwise be a breach of fiduciary duty,[69] there are two ways in which the hypothetical world can be constructed. It could be a world in which the fiduciary did not engage in the impugned activity, or it could be a world in which the fiduciary disclosed the conflict of duty and interest (or duty and duty) to the principal.[70] If the latter, it must be determined whether the principal would have given consent, and it must be decided who bears the onus of proof in that respect.

Two questions must be clearly distinguished. One is whether the principal, in order to establish liability, may rely on a hypothetical world in which the fiduciary disclosed material information to the principal, who would have taken a financially beneficial action using that information. This is not permitted. The fiduciary is not liable for loss that the principal would still have suffered even if the fiduciary had not engaged in the disloyal conduct.[71]

The other question is whether the fiduciary, in order to exclude liability, can rely on a hypothetical world in which he disclosed his conflict to the principal and the principal would have authorised the fiduciary's conduct. A decision

[68] *Novoship (UK) Ltd v Mikhaylyuk* [2014] EWCA Civ 908, [2015] QB 499 [105] (Longmore LJ speaking for the court).

[69] eg, *Queensland Mines Ltd v Hudson* (1978) 18 ALR 1 (PC); *Bristol and West Building Society v Mothew* [1998] Ch 1, 18. For company directors, see Companies Act 2006, ss 175(4)(b), (5), (6), 180.

[70] Matthew Conaglen, '*Brickenden*' in Simone Degeling and Jason NE Varuhas (eds), *Equitable Compensation and Disgorgement of Profits* (Hart 2017) 130.

[71] See *Aston Risk Management Ltd v Jones* [2024] EWHC 252 (Ch) [78].

that has caused some confusion and controversy in this area is that of the Privy Council in the Canadian case *Brickenden v London Loan & Savings Co.*[72] A solicitor acted for both the borrower and the lender in respect of the grant of a loan secured by a mortgage on the borrower's land. The solicitor failed to inform the lender that part of the loan was to be used to repay loans which the solicitor had granted to the borrower and which were secured by mortgages on the same land. Those mortgages were worthless since there were prior mortgages exhausting the value of the land. The solicitor was held liable for breach of his fiduciary duty towards the lender.[73] It does not appear from the judgments in that case that the solicitor argued that the lender would still have granted the loan had it known that part of it would be paid to the solicitor.

Nevertheless, Lord Thankerton, who delivered the Privy Council's judgment, made the following observation:

> When a party, holding a fiduciary relationship, commits a breach of his duty by non-disclosure of material facts, which his constituent is entitled to know in connection with the transaction, he cannot be heard to maintain that disclosure would not have altered the decision to proceed with the transaction, because the constituent's action would be solely determined by some other factor, such as the valuation by another party of the property proposed to be mortgaged. Once the Court has determined that the non-disclosed facts were material, speculation as to what course the constituent, on disclosure, would have taken is not relevant.[74]

This statement seems to require the court to assume, without investigation, that a disclosure of facts that a fiduciary wrongfully withheld from the principal would have made a difference to the principal's conduct. In circumstances in which the fiduciary disloyally entered into a transaction affecting the principal, rather than the principal entering into a transaction as happened in *Brickenden*, the same rule would amount to an irrebuttable presumption that the principal would not have authorised the transaction had the fiduciary sought such authorisation in advance. Thus, the hypothetical world with which the actual world is compared is a world in which the fiduciary would not have engaged in the impugned conduct.[75]

However, the highest courts of Canada, New Zealand, Hong Kong and Singapore have interpreted the *Brickenden* rule as a rebuttable presumption

---

72 [1934] 3 DLR 465.

73 Even though the solicitor was ordered to pay the bank the amount he had received out of the bank's loan to the borrower, the remedy was described as 'damages' and not as an account of profits: ibid 469.

74 ibid.

75 Matthew Conaglen, '*Brickenden*' in Simone Degeling and Jason NE Varuhas (eds), *Equitable Compensation and Disgorgement of Profits* (Hart 2017) 112, 141.

of a causal link.[76] Where it is clear that the principal, if asked, would have consented to the impugned transaction, the resulting loss is identified on that basis. But uncertainty is resolved against the fiduciary, who must thus establish the principal's hypothetical consent. Moreover, where the principal entered into a transaction in which the fiduciary had a personal interest (which was not disclosed), it is only presumed that the principal, if informed, would not have entered into *that* transaction. The *Brickenden* rule does not preclude a finding that the principal would have entered into an alternative transaction and would have suffered a loss from it.[77]

The English courts have not adopted the Brickenden rule in either form and require the principal to prove that disclosure by the fiduciary would have made a difference.[78] The relevance of what the principal would have done on disclosure is demonstrated by *Swindle v Harrison*.[79] Mrs Harrison intended to acquire a hotel and start a restaurant business. When she desperately needed a bridging loan in order to go ahead with the purchase, the solicitors advising her on the transaction offered to lend her the money through their bank. In breach of fiduciary duty, the solicitors concealed that they were entitled to half of the arrangement fee to be paid by Mrs Harrison. She took the loan and acquired the hotel, but the restaurant business proved unsuccessful. Based on the solicitors' breach of fiduciary duty, Mrs Harrison sought equitable compensation for the loss caused by the business failure. The Court of Appeal denied her claim. Even though the three judgments delivered took different routes, the

76 *Hodgkinson v Simms* [1994] 3 SCR 377, 441–42; *Amaltal Corporation Ltd v Maruha Corporation* [2007] NZSC 40, [2007] 3 NZLR 192 [30]; *Premium Real Estate Ltd v Stevens* [2009] NZSC 15, [2009] 2 NZLR 384 [40], [85]; *IQ EQ NTC Trustees Asia (Jersey) Ltd v Arboit* [2019] HKCFA 45 [118]; *Sim Poh Ping v Winsta Holding Pte Ltd* [2020] SGCA 35, [2020] 1 SLR 1199 [240]-[248]. It has been argued that the standard of proof to be satisfied by the fiduciary is higher in New Zealand than in Canada: Jamie Glister, 'Breach of Fiduciary Duty: *Brickenden* Lives On (*Premium Real Estate v Stevens*)' (2011) 5 J Eq 59, 64–68.

77 For a review of the key cases, see Sirko Harder, 'Equitable Compensation for a Fiduciary's Non-Disclosure and Hypothetical Courses of Events' (2011) 5 J Eq 22, 31–41.

78 However, the outcome of the English cases did not generally depend upon the onus of proof: John McGhee and Steven Elliott, *Snell's Equity* (34th edn, Sweet & Maxwell 2020) [7-059].

79 [1997] 4 All ER 705. See also *Satnam Investments Ltd v Dunlop Heywood & Co Ltd* [1999] 3 All ER 652, 668; *Gwembe Valley Development Co Ltd v Koshy* [2003] EWCA Civ 1048, [2004] 1 BCLC 131 [147]; *Murad v Al-Saraj* [2005] EWCA Civ 959, [2005] WTLR 1573 [110], [120], [136]; *Bank of Ireland v Jaffery* [2012] EWHC 1377 (Ch) [354]. Cf *Bristol and West Building Society v May May & Merrimans (a firm)* [1996] 2 All ER 801, 826–27.

common key reason for denying the claim was the trial judge's finding that Mrs Harrison would still have bought the hotel had she known all material facts. Thus, the case indicates the requirement of a causal link.[80]

Evans LJ in *Swindle v Harrison* stated in obiter dicta that a fiduciary who acted fraudulently or in a manner equivalent to fraud ought to be liable irrespective of what the principal would have done on disclosure.[81] This view does not seem to have been shared by the other members of the court,[82] and David Richards LJ in *Auden McKenzie (Pharma Division) Ltd v Patel* observed: 'It does not seem to accord with principle that equitable compensation should be payable only because the defendant has acted dishonestly.'[83]

Evans LJ in *Swindle v Harrison* also observed that it was for Mrs Harrrison to prove that she would not have completed the purchase if the solicitors had disclosed their personal interest in the loan transaction.[84] There have been other cases in which it was also stated that it is for the principal to disprove hypothetical consent.[85] In different contexts, however, it has been said that it is for the fiduciary to disprove the apparent causal connection between the breach of duty and the loss.[86] In light of the prophylactic purpose of the remedies for breach of fiduciary duty (namely, to deter fiduciaries from preferring their personal interests over the interests of the principal), uncertainty as to what the principal would have done on disclosure of the material facts by the fiduciary ought to be resolved against the latter.[87]

---

80 Matthew Conaglen, '*Brickenden*' in Simone Degeling and Jason NE Varuhas (eds), *Equitable Compensation and Disgorgement of Profits* (Hart 2017) 140.

81 [1997] 4 All ER 705, 718.

82 As pointed out in *Collins v Brebner* [2000] Lloyd's Rep PN 587 [57].

83 [2019] EWCA Civ 2291, [2020] BCC 316 [63]. The otherjudges agreed with David Richards LJ.

84 [1997] 4 All ER 705, 718.

85 *Nationwide Building Society v Balmer Radmore* [1999] PNLR 606, 671–72; *Gwembe Valley Development Co Ltd v Koshy* [2002] 1 BCLC 478 [277]; *Bank of Ireland v Jaffery* [2012] EWHC 1377 (Ch) [290].

86 *Mitchell v Al Jaber* [2023] EWHC 364 (Ch) [549]; *Takhar v Gracefield Developments Ltd* [2024] EWHC 1714 (Ch) [599]. Both statements relied on *Libertarian Investments Ltd v Hall* [2013] HKCFA 93, [2014] 1 HKC 368 [93] (Ribeiro PJ).

87 Weiming Tan, 'Unpacking the Enigma of Equitable Compensation for Breaches in Equity' [2022] JBL 407, 423–24.

It should be noted that an account of profits,[88] a constructive trust[89] and rescission[90] are available in cases of breach of fiduciary duty regardless of what the principal would have done on disclosure. Some have argued that the same should apply to equitable compensation for deterrent purposes.[91] However, the difference between the remedies can be justified. Equitable compensation, unlike the other remedies mentioned, may place the fiduciary in a worse position than without breach, and this may be considered inappropriate where the fiduciary can demonstrate that the principal, if informed, would have authorised the fiduciary's conduct.[92]

The Scope of Liability

The question arises whether a disloyal fiduciary must compensate all losses factually caused by his breach or whether there are principles limiting the scope of the fiduciary's liability (beyond the principle discussed in the previous section). As mentioned earlier in this chapter, the Court of Appeal in *Auden McKenzie (Pharma Division) Ltd v Patel* expressed the view that the fiduciary's liability for a particular loss is not excluded by the fact that the fiduciary could have inflicted this loss without breaching any of his duties.[93] This differs from the position at common law where the hypothetical lawful conduct of a wrongdoer does affect the amount of recoverable loss.[94] The difference may be justifiable by the deterrent function of the remedies for breach of fiduciary duty. However, the view expressed by the Court of Appeal in *Auden McKenzie* also sits uneasily with the principle discussed in the previous section, ie, the principle that the principal's hypothetical consent exonerates the fiduciary. It is

---

88 *Gray v New Augarita Porcupine Mines Ltd* [1952] 3 DLR 1 (PC); *Rama v Millar* [1996] 1 NZLR 257, 260–61 (PC). See Ch 9.

89 *Farah Constructions Pty Ltd v Say-Dee Pty Ltd* [2007] HCA 22, (2007) 230 CLR 89 [199].

90 *Swindle v Harrison* [1997] 4 All ER 705, 726; *Gwembe Valley Development Co Ltd v Koshy* [2003] EWCA Civ 1048, (2003) All ER (D) 465 [145].

91 eg, Matthew Conaglen, '*Brickenden*' in Simone Degeling and Jason NE Varuhas (eds), *Equitable Compensation and Disgorgement of Profits* (Hart 2017) 133.

92 JD Heydon, 'Causal Relationships between a Fiduciary's Default and the Principal's Loss' (1994) 110 LQR 328, 332: 'it is one thing to strip a fiduciary of profit without much inquiry; it is another to hold him accountable for all loss without inquiry into relative causes'. For further discussion, see Sirko Harder, 'Is a Defaulting Fiduciary Exculpated by the Principal's Hypothetical Consent?' (2008) 8 OUCLJ 25, 39–41.

93 [2019] EWCA Civ 2291, [2020] BCC 316.

94 See Ch 2.

difficult to see why it should make a difference whether the fiduciary's hypothetical non-wrongful conduct involves obtaining the principal's consent or some other conduct.

Another important question is whether the principles limiting the scope of liability at common law (intervening act, remoteness, etc) apply to equitable compensation for breach of fiduciary duty. It has already been mentioned that Lord Reed JSC in *AIB Group*[95] approved the decision of the Supreme Court of Canada in *Canson Enterprises Ltd v Boughton & Co*[96] to illustrate that the conduct of third parties can break the chain of causation between a breach of trust and loss factually caused by it. *Canson Enterprises* actually involved breach of fiduciary duty, and Lord Reed JSC's approval may apply in that context too.

While the Supreme Court of Canada in *Canson Enterprises* was unanimous as to the outcome, the Court was split as to the reasons. La Forest J, who spoke for four of the eight judges, stated that equitable compensation for breach of fiduciary duty is subject to the common law concepts of remoteness of damage, mitigation, and contributory negligence.[97] McLachlin J, who spoke for three judges, rejected an application of common law principles to equitable compensation.[98] Stevenson J, while generally agreeing with La Forest J, rejected the idea of a fusion of law and equity.[99]

In *Target Holdings*,[100] Lord Browne-Wilkinson refused to choose between the different views expressed in *Canson Enterprises*, but he expressly endorsed McLachlin J's statement that equitable compensation for breach of fiduciary duty is assessed with the full benefit of hindsight after taking a common sense view of causation, although foreseeability of the loss is not required.[101] The common law concept of remoteness of loss does not apply to equitable compensation for breach of fiduciary duty.[102] Neither does the avoidable loss rule.[103] However, an obvious failure of the principal to avoid a particular loss

---

95 [2014] UKSC 58, [2015] AC 1503 [135].
96 [1991] 3 SCR 534.
97 ibid 580–89.
98 ibid 542–47.
99 ibid 590–91.
100 [1996] AC 421, 438–39.
101 [1991] 3 SCR 534, 556.
102 *Novoship (UK) Ltd v Mikhaylyuk* [2014] EWCA Civ 908, [2015] QB 499 [105].
103 The concept of remoteness of loss and the avoidable loss rule are both explained in Ch 3.

may make it unjust to hold that the fiduciary's breach caused that loss.[104] This includes the failure to withdraw the fiduciary's authority once the principal has become aware that the fiduciary cannot be trusted.[105]

Neither the common law defence of contributory negligence nor the Law Reform (Contributory Negligence) Act 1947 applies to equitable compensation for breach of fiduciary duty. This does not preclude equity from developing its own apportionment regime where the unreasonable conduct of the principal contributed to the loss. In two cases, *Day v Mead*[106] and *Mouat v Clark Boyce*,[107] the New Zealand Court of Appeal upheld a reduction of equitable compensation for breach of fiduciary duty on the ground that the principal had contributed to the loss through unreasonable conduct, which was, respectively, the failure to check the solvency of a company before investing in it and the failure to obtain independent advice before providing security for a loan taken out by a relative.[108] However, the possibility of apportioning equitable compensation for breach of fiduciary duty has been rejected by the courts in Australia[109] and England.[110]

Many commentators have argued that the possibility of apportioning equitable compensation for breach of fiduciary duty would undermine the strictness of the fiduciary's duty of loyalty and impose upon the principal a duty to

---

104 *Gray v Smith* [2022] EWHC 1153 (Ch) [415]; *Bouchier v Booth* [2023] EWHC 3195 (Ch) [264].

105 *Sphere Drake Insurance Ltd v Euro International Underwriting Ltd* [2003] EWHC 1636 (Comm), [2003] Lloyd's Rep IR 525 [97].

106 [1987] 2 NZLR 443.

107 [1992] 2 NZLR 559, rev'd on the ground that there was no liability: *Clark Boyce v Mouat* [1994] 1 AC 428 (PC).

108 In *Amaltal Corporation Ltd v Maruha Corporation* [2007] NZSC 40, [2007] 3 NZLR 192 [23] fn 17, the Supreme Court of New Zealand regarded contributory negligence as irrelevant to claims for a breach of fiduciary duty that constitutes fraud, and expressly left open the relevance of contributory negligence to any equitable claim. However, this statement was an obiter dictum made in a footnote without any discussion of the issue or reference to previous cases.

109 *Pilmer v Duke Group Ltd (in liq)* [2001] HCA 31, (2001) 207 CLR 165 [86], [171]–[172]; *Rahme v Benjamin & Khouri Pty Ltd* [2019] NSWCA 211, (2019) 100 NSWLR 550 [127]–[131].

110 *Nationwide Building Society v Balmer Radmore* [1999] PNLR 606, 676–77; *Leeds & Holbeck Building Society v Arthur & Cole* [2002] PNLR 78, 80; *De Beer v Kanaar & Co (No 2)* [2002] EWHC 688 (Ch) [92]. It has been argued that since the fiduciary in *Balmer Radmore* acted with conscious disloyalty, it is an open question whether an apportionment by virtue of contributory negligence can be made where the fiduciary acted in good faith: Paul Matthews et al, *Underhill and Hayton: Law Relating to Trusts and Trustees* (20th edn, LexisNexis 2022) [91.69].

monitor the fiduciary.[111] Other commentators regard this fear as exaggerated, pointing out that *because* the principal is entitled to trust the fiduciary, the principal's conduct would rarely be considered unreasonable so as to justify a reduction of compensation even if such reduction were available in principle.[112] Where, exceptionally, the principal's conduct was unreasonable and the court considers full compensation unjust, the absence of an apportionment regime may force the court to use less precise doctrines such as lack of clean hands[113] or *novus actus interveniens*, which may lead to a denial of any compensation.[114]

BREACH OF AN EQUITABLE DUTY OF CARE

In *Permanent Building Society (in liq) v Wheeler*,[115] the Full Court of Western Australia's Supreme Court distinguished a fiduciary's equitable duty of care from a fiduciary's duty of loyalty. Ipp J, with whom Seaman J and Malcolm CJ agreed, said that the former duty, while being actionable in equity, does not stem from the requirements of trust and confidence imposed on a fiduciary,

---

[111] eg, Donal Nolan and John Davies, 'Torts and Equitable Wrongs' in Andrew Burrows (ed), *English Private Law* (3rd edn, OUP 2013) [17.202]; Joshua Getzler, 'Am I My Beneficiary's Keeper? Fusion and Loss-Based Fiduciary Remedies' in Simone Degeling and James Edelman (eds), *Equity in Commercial Law* (LBC 2005) 271; Sarah Worthington, 'Review of *Hochelaga Lectures. Fusing Common Law and Equity: Remedies, Restitution and Reform* by Andrew Burrows' (2003) 119 LQR 519, 521.

[112] J Beatson, 'Unfinished Business: Integrating Equity' in Jack Beatson, *The Use and Abuse of Unjust Enrichment: Essays on the Law of Restitution* (Clarendon Press 1991) 256; Andrew Burrows, 'Remedial Coherence and Punitive Damages in Equity' in Simone Degeling and James Edelman (eds), *Equity in Commercial Law* (LBC 2005) 384–85; Sirko Harder, 'Contributory Negligence in Contract and Equity' (2014) 13 Otago LR 307, 319–25.

[113] Lee Aitken, 'Developments in Equitable Compensation: Opportunity or Danger?' (1993) 67 Aust LJ 596, 605.

[114] Vicki Vann, *Equitable Compensation in Australia: Principles and Problems* (VDM Verlag Dr Müller 2009) 334: the 'fear that allowing a plea of contributory negligence would relieve defendants of liability is paradoxically realised by *not* allowing such a plea'. In *Lipkin Gorman v Karpnale Ltd* [1987] 1 WLR 987, a firm whose partner had stolen money from it and gambled it away was denied any relief for loss sustained after the firm had reason to be suspicious but failed to undertake even a modest investigation.

[115] (1994) 11 WAR 187.

and is not governed by the same rules as the duty of loyalty.[116] In particular, Ipp J said that the *Brickenden* rule discussed earlier in this chapter applies only to breaches of a true fiduciary obligation, carrying with it, ordinarily, the 'stench of dishonesty'.[117] He went on to make the following statement:

> It is also significant, as regards matters of policy, that the tortious duty not to be negligent, and the equitable obligation on the part of a trustee to exercise reasonable care and skill are, in content, the same. There is every reason, in my view, in such circumstances, to apply the maxim that 'equity follows the law'.[118]

Ipp J[119] quoted the following statement made by La Forest J in *Canson Enterprises Ltd v Boughton & Co*:

> Where 'the measure of duty is the same', the same rule should apply ... it would be odd if a different result followed depending solely on the manner in which one framed an identical claim.[120]

Subsequently, in *Bristol and West Building Society v Mothew*,[121] the English Court of Appeal adopted the distinction between a fiduciary's equitable duty of care and a fiduciary's duty of loyalty, and endorsed a limitation of equitable compensation for breach of the former duty by the principles limiting the scope of liability at common law. Millett LJ, with whom Otton LJ agreed on that issue, observed:

> Although the remedy which equity makes available for breach of the equitable duty of skill and care is equitable compensation rather than damages, this is merely the product of history and in this context is in my opinion a distinction without a difference. Equitable compensation for breach of the duty of skill and care resembles common law damages in that it is awarded by way of compensation to the plaintiff for his loss. There is no reason in principle why the common law rules of causation,

---

116 ibid 237–39. This doctrine is criticised by Antony Goldfinch, 'Trustee's Duty to Exercise Reasonable Care: Fiduciary Duty?' (2004) 78 Aust LJ 678; JD Heydon, 'Are the Duties of Company Directors to Exercise Care and Skill Fiduciary?' in Simone Degeling and James Edelman (eds), *Equity in Commercial Law* (LBC 2005) 185; Weiming Tan, 'Peering Through Equity's Prism: A Fiduciary's Duty of Care or a Fiduciary Duty of Care' (2021) 15 J Eq 181.

117 (1994) 11 WAR 187, 246.

118 ibid 247–48.

119 ibid 248.

120 [1991] 3 SCR 534, 586–87. La Forest J spoke for four of the eight judges. The other four judges opposed an application of common law concepts to equitable compensation, as mentioned earlier in this chapter.

121 [1998] Ch 1.

> remoteness of damage and measure of damages should not be applied by analogy in such a case.[122]

This approach has been endorsed by the New Zealand Court of Appeal[123] and the Hong Kong Court of Final Appeal.[124] However, decisions of the Supreme Court of Canada conflict with this approach,[125] and its correctness was doubted by the High Court of Australia in *Youyang Pty Ltd v Minter Ellison Morris Fletcher*:

> [T]here must be a real question whether the unique foundation and goals of equity, which has the institution of the trust at its heart, warrant any assimilation even in this limited way with the measure of compensatory damages in tort and contract.[126]

Millett LJ's statement in *Mothew* was approvingly quoted by the English Court of Appeal in *Novoship (UK) Ltd v Mikhaylyuk*.[127] However, Lord Reed JSC in *AIB Group* observed that Millett LJ's statement 'has been questioned, or given a restrictive application, in a number of other jurisdictions',[128] and the UK Supreme Court in *Pitt v Holt* described a trustee's duty to consider relevant factors before alienating trust assets as a fiduciary duty.[129]

There is a strong reason for rejecting the *Mothew* principle for a trustee's carelessness in administering the trust fund. If the common law principles

---

[122] ibid 17. He has repeated this view extra-judicially: PJ Millett, 'Equity's Place in the Law of Commerce' (1998) 114 LQR 214, 226.

[123] *Bank of New Zealand v New Zealand Guardian Trust Co Ltd* [1999] 1 NZLR 664, 681–82, 688.

[124] *IQ EQ NTC Trustees Asia (Jersey) Ltd v Arboit* [2019] HKCFA 45 [120].

[125] *Williams Lake Indian Band v Canada* [2018] SCC 4, [2018] 1 SCR 83 [46]; *Valard Construction Ltd v Bird Construction Co* [2018] SCC 8, [2018] 1 SCR 224 [17]. See Robert Flannigan, 'A Fiduciary Duty of Care for Canada' (2018) 134 LQR 368.

[126] [2003] HCA 15, (2003) 212 CLR 484 [39] (Gleeson CJ, McHugh, Gummow, Kirby and Hayne JJ).

[127] [2014] EWCA Civ 908, [2015] QB 499 [106].

[128] [2014] UKSC 58, [2015] AC 1503 [119].

[129] [2013] UKSC 26, [2013] 2 AC 108. See also *Henderson v Merrett Syndicates Ltd* [1995] 2 AC 145, 205 (Lord Browne-Wilkinson: 'fiduciary duties of care'); *White v Jones* [1995] 2 AC 207, 271 (Lord Browne-Wilkinson: 'fiduciary duties (including duties of care)').

relating to the scope of liability applied in that context, an award of equitable compensation would not always place the trust fund in the same position as if the trustee had been careful, and this would weaken the trust as an institution.[130] Similar considerations apply to a custodial fiduciary. In other contexts, the *Mothew* principle may have merit.[131]

130 JD Heydon, MJ Leeming and PG Turner, *Meagher, Gummow and Lehane's Equity: Doctrines and Remedies* (5th edn, LexisNexis 2015) [23-370].

131 Michael O'Meara, 'Causation, Remoteness and Equitable Compensation' (2005) 26 Aust Bar Rev 51, 66–69. See also Paul Matthews et al, *Underhill and Hayton: Law Relating to Trusts and Trustees* (20th edn, LexisNexis 2022) [91.53].

7. Coercive remedies

INTRODUCTION

This chapter discusses remedies that compel or restrain performance of certain actions. We refer to specific performance (an order enforcing a contract) and injunctions collectively as 'specific relief'.

To a civilian reader or a reader trained in a hybrid system, it may be surprising that remedies compelling performance are not the first and foremost remedy awarded in common law claims. After all, if a defendant has committed a breach, the 'next best' remedy is to compel the defendant to repair the breach or to prevent conduct which constitutes a breach. As a consequence, civilian or hybrid systems tend to prioritise the performance of a primary obligation, particularly in contract, and to opt for damages as a secondary remedy.

By contrast, the common law prioritises damages over compulsion because it favours autonomy. As noted in Chapter 2, the claimant is free to choose to spend their damages as they wish and, importantly, the claimant can choose not to interact with the defendant again, allowing a 'clean break' between the parties.

Specific relief is characterised by coercion. This is underlined by the fact that, if the defendant fails to comply with an order for specific relief, the court treats this as contempt of court and may enforce judgment against property by seizing it. The court may also enforce judgment against the person of the defendant by imprisoning the defendant, sequestering their assets, or imposing fines. The same measures can be imposed on those who aid and abet the defendant in non-compliance with the court's order. The intention is not to punish but to ensure compliance. As Windeyer J explained in the Australian case of *Australian Consolidated Press Ltd v Morgan*, imprisonment and sequestration:

> are used primarily to compel obedience rather than to punish disobedience; for equity acts in personam, and historically the purpose of the processes of the Court

> of Chancery was to rectify and reform the conscience of the wrongdoer. The jurisdiction was, to use Professor Ashburner's phrase, 'a cathartic jurisdiction'.[1]

The history of the common law and equity, described in Chapter 1, has also shaped the availability of specific relief. For the common law causes of action (breach of contract and tort), specific relief is generally awarded only where common law compensatory damages are 'inadequate'. This reflects the fact that both specific performance and injunctions originated in the Court of Chancery. The inadequacy hurdle arose in the eighteenth century when the Court of Chancery was concerned to avoid accusations of 'arbitrary and unprincipled interference' in common law proceedings.[2]

Whether damages are adequate for a common law cause of action depends very much on the categorisation of the subject matter of the dispute. Courts tend to be willing to award specific relief to protect real (immovable) property and are much less likely to award specific relief for other interests (such as goods, shares, and services). For equitable causes of action (a breach of trust, for example), there is no need to show that compensation is inadequate, and thus, an injunction can readily be obtained.

Before the procedural and administrative fusion of the courts with the Judicature Acts, it was also necessary for a claimant who had unsuccessfully attempted to claim specific relief in the Court of Chancery to start the claim entirely afresh in the Common Law Courts to seek damages. The Chancery Amendment Act—known as 'Lord Cairns' Act'[3]—was a pre-Judicature Act attempt to deal with the problem of circuitry of actions by giving the Court of Chancery the power to award damages in lieu of specific performance or an injunction, so that the claimant did not have to start anew. Lord Cairns' Act continues to have some relevance today, and it will also be considered in this chapter.

It is important to note that all equitable remedies are awarded on a discretionary basis and, consequently, are subject to bars to relief.

---

1 (1965) 112 CLR 483, 498. The last phrase was quoted from Denis Browne, *Ashburner's Principles of Equity* (2nd edn, Butterworth 1933) 38.

2 William Gummow, 'The Injunction in Aid of Legal Rights – An Australian Perspective' (1993) 56 Law & Contemp Probs 83, 92.

3 Chancery Amendment Act 1858 (21 & 22 Vict c 27). There was a corresponding provision bestowing the power to award injunctions upon common law courts in the Common Law Procedure Act 1854 (17 & 18 Vict c 125).

SPECIFIC PERFORMANCE

The Nature of Specific Performance

Specific performance is the remedy that enforces a contract. When a court makes a decree of specific performance, it directs a party to perform that contract according to its stipulations and terms. Specific performance may also be ordered in respect of promises enforceable by way of equitable estoppel.[4] Because equitable estoppel is an equitable doctrine, there is no need to show that damages are inadequate. Previously, specific performance was also available for contracts over land that did not comply with the formalities rules but where the parties displayed acts of part performance.[5] However, the rule of part performance was abolished in England and Wales in 1989 (although it remains in other Commonwealth jurisdictions).[6]

Some cases distinguish between specific performance in the 'limited' or 'true' sense (where the court issues an order that the defendant execute a legally binding document) and specific performance in the 'broad' sense or sense of 'quasi-specific performance' (where the contract has been executed, and the claimant simply requires the defendant to perform the obligations in the contract).[7] We deal with specific performance in the 'broad' sense here and note that it has been argued that this distinction is arbitrary,[8] and should be abolished,[9] except in the context of readiness and willingness to perform,

---

[4] In *Guest v Guest* [2022] UKSC 27, [2022] 3 WLR 911 [74]–[82], [90] (Lord Briggs, with whom Lady Arden and Lady Rose agreed), a majority of the UK Supreme Court has suggested that specific performance should be the default remedy for equitable estoppel. Cf Andrew Robertson, 'Satisfying the Minimum Equity: Equitable Estoppel Remedies after Verwayen' (1996) 20 MULR 805; B McFarlane, *The Law of Proprietary Estoppel* (3rd edn, OUP 2020); Ying Khai Liew, 'The "Prima Facie Expectation Relief Approach" in the Australian Law of Proprietary Estoppel' (2019) 39(1) OJLS 183.

[5] See, eg, *Price v Strange* [1978] Ch 337.

[6] Law of Property (Miscellaneous Provisions) Act 1989 (UK), s 2. See Peter Devonshire, 'The Doctrine of Part Performance: Where Should the Line be Drawn?' (2022) 17(2) Otago LR 277.

[7] See, eg, *Wolverhampton & Walsall Railway Co v London & North-Western Railway Co* (1873) LR 16 Eq 433, 439 (Lord Selbourne); *Pakenham Upper Fruit Co v Crosby* (1924) 35 CLR 386, 394 (Isaacs and Rich JJ); *JC Williamson Ltd v Lukey* (1931) 45 CLR 282, 297 (Dixon J).

[8] Samantha Hepburn, 'Specific Performance' in Patrick Parkinson (ed), *The Principles of Equity* (2nd edn, LBC 2003) [1702].

[9] *Australian Hardwoods Pty Ltd v Commissioner for Railways* [1961] 1 WLR 425, 433–34; PH Pettit, *Equity and the Law of Trusts* (12th edn, OUP 2012)

where it may assist in determining the obligations which the claimant must be ready and willing to perform. If this distinction is abolished, specific performance begins to resemble a form of mandatory injunction for performance of contractual promises.

The Relationship Between Specific Performance and Injunctions

As the discussion above indicates, the distinction between specific performance and injunctions is difficult to draw at times, and many issues overlap. However, we distinguish between the two because important differences remain.

First, it is generally easier to obtain an order for an injunction than an order for specific performance.[10] Specific performance is mandatory (ordering the defendant to take positive actions stipulated by the contract), but many injunctions are prohibitory (simply ordering the defendant *not* to do a thing). Prohibitory injunctions are less intrusive; hence, courts are more willing to award them.

Second, specific performance tends to apply to *all* stipulations under the contract.[11] Injunctions are available to restrain breaches of a specific clause of a contract (generally a negative covenant).

Third, injunctions are sometimes granted where specific performance would not be granted, particularly in relation to contracts for services.

Fourth, it is necessary to establish that damages are inadequate to obtain a decree of specific performance for a breach of contract. However, injunctions can be awarded for a much wider range of private law causes of action, including also tort, equitable wrongdoing, and statutory contraventions. If the cause of action is equitable or a statutory breach, there is no need to establish that damages are inadequate.

Inadequacy of Damages and the Subject Matter of the Contract

Damages are the default remedy for breach of contract, and specific performance will only be awarded if damages are 'inadequate'. In *Harnett v Yielding*, Lord Redesdale defined 'inadequacy' in the following terms:

> Unquestionably the original foundation of these decrees was simply this, that damages at law would not give the party the compensation to which he was entitled;

663–64.

[10] Janet O'Sullivan, 'Specific Performance' in John McGhee (ed), *Snell's Equity* (33rd edn, Sweet & Maxwell 2015) [17–005].

[11] *Ogden v Fossick* (1862) 4 De GF & J 426, 45 ER 1249.

> that is, would not put him in a situation as beneficial to him as if the agreement were specifically performed. On this ground, the court in a variety of cases, has refused to interfere, where from the nature of the case, the damages must necessarily be commensurate to the injury sustained. … For instance, in agreements for the purchase of stock: it is the same thing to the party where or from whom the stock is purchased, provided he receives the money that will purchase it.[12]

The question is whether damages will provide an adequate substitute for contractual performance. As Lord Redesdale indicates, this depends upon the subject matter of the contract. For a fungible item which is readily available on the market, it often will not matter whether you receive the subject matter of the contract or the money to purchase a substitute on the market. For a contract for a unique Ming vase or for land, you may want precisely what you contracted for because a substitute is not readily available. It is in the latter circumstances that damages are likely to be inadequate.

Historically, inadequacy of damages was a threshold jurisdictional issue. In other words, if damages are adequate, the court has no jurisdiction to award specific performance. There has been a move, however, to characterise it as discretionary, and to consider whether it is 'just' in the circumstances to award specific relief.[13]

Some commentators argue that 'inadequacy of damages' is unclear and should be replaced with a broader discretionary test. Elizabeth MacDonald has argued that the 'inadequacy of damages' test allows courts to dismiss specific relief too easily, without looking at whether damages are genuinely adequate for the claimant.[14] Okeoghene Odudu and Graham Virgo have argued that the test is so bedevilled by uncertainty that it should not be used in English law as a criterion for the grant of gain-based relief.[15]

It is suggested, however, that if the inadequacy of damages is understood to require the court to consider whether damages provide an adequate substitute for performance on the open market, the test can generate just outcomes.

---

12 (1805) 2 Sch & Lef 549, 553–54; [1803–13] All ER 704, 705.

13 *Beswick v Beswick* [1968] AC 58, 102; *Evans Marshall & Co Ltd v Bertola SA* [1973] 1 WLR 349, 379; *Sky Petroleum Ltd v VIP Petroleum Ltd* [1974] 1 WLR 576; *Verrall v Great Yarmouth Borough Council* [1981] QB 202; *The Stena Nautica (No 2)* [1982] 2 Lloyd's Rep 336.

14 Elizabeth MacDonald, 'The Inadequacy of Adequacy: The Granting of Specific Performance' (1987) 38 NILQ 244. See also Douglas Laycock, 'The Death of the Irreparable Injury Rule' (1990) 103 Harv L Rev 687.

15 Okeoghene Odudu and Graham Virgo, 'Inadequacy of Compensatory Damages' (2009) 17 RLR 112. Cf Katy Barnett, *Accounting for Profit for Breach of Contract: Theory and Practice* (Hart 2012) 78–80.

In what follows, we divide the principles which apply in relation to specific performance according to the subject matter of the contract. Contracts involving land are generally specifically performable. Conversely, contracts involving goods, shares, or loan contracts are often not specifically enforceable, because damages are usually an adequate remedy. Contracts for services (ie, employment contracts) are generally not specifically performable because common law courts do not wish to compel people to perform services.

It is necessary to go beyond these generalisations, however. The availability of specific performance depends upon the extent to which damages represent an adequate substitute for performance, given the availability of the subject matter of the contract on the market, and availability must always be considered in light of the facts of the case.

Contracts involving land

A contract for real property is generally presumed to be specifically enforceable,[16] subject to discretionary considerations. Courts have said that land has a 'peculiar and special value'.[17] Interests in land are therefore regarded as something for which damages cannot compensate, because one piece of land is intrinsically unique and never the same as another. Hence, in *Sudbrook Trading Estate v Eggleston*, Lord Diplock said that even if the contract for the sale of an interest in land was for commercial purposes, the lessee should still be entitled to specific performance.[18]

The purchaser is presumptively entitled to specific performance of a contract for the sale of land, and so it is said that the vendor will have the benefit of a presumptive entitlement to specific performance of payment of the purchase price on the basis of 'affirmative mutuality'[19] (ie, justice requires that both parties should be able to enforce the contract, even if damages are adequate for one party). However, in *Turner v Bladin*, the case often cited for this proposition, the contract was for payment by instalments and the land had already been conveyed to the purchaser.[20] There is a strong argument that the true basis for specific performance was inadequacy of damages.

---

[16] Provided it complies with the formalities required by s 2 of the Law of Property (Miscellaneous Provisions) Act 1989.

[17] *Adderley v Dixon* (1824) 1 Sim & St 607, 610; 57 ER 239, 240; *Dougan v Ley* (1946) 71 CLR 142.

[18] [1983] 1 AC 444, 478.

[19] Affirmative mutuality is criticised in Nicole Toy and Kenneth Yin, 'Advancing the Proposition that the Doctrine of Affirmative Mutuality is a Fallacy' (2023) 23 JCL 185.

[20] (1951) 82 CLR 463, 473 (Williams, Fullagar and Kitto JJ).

Difficult questions arise when a contract involves both a loan of money and a sale of an interest in land, as in *Loan Investment Corporation of Australasia v Bonner*.[21] The majority of the Privy Council held that the contract should not be specifically enforced, as it was a composite contract involving a commercial bargain, and mere contracts for a loan of money are not generally specifically enforceable.[22]

Contracts involving goods

Contracts involving goods are rarely specifically enforced by courts, because damages are usually adequate. Thus, in *Dominion Coal Co Ltd v Dominion Iron & Steel Co Ltd*, a contract for the sale of coal was not specifically enforceable, because coal of the same quality was readily available on the market, and damages were adequate.[23]

However, if a substitute performance cannot be easily obtained, courts will award specific performance.[24] Contracts involving unique chattels will usually be specifically performed.[25] Even if the chattel is not unique, specific performance may be awarded because the defendant is well situated to meet the claimant's needs, and the claimant cannot readily obtain a substitute performance elsewhere.[26] Sometimes, temporary market scarcity will give rise to an entitlement to specific performance.[27] Courts also sometimes award specific performance of an instalment contract to supply goods and services over a long period,[28] because a complex deal cannot be easily replaced.

---

21 [1970] NZLR 724.

22 ibid 734–35.

23 [1909] AC 293, 311.

24 See Sale of Goods Act 1979 (UK), s 52, which confirms the power but does not displace the necessity to establish the inadequacy of damages.

25 *Pusey v Pusey* (1684) 1 Vern 273, 23 ER 465; *Duke of Somerset v Cookso*n (1735) 3 P Wms 390, 24 ER 114; *Fells v Read* (1796) 3 Ves 70, 30 ER 899; *Lowther v Lord Lowther* (1806) 13 Ves Jun 95, 33 ER 230; *Lingen v Simpson* (1824) 1 Sim & St 600, 57 ER 236; *Falcke v Gray* (1859) 4 Drew 651, 62 ER 250; *Thorn v Commissioners of Her Majesty's Works and Public Buildings* (1863) 32 Beav 490, 55 ER 192; *Behnke v Bede Shipping Co Ltd* [1927] 1 KB 649, 661; *Dougan v Ley* (1946) 71 CLR 142; *Phillips v Lamdin* [1949] 2 KB 33, 41.

26 *North v Great Northern Railway Company* (1860) 2 Giff 64, 66 ER 28; *Sky Petroleum Ltd v VIP Petroleum Ltd* [1974] 1 WLR 576 (Ch); *Howard Perry & Co v British Railways* [1980] 1 WLR 1375. Cf *Société des Industries Métallurgiques SA v Bronx Engineering Co Ltd* [1975] 1 Lloyd's Rep 465.

27 *Dougan v Ley* (1946) 71 CLR 142; *Sky Petroleum Ltd v VIP Petroleum Ltd* [1974] 1 WLR 576; *Howard Perry & Co v British Railways* [1980] 1 WLR 1375.

28 See, eg, *Buxton v Lister* (1746) 3 Atk 383, 26 ER 1020; *Adderley v Dixon* (1824) 1 Sim & St 607, 610; 57 ER 239, 240; *Thomas Borthwick & Sons (Australasia)*

Contracts involving shares and stock

Compensatory damages will usually be an adequate remedy for the breach of a contract for the sale of shares in a public company, as long as substitute shares are available on the open market.[29] Courts are more willing to order specific performance of a sale of shares in a private company because of the lack of a market.[30] If shares in a public company are unavailable or if the availability is uncertain or the purchase might prejudice the claimant or a third party, specific performance may be granted.[31]

Contracts to lend money

Generally, contracts to lend money are not specifically enforceable, because damages are an adequate remedy.[32] Similarly, a contract to pay money will often not be specifically enforceable.[33] However, there are exceptions if it can be shown that damages are inadequate. Courts have been prepared to specifically enforce a contract to pay money in some circumstances, including where the contract is to relieve someone of their debt;[34] where the contract creates an annuity;[35] where the contract is to pay a third party who is incapable of enforcing the contract because of the rules against privity;[36] where the contract involves instalment payments and an interest in land;[37] where the contract is with a company to take up and pay for debentures;[38] and where the contract

---

Ltd v South Otago Freezing Co Ltd [1978] 1 NZLR 538; *Sky Petroleum Ltd v VIP Petroleum Ltd* [1974] 1 WLR 577. Cf *Fothergill v Rowland* (1873) LR 17 Eq 132, 140; *Société des Industries Métallurgiques SA v Bronx Engineering Co Ltd* [1975] 1 Lloyd's Rep 465.

29 *Cud v Rutter* (1719) 1 P Wms 570, 24 ER 521; *Hyer v Richmond Traction Co*, 168 US 471, 483 (1897); *Re Schwabacher* (1907) 98 LT 127, 128; *Chinn v Hochstrasser* [1979] Ch 447, 470.

30 *Duncuft v Albrecht* (1841) 12 Sim 189, 199; 56 ER 46, 48 (Shadwell VC).

31 *ANZ Executors and Trustees Ltd v Humes Ltd* [1990] VR 615, 630–31 (Brooking J).

32 *Rogers v Challis* (1859) 27 Beav 175; 54 ER 68; *Western Wagon & Property Co v West* [1892] 1 Ch 271, 275; *Larios v Bonany y Guerety* (1873) LR 5 PC 346 (PC); *South African Territories Ltd v Wallington* [1898] AC 309; *Loan Investment Corporation of Australasia v Bonner* [1970] NZLR 724 (PC).

33 *McIntosh v Dalwood (No 4)* (1930) 30 SR (NSW) 415, 418.

34 *McIntosh v Dalwood (No 4)* (1930) 30 SR (NSW) 415.

35 *Keenan v Handley* (1864) 2 De GJ & S 283; 46 ER 384; *Beswick v Beswick* [1968] AC 58.

36 *Beswick v Beswick* [1968] AC 58; *Gurtner v Circuit* [1968] 2 QB 587.

37 *Turner v Bladin* (1951) 82 CLR 463. Cf *Loan Investment Corporation of Australasia v Bonner* [1970] NZLR 724 (PC).

38 Companies Act 2006 (UK), s 740.

grants a mortgage or other security interest and the money has already been advanced.[39]

Although it has not traditionally been conceived of in this way (because of its common law origins), a claim in debt is said to be a form of monetary specific performance. Debt is discussed later in this chapter.

Contracts for the benefit of third parties

The common law doctrine of privity traditionally meant that a third party who is not a party to the contract cannot claim damages for breach.[40] The Contracts (Rights of Third Parties) Act 1999 (UK) now gives a direct right to a third party to sue, although, in practice, often contract out of it.[41] Section 1(5) provides that the same rules apply to the remedy of specific performance as they would if the third party were a party to the contract. Apart from the Act, the promisee (who is a party to the contract) may obtain an order of specific performance for the benefit of a third party, on the basis that damages are inadequate.[42]

Contracts involving intellectual property

Contracts involving intellectual property rights, including patents, designs, copyright, and trademarks, are generally specifically enforceable because of the unique nature of those rights.[43] Contracts for the sale of intellectual property rights may be specifically enforced.[44] So, too, may contracts to assign intellectual property rights,[45] unless they are oppressive.[46]

---

39 *Hermann v Hodges* (1873) LR 16 Eq 18; *Lamont v Osborn* (1902) 28 VLR 434; *Bridge Wholesale Acceptance Corporation (Australia) Ltd v Burnard* (1992) 27 NSWLR 415; *GE Commercial Corporation (Australia) Pty Ltd v Nichols* [2012] NSWSC 562.

40 For a comparative account of different regimes, see Hannes Unberath, *Transferred Loss: Claiming Third Party Loss in Contract Law* (Hart 2003).

41 Katy Barnett, *Damages for Breach of Contract* (2nd edn, Sweet & Maxwell 2022) [2-053].

42 *Beswick v Beswick* [1968] AC 58.

43 *Cogent v Gibson* (1864) 33 Beav 557, 55 ER 485.

44 ibid; *A H McDonald & Co Pty Ltd v Wells* (1931) 45 CLR 506, 513; *Brake v Radermacher* (1903) 20 RPC 631. Cf *Stocker v Wedderburn* (1857) 3 K & J 393, 69 ER 1163.

45 *Erskine Macdonald Ltd v Eyles* [1921] 1 Ch 631.

46 *A Schroeder Music Publishing Co Ltd v Macaulay* [1974] 3 All ER 616, 622 (Lord Reid).

Contracts for services

Courts in England and other common law jurisdictions have traditionally been reluctant to order specific performance of contracts for services (ie, employment contracts), regardless of whether these are sought by the employer or employee.[47] They are reluctant to compel parties to maintain a relationship where one party is unwilling,[48] and have sometimes likened the enforcement of contracts for service to slavery.[49] Courts are also reluctant to specifically enforce contracts where continuous supervision by the court might be necessary.[50] Andrew Tettenborn has explained that 'coerced performance is likely to be half hearted performance' and thus difficult to police.[51] Consequently, specific performance of a contract for services will be awarded rarely, although courts will sometimes award a mandatory injunction requiring a company to specifically perform an obligation.[52] Courts are now prohibited by statute from ordering specific performance of employment contracts in favour of an employer,[53] but there are instances where employees have obtained specific performance.[54]

Specific performance of an agency contract is also unlikely to be awarded, particularly when there are continuing obligations to work together, because the mutual trust and confidence between the parties have broken down.[55]

Nonetheless, as will be discussed later in this chapter, sometimes courts award an injunction to restrain the breach of a negative covenant where an employee has promised not to work for another employer, as long as the restriction is reasonable.

---

47 *Rigby v Connol* (1880) 14 Ch D 482, 487 (Jessel MR); *De Francesco v Barnum* (1890) 45 Ch D 430.

48 *Atlas Steels (Australia) Pty Ltd v Atlas Steels Ltd* (1948) 49 SR (NSW) 157, 161 (Sugarman J).

49 *De Francesco v Barnum* (1890) 45 Ch D 430, 438 (Fry LJ); P Saprai, 'The Principle against Self-Enslavement in Contract Law' (2009) 26 JCL 25.

50 *Cooperative Insurance Society Ltd v Argyll Stores (Holdings) Ltd* [1998] AC 1, 13–14 (Lord Hoffmann).

51 Andrew Tettenborn, 'Absolving the Undeserving: Shopping Centres, Specific Performance and the Law of Contract' [1998] Conv 23, 23.

52 *Lady Navigation Inc v Lauritzencool AB* [2005] EWCA Civ 579, [2005] 2 Lloyd's Rep 63.

53 See Trade Union and Labour Relations Act (Consolidation) Act 1992, s 236. 'Contract of employment' is defined in s 295(1) of that Act.

54 Andrew Burrows, *Remedies for Torts, Breach of Contract, and Equitable Wrongs* (4th edn, OUP 2019) 420–26.

55 *Chinnock v Sainsbury* (1860) 30 LJ Ch 409; *Page One Records Ltd v Britton* [1968] 1 WLR 157, 164–65 (Stamp LJ).

Other Requirements for Specific Performance

Personal remedy

Specific performance is a personal remedy because it commands an individual to do something.[56] A defendant who fails to comply is in contempt of court and subject to fines, sequestration, or imprisonment. The personal, coercive nature of the remedy means that the defendant must be physically within the jurisdiction and capable of carrying out the order of specific performance;[57] however, there is no need for the subject matter of the contract to be within the jurisdiction.[58]

Specific performance does not lie against the Crown;[59] if a remedy is sought, a declaration is appropriate.

Binding contract

A contract must be valid and binding to be specifically enforced and must not be one that the defendant is entitled to rescind because their consent was vitiated.

Specific performance will not be awarded where there was no consideration or only nominal consideration for the contract,[60] even if the contract was made by deed and did not require consideration to be valid.[61] The equitable maxim 'Equity will not assist a volunteer' refers to this situation.[62]

A court will not award specific performance of a contract that is void for uncertainty, for the obvious reason that there is no contract. If there is a contract, but there is uncertainty as to the meaning of terms or general uncertainty, a court is also unlikely to specifically enforce it.[63] If the court cannot say what the defendant is supposed to do with sufficient certainty, the court

---

[56] *Pearson v Arcadia Store, Guyra, Ltd (No 2)* (1935) 53 CLR 587, 590–91.

[57] *Jackman v Broadbent* [1931] SASR 82.

[58] *Penn v Lord Baltimore* (1750) 1 Ves Sen 444, 27 ER 1132; *Richard West & Partners (Inverness) Ltd v Dick* [1969] 2 WLR 383 (aff'd [1969] 2 Ch 424).

[59] Crown Proceedings Act 1947 (UK), s 21(1)(a).

[60] *Cannon v Hartley* [1949] 2 Ch 213, 217. However, cf *Mountford v Scott* [1975] Ch 258, where an agreement made for £1 which granted the plaintiff an option to purchase the defendant's house for £10,000 was specifically enforced on the basis that while the price of the option was nominal, the price of exercising the option was not.

[61] *Jefferys v Jefferys* (1841) Cr & Ph 138, 41 ER 443.

[62] Andrew Burrows, *Remedies for Torts, Breach of Contract, and Equitable Wrongs* (4th edn, OUP 2019) 429.

[63] See, eg, *Joseph v National Magazine Co* [1959] Ch 14.

may refuse specific performance for discretionary reasons.[64] However, if the contract has been rendered certain by subsequent actions of the parties, there will no longer be a bar to specific relief.[65]

An order of specific performance will not be made where the defendant would be required to do an illegal act.[66] The same is true for injunctions.[67]

Specific performance is unlikely to be granted where it is impossible for the defendant to carry out the terms of the contract, or where it would be futile to require the defendant to do so. Impossibility arises where it is not possible to comply with an order for specific performance and is a reason to refuse specific performance altogether.[68] Futility arises where compliance is possible, but the likelihood of achieving the outcome sought by the claimant is low. Futility sometimes leads to a refusal of specific relief,[69] although not inevitably.

Discretionary Factors and Bars for Relief

Those remedies which were originally developed in the Court of Chancery, including specific performance, are subject to discretionary considerations. Some of the discretionary considerations listed below apply to *all* equitable remedies; some only apply to specific performance or orders equivalent to specific performance.

Even if a claimant is barred from obtaining specific relief by reason of equitable discretionary factors, they will ordinarily still be entitled to compensatory damages for breach of contract.

Hardship and the public interest

Hardship acts as a bar to relief for all equitable remedies. A court will not award specific performance of a contract if it would impose undue hardship on the defendant.[70] Hardship must be weighed up with all other factors, including

---

64 *Cooperative Insurance Society Ltd v Argyll Stores (Holdings)* [1998] AC 1, 13–14.

65 *Price v Strange* [1978] Ch 337, 362.

66 *Patel v Mirza* [2016] UKSC 42, [2017] AC 467 [160] (Lord Neuberger).

67 ibid.

68 *Ferguson v Wilson* (1866) LR 2 Ch App 77.

69 For cases where specific performance was refused for futility, see *Hercy v Birch* (1804) 9 Ves 357, 32 ER 640; *New Brunswick & Canada Railway & Land Co v Muggeridge* (1850) 4 Drew 686, 699; 62 ER 263, 286 (Kindersley VC). *Hercy v Birch* is criticised in ICF Spry, *The Principles of Equitable Remedies* (9th edn, LBC 2014) 131–32.

70 *Denne v Light* (1857) 8 De GM & G 774, 44 ER 58; *Hope v Walter* [1900] 1 Ch 257; *Wroth v Tyler* [1974] 1 Ch 30.

hardship to the claimant in being denied specific performance.[71] Hardship is rarely made out, and it must be severe.

Severe hardship was established in *Patel v Ali*.[72] The defendants, the Alis, entered into a contract for the sale of their family home to the plaintiffs, the Patels, which was prima facie specifically enforceable. After the contract was signed, but before settlement, the defendants suffered terrible misfortunes. Mr Ali was bankrupted, and the sale of the property was halted after an injunction was awarded to Mr Ali's trustee in bankruptcy. Mr Ali went to prison for a year. Mrs Ali was found to have bone cancer and had her leg amputated. At the time of the application for relief, the couple had three children. Mrs Ali was from Pakistan and spoke very little English. She relied on her local community and no longer wanted to move. Goulding J refused to order specific performance of the contract of sale because of the hardship to Mrs Ali.[73] On the other hand, the plaintiffs had already suffered extensive unforeseen delays—years had elapsed since the time for settlement—and hence damages were an adequate remedy.[74]

Although Mrs Ali's hardship had arisen after the contract had been entered into, the court took it into account. However, any hardship to Mrs Ali's children was irrelevant,[75] as they were not parties to the contract.

By contrast, as will be discussed, hardship to third parties and even to the general public may sometimes be relevant when considering the award of an injunction, although it will not generally be determinative.

Financial difficulties on the part of the defendant are not usually a ground for hardship,[76] nor is an increase in the value of land after the contract was entered into.[77] However, if an agreement is unconscionable, the court may refuse to specifically enforce it.[78]

---

71 *Tamplin v James* (1880) 15 Ch D 215, 221 (James LJ); *Eastes v Russ* [1914] 1 Ch 468, 480 (Swinfen Eady LJ); *Keats v Wallis* [1953] NZLR 563, 566; *Nicholas v Ingram* [1958] NZLR 972, 974; *ANZ Executors and Trustees Ltd v Humes Ltd* [1990] VR 615, 639 (Brooking J).

72 [1984] 1 Ch 283.

73 ibid 288.

74 ibid.

75 ibid. See also *Gall v Mitchell* (1924) 35 CLR 222, 230–31, 226 (Harvey J).

76 *Pasedina (Holdings) Pty Ltd v Khouri* (1977) 1 BPR 9460.

77 *Fitzgerald v Masters* (1956) 95 CLR 420, 433 (Dixon CJ and Fullagar J).

78 *Falcke v Gray* (1859) 4 Drew 651, 62 ER 250; *Dowsett v Reid* (1912) 15 CLR 695.

Lack of clean hands

'Lack of clean hands' acts as a bar to relief for all equitable remedies, including specific performance.[79] This bar is intended to prevent claimants from misusing equitable doctrines,[80] and operates in two circumstances: first, where the claimant has misled the court, abused its process, or attempted to do so; and second, where the grant of relief would enable the claimant to achieve a dishonest purpose and it would be inequitable to grant relief.[81] A claimant may be denied relief where they have misled the defendant,[82] the court[83] or the public.[84]

Any lack of clean hands must relate to the relief sought; it does not mean general impropriety or immorality.[85] Hence, in *Moody v Cox*, Scrutton LJ said that 'the depravity, the dirt in question on the hand, [must have] … an immediate and necessary relation to the equity sued for'.[86] However, even where the claimant has 'unclean hands', if refusal of relief could cause injustice to third parties, the court may grant relief because the remedy is in the public interest.[87]

In *Quadrant Visual Communications Ltd v Hutchinson Telephone (UK) Ltd*,[88] the Court of Appeal refused to specifically enforce a contract for the sale of a mobile phone business. Among other things, the contract provided that consideration was to be paid 'free from any equity, cross claim whatsoever', but also that the plaintiff would not 'enter into any contract or commitment which is of an unusual nature or is otherwise outside the ordinary course of its business'. At completion, the plaintiff failed to disclose to the defendant that they had entered into a contract with a marketing company for a campaign in which they had promised to provide unlimited free mobile phones to anyone

---

79 *Shell UK Ltd v Lostock Garage Ltd* [1976] 1 WLR 1187, 1199 (Lord Denning); *Quadrant Visual Communications Ltd v Hutchinson Telephone (UK) Ltd* [1993] BCLC 442.

80 Nicholas Tiverios, 'Preventing the Infinite Regress: Discretion, Bars to Relief and the Structure of Equity' (2023) 82(2) Camb LJ 350, 358.

81 ICF Spry, *The Principles of Equitable Remedies* (9th edn, LBC 2014) 253–56.

82 *Summers v Cocks* (1927) 40 CLR 321.

83 *Armstrong v Sheppard & Short Ltd* [1959] 2 QB 384.

84 *Kettles and Gas Appliances Ltd v Anthony Hordern and Sons Ltd* (1934) 35 SR (NSW) 108.

85 *Jones v Lenthal* (1669) 1 Chan Cas 154, 22 ER 739; *Duchess of Argyll v Duke of Argyll* [1967] 1 Ch 302.

86 [1917] 2 Ch 71, 87–88. See also *Dering v Earl of Winchelsea* (1787) 1 Cox 318, 29 ER 1184; *Attwood v Small* (1838) 6 Cl & F 232, 7 ER 684.

87 *Vauxhall Bridge Co v Earl Spencer* (1821) Jac 64, 67; 37 ER 774, 775.

88 [1993] BCLC 442.

who held a voucher. The Court refused to award specific performance because, in view of their failure to disclose the full details of the marketing agreement, the plaintiff had not come to Court with clean hands. The reference to 'an equity' did not preclude the Court from exercising its equitable discretion.

Laches: delay with acquiescence and delay with prejudice

Delay with acquiescence and delay with prejudice (sometimes called collectively 'laches') act as a bar to relief for all equitable remedies.[89] 'Mere' delay is not enough to preclude the award of an equitable remedy.[90] Two kinds of delay will act as a bar to relief.[91] The claimant must either have apparently acquiesced to the defendant's breach such that the defendant thought they were 'in the clear', or the claimant's delay must have prejudiced the defendant or a third party. [92]

Mutuality

Mutuality acts as a bar to relief only for specific performance. There have been suggestions that it should be abolished or the concerns with which it seeks to deal should be subsumed in another bar to relief. It is derived from a statement in *A Treatise on the Specific Performance of Contracts* by Sir Edward Fry:

> A contract to be specifically enforced by the court must, as a general rule, be mutual, – that is to say, such that it might, at the time it was entered into, have been enforced by either of the parties against the other of them.[93]

The rationale is that justice requires a certain equality of enforcement (ie, if the claimant seeks to enforce the contract, the defendant must be able to enforce the claimant's obligations). The difficulty with Fry's statement is that mutuality is required 'at the time [the contract] was entered into'. So, for example, a plaintiff who was a minor at the time when a contract was made was denied

---

[89] The word 'laches' is derived from Norman French, where the term connoted 'delay'. In modern French, this word has come to mean 'cowardice'.

[90] A 12-year delay was insufficient in *Burroughes v Abbott* [1922] Ch 86, and a 26-year delay was insufficient in *Weld v Petre* [1929] 1 Ch 33 and *Fitzgerald v Masters* (1956) 95 CLR 420, 433, 440–41. However, if the property is 'commercially volatile', then the permissible delay will be much shorter: see, eg, *Edmonds v Donovan* [2005] VSCA 27, (2005) 12 VR 513 [76] (Phillips JA).

[91] *Lindsay Petroleum Co v Hurd* (1874) LR 5 PC 221, 239–40; *No 68 Ltd v Eastern Services Ltd* [2006] NZSC 42, [2006] 2 NZLR 43 [56] (McGrath J).

[92] *Lamshed v Lamshed* (1963) 109 CLR 440 (third party prejudice).

[93] Edward Fry, *A Treatise on the Specific Performance of Contracts* (GR Northcote ed, 6th edn, Stevens 1921) 219.

specific performance, because the contract could not be enforced against them at the time it was made.[94]

Fortunately, the English Court of Appeal rejected Fry's formulation in *Price v Strange*.[95] The plaintiff tenant entered into an oral agreement with the defendant landlord to have his lease renewed, in return for a promise to repair the block of flats in which he was living. Although the agreement was at first unenforceable for lack of formality, it became enforceable because of the plaintiff's acts of part performance in reliance upon the agreement. The defendant reneged on the agreement, and tried to argue that because the agreement was unenforceable at the time the contract was made, the plaintiff was not entitled to specific performance.

Goff LJ said that Fry's statement of the law was 'wrong' and that 'the true principle is that one judges the defence of want of mutuality on the facts and circumstances as they exist at the hearing'.[96] The Court judged mutuality as at the time of the hearing and awarded specific performance, subject to the plaintiff compensating the defendant for a portion of the repair works which had been done by another builder. It is suggested that this is an appropriate reformulation of the principle.

Continuous supervision

Continuous supervision acts as a bar to relief only for specific performance and orders equivalent to specific performance (eg, injunctions to restrain breach of a negative covenant). Traditionally, specific performance is strictly barred where a court would be required to constantly supervise the order.[97] However, it has subsequently been attenuated to a discretionary consideration.[98]

Nonetheless, continuous supervision remains an important discretionary consideration, even beyond personal service contracts, as *Cooperative Insurance Society Ltd v Argyll Stores (Holdings) Ltd* illustrates.[99] In that case, the House of Lords refused to specifically enforce a 35-year lease of supermarket premises in a shopping centre. The tenants decided after 16 years

94 *Flight v Bollard* (1828) 4 Russ 298; 38 ER 817. Cf *Kell v Harris* (1915) 15 SR (NSW) 473 (contract entered by infant specifically enforceable once he ratified it as an adult).

95 [1978] Ch 337.

96 ibid 356. See also *Rainbow Estates Ltd v Tokenhold Ltd* [1999] Ch 64, 69.

97 *Ryan v Mutual Tontine Westminster Chambers Association* [1893] 1 Ch 116, 123, 125, 128.

98 In *Posner v Scott-Lewis* [1997] Ch 25, 36, a case otherwise similar to *Ryan v Mutual Tontine*, continuous supervision was not a reason to refuse specific performance.

99 [1998] AC 1.

had elapsed that they no longer wished to run the supermarket because it was unprofitable. Although the landlord offered rent concessions and other inducements, the tenants closed the business without further discussion. The landlord sought specific enforcement of the lease because the supermarket was an 'anchor tenant' which brought in much other business, and it was concerned the shopping centre would fail.

Lord Hoffmann, speaking for the House of Lords, gave four reasons for the refusal of specific performance. First, it was inappropriate because of the need for continuous supervision. His Lordship distinguished between orders that require a defendant to carry on an activity over an extended time (eg, running a business), which might require repeat applications to ensure compliance with the order, and orders that simply require a defendant to achieve a one-off result, such as building contracts and repairing covenants.[100]

Second, Lord Hoffmann said that problems with continuous supervision might be indicated by a difficulty in specifying what conduct was required for compliance with its order.[101] This would mean the parties must return to court to obtain further guidance.

Third, Lord Hoffmann was concerned by the coercive nature of specific performance and the extreme sanctions for non-compliance with an order (including contempt of court), which he described as a 'sword of Damocles'.[102] He was reluctant to force the defendant to run a failing business against their best interests. Moreover, specific performance 'yokes the parties together in a continuing hostile relationship', and it was better for the parties to part.[103]

Fourth, the losing nature of the business meant an order of specific performance could put the defendant in a disadvantageous position, where they might be tempted to yield to extortionate demands for a fee to be released from the order.[104]

Readiness and willingness to perform

A claimant who seeks specific performance must show that they are ready and willing to perform their obligations.[105] Delay and acquiescence on the part of the claimant may suggest that they are not ready or willing to perform.[106]

---

100 ibid 13–14.

101 ibid. See also *Redland Bricks Ltd v Morris* [1970] AC 652, 666 (Lord Upjohn).

102 [1998] AC 1, 13.

103 ibid 16.

104 ibid 15.

105 *Green v Sommerville* (1979) 141 CLR 594 (although the bar did not succeed in that case).

106 *Foran v Wight* (1989) 168 CLR 385, 451–52.

However, the claimant need only perform essential obligations, and the court presumes that they are ready, willing, and able to do so.

This is the only area where the distinction between 'true' or 'limited' specific performance and 'broad' specific performance still has relevance. It is relevant for executory contracts but is not important where the contract sought to be specifically performed is an executed agreement,[107] because the claimant has already complied with their obligations.

Specific Restitution and Delivery Up of Property

Courts have the power to order the delivery up of goods that have been wrongfully detained. This is known as 'specific restitution' or 'specific delivery'. It is available as of right for equitable causes of action (eg, breach of fiduciary duty) and also for proprietary torts such as conversion, but only where damages are inadequate.

For proprietary torts involving goods, such as detinue,[108] conversion and trespass to goods, the default remedy was typically compensatory damages, and there was no power to award delivery up of goods. English common law courts were given the power to award delivery up in 1854.[109]

Readers trained in Roman law will be familiar with the *rei vindicatio*,[110] which allowed the claimant to demand the return of property, and which has analogues in civilian jurisdictions today. However, the common law has never had an analogous remedy.

An order for specific restitution will be made for proprietary torts only if damages are inadequate (generally when goods are unique).[111] There is a

---

107 *Bridge Wholesale Acceptance Corporation (Australia) Ltd v Burnard* (1992) 27 NSWLR 415, 423 (Clarke JA).

108 Detinue was abolished in the United Kingdom in 1977: Torts (Interference with Goods) Act 1977 (UK), s 2(1).

109 Common Law Procedure Act 1854 (17 & 18 Vict c 125), s 78. See now Torts (Interference with Goods) Act 1977 (UK).

110 Paul du Plessis, *Borkowski's Textbook on Roman Law* (6th edn, OUP 2020) 75.

111 *Pusey v Pusey* (1684) 1 Vern 273, 23 ER 465; *Duke of Somerset v Cookson* (1735) 3 P Wms 390, 24 ER 114; *Fells v Read* (1796) 3 Ves 70, 30 ER 899; *Lowther v Lord Lowther* (1806) 13 Ves Jun 95, 33 ER 230; *North v Great Northern Railway Company* (1860) 2 Giff 64, 66 ER 28; *Aristoc Industries Pty Ltd v RA Wenham (Builders) Pty Ltd* [1965] NSWR 581; *Doulton Potteries Ltd v Bronotte* [1971] 1 NSWLR 591; *Howard Perry & Co v British Railways* [1980] 1 WLR 1375; *McKeown v Cavalier Yachts Pty Ltd* (1988) 13 NSWLR 303. Damages were adequate in *Dowling v Betjemann* (1862) 2 J & H 544, 70 ER 1175; *Whiteley Ltd v Hilt* [1918] 2 KB 808, 819; *Greenwood v Bennett* [1973] QB 195, 202.

significant overlap with specific performance and goods, as many of the early cases now used to justify the specific performance of contracts involving goods were cases of specific restitution.

There is no need to show that damages are inadequate if specific restitution is sought for an equitable cause of action.[112]

Regardless of whether specific restitution is sought for a common law or an equitable breach, it will be subject to the discretionary equitable bars to relief mentioned above.[113]

Specific restitution may be refused if the defendant has increased the value of the property by making improvements to the property, leaving the claimant to a remedy in damages.[114] Alternatively, specific restitution may be awarded, but subject to an order that the claimant must pay a fair and just allowance for the increased value of the property.[115]

Debt as a Form of Specific Relief?

A debt is a definite sum of money which, under the terms of the contract, the defendant is due to pay the claimant either in return for the claimant completing a specified obligation under the contract, or upon the occurrence of a specified event.[116] This claim originated in the common law courts.

In debt, the claimant needs only to show that the contractual conditions which trigger payment have arisen and that payment has not been received.[117] There is no need to show that the defendant has breached any obligation other than a failure to pay. Nor does the claimant prove that the defendant's breach has caused loss. Mitigation generally does not apply to a debt.[118] The defences to a debt claim are limited.

Debt is therefore fundamentally different from compensation for loss: the court ensures that the defendant complies with their primary obligation to pay the sum due and does not consider loss or limitations upon liability. As a result, an action in debt has been argued by some scholars to be equivalent to specific

112 *Wood v Rowcliffe* (1847) 2 Ph 3, 45 ER 990.

113 See, eg, *Gollan v Nugent* (1988) 166 CLR 18 (unclean hands).

114 *Nash v Barnes* [1922] NZLR 303, 309.

115 *Peruvian Guano Co Ltd v Dreyfus Bros & Co* [1892] AC 166, 176; *Greenwood v Bennett* [1973] QB 195, 201–03.

116 Donald Harris, David Campbell and Roger Halson, *Remedies in Contract and Tort* (2nd edn, CUP 2005) 158. See also *Jervis v Harris* [1996] Ch 195, 202–03 (Millett LJ).

117 ibid 159. See also *Jervis v Harris* [1996] Ch 195, 202–03 (Millett LJ).

118 *Jervis v Harris* [1996] Ch 195, 202–03 (Millett LJ). For the doctrine of mitigation, see Ch 3.

performance of an obligation to pay money because it effectively requires performance of the primary obligation.[119] Nonetheless, there are important differences between specific relief and debt, reflecting the common law origins of debt. Unlike specific relief, a remedy in debt is available as of right if the conditions for the accrual of the debt are satisfied. There is no discretion.[120] Nor do any bars to relief apply where the claimant's action in debt is abusive or unmeritorious.[121]

INJUNCTIONS

Injunctions are another coercive remedy that originated in the Court of Chancery. The court orders the defendant to do something or to refrain from doing something, and the defendant must comply with the order or be in contempt of court.

Injunctions are available in a much broader variety of circumstances than specific performance. They can be granted to protect many private law rights, including rights in land, goods, and other property, economic rights (including those associated with equitable wrongs), the right to bodily integrity, the right to reputation, the right to privacy, and contractual rights. They may also be used in support of public law rights.

In earlier times, only the Court of Chancery could grant an injunction. These days, the courts' jurisdiction to grant an injunction has three sources. First, the Judicature Act reforms conferred a power to grant an injunction on common law courts, a power which continues to the current day.[122] Second, courts have an inherent jurisdiction to grant injunctions to preserve the status

---

[119] Rafal Zakrzewski, *Remedies Reclassified* (OUP 2005) 108–11; Lionel Smith, 'The Measure of Compensation Claims Against Trustees and Fiduciaries' in Elise Bant and Matthew Harding (eds), *Exploring Private Law* (CUP 2010) 363, 370–71; Andrew Tettenborn, 'Literal Enforcement of Obligations' in David Campbell and Roger Halson, *Research Handbook on Remedies in Private Law* (Edward Elgar 2019) 180, 188–89.

[120] David Winterton, 'Reconsidering *White & Carter v McGregor*' [2013] LMCLQ 5; Andrew Tettenborn, 'Literal Enforcement of Obligations' in David Campbell and Roger Halson (eds), *Research Handbook on Remedies in Private Law* (Edward Elgar 2019) 180, 189. See *White & Carter (Councils) Ltd v McGregor* [1962] AC 413, 445 (Lord Hodson).

[121] Andrew Tettenborn, 'Literal Enforcement of Obligations' in David Campbell and Roger Halson (eds), *Research Handbook on Remedies in Private Law* (Edward Elgar 2019) 180, 189.

[122] See now Senior Courts Act 1981, s 37. This ability was first conferred by the Common Law Procedure Act 1854 (17 & 18 Vict c 125).

quo and to prevent proceedings from being frustrated. Third, legislation may explicitly provide a court with the power to grant a statutory injunction.

Injunctions may be temporary or permanent. An interlocutory injunction is a temporary injunction intended to maintain the status quo before trial. It generally lasts only until the time of trial or until further order. An injunction is said to be final or 'perpetual' when it confers an ongoing right, usually granted at trial on the merits of the case. Insofar as the rules governing the grant of interlocutory injunctions differ from those governing final injunctions, they will not be considered in detail in this book. This is because while interlocutory injunctions are procedural, ensuring that the court's process is upheld, they do not finally determine the matter. Nonetheless, some of the cases we cite involve interlocutory injunctions, as many factors are relevant to both interlocutory and permanent injunctions. This is because the interlocutory injunction often mirrors the final relief sought.

Injunctions can be either 'prohibitory' (preventing a defendant from doing something which infringes the claimant's rights) or 'mandatory' (requiring the defendant to perform a positive action). Common law courts are more willing to award prohibitory injunctions than mandatory injunctions because a negative command ('you must not do that particular thing') interferes less with the defendant's autonomy than a positive command ('you must do that particular thing').[123] Nevertheless, all injunctions are subject to the court's discretion.

Injunctions may also be granted to prevent a prospective infringement of the claimant's rights if the court is satisfied that there is a high likelihood of the act occurring. In modern parlance, these are known as precautionary injunctions, but in older cases, they are known as *quia timet* injunctions. Injunctions are more flexible than specific performance because they may be interlocutory or final, prohibitory or mandatory, and may prevent future wrongdoing.

The following rubric gives guidance on how to approach the award of an injunction:

(1) Identify whether the defendant committed a legal, equitable, or statutory wrong (or, whether in the case of a precautionary or *quia timet* injunction, there is a substantial probability that they will do so).
(2) For injunctions in support of common law rights *only*, consider whether damages are adequate. Despite the general primacy of damages at

[123] See *Redland Bricks Ltd v Morris* [1970] 652, 665–66 (Lord Upjohn). Cf *National Commercial Bank Jamaica Ltd v Olint Corpn Ltd* [2009] UKPC 16; [2009] 1 WLR 1405, [20] (Lord Hoffmann) suggesting that the distinction between mandatory and prohibitory injunctions is 'barren'.

common law, for some common law torts (eg, trespass to land), injunctions could be said to be the presumptive remedy.[124]

(3) For injunctions in support of equitable rights and common law rights, consider whether a discretionary bar to relief applies. If so, the claimant may be left to a remedy in damages.

In what follows, the rules regarding the inadequacy of damages are set out.

The Relevance of Damages Being Inadequate: Only for Common Law Wrongs

Old cases suggested that a claimant must have a proprietary right before an injunction for the contravention of a common law right could be granted.[125] However, the better view is that damages are often an inadequate remedy for the infringement of property rights, although property rights are not the only rights protected by injunctions at common law. The infringement of many rights may give rise to an injunction, as the following discussion shows.

Several factors may suggest that damages are inadequate, including difficulty in assessing damages.[126] The fact that the claimant may only suffer minimal loss or damage is not necessarily a reason to refuse an injunction.[127]

Increasingly, as with specific performance, the inadequacy of damages has come to be regarded as a discretionary factor, not a jurisdictional hurdle. In *Evans Marshall & Co Ltd v Bertola SA*, Sachs LJ suggested that the test of inadequacy of damages should be reformulated as follows:

> The standard question … 'are damages an adequate remedy?' might perhaps in the light of authorities in recent years, be rewritten, 'is it just in all the circumstances that a plaintiff should be confined to his remedy in damages?'[128]

Injury to property rights in land

Several common law torts protect rights in land: trespass, private nuisance, and public nuisance.

---

[124] See, eg, *Woollerton and Wilson Ltd v Richard Costain Ltd* [1970] 1 WLR 411.

[125] See, eg, *Attorney-General v Sheffield Gas Consumers Co* (1853) 3 De GM & G 304, 320; 43 ER 119, 125; *Rigby v Connol* (1880) 14 Ch D 482, 487.

[126] *Warner Brothers Pictures Inc v Nelson* [1937] 1 KB 209, 220–21; *Evans Marshall & Co Ltd v Bertola SA* [1973] 1 WLR 349, 380 (Sachs LJ).

[127] *Evans Marshall & Co Ltd v Bertola SA* [1973] 1 WLR 349.

[128] [1973] 1 WLR 349, 379.

Courts will readily award an injunction to restrain trespass, even into airspace that the claimant is not using. Hence, for example, injunctions have been awarded to prevent the passage of a crane jib over the claimant's land,[129] or to effect the removal of an advertising sign.[130] However, at an unspecified point above the surface of the land, the actions will be too far above the land to be protected by the tort of trespass. Hence, a plaintiff was unable to restrain people from flying over his property.[131] In very minor cases of a temporary nature, the claimant will sometimes be left to their remedy in damages, as in cases where collectors accidentally chased moths or butterflies onto the claimant's land.[132]

Injunctions have also restrained defendants from committing the tort of private nuisance (ie, interference with the claimant's right to quiet enjoyment), particularly where the nuisance was ongoing.[133] Nuisances restrained by injunction include the ringing of church bells,[134] the keeping of noisy pigeons,[135] the racing of speed boats,[136] and drunken shouting,[137] but not the hitting of cricket balls into a neighbouring yard.[138] Courts have also granted precautionary or *quia timet* injunctions for prospective private nuisance.[139] The presumption in favour of an injunction for nuisance is, however, not as strong as for trespass. In fact, a minority in the Supreme Court in *Lawrence v Fen Tigers Ltd* suggested that courts should start from the presumption that damages are the appropriate remedy for nuisance, with injunctions being awarded exceptionally.[140] It should be noted that there is also the possibility of obtaining a statutory injunction for nuisance pursuant to section 1 of the Antisocial Behaviour, Crime and Policing Act 2014 (UK).

---

129 *Woollerton and Wilson Ltd v Richard Costain Ltd* [1970] 1 WLR 411; *Graham v KD Morris and Sons Pty Ltd* [1974] Qd R 1; *Anchor Brewhouse Developments Pty Ltd v Berkley House (Dockland Developments) Pty Ltd* [1987] 2 EGLR 173.

130 *Kelsen v Imperial Tobacco Co Ltd* [1957] 2 QB 334.

131 *Bernstein of Leigh (Baron) v Skyviews and General Ltd* [1978] QB 478.

132 *Fielden v Cox* (1906) 22 TLR 411.

133 *McCombe v Read* [1955] 2 QB 429, 436; *Pride of Derby and Derbyshire Angling Association Ltd v British Celanese Ltd* [1953] Ch 149, 181, 194.

134 *Soltau v De Held* (1851) 2 Sim NS 133, 61 ER 291.

135 *Fraser v Booth* (1949) 50 SR (NSW) 113.

136 *Kennaway v Thompson* [1981] QB 88.

137 *Vincent v Peacock* [1973] 1 NSWLR 466.

138 *Miller v Jackson* [1977] QB 966.

139 *Grasso v Love* [1980] VR 163.

140 [2014] UKSC 13; [2014] AC 822 [157]–[162] (Lord Sumption, with whom Lord Clarke agreed). Cf Lord Mance at [168].

Injury to property rights in goods and funds of money

Two common law torts protect rights in goods in English law: trespass to goods and conversion.[141] As with specific performance, courts are less willing to award an injunction restraining the defendant from committing a tort in relation to goods (as opposed to land). However, where the goods are unique, scarce, or irreplaceable, damages will be inadequate, and an injunction will be awarded.[142]

By contrast, where a claimant asserts a proprietary right to a fund of money or a promissory note, damages are usually considered inadequate and an injunction will be granted, particularly where it is unclear whether a payment of damages will be satisfied if the defendant becomes insolvent.[143]

Injury to intellectual property

Injunctions are readily granted for infringements of intellectual property, as damages are highly likely to be inadequate given the proprietary nature of the right. At first, these injunctions arose in the Court of Chancery's auxiliary jurisdiction; however, they are now largely buttressed by statutory provisions.[144] Nevertheless, the equitable jurisdiction still underlies the statute.

Injury to economic rights

Both the common law and equity protect economic rights. The common law does this via economic torts, and equity does this via breach of trust and breach of fiduciary duty. For equitable wrongs, there is no need to show that compensation is inadequate, and courts will readily award an injunction for equitable breaches, such as breach of trust,[145] subject to the equitable bars to relief.

Economic torts include injurious falsehood,[146] the tort of passing off, and a variety of torts involving interference with contractual relations.[147] Historically,

---

[141] As noted earlier (n 108), the tort of detinue has been abolished in England.

[142] *Collier-Garland (Properties) Pty Ltd v O'Hair* (1963) 63 SR (NSW) 500; *Aristoc Industries Pty Ltd v RA Wenham (Builders) Pty Ltd* [1965] NSWR 581.

[143] *London City Agency (JCD) Ltd v Lee* [1970] Ch 597. Cf *Bank Ltd v Medway Upper Navigation Co* [1905] 2 KB 359.

[144] Copyright, Designs and Patents Act 1988 (UK), ss 96, 103 (copyright), s 229 (designs); Patents Act 1977, s 70C; Trade Marks Act 1994 (UK), s 14.

[145] See, eg, *Fox v Fox* (1870) LR 11 Eq 142.

[146] Also called 'trade libel', 'slander of title', 'slander of goods', 'disparagement of goods', or 'malicious falsehood'.

[147] Including procuring or inducing a breach of contract, intimidation, unlawful interference, and conspiracy. In situations where an employer or the public interest is likely to be disastrously affected if an interim or interlocutory injunction is not awarded, courts will readily award an injunction: see *NWL Ltd v Woods* [1979] 1

economic torts were often used in the context of trade union disputes, but there is now a complex web of enactments dealing with trade union disputes (which will not be considered in detail here). Courts are prepared to award injunctions to prevent injurious falsehood, passing off[148] and inducing breach of contract.

Injurious falsehood occurs where the defendant makes a false statement concerning the claimant's goods or business, which is maliciously published to a third person and results in actual damage to the claimant.[149] Section 3(1) of the Defamation Act 1952 (UK) states that it is unnecessary for a claimant to prove 'special damage' with regard to slander of title, slander of goods, or other malicious falsehood if the words are calculated to cause pecuniary damage.[150] As with defamation (discussed below), which may be concurrently available, courts are concerned not to constrain freedom of speech unduly. For interim or interlocutory injunctions, if the statements are not manifestly false and the defendant indicates an intention to justify the statement, the rule in *Bonnard v Perryman* applies,[151] and an injunction will not be awarded.[152] As explained below, section 12(3) of the Human Rights Act 1998 (UK) does not affect the application of the rule in *Bonnard v Perryman*.[153]

Injury to reputation

Defamation occurs where a defendant publishes to third parties imputations which tend to harm the public reputation of the claimant.[154] A claimant seeking a final injunction restraining a threatened publication by the defendant needs to establish that the publication would be defamatory of the claimant and that the defendant has no defence. Courts can also order the removal of material from a website or to cease distributing, selling, or exhibiting defamatory material.[155]

WLR 1294, 1307 (as revised in [1980] 1 WLR 147); *Express Newspapers Ltd v McShane* [1980] AC 672, 694–695. This reflects that these torts have often been invoked in a British context in disputes between unions and employers.

148

149 *Ratcliffe v Evans* [1892] 2 QB 524, 527–28 (Bowen LJ).

150 The English Court of Appeal has recently decided that this provision is 'forward-looking' and applies to any statement likely to cause financial loss; see *George v Cannell* [2022] EWCA Civ 1067, [2023] QB 117 [27] (Warby LJ).

151 *Bonnard v Perryman* [1891] 2 Ch 269.

152 *Bestobell Paints Ltd v Bigg* [1975] FRS 421; *Easycare Inc v Bryan Lawrence & Co* [1995] FSR 597.

153 See *Cream Holdings v Banerjee* [2004] UKHL 44, [2005] 1 AC 253.

154 Within defamation, there is a distinction between written defamation (libel) and spoken defamation (slander).

155 See Defamation Act 2013 (UK), s 13.

Often interim or interlocutory injunctions are sought to restrain publication until trial, but the rule in *Bonnard v Perryman*[156] means that, because of concerns regarding free speech, these are only granted in 'exceptional' or 'very clear' cases. This is because, generally, at the stage interlocutory injunctions are sought, the merits of the case are still unclear. Section 12(3) of the Human Rights Act 1998 (UK), which stipulates that the right to freedom of expression means that the court cannot grant relief to restrain publication of material before trial unless it is 'satisfied that the applicant is likely to establish that publication should not be allowed', does not change the test for the grant of an interlocutory injunction, nor abrogate the rule in *Bonnard v Perryman*.[157] Courts tend to lean in favour of publication if there is no clear and lawful objection to it.[158]

Injury to privacy

In England and Wales, courts have interpreted the equitable doctrine of breach of confidence as giving rise to a right to privacy, in light of the Human Rights Act 1998 (UK). Courts are prepared to award injunctions to restrain breaches of privacy.[159] Sometimes courts are also prepared to award 'super-injunctions' restraining the very reporting of the injunction; however, they are reluctant to award them lightly.[160]

Injury to bodily integrity

The intentional torts covering trespass to the person are assault, battery, and false imprisonment. Injunctions to restrain battery or false imprisonment are rarely sought, since a wrongdoer will not usually announce an advance intention to commit the tort (unless there is a threat to repeat the behaviour).

---

156 [1891] 2 Ch 269. Cf *Hubbard v Pitt* [1976] QB 142.

157 See *Cream Holdings v Banerjee* [2004] UKHL 44; [2005] 1 AC 253.

158 *Maxwell Communication Corp Plc v Newspapers Publishing Plc* (CA, 1 August 1991).

159 *Campbell v MGN Ltd* [2004] UKHL 22, [2004] 2 AC 457; *Douglas v Hello! Ltd (No 3)* [2005] EWCA Civ 595, [2006] QB 125; *McKennitt v Ash* [2006] EWCA Civ 778, [2008] QB 73; *Mosley v News Group Newspapers Ltd* [2008] EWHC 1777, [2008] EMLR 679; *Murray v Big Pictures (UK) Ltd* [2008] EWCA Civ 446, [2009] Ch 481; *ZXC v Bloomberg LLP* [2022] UKSC 5, [2022] AC 1158. See Michael Tugendhat, 'Privacy Injunctions and the Rule of Law' in Jason Varuhas and Nicole Moreham (eds), *Remedies for Breach of Privacy* (Hart 2018) 29.

160 *JIH v News Group Newspapers Ltd* [2011] EWCA Civ 42, [2011] 1 WLR 1645. See also *Report of the Committee on Super-Injunctions: Super-Injunctions, Anonymised Injunctions and Open Justice*, 20 May 2011 (MR Report 2011) (London, HMSO).

Conversely, threats of assault are relatively common. Historically, equitable injunctions for common law rights traditionally protected property, not the person, and such injunctions were rare. Today, a person who is threatened would be likely to have recourse to a statutory injunction pursuant to section 1 of the Antisocial Behaviour, Crime and Policing Act 2014 (UK).[161]

Injunctions to restrain a breach of negative covenant

Sometimes, courts restrain the defendant from breaching a negative covenant in a contract (ie, a promise not to do something). Whether a clause is a negative covenant is a matter of substance, not form.[162] Sometimes, even if a clause is expressed in a positive manner, it can imply a promise not to do something.[163]

There is a line of cases suggesting that inadequacy of damages is not a relevant consideration for negative covenants, drawing on *Doherty v Allman*,[164] but cases from other Commonwealth jurisdictions have taken the opposite view.[165] It seems, however, that the other discretionary considerations operate, including delay.[166]

Notwithstanding the scepticism of *Doherty v Allman* in some quarters, inadequacy of damages was recently applied by the English Court of Appeal in *Araci v Fallon*,[167] after a jockey who had promised a certain horse upon request was restrained by injunction from riding a rival horse. While the Court found that damages were inadequate,[168] at least one judge of the Court of

---

161 'Antisocial behaviour' is defined in the Antisocial Behaviour, Crime and Policing Act 2014 (UK), s 2 as including:

(a) conduct that has caused, or is likely to cause, harassment, alarm, or distress to any person,

(b) conduct capable of causing nuisance or annoyance to a person in relation to that person's occupation of residential premises, or

(c) conduct capable of causing housing-related nuisance or annoyance to any person.

162 *Wolverhampton & Walsall Railway Co v London & North-Western Railway Co* (1873) LR 16 Eq 433, 440 (Lord Selbourne LC).

163 *Metropolitan Electric Supply v Ginder* [1901] 2 Ch 799.

164 *Doherty v Allman* (1878) 3 App Cas 709, 719–20; *McEacharn v Colton* [1902] AC 104 (PC); *Macintosh v Bebarfalds Ltd* (1922) 22 SR (NSW) 371; *Ampol Petroleum Ltd v Mutton* (1952) 53 SR (NSW) 1.

165 *JC Williamson Ltd v Lukey* (1931) 45 CLR 282, 298–300 (Dixon J); *Dalgety Wine Estates Pty Ltd v Rizzon* (1979) 141 CLR 552, 560, 573–74; *Ampol Petroleum Ltd v Mutton* (1952) 53 SR (NSW) 1; *Curro v Beyond Productions Pty Ltd* (1993) 30 NSWLR 337, 346–47.

166 *Shaw v Applegate* [1977] 1 WLR 970, 980 (Goff LJ).

167 [2011] EWCA Civ 668.

168 ibid [53] (Jackson LJ), [71] (Elias LJ).

Appeal did not think it was necessary to establish this to obtain an injunction to restrain the breach of a negative covenant.[169]

Courts are more willing to award injunctions to restrain the breach of a negative covenant than to issue a positive order for specific performance. This is because the constraints on liberty are less, and because damages are often inadequate.[170] They will be particularly ready to enforce a restrictive covenant over land, a confidentiality agreement, or a negative covenant involving intellectual property.[171]

In some situations, a court may decline to award an injunction to restrain a breach of a negative covenant. First, negative covenants in a sale of goods contract will not be enforced by injunction unless the goods are unique and damages are thereby inadequate.[172] Second, reflecting the discussion above of continuous supervision, injunctions are generally not awarded for breach of a negative covenant if the court would be required to supervise performance.[173] Third, injunctions are not generally awarded for contracts for services: the services must generally be unique, and the injunction must be of relatively brief duration.[174] This third category is considered in more detail below.

Contracts for services

As noted earlier in this chapter, courts generally refuse to award specific performance for a contract for services (ie, an employment contract). However, they may award an injunction restraining the defendant from breaching a negative covenant within a contract for services if the defendant has agreed not to provide their services to any person other than the claimant. Sometimes, courts will award injunctions to restrain breaches of 'non-compete' clauses, where the defendant promises not to compete with the claimant's business for a certain period of time, as long as the injunction is not too broad.[175]

---

169 ibid [70] (Elias LJ).

170 Andrew Burrows, *Remedies for Torts, Breach of Contract, and Equitable Wrongs* (4th edn, OUP 2019) 455–56.

171 *One Step Support Ltd v Morris-Garner* [2018] UKSC 20; [2019] AC 649 [91]–[93] (Lord Reed JSC).

172 *Sky Petroleum Ltd v VIP Petroleum Ltd* [1974] 1 WLR 576.

173 *JC Williamson Ltd v Lukey* (1931) 45 CLR 282, 299–300 (Dixon J).

174 *Lumley v Wagner* (1852) 1 De GM & G 604, 42 ER 687.

175 *Herbert Morris Limited v Saxelby* [1916] AC 688 (clause too broad to be protected by injunction); *Scorer v Seymour-Jones* [1966] 1 WLR 1419 (injunction awarded); *Lansing Linde Limited v Kerr* [1991] 1 WLR 250 (clause too broad to be protected by injunction); *Planon Ltd v Gilligan* [2022] EWCA Civ 642 (injunction declined on the basis of delay).

Historically, courts have safeguarded the right of individuals to work in their chosen trade or profession without unfair restriction, and, as a result, they scrutinise restraints on employment closely, including negative covenants. The common law doctrine of restraint of trade provides that contractual obligations restricting someone's ability to trade are void by reason of illegality unless they are reasonable and in the interests of both contracting parties and of the public at large.[176] Hence, this must be considered as a factor in the enforceability of a negative covenant. On the other hand, the possession of confidential information or trade secrets by an employee might be a factor suggesting an injunction should be awarded.[177]

Although English courts do not explicitly mention uniqueness as a criterion, as a matter of practice, courts award injunctions to restrain breaches of negative covenants when services are 'unique', such as those offered by opera singers[178] and actors and actresses.[179] More 'ordinary' employees, such as managers,[180] salespersons,[181] porters,[182] and other ordinary employees[183] are less likely to be restrained from working for a competitor.

There are two reasons for this. First, if a service is unique, damages will be inadequate because an employee with equivalent skills cannot be found elsewhere. Second, courts do not wish to prevent 'ordinary' employees from working. They are concerned that 'ordinary' employees will, in effect, be rendered unemployable because they will be prevented by the injunction from undertaking a wide variety of activities. For similar reasons, the length of these injunctions tends not to be very long, even for unique services.

In *Lumley v Wager*,[184] the court was prepared to prevent Ms Wagner, an opera singer and niece of the composer Richard Wagner, from singing for a rival opera house in breach of a negative covenant, for three months. Conversely, in *Page One Records v Britton*,[185] members of a pop group called 'The Troggs' were not restrained from employing a new manager, in breach

---

176 *Mason v The Provident Clothing and Supply Co Ltd* [1913] AC 724.

177 *Herbert Morris Limited v Saxelby* [1916] AC 688, 709 (Lord Parker).

178 *Lumley v Wagner* (1852) 1 De GM & G 604, 42 ER 687.

179 *Grimston v Cuningham* (1894) 1 QB 125; *Warner Brothers Pictures Inc v Nelson* [1937] 1 KB 209; *Marco Productions Ltd v Pagola* [1945] 1 KB 111.

180 *Whitwood Chemical Company v Hardman* [1891] 2 Ch 416; *Davis v Foreman* [1894] 3 Ch 654; *Mortimer v Beckett* [1920] 1 Ch 571; *Page One Records v Britton* [1968] 1 WLR 157; *Warren v Mendy* [1989] 1 WLR 853.

181 *Ehrman v Bartholomew* [1898] 1 Ch 671.

182 *Ryan v Mutual Tontine Westminster Chambers Association* [1893] 1 Ch 116.

183 *Rely-A-Bell Burglar and Fire Alarm Company Ltd v Eisler* [1926] 1 Ch 609.

184 (1852) 1 De GM & G 604, 42 ER 687.

185 [1968] 1 WLR 157.

of a negative covenant with their previous manager. The judge found that the band members were 'simple persons of no business experience and could not survive without the services of a manager' and the agreement still had four years to run.[186] It was inappropriate to compel the parties to continue to work together, particularly for such a long time.

Precautionary or Quia Timet Injunctions

A precautionary[187] injunction (also known as a *quia timet* injunction)[188] is awarded where no damage has been sustained by the claimant, but 'there must be a sufficiently real and imminent risk of a tort being committed'.[189] 'Imminent' simply means that 'the injunction must not be granted prematurely'.[190] Such cases are highly fact-specific. Among other things, the court must balance the probability of harm, the gravity of injury, and the likely consequences, as well as considerations of hardship to both parties.[191]

Discretionary Factors and Bars to Relief

Hardship and the public interest

The nature of hardship as a general bar for all equitable remedies has already been described above.

There are differences in the way hardship is applied to injunctions when compared to specific performance. As noted above, hardship to third parties (including the general public) is not generally taken into account for specific performance. Traditionally, this was also the case for injunctions. Hence, in *Shelfer v City of London Electric Lighting Co*,[192] an injunction to restrain a nuisance was granted even though this inconvenienced the general public.

More recent cases suggest that the public interest or impact on third parties may be a factor to deny an injunction, although seldom determinative.[193]

---

186 ibid 166.

187 See *High Speed Two (HS2) Ltd v Four Categories of Persons Unknown* [2022] EWHC 2360 (KB) [99] (Knowles J).

188 *Quia timet* means 'because he is afraid' in Latin.

189 *Ineos Upstream Ltd v Persons Unknown* [2019] EWCA Civ 515, [2019] 4 WLR 100 [34](1) (Longmore LJ speaking for the court).

190 *Hooper v Rogers* [1975] Ch 43, 49–50 (Russell LJ).

191 *Fletcher v Bealey* (1885) 28 Ch D 688, 698.

192 [1895] 1 Ch 287.

193 *Miller v Jackson* [1977] QB 966; *Lawrence v Fen Tigers Ltd* [2014] UKSC 13, [2014] AC 822.

In *Miller v Jackson*,[194] a majority of the English Court of Appeal declined to award an injunction restraining members of the Lintz cricket club from playing, despite the plaintiff's complaints of nuisance and negligence, on the basis that cricket was in the public interest. However, in *Kennaway v Thompson*,[195] a differently constituted Court of Appeal declined to follow *Miller v Jackson* and restrained speed-boat racing outside the plaintiff's house. In *Lawrence v Fen Tigers Ltd*,[196] the Supreme Court suggested that the public interest was relevant, but not determinative. The claimants sought an injunction to restrain the noise from a speed track raceway, but the injunction was refused. Lord Neuberger PSC, for the majority, held that the public interest would be relevant in most cases, although rarely determinative.[197] By contrast, Lord Sumption JSC, for the minority, was doubtful that judges were capable of effectively ascertaining the public interest.[198]

Public interest concerns were also a reason to refuse a mandatory injunction to tear down houses built in breach of a restrictive covenant in *Wrotham Park Estate Co Ltd v Parkside Homes Ltd*, with Brightman J saying that it would be 'an unpardonable waste' of much-needed housing.[199]

Lack of clean hands

Just as with specific performance, 'lack of clean hands' operates as a discretionary bar to the award of an injunction, even for purely equitable causes of action. For example, in *Hubbard v Vosper*,[200] the defendant Vosper, a former minister of the Church of Scientology, wrote a book alleging that the church authorised extreme actions (even killing) against persons in a state of 'enemy' with the church. The church sought to restrain the publication for breach of confidence. It did not come to court with clean hands insofar as any confidential information pertained to the sanctions against the church's 'enemies', and an injunction was refused.[201]

Laches: delay with acquiescence and delay with prejudice

As for specific performance, delay with acquiescence and delay with prejudice on the part of the claimant may be a reason to deny the award of an injunction. The cases are highly fact-specific; depending upon the situation in question,

---

194 [1977] QB 966.
195 [1981] QB 88.
196 [2014] UKSC 13, [2014] AC 822.
197 ibid [118], [124].
198 ibid [158].
199 [1974] 1 WLR 798, 811.
200 [1972] 2 QB 84.
201 ibid 100–01 (Megaw LJ).

a lengthy delay may not constitute laches, or a short delay may result in the refusal to award an injunction.[202]

Delay is also a significant reason why a court may choose to award damages in lieu of an injunction pursuant to Lord Cairns' Act.

Mandatory injunctions that are equivalent to specific performance

If a mandatory injunction is effectively equivalent to specific performance, the discretionary factors applying to an award of specific performance (such as continuous supervision and readiness and willingness) apply in the same way.

It is also important to note that the need for continuous supervision sometimes informs the courts' reluctance to restrain breaches of restrictive covenants by means of an injunction.

DAMAGES IN LIEU OF SPECIFIC RELIEF

As noted at the outset of this chapter, prior to the enactment of the Judicature Acts, claimants faced the problem that, with two different court systems, if they failed in one court, they had to start their action afresh in the other court (an issue known as circuitry of actions).[203]

For the Court of Chancery, the legislature sought to solve this problem by Lord Cairns' Act in 1858.[204] Section 2 of that Act provided that the Court of Chancery could award damages in addition to, or in lieu of, specific performance or an injunction:

> In all cases in which the Court of Chancery has jurisdiction to entertain an application for an injunction against a breach of any covenant, contract or agreement, or against the commission or continuance of any wrongful act, or for the specific performance of any covenant, contract or agreement, it shall be lawful for the same court, if it shall think fit, to award damages to the party injured either in addition to or in substitution for such injunction or specific performance, and such damages may be assessed in such manner as the court shall direct.

A statutory ability to award damages in addition to or in lieu of specific relief remains in English law, but it now exists in a 'simplified' version, in section 50 of the Senior Courts Act 1981 (UK):

---

[202] See, eg, *Wroth v Tyler* [1974] 1 Ch 30, 53, where a delay of a few months was important.

[203] Michael Bryan, 'Injunctions and Damages: Taking Shelfer off the Shelf' (2016) 28 SAcLJ 921, 927.

[204] Chancery Amendment Act 1858 (21 & 22 Vict c 27).

> If the Court has jurisdiction to entertain an application for an injunction or specific performance, it may award damages in addition to, or in substitution for, an injunction or specific performance.

The 'simplified' version may give the provision a wider operation, encompassing not only damages in lieu of injunctions for common law wrongs but also for equitable wrongs.[205] Many other Commonwealth jurisdictions have similar provisions, either based on the original provision or the 'simplified' version.

Although the original Act was enacted to deal with a very specific problem, the broad wording and discretion conferred on the court mean that it has been used for purposes which go well beyond the original legislative intention, to allow for flexible or novel remedial responses.[206]

Sometimes, damages awarded under this legislation are known as 'equitable damages', which are distinct from 'equitable compensation'. However, to avoid confusion, we call awards under this style of legislation 'Lord Cairns' Act damages'.

Lord Cairns' Act damages are primarily awarded for proprietary torts such as trespass and for breaches of a negative covenant where no other relief is available (either because it is impossible or for discretionary reasons). Their calculation varies according to the facts of the individual case, and there is no singular rule applying to all cases.

Although Lord Cairns' Act is one of the bases upon which a court can order a 'reasonable fee' for the breach of a private law right, we have chosen to consider these awards here because of their close relationship with specific relief, and because Lord Reed in *One Step (Support) Pty Ltd v Morris-Garner* saw them as distinct from negotiating damages or user damages.[207] Cases where 'reasonable fees' have been awarded without reliance on Lord Cairns' Act will be considered in Chapter 8.

Jurisdiction to Award Lord Cairns' Act Damages

Section 50 of the Senior Courts Act 1981 (UK) specifies that damages may be awarded where the court has jurisdiction to 'entertain an application' for an injunction or specific performance. Lord Reed in *One Step (Support) Pty Ltd v*

---

205 *Giller v Procopets* [2008] VSCA 236, (2008) 24 VR 1, on the equivalent provision in Victoria, Australia.

206 Katy Barnett and Michael Bryan, 'Lord Cairns's Act: A Study in the Unintended Consequences of Legislation' (2015) 9 J Eq 150. It has been argued these extended purposes are illegitimate: see Daniel Reynolds, 'Rethinking Equitable Damages' (2019) 13 J Eq 46.

207 [2018] UKSC 20, [2019] AC 649 [44].

Morris-Garner said that '[t]he power to award damages in substitution for an injunction is dependent on the courts having jurisdiction to grant an injunction, determined as at the commencement of the proceedings'.[208]

However, the award of an injunction or specific performance is itself discretionary. This led Jolowicz to lament that 'a discretionary power to substitute damages for a remedy which is itself discretionary is a logical monstrosity'.[209] In other words, the award of this remedy involves two successive exercises of discretion, making its availability difficult to predict.

The court can award Lord Cairns' Act damages only when the bars to specific relief are discretionary rather than jurisdictional. However, as discussed earlier in this chapter, the distinction between jurisdiction and discretion has been broken down for specific performance and injunctions.

Modern courts tend to treat formerly jurisdictional hurdles as discretionary factors. For example, mutuality was previously regarded as a matter of jurisdiction but appears now to be discretionary. More fundamentally, it is unclear whether the inadequacy of damages is a matter of jurisdiction or discretion. Historically, it was thought to be a question of jurisdiction; in other words, where common law damages were adequate, a court had no power to award specific relief. However, particularly in the context of injunctions, it seems that inadequacy of damages is a discretionary factor, and perhaps even replaced by a question of whether it is 'just' in the circumstances.

This makes it more difficult to ascertain whether Lord Cairns' Act damages are available. Perhaps the better view may be that, where common law compensatory damages for loss are adequate, that measure should prevail.

Courts have struggled to ascertain when Lord Cairns' Act damages can be awarded when equitable discretionary bars apply. In some cases, it has been said that the claimant must be entitled to specific relief without the operation of any discretionary bars. In other cases, it has been said that the claimant needs only to establish that the court could theoretically have awarded specific relief at the time when the litigation began (but specific relief is unavailable because of discretionary factors). The latter view is preferable because it makes no sense to confine the availability of Lord Cairns' Act damages to the situation where a claimant is least likely to need them. Certainly, case law indicates that there is no need for the claimant to have actually sought specific relief and been refused.[210]

---

[208] ibid [45].

[209] JA Jolowicz, 'Damages in Equity – A Study of Lord Cairns' Act' (1975) 34 Camb LJ 224, 240.

[210] *Pell Frischmann Engineering Ltd v Bow Valley Iran Ltd* [2009] UKPC 45, [2011] 1 WLR 2370 [48]. However, reservations were expressed in *One Step*

Factors Influencing the Exercise of the Jurisdiction

The categories of cases below are not mutually exclusive, and sometimes a case will fit into several categories.

Where specific relief is no longer available or in addition to specific relief
Often, these cases arise when the claimant comes to court 'too late' to obtain specific performance or an injunction and seeks damages in lieu of equitable relief.[211] For these cases, it needs to have been hypothetically possible to award specific relief when proceedings are issued.

The original legislators also intended to allow for damages in addition to specific relief, and courts have often awarded specific relief as well as Lord Cairns' Act damages. The measure of these damages is discussed below.

To provide a middle ground between no relief and an injunction
In some circumstances, only nominal damages are available at common law for a particular breach—often for proprietary torts such as trespass and nuisance, or breaches of a negative covenant where there is no factual loss—but a court does not wish to award specific relief. Lord Cairns' Act gives the court a 'middle ground' solution, often via a 'reasonable fee' award (discussed in Chapter 8). However, courts do not exercise a simple binary choice between an injunction and damages. Even when a court awards an injunction, its operation may be suspended for an extended period, or stringent limits may be placed on it.[212]

Courts are sometimes concerned that an award of Lord Cairns' Act damages looks like a judicial expropriation of rights. In *Krehl v Burrell*, Jessel MR said that Lord Cairns' Act 'never could have been meant to invest the Court of Chancery with a new statutory power … to compel people to sell their property without their consent at a valuation'.[213] In *Shelfer v City of London*

(Support) Pty Ltd v Morris-Garner [2018] UKSC 20; [2019] AC 649 [45] (Lord Reed, with whom Lady Hale, Lord Wilson and Lord Carnwath agreed).

211 See, eg, *Catton v Wyld* (1863) 55 ER 105; 32 Beav 266; *Fritz v Hobson* (1880) 14 Ch D 542; *Davenport v Rylands* (1865) LR 1 Eq 302; *Chapman, Morsons & Co v The Guardians of the Auckland Union* (1889) 23 QBD 294; *Johnson v Agnew* [1980] AC 367.

212 Mark Pennini, 'Damages in lieu of an Injunction in Australia: Shelfer, Fen Tigers and Public Interests' (2022) 16 J Eq 239, 259–60. See also Robert Palmer and Ben Pontin, 'Injunctions Through the Lens of Nuisance' in Roger Halson and David Campbell (eds), *Research Handbook on Remedies in Private Law* (Edward Elgar 2019) 294, 298.

213 (1878) 7 Ch D 551, 554.

Electric Co, Lindley LJ expressed similar concerns by stating that 'a person committing a wrongful act … is not thereby entitled to ask the court to sanction his doing so by purchasing his neighbour's rights'.[214]

On the other hand, courts are also concerned to ensure that claimants cannot demand an exorbitant fee from a defendant for the right to breach the injunction. Hence, in *Isenberg v East India House Estate Co Ltd*, Lord Westbury LC said:

> I hold it, therefore, to be the duty of the Court in such a case as the present not, by granting a mandatory injunction, to deliver over the Defendants to the Plaintiff bound hand and foot, in order to be made subject to any extortionate demand that he may by possibility make, but to substitute for such mandatory injunction an inquiry before itself, in order to ascertain the measure of damage that has been actually sustained.[215]

Hence, there are risks associated with awards of both injunctions and Lord Cairns' Act damages.

In making a choice, generally between nominal damages, specific relief, and Lord Cairns' Act damages, the courts assess a range of factors, including the nature of the injunction sought, the nature of the wrong committed, how the claimant objected to that wrong, and the nature of the defendant's response to any objection. If the wrong is one where courts readily award an injunction, if the injunction is prohibitory, if the claimant has made their objection to the wrong clear, and/or if the defendant has continued the wrong, then the courts are more likely to award an injunction than Lord Cairns' Act damages. By contrast, if the wrong is one where the courts are generally reluctant to award an injunction, if the injunction is mandatory, and/or if the claimant has delayed in bringing action against the defendant or has acquiesced in some way to the wrongdoing, the courts are more likely to award Lord Cairns' Act damages than an injunction.

Even if neither the claimant nor the defendant has sought Lord Cairns' Act damages, the court may exercise its discretion to award them if the claimant has sought specific relief, and the court decides it is more appropriate to award damages in lieu.[216]

214 [1895] 1 Ch 287, 322.

215 (1863) 3 De GJ & S 263, 273; 46 ER 637, 641.

216 *Betts v Neilson* (1868) LR 3 Ch App 429, 441 (Lord Chelmsford); *Catton v Wyld* (1863) 32 Beav 266, 55 ER 105; *Lady Stanley of Alderley v Earl of Shrewsbury* (1875) LR 19 Eq 616.

To provide relief for future losses

Common law compensatory damages can be awarded only in respect of wrongdoing that occurred before the commencement of proceedings. This provides particular difficulties for claimants who are victims of torts such as nuisance and trespass where the wrong may have ongoing consequences.

For example, if the defendant has caused a nuisance by creating subsidence of the claimant's land, because damage is the gist of the action, the claimant would need to return to court repeatedly when fresh damage occurs. However, Lord Cairns' Act damages can accommodate the possibility of future loss and damage by making an award in lieu of the injunction that might otherwise be ordered.[217]

It is unnecessary for a past injury to have occurred for Lord Cairns' Act damages to be available. Sometimes Lord Cairns' Act damages may be awarded in lieu of a precautionary or *quia timet* injunction (which restrains a threatened wrong),[218] or in lieu of specific performance for an anticipatory breach of contract.[219] Michael Bryan has noted that this is one of the few areas where Lord Cairns' Act provisions are necessary.[220]

To provide novel forms of relief

Jolowicz argues, 'recognition of this novel jurisdiction [to award Lord Cairns' Act damages] is equivalent to recognition – to the extent allowed by the Act – of an actual, though limited, fusion of law and equity'.[221] Lord Cairns' Act allows a court to award a remedy which is not traditionally available for a particular cause of action, as long as it is made in lieu of specific relief.[222]

A good illustration is the Australian case, *Giller v Procopets*.[223] Aggravated damages are generally available only for common law torts and not for equitable wrongdoing. However, in this case, the Victorian Court of Appeal used the local Lord Cairns' Act provision to buttress an award of aggravated damages

---

[217] *Leeds Industrial Cooperative Society Ltd v Slack* [1924] AC 851; *Hooper v Rogers* [1975] Ch 43; *Jaggard v Sawyer* [1995] 1 WLR 269, 276–77 (Sir Thomas Bingham MR).

[218] *Barbagallo v J & F Catelan Pty Ltd* [1986] 1 Qd R 245.

[219] *Oakacre Ltd v Claire Cleaners (Holdings) Ltd* [1982] Ch 197; *Hasham v Zenab* [1960] AC 316.

[220] Michael Bryan, 'Injunctions and Damages: Taking Shelfer off the Shelf' (2016) 28 SAcLJ 921, 927–28.

[221] JA Jolowicz, 'Damages in Equity – A Study of Lord Cairns' Act' (1975) 34 Camb LJ 224, 227.

[222] ibid 227–28.

[223] [2008] VSCA 236, (2008) 24 VR 1.

for an equitable breach of confidence after the defendant had released videos of himself and the claimant in intimate relations following their breakup.

The Status of the Shelfer Criteria

In *Shelfer v City of London Electric Co*,[224] the English Court of Appeal laid out a set of criteria for the award of Lord Cairns' Act damages. This effectively created a presumption that an injunction should be awarded (at least in nuisance) *unless* the 'good working rule' of AL Smith LJ below applied:

(1) the injury to the plaintiff's legal right is small;
(2) the injury is capable of being quantified in money;
(3) the injury can be compensated by a small monetary payment; and
(4) it would be oppressive to the defendant to grant the injunction.[225]

In *Lawrence v Fen Tigers Ltd*,[226] the UK Supreme Court considered and revised the *Shelfer* rules. The claimants moved into a bungalow near a speed track raceway which had been in operation for over 20 years at this point. They sought an injunction in nuisance, restraining the operator of the raceway from making noise above certain levels. The Supreme Court declined to award an injunction and instead awarded Lord Cairns' Act damages in lieu. The majority added 'public interest' considerations to the *Shelfer* rules and said that the *Shelfer* rules should be applied flexibly, not rigidly.[227] The minority, however, held that the *Shelfer* rules should be abolished, and the presumption created by *Shelfer* should be reversed, so that in cases of nuisance, damages were the presumptive remedy, not an injunction.[228]

The Basis of Assessment

Timing

Sometimes, Lord Cairns' Act has been used to change the date of the assessment of damages, as in *Wroth v Tyler*.[229] The plaintiff sought specific performance of a contract for the sale of a house. The court declined to award specific performance because of the potential hardship to the defendant's wife,

224 [1895] 1 Ch 287.
225 ibid 322–23.
226 [2014] UKSC 13, [2014] AC 822.
227 ibid [100]–[127] (Lord Neuberger, with whom Lord Mance and Lord Carnwath agreed).
228 ibid [157]–[161] (Lord Sumption, with whom Lord Clark agreed).
229 [1974] 1 Ch 30.

a third party, who had registered an interest in the house under the Matrimonial Homes Act 1967 (UK). Mr Justice Megarry awarded Lord Cairns' Act damages in lieu of specific performance, measured by the difference between the value of the house as at the date of judgment and the value as at the date of the contract, rather than by the difference between the value as at the date of breach and at the date of the contract (as would ordinarily be the case for common law damages).[230] The value of the house had gone up steeply since the date of the breach and Megarry J said that this measure of damages better reflected the right to performance of the contract lost by the plaintiff.[231]

However, in *Johnson v Agnew*, Lord Wilberforce cast doubt on the correctness of *Wroth v Tyler* and held that the principles governing the calculation of Lord Cairns' Act damages and common law damages were the same.[232] However, he left open the date as at which Lord Cairns' Act damages are to be assessed.[233]

Johnson v Agnew should be read narrowly after *One Step Support Ltd v Morris-Garner*. In that case, Lord Reed said that *Johnson v Agnew* could not mean that Lord Cairns' Act damages must always be measured in the same way as common law damages, particularly given that Lord Cairns' Act damages are available on a different basis, in different circumstances, and in respect of different types of wrong (past wrongs for common law damages, and future or continuing wrongs for Lord Cairns' Act damages).[234]

'Reasonable fee' awards

Courts sometimes award a 'reasonable fee' in lieu of specific relief. This most commonly occurs in cases involving breach of negative covenants or trespass to land, particularly when a court wishes to choose an option between an injunction and nominal or no damages.

Such damages have also occasionally been awarded for nuisance, although later English cases suggest that reasonable fee awards are not available for nuisance. The basis and means of measuring reasonable fee awards (whether under Lord Cairns' Act or otherwise) have been contested (as discussed in more detail in Chapter 8). In *One Step Support Ltd v Morris-Garner*, Lord Reed suggested that reasonable fee awards made pursuant to Lord Cairns' Act are compensatory and provide a monetary substitute for the injunction:

---

230 The date of assessment of common law damages is discussed above.
231 [1974] 1 Ch 30, 57–58.
232 [1980] AC 367, 400.
233 ibid.
234 [2018] UKSC 20, [2019] AC 649 [47] (Lord Reed, with whom Lady Hale, Lord Wilson and Lord Carnwath agreed).

> Damages awarded in substitution for an injunction are, as one might expect, a monetary substitute for an injunction. As Viscount Finlay stated in *Leeds Industrial Co-operative Society Ltd v Slack* … "the power to give damages in lieu of an injunction must in all reason import the power to give an equivalent for what is lost by the refusal of the injunction". Where it is likely that the refusal of an injunction will result in the claimant's sustaining loss and damage as a consequence of the tort, breach of contract or other wrongful act which the court has declined to prevent, the damages should provide compensation for that loss and damage.[235]

Further information on how to calculate reasonable fees is contained in Chapter 8.

Where specific relief was impossible or in addition to specific relief

When Lord Cairns' Act damages are awarded because specific relief was genuinely impossible at the time of trial, courts generally award damages for losses flowing from the wrongdoing. Thus, in *Catton v Wyld*,[236] damages reflected the losses suffered during the period that a wall had been pulled down, and in *Fritz v Hobson*,[237] damages reflected the loss of custom a shop owner suffered while the entrance to his shop was blocked by an obstruction.

When Lord Cairns' Act damages are sought in addition to specific relief, the court is careful not to award double relief (ie, both specific relief and damages in substitution for it). Generally, damages awarded in addition to specific relief are compensatory and arise in cases where some obligations can be enforced, and others cannot. For example, a court may order specific performance of part of a contract, and Lord Cairns' Act damages in respect of the balance of the agreement, as in *Grant v Dawkins*,[238] where the court compensated the plaintiff for the cost of discharging mortgages over the property so that specific performance could be effected.

Future wrongdoing

Generally, Lord Cairns' Act damages for future wrongdoing are compensatory.[239] For nuisance involving subsidence, damages are measured according to the anticipated cost of repair of the future subsidence, as well as any projected loss of land.[240] Similarly, damages for an anticipatory breach of contract

---

235 ibid [44].
236 (1863) 32 Beav 266, 55 ER 105.
237 (1880) 14 Ch D 542.
238 [1973] 1 WLR 1406.
239 *Leeds Industrial Cooperative Society Ltd v Slack* [1924] AC 851, 857 (Viscount Finlay).
240 *Hooper v Rogers* [1975] Ch 43; *Barbagallo v J & F Catelan Pty Ltd* [1986] 1 Qd R 245.

reflect the costs arising from the delay of the defendants in completing the contract.[241] However, where it is impossible to calculate the future loss, courts (arguably) make gain-based awards, as in the 'right to light' cases. When the defendant's building impedes the claimant's right to light in the future, damages are calculated as a 'share of the profits' that the defendant would make from the building.[242]

Discretionary Factors and Bars to Relief

The general equitable discretionary bars apply to Lord Cairns' Act damages, including hardship and the public interest, lack of clean hands, and delay and acquiescence. However, if (for example), specific relief has been barred because it will cause undue hardship to the defendant, Lord Cairns' Act damages will not necessarily be barred for the same reason. The court must consider—independently of whether an order of specific performance will cause hardship to the defendant—whether an award of Lord Cairns' Act damages will cause hardship to the defendant. In fact, this is the very situation where Lord Cairns' Act damages are useful: they allow a court to recognise the claimant's interest notwithstanding the operation of a discretionary bar precluding specific relief.

Although all bars to relief apply, the only bar to relief that will be discussed in detail here is delay and acquiescence. In *Sayers v Collyer*, Fry LJ said that 'acquiescence may be either an entire bar to all relief, or it may be a ground for inducing the court to act under the powers of Lord Cairns' Act'.[243] Sometimes, as in *Sayers v Collyer* itself, delay and acquiescence on the part of the claimant result in the denial of any relief,[244] but more usually it is an important factor in why a court chooses to award Lord Cairns' Act damages in lieu of specific relief.[245] In other words, the claimant's right should be recognised by the court, but they have acquiesced or delayed in enforcing the right to such an extent that it would be unfair to impose an injunction on the defendant, and so damages are awarded in lieu.

---

241 *Oakacre Ltd v Claire Cleaners (Holdings) Ltd* [1982] Ch 197, 203.

242 *Tamares (Vincent Square) Ltd v Fairpoint Properties (Vincent Square) Ltd (No 2)* [2007] EWHC 212 (Ch), [2007] 1 WLR 2167; *HKRUK II (CHC) Ltd v Heaney* [2010] EWHC 2245 (Ch).

243 (1884) 28 Ch D 103, 110.

244 ibid. See also *Sobey v Sainsbury* [1913] 2 Ch 513.

245 *Eastwood v Lever* (1863) 4 De GJ & Sm 114, 46 ER 859; *Shaw v Applegate* [1977] 1 WLR 970.

8. Vindicatory remedies

INTRODUCTION

This chapter considers remedies that vindicate the rights of the claimant. Jason Varuhas has argued that the law allows the redress of certain rights in a way that affirms and reinforces the importance of particular interests.[1] The interests protected by vindicatory awards are often associated with the torts actionable per se (ie, those torts which are actionable without proof of damage). However, breach of contract is also actionable per se.

In what follows, we look at remedies available under common law that could be said to have a vindicatory aspect, not only compensation of factual loss. Of course, in a broad sense, all remedies have vindication of rights at their heart, but it is suggested that this function is the thread that draws together the disparate remedies listed below.

REASONABLE FEE AWARDS

'Reasonable fees' are awarded when defendants have wrongfully used certain property or infringed certain rights. The court awards the objectively ascertained fee notionaly reflecting the amount that the parties would have agreed upon for permitting the defendant's conduct. Reasonable fee awards may arise in various ways, including through an award of compensation, via an action for money had and received awarded as a result of a 'waiver of tort', as 'restitutionary damages', or (as discussed in the previous Chapter 7) under Lord Cairns' Act in lieu of an injunction. They are generally awarded for certain common law wrongs, namely, some (but not all) proprietary torts, and for breach of a negative covenant in contract.

The need for a 'reasonable fee' to be awarded can be illustrated with the following scenario, taken from Lord Shaw's speech in *Watson, Laidlaw & Co Ltd v Pott, Cassels & Williamson*.[2] If you borrow my horse without my permission

---

[1] Jason Varuhas, 'The Concept of 'Vindication' in the Law of Torts: Rights, Interests and Damages' (2014) 34 OJLS 253.

[2] (1914) SC 18, 31.

and ride him, and I was not in the business of hiring him out, I have not suffered a *factual* loss which can be readily compensated. In fact, my horse might be better off for the exercise. However, it is incontrovertible that by using my horse without my permission, you have committed a proprietary tort. Common law courts have held that I should be entitled to 'user damages' reflecting the value of your use of my horse. *The Mediana* confirms that it is immaterial that I would not have used the horse while you were using it; I am still entitled to damages.[3] It is in these situations, where the claimant has not suffered a factual loss in the ordinary sense, yet the situation still calls for damages, that courts award reasonable fees. Courts may also award a 'reasonable fee' to highlight that the defendant ought to have sought consent to infringe the claimant's right, in which case it is effectively a compulsory licence fee imposed ex post facto on the defendant.

It must be observed that, at different times and in different cases, a variety of terms have been used to denote reasonable fee awards, such as 'restitutionary damages', 'Wrotham Park damages', 'licence fee damages', 'user awards' and 'bargaining damages'. However, the primary authority on this topic in England and Wales, *One Step Support Pty Ltd v Morris-Garner*,[4] has clarified the matter of terminology. In the leading speech, Lord Reed outlined three kinds of reasonable fee awards:

(1) 'User damages' in tort, which are awarded when there is the commission of a proprietary tort. The claimant is said to lose 'his right to obtain the economic value of the use in question, and [the defendant] should therefore compensate him for the consequent loss'.[5]
(2) 'Negotiating damages' in contract, which are awarded when there is a breach of a negative obligation (particularly restrictive covenants, intellectual property, or confidential information). The claimant is said to lose 'a valuable asset, and his loss can therefore be measured by determining the economic value of the asset in question. The defendant has taken something for nothing, for which the claimant was entitled to require payment'.[6]
(3) 'Lord Cairns' Act damages' (in the sense described in Chapter 7) which are awarded under Lord Cairns' Act as 'a monetary substitute for an injunction',[7] according to Lord Reed. These cases arise in contract for

---

[3] *The Mediana* [1900] AC 113, 117 (Lord Halsbury LC).
[4] [2018] UKSC 20; [2019] AC 649 ('*One Step*').
[5] ibid [30]. Lady Hale, Lord Wilson and Lord Carnwath agreed with Lord Reed.
[6] ibid [92].
[7] ibid [44].

breaches of negative covenant and in tort, when an injunction is denied on discretionary grounds.

Prior to Lord Reed's speech, there had been confusion regarding the normative basis for reasonable fee awards, with case law and academic commentary pointing in many different directions.

(1) Compensation for actual loss, namely loss of an opportunity to bargain for a release fee;[8]
(2) Substitutive compensation, namely compensation for the loss of the valuable rights associated with the contract or property in question;[9]
(3) Restitution, namely the reversal of a benefit received by the defendant at the claimant's expense;[10]
(4) Both compensation and restitution simultaneously;[11]

---

8 *Jaggard v Sawyer* [1995] 1 WLR 269, 291 (Millett LJ); *Gafford v Graham* (1999) 77 P & CR 73, 86 (Nourse LJ); *World Wide Fund for Nature v World Wrestling Federation Entertainment Inc* [2007] EWCA Civ 286; [2008] 1 WLR 445 [29] (Chadwick LJ); *One Step* (n 4) [115]–[123] (Lord Sumption); RJ Sharpe and Stephen M Waddams, 'Damages for Lost Opportunity to Bargain' (1982) 2 OJLS 290; Andrew Phang and Pey-Woan Lee, 'Rationalising Restitutionary Damages in Contract Law – An Elusive or Illusory Quest?' (2001) 17 JCL 240, 252–53.

9 *Turf Club Auto Emporium Pte Ltd v Yeo Boong Hua* [2018] SGCA 44; [2018] 2 SLR 655 [206]–[207]; Mitchell McInnes, 'Account of Profits for Common Law Wrongs' in Simone Degeling and James Edelman (eds), *Equity in Commercial Law* (LBC 2004) 416–18; Mitchell McInnes, 'Gain, Loss and the User Principle' (2006) 14 RLR 76, 84–86. See also Francisco Giglio, *The Foundations of Restitution for Wrongs* (Hart 2007). Cf Craig Rotherham, '"Wrotham Park Damages" and Accounts of Profits' [2008] LMCLQ 25, 45–52. Other rights-based interpretations include Kit Barker, 'Damages Without Loss': Can Hohfeld Help?' (2014) 34 OJLS 631 and Robert Stevens, *Torts and Rights* (OUP 2007) 60.

10 *Strand Electric & Engineering Co Ltd v Brisford Entertainments Ltd* [1952] 2 QB 246 (CA) 252 (Somervell LJ), 253 (Denning LJ); *LJP Investments v Howard Chia Investments* (1989) 24 NSWLR 499; *Gaba Formwork Contractors Pty Ltd v Turner Corp Ltd* (1991) 32 NSWLR 175, 188 (Giles J); *Bunnings Group Ltd v Chep Australia Ltd* [2011] NSWCA 342; (2011) 82 NSWLR 420 [194]–[199], [205] (Giles JA); Jack Beatson, 'The Nature of Waiver of Tort' in Jack Beatson (ed), *Use and Abuse of Unjust Enrichment* (Clarendon Press 1991) 206, 232; Sarah Worthington, 'Reconsidering Disgorgement for Wrongs' (1999) 62 Mod LR 218; James Edelman, *Gain-Based Damages: Contract, Tort, Equity and Intellectual Property* (Hart 2002) 65–78.

11 *Inverugie Investments Ltd v Hackett* [1995] 1 WLR 713, 718 (Lord Lloyd); *Hampton v BHP Billiton Minerals Pty Ltd (No 2)* [2012] WASC 285 [355]–[359],

(5) Property-right-based analyses, which focus on the fact that awards are linked to the presence of a property right or property-like right;[12] and
(6) Disgorgement of a gain, namely removal of part or all of the profits received as a result of the breach.[13]

After *One Step*, however, Lord Reed's analysis confirms that the normative basis for these awards in England and Wales is point (2), namely, substitutive compensation reflecting the loss of the valuable rights associated with the contract or property.

General Methods of Calculation

It is difficult to discern a general pattern for the calculation of reasonable fee awards. In *Marathon Asset Management LLP v Seddon*,[14] Leggatt J proposed a scheme which, while expressed in terms that presume these awards to be gain-based, remains very helpful. However, in what follows, the word 'benefit' has been replaced by the word 'interest':

(1) If there was an alternative means by which the defendant could have obtained the interest, the interest will be valued at the market value.[15]
(2) If the defendant could not have obtained the interest from another source, it should be asked whether it was reasonable to expect the claimant to sell the interest to the defendant for a reasonable fee. The interest will be valued by reference to the reasonable fee the claimant could have charged.[16]

---

[342]–[354]; *ACES System Development Pte Ltd v Yenty Lily* [2013] SGCA 53; [2013] 4 SLR 1317 [38]; David Brennan, 'The Beautiful Restitutionary Heresy of a Larrikin' (2011) 33 Syd LR 209; Kelvin FK Low, 'The User Principle: Rashomon Effect or Much Ado about Nothing' (2016) 28 SAcLJ 984. Cf Kit Barker, '"Damages Without Loss": Can Hohfeld Help?' (2014) 34 OJLS 631, 646.

12 *Hospitality Group Pty Ltd v Australian Rugby Union Ltd* [2001] FCA 1040; (2001) 110 FCR 157, [167]–[168] (Emmett J), drawing on Daniel Friedmann, 'Restitution of Benefits Obtained through the Appropriation of Property or the Commission of a Wrong' (1980) 80 Colum L Rev 504; Peter Jaffey, 'Licence Fee Damages' (2011) RLR 95; Sirko Harder, *Measuring Damages in the Law of Obligations: The Search for Harmonised Principles* (Hart 2010) 216.

13 *Kansas v Nebraska*, 135 S Ct 1042, 1058 (2015); *Marathon Asset Management LLP v Seddon* [2017] EWHC 300 (Comm); [2017] ICR 791 [192]–[202]; Katy Barnett, *Accounting for Profit for Breach of Contract: Theory and Practice* (Hart 2012) Ch 6.

14 [2017] EWHC 300 (Comm); [2017] ICR 791 ('*Marathon Asset*').

15 ibid [232].

16 ibid [233].

(3) If the defendant could not reasonably have been expected to purchase the interest from elsewhere and it was not reasonable for the claimant to sell, the interest should be assessed according to the profit made by the defendant as a result of the breach.[17]

While the final point appears to take a profit-based approach, it could still be justified as substitutive compensation if the profit is used as a proxy for the claimant's loss. It should be noted that Lord Reed in *One Step* referred to *Marathon Asset* with apparent approval.[18]

We now consider the categories of cases in which reasonable fee awards have been made: in equity, in intellectual property law, in tort, and in contract.

Reasonable Fees in Equity

Reasonable fee awards have been made for breach of confidence, particularly in the context of trade secrets. For example, in the *Seager v Copydex* cases,[19] where the defendant mistakenly believed it was legally entitled to use the plaintiff's confidential information, the Court of Appeal declined to award an injunction or a full account of profits, but instead awarded a reasonable fee reflecting the market value of the confidential information. The Court of Appeal did not identify an equitable basis for this, nor did it purport to grant damages in lieu of an injunction.

In *Vercoe v Rutland Fund Management Ltd*,[20] Sales J awarded a reasonable fee for concurrent breach of contract and breach of confidence. His Honour said that in light of *Attorney General v Blake* (discussed in Chapter 9), accounts of profits should only be awarded exceptionally, and only in cases where there was a proprietary right akin to an intellectual property right.

Intellectual Property: 'User Damages'

Intellectual property infringements have been treated by courts as analogous to the wrongful use of corporeal property; hence, 'user damages' may

17 ibid [236].

18 *One Step* [2018] UKSC 20; [2019] AC 649 [75] (Lord Reed, with whom Lady Hale, Lord Wilson and Lord Carnwath agreed).

19 *Seager v Copydex (No 1)* [1967] 1 WLR 923; *Seager v Copydex (No 2)* [1969] 1 WLR 809.

20 [2010] EWHC 424 (Ch), [2010] Bus LR 141 [341].

be awarded. The tort of passing off is regarded as an intellectual property infringement and may also give rise to a reasonable fee award.[21]

For a single use, damages are calculated on a licence fee basis.[22] For multiple uses, damages are assessed on a royalty basis.[23] The court must consider what a willing licensee would have paid and what a willing licensor would have accepted, in light of the characteristics of the parties in dispute,[24] and have an eye to the position the claimant would have been in had the defendant behaved properly.[25]

Section 97(1) of the Copyright, Designs and Patents Act 1988 (UK) provides for an 'innocent infringement' defence:

> Where in an action for infringement of copyright it is shown that at the time of the infringement the defendant did not know, and had no reason to believe, that copyright subsisted in the work to which the action relates, the plaintiff is not entitled to damages against him, but without prejudice to any other remedy.

Likewise, sections 191J(1) and 233(1) of the same Act also provide for an 'innocent infringement' defence for a performer's property right and for a primary infringement of a design right. Insofar as a reasonable fee is regarded as a species of compensatory damages, the 'innocent infringement' defence will provide a defence in these circumstances.

Tort: 'User Damages'

'User damages' awards are made primarily for certain torts that involve a direct interference with property (ie, trespass to land, trespass to goods, and conversion).[26] The availability of user damages for nuisance is contested, and they are unlikely to be available for non-proprietary torts.

Historically, user damages were often awarded under a doctrine known as 'waiver of tort'. Here, the claimant proceeded against the defendant on the fiction that the claimant had consented to the defendant dealing with the claimant's property, but that the defendant had made an implied promise that they would account to the claimant for the proceeds of the profit. As a result, the

---

21 See, eg, *Winnebago Industries Inc v Knott Investments Pty Ltd (No 4)* [2015] FCA 1327; (2015) 241 FCR 271.

22 *Chabot v Davies* [1936] 3 All ER 211, 228.

23 *Lewis Trusts v Bambers Stores* [1982] FSR 281.

24 *General Tire and Rubber Co v Firestone Tyre and Rubber Co Ltd* [1975] 1 WLR 819, 824–26 (Lord Wilberforce).

25 *Penn v Jack* (1867) LR 5 Eq 81, 84.

26 Such damages were also available for detinue before it was abolished in the UK by s 2(1) of the Torts (Interference with Goods) Act 1977 (UK).

claimant was entitled to an *indebitatus assumpsit* or 'action for money had and received' (a restitutionary remedy discussed in Chapters 9 and 10). However, the 'waiver of tort' fiction was debunked by the House of Lords in *United Australia Ltd v Barclays Bank*,[27] in which it was observed that there was no true 'waiver' of the wrong. Rather, the claimant was electing between compensatory and restitutionary remedies.

'User damages' in tort do not spring from a single source, and the results in case law have been achieved by varied pathways. This variability helps explain the controversy over the normative justification for user fees. The pathways according to which courts have awarded 'user damages' in tort include:

- A compensatory alternative to other loss-based awards, as suggested by *One Step*;
- A restitutionary award, reflecting the history of 'waiver of tort', and the 'wayleave' and 'mesne profit' cases (discussed below), where a claimant can elect to go down a restitutionary path rather than a compensatory path; or
- Lord Cairns' Act damages, ie, in lieu of an injunction to restrain the commission of a proprietary tort.

Torts protecting proprietary interests in land

Historically, user damages were given in two kinds of cases of trespass, pursuant to the doctrine of waiver of tort. First, in the 'wayleave' cases, the defendant uses the claimant's land without denying the claimant possession.[28] For example, if I cross your property without permission, I do not deny your possession, but I infringe your right to possession. Second, in the 'mesne profit' cases, the defendant wrongfully withholds possession of the land from the claimant, typically after the expiry of a lease.[29] For example, you may be entitled to 'mesne profits' if I wrongfully remain in your property after the expiry of my lease. Sometimes user damages for trespass to land are also awarded in lieu of an injunction pursuant to Lord Cairns' Act.[30] It is clear, in any case, that

---

27 [1941] AC 1.

28 See, eg, *Martin v Porter* (1839) 5 M & W 351, 151 ER 149; *Jegon v Vivian* (1871) LR 6 Ch 742; *Phillips v Homfray* (1871) LR 6 Ch App 770; *Whitwham v Westminster Brymbo Coal & Coke Company* [1896] 2 Ch 538.

29 See, eg, *Elliott v Boynton* [1924] 1 Ch 236; *Wilson v Kelly* [1957] VR 147; *Swordheath Properties Ltd v Tabet* [1979] 1 WLR 285; *Ministry of Defence v Ashman* [1993] 2 EGLR 102; *Ministry of Defence v Thompson* [1993] 2 EGLR 107; *Lollis v Loulatzis* [2007] VSC 547.

30 See eg, *Bracewell v Appleby* [1975] Ch 408; *Jaggard v Sawyer* [1995] 1 WLR 269.

user damages are available for trespass to land even where no physical damage to land occurs, to vindicate the owner's right to exclusive possession.

English courts have sometimes awarded user damages for nuisance.[31] However, two English cases suggest that user damages are unavailable for the tort of nuisance, even though it is a proprietary tort. In *Stoke-on-Trent City Council v W and J Wass Ltd*,[32] user damages were refused for nuisance in the form of an infringement of a market right. Furthermore, a majority of the English Court of Appeal in *Forsyth-Grant v Allen* said in obiter dicta that user damages (which were regarded as restitutionary at that time) were inappropriate for nuisance because this tort did not involve misappropriation of rights, unlike trespass, conversion, or intellectual property infringement.[33]

Torts protecting proprietary interests in goods

In *Strand Electric & Engineering Co Ltd v Brisford Entertainments Ltd*,[34] it was established that a claimant may also be entitled to 'user damages' where a defendant has committed a tort against goods. In that case, the plaintiff, Strand Electric, hired out electric switchboards to a theatre company. Brisford Entertainment, the defendant, owned the theatre. It repossessed the building from the theatre company which had been using the premises, but refused to return the switchboards to the plaintiff because the property could be more readily marketed with the switchboards in situ. The plaintiff brought an action in detinue, claiming the return of its goods and damages for the period of detention.

The trial judge awarded user damages; however, he discounted the damages to reflect the fact that the plaintiff might not have hired out all the switchboards. On appeal, the English Court of Appeal unanimously held that the plaintiff was entitled to the full hiring charge for the whole period of the goods' detention without any discount. Somervell LJ and Denning LJ specifically drew parallels between the unlawful detention of the goods and the mesne profit cases mentioned above.[35]

The Court of Appeal judges expressed two competing views about the normative basis of the award. Denning LJ saw user damages as based on

---

31 *Bracewell v Appleby* [1975] Ch 408; *Carr-Saunders v Dick McNeil Associates Ltd* [1986] 1 WLR 922.

32 [1988] 1 WLR 1406.

33 *Forsyth-Grant v Allen* [2008] EWCA Civ 505; [2008] 2 EGLR 16 [32] (Patten LJ, with whom Mummery LJ agreed). Toulson LJ (at [47]) left open the question of whether a restitutionary award can be awarded for nuisance.

34 [1952] 2 QB 246.

35 ibid 252 (Somervell LJ), 253 (Denning LJ).

restitutionary principles.[36] In his view, the hiring charge reflected the fact that the defendant had wrongfully used the goods for its own purposes. The user damages reversed the benefit the defendant had received from the use of the goods, and it was irrelevant that the plaintiff had suffered no loss.

Romer LJ saw user damages as compensatory.[37] He said that three important facts indicated that user damages were appropriate: (1) the equipment which the defendant detained was profit-earning; (2) the plaintiff normally hired out the equipment in its business; and (3) during the period of wrongful detention, the defendant used the property for its own ends. User damages were said to reflect the losses made by the plaintiff, and the question of the profit or benefit which the defendant had derived from the wrongful act did not arise.

Other torts

English law tends to suggest that user damages for non-proprietary torts will not be made. For instance, in *Halifax Building Society v Thomas*,[38] the English Court of Appeal refused to allow 'waiver of tort' for the tort of deceit. In *Devenish Nutrition Ltd v Sanofi-Aventis SA (France)*,[39] the English Court of Appeal held that *Stoke-on-Trent City Council v W and J Wass Ltd* (mentioned above) stood for the proposition that user damages were unavailable for non-proprietary torts. The Court of Appeal declined to award user damages for breach of statutory duty.

Although there may be good reasons why such awards are unavailable, these reasons should be developed in a more coherent fashion.[40] At present, the conclusions in these cases are not reached on a principled basis.

Contract: 'Negotiating Damages'

'Negotiating damages' for breach of contract typically arise in instances of breach of negative covenant, where the loss is difficult to calculate on the traditional expectation measures such as the difference in value.

In *Wrotham Park Estate Co Ltd v Parkside Homes Ltd*,[41] Brightman J clearly awarded 'negotiating damages' for breach of a restrictive covenant, in lieu of an injunction restraining the breach, pursuant to Lord Cairns' Act. The normative basis of that award remains contested, both by scholars and in case

---

36 ibid 254–55.

37 ibid 256.

38 [1996] Ch 217.

39 [2008] EWCA Civ 1086; [2009] Ch 390.

40 Craig Rotherham, 'Gain-Based Relief in Tort after *Attorney General v Blake*' (2010) 126 LQR 102, 110–11.

41 [1974] 1 WLR 798.

law. The defendants were property developers who built more houses than the plaintiffs would have permitted, in breach of a restrictive covenant in favour of the plaintiffs' land. The plaintiffs had notified the developers about this covenant shortly after the developers purchased the land, and a writ claiming a mandatory injunction was served on the defendants before substantial construction began. However, the plaintiffs chose not to seek an interlocutory injunction because they were advised (wrongly) that it would not have been available. Later, the plaintiffs sought a mandatory injunction to demolish the houses. By the time the matter came to trial, the houses had been built. Brightman J refused to award an injunction as it would be an 'unpardonable waste'.[42] However, he awarded the plaintiffs damages in lieu of an injunction pursuant to Lord Cairns' Act (discussed in Chapter 7) and calculated these damages at 5 percent of the anticipated profit of the defendants. Lord Nicholls, in *Attorney-General v Blake*, had suggested that the award in *Wrotham Park* was gain-based.[43] However, Lord Reed in *One Step* rejected Lord Nicholls' characterisation, and instead, categorised the award as compensatory.[44]

In *One Step* itself, negotiating damages were refused because contractual damages on the ordinary measure of difference in value could be calculated. Ms Morris-Garner developed a business providing support for young people leaving government care. She sold the business to One Step (Support) Ltd ('One Step'), whereupon the business was run by Mr Costelloe, but she remained a part-owner and director. In 2006, Ms Morris-Garner sold her interest in One Step to Mrs Costelloe, when her relationship with the Costelloes soured. She signed a deed in which she agreed (among other things) not to use confidential information from One Step and not to compete with One Step for a year after the deed was signed. However, Ms Morris-Garner and her partner had already incorporated a company named Positive Living Limited ('Positive Living'), which began to operate in a similar geographical area to One Step, providing similar services. In 2007, Mr Costelloe instructed solicitors to restrain Positive Living from competing with One Step, but Positive Living denied that it was, and the proceedings were discontinued. However, in 2008, when One Step's business continued to decline, it discovered that the 2007 denial was false. It sought what were known as '*Wrotham Park*' damages (now 'negotiating damages'). Presumably, it did so because the loss was speculative and difficult to calculate and because it hoped to obtain some part of the gains Positive Living had made by breaching the covenant.

---

42 ibid 811.

43 *Attorney-General v Blake* [2001] 1 AC 268, 283.

44 *One Step* [2018] UKSC 20; [2019] AC 649 [73].

According to Lord Reed, delivering the majority speech, an award of negotiating damages is available where difference-in-value damages were impossible to calculate, and the breach of contract 'result[ed] in the loss of a valuable asset created or protected by the right which was infringed'.[45] In this case, it was possible to calculate damages for breach of contract on a difference-in-value basis,[46] by comparing the position as if the contract had been performed (ie, Ms Morris-Garner had not created a rival company) and the actual position (ie, Ms Morris-Garner created Positive Living, which caused One Step's business to decline). One Step suffered pecuniary losses between £3.4m and £4.6m, and further consequential loss of profits when the negative covenant expired, based on a comparison between projected sales in the absence of Positive Living and actual sales made. One Step also suffered other losses which, as Lord Reed noted, would be harder to quantify (including damage to the value of the business, effect on its profits, an increase in management costs, and a loss of goodwill).

Although in this case the claimant was awarded expectation damages on a difference in value measure, Lord Reed made several observations about 'negotiating damages'. First, he said that 'negotiating damages' were compensatory:

> ... There are certain circumstances in which the loss for which compensation is due is the economic value of the right which has been breached, considered as an asset. The imaginary negotiation is merely a tool for arriving at that value. The real question is as to the circumstances in which that value constitutes the measure of the claimant's loss.[47]

Lord Reed also said that the kinds of circumstances where negotiating damages might arise were cases of negative covenants concerning restrictive covenants, intellectual property, and breach of confidentiality, as in these cases, the claimant had been deprived of a valuable asset, which could be measured by considering the economic value of that asset.[48] He rejected any suggestion that negotiating damages were restitutionary,[49] or represented a partial or total disgorgement of profit.[50] Lord Sumption, in the minority, found that there was still a role for gain-based measures in the calculation of reasonable fees.[51]

Lord Reed recognised that there were problems with the opportunity to bargain analysis, acknowledging that the assessment of a hypothetical release fee

45 ibid [92].
46 ibid [98]–[99].
47 ibid [91].
48 ibid [92].
49 ibid [79].
50 ibid [81]–[82].
51 ibid [110]–[111].

was 'a difficult and uncertain exercise', and that in the early cases, judges had tended to estimate fees 'in a rough and ready way' (replaced in later cases by expert evidence from forensic accountants).[52] Despite this, his Lordship opined that 'the fact that the claimant might in reality have been unwilling to release the defendant from the obligation is not necessarily a problem'.[53] However, it appears from Lord Reed's speech that the hypothetical bargain must be one which a reasonable person in the claimant's position would accept; if it is not, Lord Reed seems to suggest that the award would be inappropriate but does not suggest an alternative method of calculation.[54]

Shortly after *One Step* was handed down, Singapore's Court of Appeal handed down a unanimous decision in *Turf Club Auto Emporium Pte Ltd v Yeo Boong Hua*,[55] which comes to a conclusion similar to that in *One Step*.[56] Negotiating damages were held to be compensatory and available only where there was a breach of a negative covenant, and when orthodox compensatory damages and specific relief were unavailable.[57] Moreover, negotiating damages would not be awarded where it would be irrational or unrealistic to expect the parties to bargain for a release, even on a hypothetical basis.[58] *Turf Club* also held that these species of damages are not subject to the limitations of causation and remoteness.[59]

Nonetheless, *Turf Club* differs from *One Step* in three respects. First, the Court did not regard it as important whether these awards were known as 'negotiating damages' or '*Wrotham Park*' damages.[60] Second, the Court did not confine negotiating damages to contracts involving economically valuable assets, because it considered that the meaning of 'asset' was unclear.[61] Finally, by contrast to Lord Reed in *One Step*, Singapore's Court of Appeal did not distinguish between 'reasonable fee' damages awarded in the absence of Lord Cairns' Act, and those available pursuant to Lord Cairns' Act, but integrated Lord Cairns' Act damages into their general analysis.[62]

---

52 ibid [74].
53 ibid [75].
54 ibid.
55 [2018] SGCA 44; [2018] 2 SLR 655.
56 ibid [271]–[276].
57 ibid.
58 ibid [217]–[241].
59 ibid [248].
60 ibid [270].
61 ibid [278]–[281].
62 ibid [284]–[286].

Vindicatory Aspect to 'Reasonable Fees'

It is clear that, after *One Step*, there is a vindicatory aspect to the awards of 'user damages', 'negotiating damages' and Lord Cairns' Act damages, because Lord Reed characterised them as effecting substitutive compensation. In other words, they compensate for the loss of a valuable right (in one way or another). This is why they are not subject to limitations such as remoteness and mitigation.

SELF-HELP REMEDIES

Self-help remedies allow the claimant to make good on their own rights without the intervention of the courts. Hence, they are not remedies in the strict sense of the word because the court makes no order. Instead, the claimant is given the liberty to redress their grievance by vindicating their own rights, thus affirming the importance of certain interests. Claimants have the liberty to respond reasonably to trespass to land, trespass to the person, and wrongful interference with goods. Self-help remedies are also available for breach of contract, most prominently by providing for liquidated damages. It is necessary to discuss the situations in which the courts leave room for self-help.

Unsurprisingly, the law is wary of allowing parties to resolve disputes by themselves, and 'self-help' is always subject to the qualification that it must be reasonable. Evidently, some responses to a dispute might have tortious or criminal consequences. For example, in the Australian case of *Croucher v Cachia*,[63] neighbours had a dispute over the boundary of their properties. When the plaintiff was clipping his hedge at the boundary, the defendant stated that the clippings from the plaintiff's hedge should not fall onto the defendant's driveway. A violent scuffle ensued, and the defendant severely injured the plaintiff's hand and thumb with gardening shears. The court found that the defendant committed the torts of trespass to the person and negligence. This recourse to self-help was unreasonable.

Indeed, civil recourse theorists argue that an important function of tort law is to prevent persons from engaging in violent recourse against one another when they have been wronged, by ensuring that courts vindicate the rights of the victim in a public forum instead.[64] Self-help remedies in tort are exceptional,

---

63 [2016] NSWCA 132; (2016) 95 NSWLR 117.

64 See, eg, Benjamin Zipursky, 'Rights, Wrongs and Recourse in the Law of Torts' (1998) 51 Vand L Rev 1; Benjamin Zipursky, 'Civil Recourse, Not Corrective Justice' (2003) 81 Georgetown LJ 695; John Goldberg and Benjamin Zipursky, 'Torts as Wrongs' (2010) 88 Tex L Rev 917; John Goldberg and Benjamin Zipursky, 'Civil Recourse Revisited' (2011) 39 Fla St U L Rev 340; Benjamin Zipursky,

and there is a strong requirement that any self-help must be reasonable. In contract, parties have greater freedom to bargain for remedies but, again, courts are concerned to prevent remedies that are harsh or unfair, particularly where bargaining power is unequal.

Tort and Self-Help

Some proprietary torts allow claimants to have recourse to self-help remedies, including trespass to land, trespass to goods, trespass to persons, and nuisance. These allow persons to defend themselves or their property from tortious interference, but courts are clear that any self-help must be reasonable. As Percy Winfield observed, 'self-help has always been reckoned as a perilous remedy owing to the stringent rules against its abuse'.[65]

Section 3 of the Criminal Law Act 1967 (UK) provides that:

(1) A person may use such force as is reasonable in the circumstances in the prevention of crime, or in effecting or assisting in the lawful arrest of offenders or suspected offenders or of persons unlawfully at large.
(2) Subsection (1) above shall replace the rules of the common law on the question when force used for a purpose mentioned in the subsection is justified by that purpose.

Consequently, more broadly, a person may use reasonable force to protect themselves from a crime, including threats to the person and protection of land and goods, as long as the conduct itself is not criminal.

Eviction of trespassers and protection of land and goods from trespass

A person in possession of land may evict a trespasser, but only using 'reasonable' force.[66]

Generally, force is unjustified unless the trespasser has been asked to leave and has been given a reasonable opportunity to leave, but refused to do so.[67] However, if a trespass is committed with force and with 'a strong hand', a

---

'Substantive Standing, Civil Recourse, and Corrective Justice' (2011) 39 Fla St U L Rev 299; Andrew Robertson, 'On the Function of the Law of Negligence' (2013) 33 OJLS 31; John Goldberg and Benjamin Zipursky, *Recognizing Wrongs* (HUP 2020).

[65] PH Winfield, *The Province of the Law of Tort* (CUP 1931) 233.

[66] *Hemmings v Stoke Poges Golf Club* [1920] 1 KB 820; *Cowell v Rosehill Racecourse Co Ltd* (1937) 56 CLR 605, 631 (Dixon J).

[67] *Green v Goddard* (1795) 2 Salk 641, 91 ER 541; *Polkinhorn v Wright* (1845) 8 QB 197, 115 ER 849.

possessor may respond with force, as the intruder's conduct indicates that a request to leave would be futile.[68] However, if the trespasser does not threaten to harm the property or the possessor, the possessor may only use minimal force.[69] Particularly difficult questions arise regarding the extent of the right of a landowner to evict a thief or burglar from the property.[70] This issue will be discussed in the context of self-defence of property.

The law regarding the right of a landowner to repossess a property from an occupier (such as a tenant or a squatter) is complex because of the other rules relating to the eviction of persons in possession of land,[71] which may impact the availability of any general law remedy.

Previously, the repossession of property was governed by the old Statutes of Forcible Entry, which made it an offence to forcibly enter the land 'with a strong hand' or with a multitude of people.[72] In *McPhail v Persons Unknown*,[73] the English Court of Appeal held that landowners could evict squatters without a court order, as long as they used no more force than was reasonably necessary. It was found that the Statutes of Forcible Entry did not preclude owners from using force to evict the squatters, because the squatters themselves had entered using force ('with a strong hand') which was precluded by the statute.[74] As a consequence, the Statutes of Forcible Entry were repealed by the Criminal Law Act 1977 (UK). Section 6 of that Act now creates an offence where a person uses or threatens unauthorised violence (whether against persons or property) for the purpose of securing entry into any premises, if there is known to be a person inside opposing entry. This is the case even if the person inside is a squatter. There is an exception under section 6(1A) for displaced residential occupiers or their representatives.

There is also a question of damage to goods. In the nineteenth century, English courts began to doubt that landowners were entitled to use force to

68 ibid.

69 ibid.

70 See generally Brian Hogan, 'Defence of Property' (1994) 144 New LJ 466.

71 See, eg, the Protection from Eviction Act 1977 (UK), ss 2 and 3, which make it a crime to evict tenants without using proceedings in the court.

72 Statute of Forcible Entry 1381 (15 Rich II, c 7); Statute of Forcible Entry 1391 (15 Rich II, c 2); Statute of Forcible Entry 1429 (8 Hen VI, c 9). See *R v Mountford* [1972] 1 QB 28 for a history of these statutes. The medieval term for forcible entry was trespass *vi et armis* ('with force and arms'). These were all repeated by the Criminal Law Act 1977 (UK), s 13(2).

73 [1973] Ch 447, 455.

74 ibid 456, 461–62.

evict an occupier or their chattels,[75] but in *Hemmings v Stoke Poges Golf Club* the English Court of Appeal held that a landlord was not liable for assault and damage to goods occurring during the eviction of a tenant who had overstayed his lease.[76] Thus, at common law, it appears that a landlord may repossess a property from a former tenant using reasonable force, as long as the landlord first asks the tenant to leave and gives them a reasonable opportunity to leave. However, sections 2 and 3 of the Protection from Eviction Act 1977 (UK) make it unlawful to evict tenants without using proceedings in the court.

The net effect of this legislation is to encourage landowners to seek court orders before exercising any force. If an owner obtains an order for possession via proceedings in court, the use of force by the bailiff is not unauthorised violence.

Reasonable force may be used to remove protesters who deliberately obstruct lawful work being undertaken on a property.[77] However, courts are wary of encouraging self-help in these circumstances, and it has been observed that breaches of the peace and disputes as to whether reasonable force was used are likely to arise as soon as one person lays hands on another to remove them from their land.[78]

Self-defence of property

A possessor of land or goods may use reasonable force to protect their land or goods. Historically, a possessor of land and goods could go to extreme lengths to protect their property. In *Semayne's Case*, it was famously said: 'The house of every one is his castle, and if thieves come to a man's house to rob or murder, and the owner or his servants kill any of the thieves in defence of himself and his house, it is no felony and he shall lose nothing.'[79] However, from 1827 onwards, the use of 'spring guns', 'man traps' and other instruments that may cause death or inflict grievous bodily harm was outlawed in the United Kingdom.[80] Hence, in *Bird v Holbrook*, when the teenage neighbour of

---

[75] See, eg, *Pollen v Brewer* (1859) 7 CB (NS) 371; *Clifton Securities v Huntley* [1948] 2 All ER 283.

[76] *Hemmings v Stoke Poges Golf Club* [1920] 1 KB 820.

[77] *Holmes v Bagge* [1853] 1 E & B 782, 786–87; 118 ER 629, 631 (Lord Campbell CJ); *R v Chief Constable of Devon and Cornwall* [1982] 1 QB 458, 470, 473.

[78] *R v Chief Constable of Devon and Cornwall* [1982] 1 QB 458, 473 (Lawton LJ). See also *Sedleigh-Denfield v O'Callaghan* [1940] AC 880, 911 (Lord Wright).

[79] (1604) 5 Co Rep 91a, 91a; 77 ER 194, 194. Still retained in US law as the 'castle doctrine'.

[80] Spring Guns Act 1827 (7 & 8 Geo. 4, c. 18). Later replaced by the Offences against the Person Act 1861 (24 & 25 Vict., c. 100), s 31, still in force.

a landowner was badly injured by a spring gun[81] after he entered the landowner's garden to retrieve a straying peahen, this was an unreasonable defence of property.[82] Landowners can still install spiked barriers to protect property,[83] and keep guard dogs,[84] as their utility outweighs the chance that a trespasser may suffer an injury.

Defence of goods must also be reasonable. In *Poland v John Parr & Sons*,[85] a man was walking home when he saw a boy whom he thought was stealing sugar from his employer's wagon. He hit the boy on the back of the neck, causing the boy to fall. The wheel of the wagon went over the boy's foot and, as a result, his leg had to be amputated. It was clear that the man was entitled and authorised to protect his employer's goods, but the employer was vicariously liable for his conduct because the force was excessive.[86]

Self-defence of the person

A person may act with reasonable force to defend themselves or a third person. The defendant must have had an honest and reasonable belief that he or she was about to be attacked by the claimant and must have used reasonable and necessary force to defend him or herself, or a third party. The burden of proof lies on the defendant, and the defendant must be both reasonable and honest.[87] This is in contrast to criminal law, where the defendant's belief need only be honest.

While the court does not require the defendant to 'very nicely measure the weight of the blows',[88] if the force used is unreasonable, then the defence will not apply. In *McAleer v PSNI*,[89] four police officers in Omagh in Northern Ireland were attempting to arrest a man, but they were surrounded by 15 to 20 hostile locals, including Ms McAleer. A police constable warned Ms McAleer to stop abusing her and pushing against her and asked her to step back. Ms

---

[81] A 'spring gun' is a gun rigged to fire a bullet when someone trips a tripwire. This spring gun was installed to protect tulip bulbs.

[82] (1828) 4 Bing 628, 130 ER 911. However, cf *Jordin v Crump* (1841) 8 M & W 783, 789; 151 ER 1256, 1259.

[83] *Deane v Clayton* (1817) 7 Taunt 489, 129 ER 196.

[84] *Brock v Copeland* (1794) 1 Esp 200, 170 ER 328.

[85] [1927] 1 KB 236.

[86] ibid 242–245. Cf *Bonette v Woolworths Ltd* (1937) 37 SR (NSW) 132, 151 (Jordan CJ), which held that an employee may protect goods but has no authority to punish a person who has dealt with them improperly.

[87] *Bici v Ministry of Defence* [2004] EWHC 786; *Chief Constable of Merseyside v McCarthy* [2016] EWCA Civ 1257 [30].

[88] *McAleer v PSNI* [2014] NIQB 53, [7] (Gillen J).

[89] ibid.

McAleer did not obey. The police constable hit Ms McAleer twice on the upper thigh, with a baton, and Ms McAleer suffered severe bruising. The court found that the constable's belief that Ms McAleer was aggressive was both reasonable and borne out by the evidence but that disproportionate force had been used, and the proper procedure was to aim for the lower legs. For this reason, the defence did not apply.[90]

Conversely, in *Cross v Kirkby*,[91] it was found that self-defence was available. Mr Cross and Mrs Davis, his partner, were anti-hunting activists who attempted to disrupt a fox hunt, including by trespassing on land. Mr Cross had already threatened to hit other people with his baseball bat, seized a man by the throat, and pushed another man over. Mr Kirkby attempted to gently escort Mrs Davis off the land, and she attempted to bite him. Mr Kirkby then backed off and tried to walk away, but Mr Cross ran at Mr Kirkby, wielding a baseball bat, and screamed, 'You're fucking dead, Kirkby', smashed the bat on the ground, splitting it into two pieces, and ran after Mr Kirkby, hitting him with the bat from behind. Mr Kirkby seized the handle of the bat from Mr Cross and hit him on the side of the head with it, causing Mr Cross a serious skull fracture which rendered him epileptic. It was found that Mr Kirkby's action was justified, first, because onlookers gave evidence that they believed Mr Kirkby was at serious risk, and secondly, because Mr Kirkby said that he reacted instinctively to defend himself, seizing the same weapon with which Mr Cross had attacked him.[92]

Recaption, replevin and specific restitution

As noted in Chapter 7, a person whose goods have been wrongfully taken may be able to obtain an order for specific restitution of the goods, but generally, this is only available if the goods are unique. Previously, the recovery of goods was often dealt with by self-help because of the limitations of court orders. Recaption allowed a person with an immediate right to possession to retake wrongfully possessed goods using reasonable force, but this has been abolished in English law.[93] Replevin establishes a similar right to recaption but developed in debtor and creditor law. A secured creditor may file a writ of replevin to obtain possession of goods over which the creditor has security, upon providing a bond or other security to the sheriff, until the court decides the final entitlement to the goods (sometimes called 'levying distress' on goods).[94]

---

90 ibid [11]–[12].
91 [2000] EWCA Civ 426.
92 ibid [32]–[35].
93 Tribunals, Courts and Enforcement Act 2008 (UK), s 65 and sch 12.
94 Lee Aitken, 'The Abandonment and Recaption of Chattels' (1994) 68 Aust LJ 263, 280.

The extent of availability of replevin in England and Wales is unclear.[95] It may extend to persons beyond creditors and is (at least theoretically) available to all kinds of takings amounting to trespass.

Abatement of nuisance

A person who has an action in nuisance may remove the source of the inconvenience through the self-help remedy of abatement. For example, if branches are overhanging a person's fence, or roots are growing into a person's land, the person has a right to remove the branches or roots up to the boundary line, as long as the person returns them to the other person's land. 'Abatement' only refers to the act of removing the source of the nuisance and does not extend to acts undertaken to alleviate the effects of the interference.

A person may only do what is necessary to avert the harm, and recovery of damages is restricted once abatement occurs. The least harmful way must be adopted, unless it would injure a third party or the public. In the Australian case of *Traian v Ware*,[96] it was found that the defendants' abatement was unreasonable. The plaintiffs and the defendants farmed adjoining blocks of land situated on a slope. The plaintiffs' land was downhill from the defendants' land. Fifteen years earlier, a previous owner of the plaintiffs' land had built an earthen bank at the top of the block to prevent it from being flooded by water running down from the defendants' land. During heavy rain, water collected at the bank and pooled on the defendants' land. The defendants entered the plaintiffs' land three times and cut a breach in the bank, without notice, flooding the plaintiffs' land and damaging their crops and orchards. The plaintiffs sued the defendants for damages in nuisance and trespass and sought an injunction to restrain the defendants from cutting the bank again. The defendants counterclaimed for a declaration that they were entitled to have the natural flow of water unimpeded, and for an injunction to prevent the bank from being repaired. Martin J held that the plaintiffs had an obligation to receive the natural flow of the water from the defendants' land and that the bank was a nuisance. However, the defendants had neither given notice to the plaintiffs nor asked for permission to cut the bank. Consequently, Martin J said the defendants were liable for trespass because of their 'unauthorised and high handed' conduct.[97] The defendants were not entitled to an injunction as they elected to abate. However, a declaration was made that the defendants were entitled to have the natural flow of water discharged onto the plaintiffs' land henceforth.

95 ibid 280–81.
96 [1957] VR 200.
97 ibid 208.

Contract and Self-Help

Contract law allows more latitude in self-help as contracts arise consensually, and the common law is predicated on the basis of freedom of contract.

Rescission

Rescission can be seen as a form of self-help, in at least some cases. If the defendant has supplied the claimant with defective goods, the claimant may simply elect to return the defective goods to the defendant and the defendant may return the purchase price to the claimant, without any recourse to a court. This is arguably a form of self-help,[98] although the rescission of the transaction is conducted in the shadow of the law. However, other cases of rescission (particularly equitable rescission) require court intervention because the courts must intervene and make adjustments to achieve 'practical justice'. Rescission is discussed in detail in Chapter 10.

Liquidated damages and penalties

A liquidated damages clause stipulates the damages available for breach, sometimes also known as an 'agreed damages' clause. A liquidated damages clause can be seen as a form of self-help because the parties agree to estimate the losses flowing from the breach of contract rather than obtaining a judicial assessment of the loss. A typical liquidated damages clause might stipulate: 'For a breach of cl 57 of this agreement, liquidated damages of £10,000 shall be payable.' Parties to a contract often agree to damages to bypass the expense and hostility of litigation and to increase certainty in respect of their obligations.

Nonetheless, sometimes the court will not allow certain liquidated damages clauses to be enforced if it decides the clause is a 'penalty'. According to this doctrine, a clause will not be enforceable if the payment of money or obligation is imposed *in terrorem* of the defaulting party (ie, intended to intimidate them into performance) as opposed to a clause which protects a 'legitimate interest' of the innocent party. This may seem to be an anomalous development in the common law: why only prevent these kinds of clauses and not others?

In fact, in *Cavendish Square Holding BV v Makdessi*,[99] the United Kingdom Supreme Court was invited to abolish the rule but declined to do so. However, the operation of the rule has been curtailed because the Court held that clauses will only be invalidated as penalties if the sum of liquidated damages is

[98] *Alati v Kruger* (1955) 94 CLR 216, 225–26.

[99] [2015] UKSC 57; [2016] AC 1172, [36] (Lord Neuberger and Lord Sumption).

extravagant and unconscionable in comparison to the 'legitimate interest' of the party imposing the detriment. The range of permissible 'legitimate interests' is wide.

There are three questions that must be answered to ascertain whether a clause will be a penalty rather than a valid liquidated damages clause:

1. Is this a clause to which the penalties doctrine applies?
2. If so, is the clause, in fact, penal?
3. If so, what are the consequences?

Each question will be dealt with in turn.

In English law, the penalties doctrine applies to a clause only where the detriment is imposed upon a breach of contract, or upon an event that cannot occur without breach. It is important to note that the rule against penalties applies beyond situations involving the payment of a stipulated sum and may also apply to clauses which prevent the breaching party from receiving a sum to which it would otherwise be entitled, to provisions which require a breaching party to transfer property at less than its full value, to deposits, and to forfeiture clauses, but only if the detriment is imposed as a result of a breach or an event which cannot occur without breach.

The following clause (the 'Breach Example Clause') would attract the application of the penalties doctrine:

(a) *Alphonse leases his hat shop to Bertha for £100 per week, on the condition that the shop is not used on weekends.*
(b) *If Bertha uses the shop on weekends, she agrees to pay Alphonse £500 for each breach.*

The payment of £500 may or may not, in fact, be a penalty (that is a separate question). However, the doctrine is prima facie applicable to the clause because the payment of £500 pursuant to clause (b) is triggered by a breach of clause (a).

The desire to avoid the penalties doctrine has led parties to draft clauses permissively, so that any negative consequences are not imposed as a result of breach or an event which cannot occur without breach. As an example, the Breach Example Clause could be redrafted as follows ('the Permissive Example Clause') to avoid triggering the penalties doctrine:

(a) *Alphonse leases his hat shop to Bertha for £100 per week for use Monday to Friday.*

(b) *Bertha agrees to pay Alphonse £500 each time the property is used on the weekend.*

In the Permissive Example Clause, the payment of £500 pursuant to (b) is not triggered by a breach. Bertha has simply agreed to pay £500 if the property is used on weekends.

It is immediately evident, however, that while the forms of the clauses are different, in substance, they produce the same result: Bertha pays £100 per week to use the hat shop from Monday to Friday, and Bertha pays £500 to Alphonse every time the hat shop is used on a weekend.

The widespread use of permissive drafting led the High Court of Australia to revive the equitable doctrine against penalties in *Andrews v Australia and New Zealand Banking Group Ltd*,[100] to ensure that permissively drafted clauses may be subject to the equitable rule against penalties. In a unanimous judgment, the Court suggested that the equitable doctrine against penalties would render voidable 'collateral stipulations' imposing detriment upon the breaching party, but this doctrine did not apply to 'additional stipulations' where the breaching party simply agreed to pay more for an extra right. The case has been strongly criticised, in part on the basis that it is uncommercial, and in part on the basis that the distinction between 'collateral stipulations' and 'additional stipulations' is difficult to apply in practice.[101] In *Cavendish v Makdessi*, the United Kingdom Supreme Court rejected *Andrews*, and confirmed that the doctrine is confined to detriments triggered by a breach of contract.[102]

Lord Neuberger and Lord Sumption, with whom Lord Carnwath agreed, said that the English penalties doctrine applies only to 'secondary obligations', which are said to arise when 'a contract contains an obligation on one party to perform an act, and also provides that, if he does not perform it, he will pay the other party a specified sum of money'.[103] The penalties doctrine does not apply to 'primary obligations'. Nor does it apply to 'conditional primary obligations', which are said to arise when 'the contract does not impose (expressly

---

100 [2012] HCA 30; 247 CLR 205, [10] (French CJ, Gummow, Crennan, Kiefel and Bell JJ) ('*Andrews*').

101 See John Carter, Wayne Courtney, Elisabeth Peden, Andrew Stewart and Gregory Tolhurst, 'Contractual Penalties: Resurrecting the Equitable Jurisdiction' (2013) 30 JCL 99; Sirko Harder, 'The Scope of the Rule against Contractual Penalties: A New Divergence' in Andrew Robertson and Michael Tilbury (eds), *Divergences in Private Law* (Hart 2016) 135. Cf Paul S Davies and Peter G Turner, 'Relief against Penalties without a Breach of Contract' (2013) 72 CLJ 20.

102 [2015] UKSC 67; [2016] AC 1172, [42] (Lord Neuberger and Lord Sumption, with whom Lord Carnwath agreed).

103 ibid [13].

or impliedly) an obligation to perform the act, but simply provides that, if one party does not perform, he will pay the other party a specified sum'. [104]

Applying this analysis to our example clauses above, the Breach Example Clause would be a 'secondary obligation' and subject to the rule against penalties. However, the Permissive Example Clause would probably be a 'conditional primary obligation', and therefore not subject to the rule against penalties, *unless* the court decided that the clause impliedly required Bertha not to use the hat shop on weekends.

Lord Neuberger and Lord Sumption went on to say that they recognised that the effects of this distinction could be capricious, and that 'the classification of terms for the purpose of the penalty rule depends on the substance of the term and not on its form or on the label which the parties have chosen to attach to it'.[105] However, one of the current authors has observed that although courts in England and Wales have made statements regarding substance over form before, the drafting of the contract has always been paramount.[106] Consequently, it is unclear when a permissively drafted clause may be found to be in substance a 'secondary obligation'.

In *Cavendish v Makdessi* itself, the judges disagreed upon the application of the distinction between 'secondary obligations' and 'primary obligations'. The case involved two conjoined appeals with different facts. In the first appeal, Makdessi sold the majority shareholding in an advertising company to Cavendish Square Holding BV ('Cavendish'). Both were experienced commercial parties, represented by lawyers in negotiations. The purchase price reflected the company's goodwill and was to be paid in instalments. Makdessi undertook not to compete with the company for two years but breached his obligation. Clause 5.1 of the contract of sale provided that, if Makdessi breached the obligation not to compete, he would not receive the final two instalments of the purchase price. Clause 5.6 further provided that, if Makdessi breached the obligation not to compete, Cavendish had the right to buy Makdessi's remaining shares in the company at a set price which excluded the company's goodwill. Makdessi sought to argue that both clauses were unenforceable as penalties.

Lord Neuberger and Lord Sumption held that Cl 5.1 was a 'primary obligation': it was a price adjustment clause that was 'in no way a secondary

104 ibid.

105 ibid [14].

106 Sirko Harder, 'The Scope of the Rule against Contractual Penalties: A New Divergence' in Andrew Robertson and Michael Tilbury (eds), *Divergences in Private Law* (Hart 2016) 54–58.

provision', as it was not a contractual alternative to damages at law.[107] Lord Hodge thought that this argument was 'strong' but added that even if Cl 5.1 were a secondary provision, he would not regard it as in fact a penalty.[108] Lord Neuberger and Lord Sumption found that Cl 5.6 was a 'primary obligation', because it reflected the reduced price that Cavendish was prepared to pay for the company if Makdessi competed with it.[109] They emphasised that the obligation imposed by Cl 5.6 was additional to, and not in substitution for, the obligation to pay damages at law.[110] Lord Hodge thought that this was a 'strong' argument, but he still construed it as a 'secondary obligation', for 'if all such clauses were treated as primary obligations, there would be considerable scope for abuse'.[111] Lord Mance applied the 'legitimate interest' test to each clause without considering how they should be characterised.[112]

Consequently, while Lord Neuberger and Lord Sumption (with whom Lord Carnwath agreed) found that the clauses were not subject to the penalty doctrine, a majority of the Court seemed to have been prepared to find that these clauses were subject to the doctrine,[113] but that Cavendish had a 'legitimate interest' which was proportionate to the detriment imposed upon Makdessi. The test proposed by Lord Neuberger and Lord Sumption requires a determination as to whether an obligation arising on the breach of another obligation is a secondary obligation or a conditional primary obligation, but, as Sarah Worthington has observed, there is no obvious test to allow parties to distinguish between the two.[114] Barnett and Harder have suggested that it must be ascertained whether the impugned obligation belongs to the core terms of the bargain: in other words, it must be essential to the achievement of its

107 [2015] UKSC 67, [2016] AC 1172, [74]. In any case, it was observed at [75] that Cavendish had a 'legitimate interest' in Makdessi's observance of the restrictive covenant.

108 ibid [270] (Lord Hodge, with whom Lord Clarke and Lord Toulson agreed on this issue).

109 ibid [81] (Lord Neuberger and Lord Sumption, with whom Lord Carnwath agreed).

110 ibid [80]. At [82], it was noted that the legitimate interest also justified Cl 5.6.

111 ibid [280] (Lord Hodge, with whom Lord Clarke and Lord Toulson agreed on this issue). At [282], Lord Hodge said that Cl 5.6 was not a penalty as it was not exorbitant when measured against Cavendish's legitimate interest in Makdessi not competing with the company.

112 ibid [182]–[185].

113 ibid [170] (Lord Mance), [226]–[227] (Lord Hodge). Lord Toulson agreed with Lord Mance and Lord Hodge on this issue.

114 Sarah Worthington, 'Penalty Clauses' in Graham Virgo and Sarah Worthington (eds), *Commercial Remedies: Resolving Controversies* (CUP 2017) 375–78.

purpose.[115] As noted above, Lord Neuberger and Lord Sumption emphasised that the detriments imposed by the disputed clauses in *Cavendish v Makdessi* were additional to, and not in substitution of, an obligation to pay damages at law, and that this led them to conclude they were not subject to the penalty doctrine. This seems to lead to the somewhat counterintuitive position that a detriment imposed above and beyond ordinary damages will be less likely to attract the doctrine.[116]

The second question, once it is established that the rule against penalties applies, is whether the clause is in fact penal. This is both a question of law,[117] and a question of construction.[118] In *Cavendish v Makdessi*, it was stated that if the amount payable pursuant to the clause is greater than a 'genuine pre-estimate' of the losses flowing from the breach of contract, it will not be penal if the party imposing the detriment has a 'legitimate interest' in doing so. [119]

The use of the words 'genuine pre-estimate' of losses reflects the earlier test of whether a clause is in fact a penalty, outlined by Lord Dunedin in *Dunlop Pneumatic Tyre Co Ltd v New Garage & Motor Co Ltd*.[120] For many years, this was the sole test used to determine whether a clause was a penalty,[121] and it is still applied in Singapore.[122] In *Dunlop*, Lord Dunedin said that a detriment will be a penalty if the sum stipulated is 'extravagant and unconscionable

---

115 Katy Barnett and Sirko Harder, 'A Comparative Consideration of the Penalties Doctrine in England and Australia' in Russell L Weaver, Steven I Friedland, Laetitia Tranchant and Guilhem Gil (eds), *Twenty-First Century Remedies: Comparative Perspectives* vol X (CAP 2020) 115, 121.

116 ibid.

117 *Sainter v Ferguson* (1849) 7 CB 716, 727; *Cargill International Trading Pte Ltd v Uttam Galva Steels Ltd* [2019] EWHC 476 (Comm), [37] (Bryan J).

118 *Cavendish v Makdessi* [2015] UKSC 67; [2016] AC 1172, [9] (Lord Neuberger and Lord Sumption, with whom Lord Carnwath agreed), [243] (Lord Hodge). See Francis Dawson, 'Determining Penalties as a matter of Construction' [2016] LMCLQ 207.

119 *Cavendish v Makdessi,* ibid [32] (Lord Neuberger and Lord Sumption, with whom Lord Clarke and Lord Carnwath agreed), [152] (Lord Mance, with whom Lord Clarke and Lord Toulson agreed), [255] (Lord Hodge, with whom Lord Clarke and Lord Toulson agreed).

120 [1915] AC 79, 86. See also Lord Parker at 97 and Lord Parmoor at 101. For detailed discussion of Lord Dunedin's test and its subsequent application, see John Carter, Wayne Courtney and Gregory Tolhurst, 'Assessment of Contractual Penalties: *Dunlop* Deflated' (2017) 34 JCL 4, 12–17.

121 Hugh Beale (ed), *Chitty on Contracts*, Vol 2, (35th edn, Sweet & Maxwell 2023) [29-211].

122 *Denka Advantech Private Ltd v Seraya Energy Pte Ltd* [2020] SGCA 119, [151] (Leong JA); *Ethoz Capital Ltd v Im8ex Pte Ltd* [2023] SGCA 3, [65].

in comparison with the greatest loss that could conceivably be proved to have followed from the breach' (the genuine pre-estimate of loss test).[123] Under the *Dunlop* test, if the sum does not constitute a genuine pre-estimate of loss at the time that the contract is made, it will be a penalty. A clause is presumed to be a penalty if a single lump sum is payable on the occurrence of one or more or all of several events, some of which are serious and others are not; however, the party imposing the detriment may rebut this presumption with evidence to the contrary. Finally, if the consequences of the breach are such as to make a precise pre-estimate impossible, the sum may still be a genuine pre-estimate. In fact, this is precisely the situation where a liquidated damages clause might be useful (to get around the uncertainty of calculation).[124]

However, *Cavendish v Makdessi* establishes that even if the detriment imposed upon the parties is greater than the greatest loss that could conceivably have been proved to have followed from the breach, the clause is permissible if the party imposing the detriment is protecting a 'legitimate interest' under the contract (as opposed to deterring breach).[125] The 'legitimate interest' test has been adopted by courts in Australia and New Zealand,[126] but rejected in Singapore.[127] It is suggested that the new test makes it harder for a clause to in fact constitute a penalty, as the category of what counts as a 'legitimate interest' is potentially broad and includes the protection of commercial interests.

In the English Court of Appeal case preceding the first of the conjoined appeals in *Cavendish v Makdessi*, Christopher Clarke LJ said that deterrence was not recognised as a 'commercial justification' for the imposition of Cls 5.1 and 5.6,[128] and would have held that the clauses were penalties. However, as discussed above, a majority of the Supreme Court seems to have held that the clauses were subject to the penalty doctrine, but that Cavendish had a

---

123 A corollary of this is that if the breach consists only of not paying a sum of money, the clause will be a penalty if the sum stipulated is greater than the sum which ought to have been paid.

124 [1915] AC 79, 87.

125 The 'legitimate interest' test originates from the speech of Lord Robertson in *Clydebank Engineering and Shipbuilding Co Ltd v Yzquierdo E Castanada* [1906] AC 6.

126 *Paciocco v Australian & New Zealand Banking Group* [2016] HCA 28, (2016) 258 CLR 525; *127 Hobson Street Ltd v Honey Bees Preschool Limited* [2020] NZSC 53.

127 *Denka Advantech Private Ltd v Seraya Energy Pte Ltd* [2020] SGCA 119 [151] (Leong JA); *Ethoz Capital Ltd v Im8ex Pte Ltd* [2023] SGCA 3 [65]. See also Nettle J's dissenting judgment in *Paciocco v Australian & New Zealand Banking Group* [2016] HCA 28, (2016) 258 CLR 525.

128 *Makdessi v Cavendish Square Holdings BV* [2013] EWCA Civ 1359, [2014] 2 All ER (Comm) 125 [104]–[123].

'legitimate interest' in imposing them, namely deterrence from breaching the promise not to compete.

In *ParkingEye v Beavis*, the second of the conjoined appeals considered by the Supreme Court in the *Cavendish v Makdessi* appeal, the 'legitimate interest' test was used to validate a fee which would otherwise in fact be a penalty under the *Dunlop* test. In the second appeal, notices at a shopping centre car park stipulated that the maximum stay allowable for customers was two hours, that parking was free for two hours, and that £85 would be charged thereafter (reduced to £50 if paid within 14 days). Beavis parked his car at the car park for almost three hours, and he was charged £85. He argued that this sum was a penalty. The operator of the car park, ParkingEye Ltd ('ParkingEye') conceded that the fee was not a pre-estimate of loss. This would have rendered the fee a penalty under *Dunlop*.

However, the Supreme Court held that the £85 fee was not a penalty because it was not out of all proportion to ParkingEye's 'legitimate interest' in customers adhering to the two-hour maximum stay period. There was an interest in keeping car park spaces available for shoppers visiting the shopping centre, and to deter commuters and other long-stay motorists from parking there, and the fee was found to be proportionate to that interest.[129]

The test from *Cavendish v Makdessi* requires a court to assess whether the detriment imposed by the impugned clause is 'extravagant and unconscionable' and out of all proportion to the 'legitimate interest' of the party imposing the detriment. However, as Lord Neuberger and Lord Sumption correctly noted, the 'extravagant and unconscionable' test is not easily applied to more complex cases.[130]

Where, as is often the case, the detriment is an obligation to pay a stipulated sum of money and the primary obligation is not an obligation to pay money, the 'legitimate interest' test requires the court to compare the sum of money to the other party's interest in obtaining something other than money. This can be difficult, particularly if the innocent party's interest is not purely commercial.[131] To illustrate the difficulty, in the ParkingEye case, clearly, a fee of £1m

---

129 [2015] UKSC 67, [2016] AC 1172, [98]–[100] (Lord Neuberger and Lord Sumption), [198]–[199] (Lord Mance), [286]–[287] (Lord Hodge). The defendant also relied on unfair terms legislation, but that argument was also unsuccessful (Lord Toulson dissenting).

130 [2015] UKSC 67, [2016] AC 1172 [22] (Lord Neuberger and Lord Sumption).

131 There is no reason why non-commercial interests should be unable to justify the imposition of consequences that go beyond compensation of loss: see Man Yip and Yihan Goh, 'Convergence Between Australian Common Law and English Common Law: The Rule against Penalties in the Age of Freedom of Contract' (2017) 46 CLWR 61, 66.

would have been extravagant and unconscionable, but it is less clear that a fee of £250 would be. Lord Dunedin's test in *Dunlop* (at least arguably) requires a court to test whether the detriment was genuinely imposed to compensate for loss, or for other reasons.[132] In order to assess the proportionality of a detriment to a contracting party's legitimate interest, the court may be required to consider whether the detriment imposed reflects a reasonably foreseeable loss, and hence, it may be that the rejection of Lord Dunedin's *Dunlop* test was premature.[133]

The third question is, if a clause is in fact a penalty, what the consequences will be. Under English law, a clause which is in fact a penalty is void and unenforceable. In effect, this means that the party seeking to rely on the clause can only recover the amount that would be recoverable as ordinary expectation damages in contract.[134] In a situation where a claimant actually suffers a greater loss than they can recover pursuant to a liquidated damages clause, they may wish the clause to be rendered void so that they obtain more generous damages.[135] However, some judges have held that the rule exists to protect defendants and that it cannot be used in this way.[136]

It should also be noted for completeness that other statutory regimes may render certain clauses unenforceable. In the second appeal in *Beavis v ParkingEye Ltd*, Mr Beavis attempted to argue that the payment of the fee was unenforceable as an 'unfair term' pursuant to the Unfair Terms in Consumer Contracts Regulations 1999.[137] A majority of the court found that it was not an unfair term, essentially using the same reasoning as they had used to establish the inapplicability of the penalty doctrine.[138]

---

132 John Carter, Wayne Courtney and Gregory Tolhurst, 'Assessment of Contractual Penalties: *Dunlop* Deflated' (2017) 34 JCL 4, 2–17.

133 ibid 31.

134 *Jobson v Johnson* [1989] 1 WLR 1026, 1040 (Nicholls LJ).

135 See, eg, *Wall v Rederiaktiebolaget Luggude* [1915] 3 KB 66; *Harrison v Wright* (1811) 13 East 343, 104 ER 402; *Dingwall v Burnett* [1912] SLR 882 (Scottish Court of Sessions); *Leeds Shipping Co Ltd v Société Française Bunge* [1957] 2 Lloyd's Rep 182.

136 *Lord Elphinstone v Monklands Iron & Coal Co* (1886) 11 App Cas 332, 348 (Lord Fitzgerald); *Public Works Commissioner v Hills* [1906] AC 368, 385; *Eisley v JG Collins Insurance Agencies Ltd* (1978) 83 DLR (3d) 1 (SCC). The question was left open in *Cellulose Acetate Silk Co Ltd v Widnes Foundry Ltd* [1933] AC 20, 26 (Lord Atkin) and *Robophone Facilities Ltd v Blank* [1966] 1 WLR 1428, 1446–47 (Diplock LJ).

137 The Regulations have been superseded by Part 2 of the Consumer Rights Act 2015.

138 *Cavendish Square Holding BV v Makdessi* [2015] UKSC 67; [2016] AC 1172 [99] (Lord Neuberger and Lord Sumption, with whom Lord Carnwath agreed and

Other stipulated contractual remedies

A claimant may draft a contract so as to allow them to claim in debt instead of in damages. A claim in debt differs from a claim in damages for breach of contract: the claimant need only establish that the sum has become due upon the occurrence of a specific event. The rules of remoteness and mitigation do not apply. The rule against penalties was said not to apply to acceleration of a debt in the Australian case, *O'Dea v Allstates Leasing System (WA) Pty Ltd*.[139] The rule against penalties will still apply if the contract provides that upon the defendant's failure to pay the specified sum, a larger sum becomes payable. A debt may also be a penalty where the real substance of the acceleration of the debt is to operate as a penalty for non-performance. A debt may also be subject to relief against forfeiture.

Self-help remedies in contract are not restricted to terms stipulating payment of money. Parties sometimes stipulate that they are only liable for damages and that the remedy of specific performance is excluded. Generally, however, courts presume that contracting parties do not intend to exclude remedies available under the general law, and such a clause will be effective only if the parties have used clear words to indicate that they intend to exclude contractual remedies which otherwise arise by operation of law.

Sometimes parties stipulate a remedy by means of a termination clause, which provides that upon the occurrence of a breach, the non-breaching party has a choice (unless other elections are also involved) to affirm or terminate the contract. This constitutes a self-help act because the claimant is exercising their right to terminate without the imprimatur of the court. The common law gives a right to terminate a contract for a breach of an 'essential' term or for a serious breach of an 'innominate' or 'intermediate' term. However, contracting parties may include a clause that entitles one or both parties to terminate the contract more easily than under the general law. Parties may declare in the contract that certain terms are so important to them that their breach will give rise to the right to end performance, no matter how minor these breaches appear. Contracts might also detail when or how termination will occur. This allows a non-breaching party to exercise their right to exit the contract without involving a court. Termination clauses protect the party who relies on them to end the contract and give the other party an incentive to perform. These clauses have sometimes been held to be a penalty, particularly when damages are also to be paid upon termination.

---

with whom Lord Clarke agreed on this point), [184] (Lord Mance), [285]–[286] (Lord Hodgson). Lord Toulson dissented on this point and would have found the fee to be unfair.

[139] (1983) 152 CLR 359, 366; applied in *Kallinicos v Hunt* [2008] NSWSC 149 [12]–[15].

EXEMPLARY DAMAGES AND AGGRAVATED DAMAGES

The Nature of Exemplary Damages

Exemplary damages are a separate category of award. They do not compensate for loss but seek to punish and deter defendants.[140] They also attempt to assuage any anger arising from the wrongdoing and to discourage claimants from seeking aggressive self-help. In the early nineteenth-century case *Merest v Harvey*, it was noted that exemplary damages deterred duelling.[141] Public punishment of the defendant has a vindicatory aspect.[142] Hence, in *Wilkes v Wood*, Pratt LCJ said that exemplary damages were awarded 'as a punishment to the guilty, to deter from any such proceeding for the future, and as proof of the detestation of the jury to the action itself'.[143]

Importantly, exemplary damages are payable not to the state, but to the claimant. This contributes to the controversy over exemplary damages—while there may be a reason to punish the defendant, it is more difficult to establish why such damages should be paid to the claimant above any other, particularly in a private law context.[144] In the United States, these damages are known as 'punitive damages', but in England and Wales and other Commonwealth jurisdictions, they tend to be known as 'exemplary damages'.[145] Courts in the United States are more willing to impose punitive awards, whereas in England and Wales and other Commonwealth jurisdictions, these awards are exceptional.[146]

---

[140] *Rookes v Barnard* [1964] AC 1129, 1221 (Lord Devlin); *Uren v John Fairfax & Sons Pty Ltd* (1966) 117 CLR 118, 129–30 (Taylor J), 149 (Windeyer J).

[141] *Merest v Harvey* (1814) 5 Taunt 442, 444; 128 ER 761, 761 (Heath J). In that case, the defendant trespassed on the plaintiff's land, shot at his game, and drunkenly insulted him, actions which could have sparked a duel (but, in the event did not).

[142] Joel Feinberg, 'The Expressive Function of Punishment' in Joel Feinberg (ed), *Doing and Deserving* (PUP 1970) 95, 104.

[143] (1763) Lofft 1, 19; 98 ER 489, 498–99.

[144] Ernest Weinrib, 'Restitutionary Damages as Corrective Justice' (2000) 1 Theo Inq Law 1, 2–3; Ernest Weinrib, 'Punishment and Disgorgement as Contract Remedies' (2003) 78 Chi-Kent L Rev 55.

[145] Michael Tilbury and Harold Luntz, 'Punitive Damages in Australian Law' (1995) 17 Loy LA Int & Comp LJ 769, 773–75. Cf NJ McBride, 'A Case for Awarding Punitive Damages in Response to Deliberate Breaches of Contract' (1995) 24 Anglo-American Law Rev 369, who prefers the term 'punitive damages'.

[146] John D McCamus, 'Prometheus Bound or Loose Cannon? Punitive Damages for Pure Breach of Contract in Canada' (2004) 41 San Diego L Rev 1491, 1493–94.

As Lord Devlin observed in *Rookes v Barnard*, damages with the aim of punishment appear to be anomalous because punishment is generally thought to be the province of the criminal law:

> It may well be thought that this confuses the civil and criminal functions of the law; and indeed, so far as I know, the idea of exemplary damages is peculiar to English law.[147]

The availability of exemplary damages in a private law context persists because of the history of tort, as Windeyer J noted in the Australian case, *Uren v John Fairfax & Sons Pty Ltd*:

> Compensation is the dominant remedy if not the purpose of the law of torts today. But fault still has a place in many forms of wrongdoing. And the roots of tort and crime in the law of England are greatly intermingled. Some things that today are seen as anomalies have roots that go deep, too deep for them to be easily uprooted.[148]

Prosecution of crime was a private matter until the nineteenth century in England; hence, parties often utilised civil actions in tort to deal with wrongdoing which would now be dealt with by the criminal law. The modern distinction between tort and crime is relatively recent.[149]

Until 1964, juries were solely responsible for awarding damages, and there was no need for a jury to explain the bases upon which they made awards. It is possible that some awards of damages had either partly or entirely punitive bases, but we cannot know for sure.[150]

In the Privy Council case *W v W*, Lord Hoffmann noted the important differences between criminal prosecution and an action for exemplary damages:

> The procedure is of course radically different and so is the standard of proof. A prosecution is generally speaking initiated and controlled by the state. A civil action is initiated and controlled by the victim. Thus the prosecution of an action for exemplary damages enables the victim publicly to vindicate his or her version of events and inflict punishment, even revenge, in ways which a criminal prosecution

---

147 [1964] AC 1129, 1221 (Lord Devlin).

148 (1966) 117 CLR 118, 149–50.

149 Kit Barker, 'Punishment in Private Law – No Such Thing (Any More)' in Elise Bant, Wayne Courtney, James Goudkamp and Jeannie M Paterson (eds), *Punishment and Private Law* (Hart 2021) 35, 37–39.

150 Nicholas Sinanis has argued that the roots of exemplary damages go back further than 1763, the date often given for the emergence of exemplary damages: see Nicholas Sinanis, 'Aggravation in Tort before 1763' (2022) 43 J Leg Hist 24; Nicholas Sinanis, 'The North Briton No 45 and the Doctrinal Origins of Exemplary Damages' (2023) 82(2) Camb LJ 321.

> may not satisfy. Punishment takes the form of damages which go to the victim rather than imprisonment or a fine which can afford her only a more indirect satisfaction. Allowing the victim to pursue such a claim may have a therapeutic value which mitigates the effects of the offence.[151]

In *Rookes v Barnard,* Lord Devlin distinguished between cases where damages were awarded to punish and cases where damages were compensatory. Aggravated damages are said to be compensatory, despite having a partly punitive element, because they compensate the claimant for the wrongful manner in which the harm occurred. Exemplary damages arise where the sole purpose of the awards is punishment and deterrence.[152]

The Limitations Upon Exemplary Damages in English Law

Generally, exemplary damages are only available for torts in England and Wales. They are generally not currently available for breach of contract,[153] or for equitable wrongdoing.

In *Rookes v Barnard*, the House of Lords further limited the situations for which exemplary damages can be awarded in England and Wales. Lord Devlin said that exemplary damages should only be awarded in three categories of cases:

1. where there were oppressive, arbitrary, or unconstitutional acts by servants of the government;
2. where the defendant cynically calculated that the profit to be made by his conduct might well exceed the compensation payable to the plaintiff; or
3. where statute authorises awards of exemplary damages.[154]

---

151 [1999] 2 NZLR 1, 3 (PC).

152 [1964] AC 1129, 1221. For a discussion of the historical context of this decision, see Nicholas Sinanis, 'Punishment in Tort: The Context of Ideas in *Rookes v Barnard*' (2022) 15 J Tort L 29. The distinction between exemplary and aggravated damages has been criticised as incoherent: James Goudkamp and Eleni Katsampouka, 'Punitive Damages: Ten Misconceptions' in Elise Bant, Wayne Courtney, James Goudkamp and Jeannie M Paterson (eds), *Punishment and Private Law* (Hart 2021) 187.

153 *Addis v Gramophone Co Ltd* [1909] AC 488. Cf Canada: *Vorvis v Insurance Corporation of British Columbia* [1989] 1 SCR 1085; *Royal Bank of Canada v W Got & Associates Electric Ltd* [1999] 3 SCR 408; and especially *Whiten v Pilot Insurance Co* [2002] 1 SCR 595. Cf *Performance Industries Ltd v Sylvan Lake Golf & Tennis Club Ltd* [2002] SCR 678.

154 [1964] AC 1129, 1226–27.

The House of Lords eventually confirmed the validity of these limiting factors in *Cassell & Co Ltd v Broome*.[155] However, these limitations have been rejected in many other common law jurisdictions, including Australia,[156] New Zealand,[157] Singapore,[158] and Canada.[159] In *Uren v John Fairfax & Sons Pty Ltd*, the High Court of Australia explicitly rejected the criteria in *Rookes v Barnard* on the basis that there was no reason, in category one, to distinguish between a 'servant of the government' and a private individual doing government work, nor was the restriction to cynical profit in category two sensible or based on any rational policy basis.[160] This was the first time the High Court of Australia had departed from English authority, and the act represented an important step in the separation of English and Australian law.[161] Hong Kong is the only jurisdiction to have accepted the *Rookes v Barnard* categories uncritically.[162]

After *Rookes v Barnard*,[163] the English courts sought to constrain the availability of exemplary damages even further, after the Court of Appeal held in *AB v South West Water Services Ltd*[164] that *Cassell v Broome*[165] required the tort in question to be one for which exemplary damages would have been available prior to 1964. However, the 'cause of action' limitation was subsequently overturned by the House of Lords in *Kuddus v Chief Constable of Leicestershire Constabulary*.[166] It is now only necessary for the case to fall into one of the three categories.

155 [1972] AC 1027.

156 *Uren v John Fairfax & Sons Pty Ltd* (1966) 117 CLR 118; *Australian Consolidated Press Ltd v Uren* (1967) 117 CLR 185.

157 *Taylor v Beere* [1982] 1 NZLR 81 (NZCA).

158 *ACB v Thomson Medical Pte Ltd* [2017] SGCA 20, [2017] 1 SLR 918 [162]–[169], [176].

159 *Vorvis v Insurance Corporation of British Columbia* [1989] 1 SCR 1085, 1105.

160 (1966) 117 CLR 118, 132–33, 136–37 (Taylor J).

161 The Privy Council upheld the High Court's decision: *Australian Consolidated Press Ltd v Uren* [1969] 1 AC 590 (PC).

162 *China Light & Power Co Ltd v Ford* [1996] 2 HKC 23 (HKCA); *Allan v Ng & Co* [2012] 2 HKC 266 (HKCA). Malaysia has also accepted the categories in *Sistem Televisyen Malaysia Bhd v Nurullah bt Zawawi* [2015] 6 MLJ 703 (MCA) [31]–[32]; *Zulkiply bin Taib v Prabakar a/l Bala Krishna* [2015] 2 MLJ 607, [14], but not without doubt and criticism: see *Cheong Fatt Tze Mansion Sdn Bhd v Hotel Continental Sdn Bhd* [2011] 4 MLJ 354, [53] (MHC).

163 [1964] AC 1129.

164 [1993] QB 507.

165 [1972] AC 1027.

166 [2001] UKHL 29, [2002] 2 AC 122.

The Law Commission of England and Wales said in 1997 that the three categories of *Rookes v Barnard* were not 'consistent with either sound principle or sound policy'.[167] The Commission recommended that the categories be abolished and a more principled approach be taken.[168]

We suggest that the criticisms by the Law Commission of England and Wales have basis, and that if exemplary damages are to be retained as a category, there is no reason to confine them to the three categories in *Rookes v Barnard*.

Exemplary damages for oppressive, arbitrary or unconstitutional acts by servants of government

As noted above, in *Uren v John Fairfax & Sons Pty Ltd*, Taylor J of the High Court of Australia explicitly rejected category one in *Rookes v Barnard* on the basis that there was no reason to distinguish between a 'servant of the government' and a private individual doing government work.[169] The cogency of this criticism can be seen from *AB v South West Water Services Ltd*,[170] a case where a nationalised government corporation failed to warn the public that drinking water had been contaminated by aluminium sulphate. The corporation was later privatised. It was found that the corporation did not carry out governmental functions and their conduct was not an exercise of executive power derived from government.[171]

As in other Commonwealth jurisdictions, exemplary damages are now most frequently awarded in the first category in cases involving misuse of police power, including false imprisonment, assault, malicious prosecution, trespass, and intimidation.[172]

---

167 Law Commission, *Aggravated, Exemplary and Restitutionary Damages* (Law Com No 247, 1997) [1.2].

168 ibid [1.7].

169 (1966) 117 CLR 118, 132–33 (Taylor J).

170 [1993] QB 507.

171 [1993] QB 507, 525 (Stuart-Smith LJ); 531–32 (Sir Thomas Bingham MR).

172 See, eg, *White v Metropolitan Police Commissioner*, The Times, 24 April 1982; *George v Metropolitan Police Commissioner*, The Times, 11 April 1984; *Holden v Chief Constable of Lancashire* [1987] QB 380; *Connor v Chief Constable of Cambridgeshire*, The Times, 8 August 1989; *Makanjuold v Metropolitan Police Commissioner*, The Times, 8 August 1989; *Treadaway v Chief Constable of West Midlands*, The Times, 15 October 1994; *Thompson v Metropolitan Police Commissioner* [1998] AC 498.

Cases have arisen involving false imprisonment where governments have detained asylum seekers and foreign nationals who commit crimes.[173] In *Muuse v Secretary of State for the Home Department*,[174] Mr Muuse was awarded exemplary damages of £27,500 for false imprisonment after the British government detained him without giving reasons and attempted to deport him to Somalia, despite the fact that he held Dutch citizenship. The detention was not only unconstitutional but an outrageous and arbitrary exercise of executive power.

Muuse can be compared with *R (Lumba) v Secretary of State for the Home Department*.[175] In that case, foreign nationals were imprisoned for criminal offences, but after their criminal sentence was completed, the Home Secretary detained them pursuant to the Immigration Act 2016 (UK). The detention was unlawful because of a procedural flaw, but the plaintiffs could have been detained lawfully in any event. The plaintiffs sought damages for false imprisonment, including exemplary damages and vindicatory damages. A majority of the Supreme Court held that, although the detention was unlawful and the plaintiffs were falsely imprisoned, they were only entitled to nominal damages, not exemplary damages,[176] because their detention could have been achieved lawfully.[177] The question of 'vindicatory damages' will be dealt with below.

Exemplary damages for cynical profit-making

Category two of *Rookes v Barnard* was at issue in *Cassell & Co Ltd v Broome*,[178] after Captain Jack Broome sought damages for libel against David Irving, the author of a book called *The Destruction of Convoy PQ-17*, and Cassell & Co Ltd, its publisher. The book criticised Broome's conduct during World War II and blamed him for the disastrous fate of an Arctic Convoy, despite the fact that Broome's superiors had absolved him of any blame. It was found that the publication was libellous, and the jury awarded Broome £15,000 in compensatory damages and £25,000 in exemplary damages. The House of Lords upheld the award, but also made it clear that simply carrying

---

173 See *Muuse v Secretary of State for the Home Department* [2010] EWCA Civ 453; *R (Lumba) v Secretary of State for the Home Department* [2011] UKSC 12, [2012] 1 AC 245.

174 [2010] EWCA Civ 453.

175 [2011] UKSC 12, [2012] 1 AC 245.

176 ibid [62]–[88] (Lord Dyson), [170] (Lord Hope), [194] (Lord Walker), [208]–[211] (Lady Hale), [221] (Lord Collins), [239]–[247] (Lord Kerr). Lord Phillips, Lord Brown and Lord Rodger dissented.

177 ibid [90]–[96] (Lord Dyson, with whom Lord Collins, Lord Kerr, Lord Hope, Lord Walker and Lady Hale agreed on this point).

178 *Cassell* [1972] AC 1027.

out a tort while undertaking a profit-making business was not enough to justify an award. Lord Hailsham said:

> What is necessary in addition is (i) knowledge that what is proposed to be done is against the law or a reckless disregard whether what is proposed to be done is illegal or legal, and (ii) a decision to carry on doing it because the prospects of material advantage outweigh the prospects of material loss. It is not necessary that the defendant calculates that the plaintiff's damages if he sues to judgment will be smaller than the defendant's profit.[179]

In fact, as Lord Hailsham noted, the defendant might contemplate or hope that the plaintiff did not sue at all.[180] Lord Morris adopted a similar test, saying:

> I do not think that the word 'calculated' was used to denote some precise balancing process. The situation contemplated is where someone faces up to the possibility of having to pay damages for doing something which may be held to have been wrong but where nevertheless he deliberately carries out his plan because he thinks that it will work out satisfactorily for him. He is prepared to hurt somebody because he thinks that he may well gain by so doing even allowing for the risk that he may be made to pay damages.[181]

On the basis of these tests, the conduct of the author and the publisher fell into the second category, and the awards were upheld.

Given the reference to 'profit-making activity', there could be said to be an overlap between exemplary damages and gain-based relief in English law. However, the functions of the two awards are different. The first punishes, and the second strips gain. In *Cassell v Broome*, Lord Diplock said, of the second category of *Rookes v Barnard*:

> It too may be a blunt instrument to prevent unjust enrichment by unlawful acts. But to restrict the damages recoverable to the actual gain made by the defendant if it exceeded the loss caused to the plaintiff, would leave a defendant contemplating an unlawful act with the certainty that he had nothing to lose to balance against the chance that the plaintiff might never sue him or, if he did, might fail in the hazards of litigation. It is only if there is a prospect that the damages may exceed the defendant's gain that the social purpose of this category is achieved—to teach a wrong-doer that tort does not pay.[182]

Therefore, the amount of exemplary damages awarded under the second category of *Rookes v Barnard* is not restricted to the actual profit made.

---

179 ibid 1079 (Lord Hailsham).
180 ibid.
181 ibid 1094.
182 ibid 1130.

Subsequently to *Cassell v Broome*, many of the cases falling under the second category of *Rookes v Barnard* involve actions by tenants against landlords for trespass and nuisance.[183] Exemplary damages have also been awarded for economic torts including interference with business,[184] and insurance fraud.[185] Finally, in a terrible case, exemplary damages under the second category of *Rookes v Barnard* were awarded for conspiracy, false imprisonment, and assault, after the defendant forced several women from Moldova to work as prostitutes against their will.[186]

Exemplary damages available under statute

The third category in *Rookes v Barnard* is for situations where statutes give courts the power to award exemplary damages for specific statutory breaches. A clear example of this is section 34 of the Crime and Courts Act 2013 (UK), which provides that a court may award exemplary damages against publishers of news-related content where the defendant publisher has shown a deliberate or reckless disregard of an outrageous nature for the claimant's rights, and it is appropriate to punish the defendant.[187]

A more difficult question is whether exemplary damages are available under intellectual property statutes that provide for 'additional damages' in the event of 'flagrant' breaches. So, for example, section 97(2) of the Copyright, Designs and Patents Act 1988 (UK) provides:

> The court may in an action for infringement of copyright having regard to all the circumstances, and in particular to—
> (a) the flagrancy of the infringement, and
> (b) any benefit accruing to the defendant by reason of the infringement,
>
> award such additional damages as the justice of the case may require.

---

[183] See, eg, *Drane v Evangelos* [1978] 1 WLR 455; *Guppys (Bridport) Ltd v Brookling* (1983) 14 HLR 1; *Design Progression Ltd v Thurloe Properties Ltd* [2004] EWHC 383 (Ch). See also James Goudkamp and Eleni Katsampouka, 'An Empirical Study of Punitive Damages' (2018) 38 OJLS 90.

[184] *Borders (UK) Ltd v Commissioner of Police of the Metropolis* [2005] EWCA Civ 197; *Messenger Newspaper Group Ltd v National Graphical Association* [1984] IRLR 397.

[185] *AXA Insurance UK Plc v Financial Claims Solutions* [2018] EWCA Civ 1330.

[186] *AT v Dulghieru* [2009] EWHC 225 (QB).

[187] See also Crimes and Courts Act 2013 (UK), ss 35–42, for further details about when and how the provisions apply.

In *Williams v Settle*,[188] a case pre-dating *Rookes v Barnard*, the judges awarded what they considered to be 'exemplary damages' under a predecessor of section 97(2). After *Rookes v Barnard*, *Williams v Settle* has subsequently been thought to be more explicable as an award of aggravated damages in a series of later cases.[189] It will therefore be considered below in that category. It remains unclear whether exemplary damages could theoretically be awarded as 'additional damages': the question was left open by Lord Devlin in *Rookes v Barnard*,[190] their availability was doubted in some cases.[191] The unreality of treating the damages in *Williams v Settle* as purely aggravated, and the doubt about the nature of the damages awarded under these intellectual property statutory provisions, demonstrates further the problems with the *Rookes v Barnard* categories.

Calculation of exemplary damages

There is no certain measure for exemplary damages. Although any pecuniary award assessed by a court will be uncertain in some sense, compensatory damages are tied to the loss suffered by the claimant and gain-based relief is tied to the gain received by the defendant, providing some limit on recovery. Exemplary damages are not tied to any particular factual consequence: it is only necessary that the amount awarded be sufficient to deter and punish the defendant.

Lord Devlin indicated in *Rookes v Barnard* that an award of exemplary damages should be moderate.[192] As James Goudkamp and Eleni Katsampouka have illustrated with their helpful empirical study of these awards, English courts have indeed exercised moderation in fixing awards of exemplary damages, with most cases from January 2000 to December 2015 in England, Wales, and Northern Ireland awarding sums falling between £388 and £33,851.[193]

---

188 [1960] 1 WLR 1072, 1081–83 (Sellers LJ), 1086–87 (Willmer LJ), 1087–88 (Harman LJ).

189 *Rookes v Barnard* [1964] AC 1129, 1225 (Lord Devlin); *Redrow Homes Ltd v Bett Brothers plc* [1999] 1 AC 197; *Nottinghamshire Healthcare NHS Trust v News Group Newspapers Ltd* [2002] EWHC 408; [2002] RPC 49.

190 *Rookes v Barnard* [1964] AC 1129, 1225 (Lord Devlin); *Cassell v Broome* [1972] AC 1027, 1080 (Lord Hailsham).

191 *Cassell v Broome* [1972] AC 1027, 1134 (Lord Kilbrandon); *Beloff v Pressdrum Ltd* [1973] 1 All ER 241, 265 (Ungoed-Thomas J); *Nottinghamshire Healthcare NHS Trust v News Group Newspapers Ltd* [2002] EWHC 408; [2002] RPC 49, [51] (Pomfrey J).

192 [1964] AC 1129, 1227–28 (Lord Devlin).

193 James Goudkamp and Eleni Katsampouka, 'An Empirical Study of Punitive Damages' (2018) 38 OJLS 90, 116.

In calculating the quantum of exemplary damages, it is necessary for the courts to take into account the means of the defendant and any mitigating circumstances.[194] It is possible for a party to be vicariously liable for the conduct of an employee for whom they are responsible, as in the case of police officers who misuse their power.[195]

Cases involving either multiple defendants or multiple claimants can give rise to awards of exemplary damages, but the rules differ. *Cassell & Co Ltd v Broome*,[196] mentioned previously, was a case involving two defendants (author and publisher). The House of Lords laid down in that case that exemplary damages must not exceed the lowest sum any of the defendants are liable to pay in damages. It therefore followed that if there is a chance that one defendant out of several will not be liable, then that defendant should not be sued if exemplary damages are sought, because they may be precluded by this rule.

Conversely, where there are multiple claimants, the court first decides on the appropriate sum (because the focus is on punishing the defendant) and then decides how to divide the amount amongst the claimants.[197] In *AB v South West Water Services Ltd*,[198] one of the factors militating against an award of exemplary damages was that it was a class action, and there was no clear indication as to how such an award would be shared among the members of the group or others affected.

In light of concerns about the uncertainty of the quantum of exemplary damages, there is strong merit to the English Law Commission's suggestion that there should be 'guideline' awards and lists of factors to assist courts in arriving at a suitable sum.[199]

Normative Objections to Exemplary Damages Generally

Some scholars have argued that punishment should not enter into private law remedial responses because this is an inappropriate goal for private law to pursue.[200] A punitive award is said to be illegitimate because it focusses only on the blameworthiness of the defendant and not on the correlative relationship

---

194 *Rookes v Barnard* [1964] AC 1129, 1228 (Lord Devlin).

195 *Rowlands v Chief Constable of Merseyside Police* [2006] EWCA Civ 1773, [2007] 1 WLR 1065.

196 *Cassell* [1972] AC 1027.

197 *Riches v News Group Newspapers* [1986] QB 256.

198 [1993] QB 507.

199 Law Commission, *Aggravated, Exemplary and Restitutionary Damages* (Law Com No 247, 1997) [5.32].

200 Ernest Weinrib, 'Punishment and Disgorgement as Contract Remedies' (2003) 78 Chi-Kent L Rev 55, 86–87; Allan Beever, 'The Structure of Aggravated

between the parties.[201] It is also said that the proper party to enforce the broader regime of rights is the state, using criminal law.[202] Moreover, it has been argued that a retributive rationale requires the extra procedural and evidentiary constraints which are associated with the criminal law protections for the accused.[203] For scholars who accept that corrective justice is the proper explanation for private law remedies, it has been said that punishment is incompatible with normative corrective justice.[204]

Other scholars have attempted to refute these arguments. Robert Stevens points out that retribution in private law is used in a narrower sense than in criminal law, as it focusses on the infringement and vindication of a private right.[205] James Edelman, Ralph Cunnington, and Peter Jaffey observe that the reality is that courts do not always behave as though punishment is solely the province of criminal law.[206] Cunnington argues that the true division is not between punishment and compensation but between individual enforcement of rights and a public attribution of blame by the state.[207] Both Cunnington and Stevens have argued that exemplary damages are not a criminal punishment

---

and Exemplary Damages' (2003) 23 OJLS 87; Stephen Todd, 'A New Zealand Perspective on Exemplary Damages' (2004) 33 CLWR 255.

201 Ernest Weinrib, 'Punishment and Disgorgement as Contract Remedies' (2003) 78 Chi-Kent L Rev 55; Kit Barker, 'Punishment in Private Law – No Such Thing (Any More)' in Elise Bant, Wayne Courtney, James Goudkamp and Jeannie M Paterson (eds), *Punishment and Private Law* (Hart 2021) 35, 47–50. Cf Pey Woan Lee, 'Contract Damages, Corrective Justice and Punishment' (2007) 70 Mod LR 887.

202 Bruce Chapman and Michael Trebilcock, 'Punitive Damages: Divergence in Search of a Rationale' (1989) 40 Ala L Rev 741, 782.

203 ibid 804–05; Ernest Weinrib, 'Punishment and Disgorgement as Contract Remedies' (2003) 78 Chi-Kent L Rev 55, 100–01; Peter Jaffey, *The Nature and Scope of Restitution* (Hart 2000) 376–78; *Cassell & Co Ltd v Broome* [1972] AC 1027, 1100 (Lord Morris).

204 Ernest Weinrib, *The Idea of Private Law* (OUP 2012) 74; Ernest Weinrib, 'Punishment and Disgorgement as Contract Remedies' (2003) 78 Chi-Kent L Rev 55. Cf Pey Woan Lee, 'Contract Damages, Corrective Justice and Punishment' (2007) 70 Mod LR 887.

205 Robert Stevens, *Torts and Rights* (OUP 2007) 85. Cf Peter Jaffey, The Nature and Scope of Restitution (Hart 2000) 376–78, 376.

206 James Edelman, *Gain-Based Damages: Contract, Tort, Equity and Intellectual Property* (Hart 2002) 19; Ralph Cunnington, 'Should Punitive Damages Be Part of the Judicial Arsenal in Contract Cases?' (2006) 26 LS 369, 380–81; Peter Jaffey, *The Nature and Scope of Restitution* (Hart 2000) 376–78.

207 Ralph Cunnington, 'Should Punitive Damages Be Part of the Judicial Arsenal in Contract Cases?' (2006) 26 LS 369, 381.

because they do not supplement the criminal law, and the stigma and approbation which attach to criminal offences enforced by the state do not apply to exemplary damages.[208]

The Distinction Between Exemplary Damages and Aggravated Damages

As noted above, Lord Devlin in *Rookes v Barnard* distinguished between exemplary damages (which have a primarily punitive and deterrent rationale) and aggravated damages (which have a partly punitive and partly compensatory rationale).[209] He explained that aggravated damages can be awarded where the defendant exercised 'malevolence or spite' or the manner of committing the wrong was 'such as to injure the plaintiff's proper feelings of dignity and pride'.[210] All Commonwealth jurisdictions have adopted this division, despite their reluctance to embrace the three categories from *Rookes v Barnard*. In *Uren*, Windeyer J of the High Court of Australia distinguished between the two categories in the following way:

> aggravated damages are given to compensate the plaintiff when the harm done to him by a wrongful act was aggravated by the manner in which the act was done: exemplary damages, on the other hand, are intended to punish the defendant, and presumably to serve one or more of the objects of punishment – moral retribution or deterrence.[211]

Aggravated damages compensate for intangible injuries, including mental distress and physical inconvenience. There is no need for the claimant to suffer a recognised psychiatric illness; indeed, aggravated damages are precisely 'compensation for mental suffering falling short of a recognised psychiatric illness'.[212]

Witzleb, Bant, Degeling, and Barker observe that the division between exemplary damages and aggravated damages requires a further distinction between three categories of damages:

1. compensatory damages *simpliciter*;
2. aggravated compensatory damages; and

[208] Ralph Cunnington, 'Should Punitive Damages Be Part of the Judicial Arsenal in Contract Cases?' (2006) 26 LS 369; Robert Stevens, *Torts and Rights* (OUP 2007) 86.
[209] [1964] AC 1129, 1221.
[210] ibid.
[211] *Uren v John Fairfax & Sons Pty Ltd* (1966) 117 CLR 118, 149.
[212] *New South Wales v Corby* [2010] NSWCA 27, (2010) 76 NSWLR 439 [48] (Basten JA).

3. exemplary damages.[213]

Unfortunately, the distinction between all these kinds of damages is difficult to draw in practice. First, various academics have argued that the distinction between aggravated damages and exemplary damages is illusory and ultimately unsustainable. In *Carson v John Fairfax & Sons Ltd*, McHugh J of the High Court of Australia dissented, and argued that there is an 'element of punishment' in awards of aggravated damages.[214] Second, it can also be hard to distinguish between compensatory damages *simpliciter* and aggravated damages if damages are awarded for torts that involve intangible as well as tangible harm.

The Ontario Law Reform Commission has recommended that aggravated damages should be abolished because they are confusing, and that instead, damages for loss of pride and dignity should be awarded as a new head of non-pecuniary loss.[215] The English Law Commission thought that aggravated damages awards should be equated with damages for mental distress.[216] However, aggravated damages also clearly compensate for physical inconvenience, as Burrows has noted.[217]

Availability of Aggravated Damages in the Law of England and Wales

Because aggravated damages are awarded to compensate a person for mental distress or injured feelings, they cannot be awarded to a company.[218]

---

213 Normann Witzleb, Elise Bant, Simone Degeling and Kit Barker, *Remedies: Commentary and Materials* (7th edn, LBC 2020) [8.120].

214 (1993) 178 CLR 44, 108.

215 Ontario Law Reform Commission, *Report on Exemplary Damages* (1991) ch 5.

216 Law Commission, *Aggravated, Exemplary and Restitutionary Damages* (Law Com No 247, 1997) [2.39]–[2.43].

217 Andrew Burrows, *Remedies for Torts, Breach of Contract, and Equitable Wrongs* (4th edn, OUP 2019) 283–84.

218 *Collins Stewart Ltd v The Financial Times Ltd* [2005] EWHC 262 (QB); [2006] EMLR 5; *Eaton Mansions (Westminister) Ltd v Stinger Compania de Inversion SA* [2013] EWCA Civ 1308; [2014] HLR 4.

Aggravated damages available for tort

Aggravated damages are most frequently awarded for torts actionable per se, including assault and battery,[219] defamation,[220] false imprisonment,[221] trespass to land,[222] trespass to goods,[223] and malicious prosecution.[224] They have also been found to be available for nuisance,[225] deceit,[226] malicious falsehood,[227] and for breach of privacy.[228] However, in English law, they are generally not available for negligence, as confirmed by *AB v South West Water Services Ltd*.[229] This is the case even if the negligence is accompanied by an intentional tort.[230]

Aggravated damages available for some statutory causes of action

As noted earlier, there is an ability under some intellectual property statutes to award 'additional damages'. An award of 'additional damages' was made in *Williams v Settle*.[231] The defendant, a professional photographer, photographed the plaintiff's wedding. The copyright in the photographs vested in the plaintiff. Two years later, when the plaintiff's wife was expecting her first child, her father disappeared and was later discovered to have been murdered, attracting

---

219 See, eg, *W v Meah* [1986] 1 All ER 935.

220 See, eg, *McCarey v Associated Newspapers Ltd* [1965] 2 QB 86.

221 See, eg, *Prison Officers Association v Iqbal* [2009] EWCA Civ 1312, [2010] QB 732; *Alseran v Ministry of Defence* [2017] EWHC 3289, [2018] 3 WLR 95.

222 See, eg, *Drane v Evangelou* [1978] 1 WLR 455; *McMillan v Singh* (1984) 17 HLR 120.

223 See, eg, *Owen and Smith v Reo Motors (Britain) Ltd* (1934) 151 LT 274; *Piper v Darling* (1940) 67 Lloyd's Law Rep 419; *Yearworth v North Bristol NHS Trust* [2009] EWCA Civ 37, [2009] 2 All ER 986.

224 See, eg, *Thompson v Metropolitan Police Commissioner* [1998] QB 498.

225 See, eg, *Bone v Seale* [1975] 1 WLR 797.

226 See, eg, *Mafo v Adams* [1970] 1 QB 548.

227 See, eg, *Khodaparast v Shad* [2000] 1 All ER 545.

228 See, eg, *Gulati v MGN Ltd* [2015] EWCA Civ 1291, [2017] QB 149; *Sir Cliff Richard v BBC* [2018] EWC 1837 (Ch).

229 [1993] QB 507, 527–28.

230 *Alleyne v Chief Commissioner of Police of the Metropolis* [2012] EWHC 3955 (QB), [80]–[83]. Cf, however, *Ashley v Chief Constable of Sussex Police* [2008] UKHL 28, [2008] 1 AC 962, where the Chief Commissioner agreed to pay aggravated damages to the family of a man shot in a police raid. At [102], Lord Woolf observed that if aggravated damages were always rejected for negligence, then claimants would be forced to plead assault and battery rather than negligence, in order to recover for mental distress (necessitating a return to what he called 'the bad old days of the forms of action').

231 [1960] 1 WLR 1072.

media attention. The defendant sold some of the photographs to newspapers and one, showing a family wedding photograph, was later published in two national newspapers. At that time, the operative provision was section 17(3) of the Copyright Act 1956 (UK):

> Where in an action under this section an infringement of copyright is proved or admitted, and the court, having regard (in addition to all other material considerations) to—
> (a) the flagrancy of the infringement, and
> (b) any benefit shown to have accrued to the defendant by reason of the infringement, is satisfied that effective relief would not otherwise be available to the plaintiff,
>
> the court, in assessing damages for the infringement, shall have power to award such additional damages by virtue of this subsection as the court may consider appropriate in the circumstances.

The English Court of Appeal awarded £1,000 in 'exemplary damages' on the basis that the defendant's conduct had been scandalous, flagrant, and intrusive.[232] As noted above, it has been thought to be more explicable as an award of aggravated damages than as exemplary damages in a series of later cases.[233] However, in *Phonographic Performance Ltd v Ellis*, the Court of Appeal observed that a categorisation of 'additional damages' as aggravated damages would mean that 'they are only recoverable by natural persons who are not the most frequent of claimants in intellectual property cases'.[234] The Court concluded that 'additional damages' may include damages designed to punish or deter.[235] Other statutes explicitly allow for awards for injured feelings for discrimination,[236] or alarm or distress arising from harassment.[237] Finally, a person may obtain damages for distress if their rights under the Human Rights Act 1998 (UK) have been infringed by a public authority.[238]

---

232 ibid 1081–83 (Sellers LJ), 1086–87 (Willmer LJ), 1087–88 (Harman LJ).

233 *Rookes v Barnard* [1964] AC 1129, 1225 (Lord Devlin); *Redrow Homes Ltd v Bett Brothers plc* [1999] 1 AC 197; *Nottinghamshire Healthcare NHS Trust v News Group Newspapers Ltd* [2002] EWHC 408, [2002] RPC 49.

234 [2018] EWCA Civ 2812, [2019] Bus LR 542 [32] (Lewison LJ speaking for the Court).

235 ibid [36].

236 Equality Act 2010 (UK), s 119.

237 Protection from Harassment Act 1997 (UK), s 3(2).

238 *R (on the application of Bernard) v Enfield London Borough Council* [2002] EWHC 2282 (Admin), [2003] HRLR 4.

Aggravated damages not generally available for breach of contract

Generally, English law does not compensate for non-pecuniary losses arising from a breach of contract. Bingham LJ said in *Watts v Morrow*, 'a contract-breaker is not in general liable for any distress, frustration, anxiety, displeasure, vexation, tension or aggravation which his breach of contract may cause to the innocent party'.[239] Lord Steyn approvingly quoted these words in *Farley v Skinner*.[240] In *Watts v Morrow*, Bingham LJ opined that the reasons for this are not that such losses are unforeseeable—in fact, they are often entirely within the contemplation of the parties—but considerations of policy.[241]

The situations in which damages might be awarded for non-pecuniary loss are discussed in greater detail in Chapter 4 in contract.

Aggravated damages not generally available for equitable wrongdoing

Aggravated damages are not generally available for equitable wrongdoing, for similar reasons to those mentioned regarding contract damages. The main area where aggravated damages may be at issue is in the context of a breach of confidence where the breach is personal rather than commercial.

In *Campbell v MGN Ltd*,[242] the House of Lords was prepared to award £2,500 for mental distress and £1,000 aggravated damages for what was characterised as a breach of confidence. Ms Campbell, a famous model, was filmed leaving a drug and alcohol rehabilitation centre run by Narcotics Anonymous after she had publicly stated that she was not a drug addict. Similarly, an award of damages for mental distress (including aggravated damages) in the sum of £60,000 was made in *Mosley v News Group Newspapers*,[243] for disclosure of Mr Mosley's private involvement in sexual activities with five prostitutes. Mr Mosley was then the President of the Fédération Internationale de l'Automobile. In *Douglas v Hello Ltd (No 6)*,[244] the English Court of Appeal made an award of aggravated damages of £3,750 to each of Michael Douglas and Catherine Zeta-Jones after a photographer took unauthorised photographs of their wedding. This was not overturned on appeal.[245] However, since these cases, it has been found in *Vidal-Hall v Google Inc* that these cases were not cases of breach of confidence but instead were best characterised as instances

239 [1991] 1 WLR 1421, 1445.
240 [2001] UKHL 49, [2002] 2 AC 732, [16].
241 [1991] 1 WLR 1421, 1445. Cf however, *Farley v Skinner* [2002] 2 AC 732, [98], [104], where Lord Scott considered it a matter of contemplation of the parties.
242 [2004] UKHL 22, [2004] 2 AC 475.
243 [2008] EWHC 1777 (QB), [2008] EMLR 20.
244 [2005] EWCA Civ 595, [2006] QB 125.
245 *OBG Ltd v Allan* [2007] UKHL 21, [2008] 1 AC 1.

of the tort of misuse of private information.[246] The nature of awards for equitable wrongdoing is discussed in more detail in Chapter 6.

'Vindicatory Damages'

Vindicatory damages are a novel head of damages said to be available for violations of constitutional or human rights in some jurisdictions. They are prevalent in the West Indies, where written constitutions enshrine certain fundamental rights,[247] and have also been recognised in New Zealand,[248] which has a Bill of Rights. In *Attorney General of Trinidad and Tobago v Ramanoop*, the Privy Council said that such an award might be needed to reflect the sense of public outrage, emphasise the gravity of the breach, and deter further breaches.[249] Importantly, the availability of such damages does not require any factual loss and has been sought in circumstances where the claimant would have suffered the loss anyway, but it has been argued that it is necessary to vindicate the claimant's rights with a normative award.

Vindicatory damages do not seem to be available in the United Kingdom after *R (Lumba) v Secretary of State for the Home Department*.[250] As noted earlier, a majority of the Supreme Court held that the plaintiffs in that case were only entitled to nominal damages for false imprisonment, not exemplary damages.[251] Nor, according to the majority, were they entitled to vindicatory damages.[252] Lord Hope cautioned against analogising vindicatory damages with punitive or exemplary damages, saying:

> Although such an award is likely in financial terms to cover much the same ground as an award by way of punishment in the sense of retribution, punishment in that

---

246 [2015] EWCA Civ 311, [2016] QB 1003.

247 See. eg, *Attorney-General of Trinidad and Tobago v Ramanoop* [2005] UKPC 15, [2006] 1 AC 328; *Merson v Cartwright and Attorney General* [2005] UKPC 38; *Subiah v Attorney-General of Trinidad and Tobago* [2008] UKPC 47; *Fraser v Judicial and Legal Services Commission* [2008] UKPC 25; *Graham v Police Service Commission and Attorney-General of Trinidad and Tobago* [2011] UKPC 46; *Welch v Attorney General of Antigua and Barbuda* [2013] UKPC 1.

248 *Taunoa v Attorney-General* [2007] NZSC 70, [2008] 1 NZLR 429.

249 [2005] UKPC 15, [2006] 1 AC 328, [19].

250 [2011] UKSC 12, [2012] 1 AC 245.

251 ibid [62]–[88] (Lord Dyson); [170] (Lord Hope); [194] (Lord Walker); [208]–[211] (Lady Hale); [221] (Lord Collins); [239]–[247] (Lord Kerr). Lord Phillips, Lord Brown and Lord Rodger dissented.

252 ibid [101] (Lord Dyson), [222]–[237] (Lord Collins), [253]–[256] (Lord Kerr). Dissenting on this point: [176]–[179] (Lord Hope), [195] (Lord Walker), [217] (Lady Hale).

> sense is not its object. The expressions 'punitive damages' or 'exemplary damages' are therefore best avoided. Allowance must be made for the importance of the right and the gravity of the breach in the assessment of any award. Its purpose is to recognise the importance of the right to the individual, not to punish the executive. It involves an assertion that the right is a valuable one as to whose enforcement the complainant has an interest. Any award of damages is bound, to some extent at least, to act as a deterrent against further breaches. The fact that it may be expected to do so is something to which it is proper to have regard.[253]

In a private law context, in jurisdictions which lack constitutional rights or Bills of Rights, Varuhas has argued that 'normative damages' should be available for torts actionable per se, such as false imprisonment and trespass.[254] Conversely, Descheemaeker has argued that vindicatory damages are not compensatory, nor can they be justified as analogous to exemplary damages, because exemplary damages are defendant-focused, whereas vindicatory damages are claimant-focused.[255]

The High Court of Australia also refused to recognise a right to vindicatory damages: in *Lewis v Australian Capital Territory*,[256] another case where the plaintiff's imprisonment suffered from a procedural flaw, but the plaintiff could have been detained lawfully (and in fact, because of strange legislative drafting, the authority deciding his imprisonment had no choice but to do other than detain him because of his repeated failure to attend periodic detention). The High Court accepted the decision of the majority in *R (Lumba) v Secretary of State for the Home Department*.[257] Gordon J, with whom Kiefel CJ and Keane J agreed, said that there was 'no need, nor … any basis in principle, for the Court to recognise a separate head of vindicatory damages' because other remedies, such as exemplary damages, aggravated damages, and nominal damages already performed a vindicatory role.[258] Edelman J, with whom Gageler J agreed, found that damages (apart from exemplary damages) were concerned with loss, and hence there was no need for an award which did not compensate but which sought to vindicate a right.[259]

253 ibid [178] (Lord Hope).

254 Jason Varuhas, 'The Concept of "Vindication" in the Law of Torts: Rights, Interests and Damages' (2014) 34 OJLS 253; Jason Varuhas, *Damages and Human Rights* (Hart 2016).

255 Eric Descheemaeker, 'Against Normative Damages' (2023) 76 CLP 35, 40–41.

256 [2020] HCA 26, (2020) 271 CLR 192.

257 [2011] UKSC 12, [2012] 1 AC 245.

258 [2020] HCA 26, (2020) 271 CLR 192 [104], [109]–[121].

259 ibid [170]–[172].

DECLARATORY RELIEF AND FORMS OF NOMINAL DAMAGES

Sometimes the court simply wishes to make a declaration as to the rights of the parties. Obviously, this has a vindicatory aspect, as it allows the rights of the parties to be confirmed.

There are two ways in which the court does this. The first is via a formal declaration of the rights or obligations of the parties. The second is via an award of nominal damages, which is arguably an historical anomaly that derives from the fact that at common law (in the narrow sense), the courts could not award declarations until the UK Judicature Acts (Judicature Act 1873 and Judicature Act 1875) were passed.

In the absence of the ability to award a declaration, the common law courts developed nominal damages as an analogue to a declaratory judgment, to signal the breach of rights by the award of a token sum. These awards are usually made for common law wrongs actionable per se, where the claimant has a right to a verdict in their favour because a legal right has been infringed, but they cannot otherwise show any loss. Now that declarations are available more broadly, there is a question as to whether nominal damages should have a continuing role, outside two relatively narrow situations (ie, where there have been factual difficulties in calculating loss, and where the court wishes to signal contempt).

In what follows, declarations are considered first, followed by nominal damages.

Declarations

A declaratory judgment is an order made by a court that conclusively pronounces the existence or non-existence of certain legal rights or obligations concerning parties to proceedings. As noted above, it has equitable origins, but its availability for any sort of legal right was conferred by statute.[260] The procedural rule supporting the availability of this remedy is CPR 40.20, which states: 'The court may make binding declarations whether or not any other remedy is claimed.' Because the declaration has become divorced from its origins in the court of Chancery, it is no longer subject to the equitable bars to relief, although it remains discretionary.[261]

---

260 Supreme Court of Judicature Act 1873 (36 & 37 Vict. c. 66); Supreme Court of Judicature Act 1875 (38 & 39 Vict. c. 77); Rules of the Supreme Court 1883, Ord 25 r 5.

261 *Messier-Dowty Ltd v Sabena SA* [2000] 1 WLR 2040, 2050; *Panasonic Holdings Corp v Xiaomi Technology UK Ltd* [2024] EWCA Civ 1143 [27] (Arnold LJ).

A declaration is not an enforceable order of the court, and thus it stands in contrast to judgments for damages or specific relief (for example), which are executory and can be enforced against a defendant. A declaration can also be contrasted with constitutive or investitive judgments (which create a new right in the party) and with interlocutory judgments (which maintain the status quo before trial). Declaratory judgments are final, non-investitive, and cannot be followed up by any process of execution.

Declarations are an important remedy not only in private law but also in public law and are even available (subject to certain restrictions) in criminal law. This book focusses on declarations in private law.

A positive declaration creates a *res judicata* or an issue estoppel which prevents the matter from being reopened in litigation between the same parties. A positive declaration establishes the existence of a certain legal position relevant to the parties. Courts can also make a negative declaration (ie, that the claimant has no cause of action or that the defendant has not infringed the law), but they exercise this power sparingly.[262]

The weakness of declarations is their lack of enforceability. This is particularly the case when the defendant fails to respect the claimant's rights, even after the court has declared them. However, declarations do have many strengths, including that they are relatively quickly obtainable and relatively inexpensive to seek, that they are available where no other relief (including an injunction) is possible, and that they may minimise the possibility of protracted litigation and prevent irreparable injury from occurring.[263]

In a private law context, declarations are useful in disputes over status and may be used in property law and contract law when parties seek to establish the status of property rights, or of an agreement, or of actions taken in relation to that agreement.[264] They may also be used in disputes over the right to consent to or refuse medical treatment, where the ability to obtain a swift resolution of the dispute can be pivotal.

To obtain a declaration, the claimant must establish three things: (1) that the court has jurisdiction to grant the remedy; (2) that they have standing to claim

---

[262] *Messier-Dowty Ltd v Sabena SA (No 2)* [2000] 1 WLR 2040, 2050 (Lord Woolf MR); *Greenwich Healthcare National Health Service Trust v London and Quadrant Housing Trust* [1998] 3 All ER 437.

[263] Andrew Burrows, *Remedies for Torts, Breach of Contract, and Equitable Wrongs* (4th edn, OUP 2019) 506.

[264] See, eg, *Harrison v Duke of Rutland* [1893] 1 QB 142 (declaration of trespass); *Burdett-Coutts v Hertfordshire County Council* [1984] IRLR 91 (declaration that contract had been breached); *Royal Devon and Exeter NHS Foundation Trust v ATOS IT Services UK Ltd* [2017] EWCA Civ 2196, [2018] 2 All ER (Comm) 535 (declaration of correct interpretation of a contractual clause).

the remedy; and (3) that there are no discretionary reasons why a declaration should not be granted.

The jurisdiction to grant an injunction is very wide, and traditionally may only be excluded by clear words in a statute.[265] Additionally, there must be a defendant or a 'contradictor': someone who will object to the declaration if necessary.[266]

A claimant who seeks declaratory relief must establish that they have sufficient standing to do so. This entails establishing a sufficient interest in the subject matter of the dispute. For private rights, standing is generally uncontroversial, as long as the claimant is a party to the contract or tort. However, if a party before the court is not a party to the contract, this may be a reason to refuse a declaration, as the issue is not one between the parties.[267] For a declaration in respect of public rights, obtaining standing may be more controversial. The proper claimant is usually the Attorney-General, who may act either in their own right or on behalf of a third party. *Boyce v Paddington Borough Council* established that, unless it is provided otherwise by statute, a private claimant may only act to enforce a public right without joining the Attorney-General in two situations: (1) where the interference with the public right is such that the claimant's private right is also interfered with; and (2) where no private right is interfered with, but the claimant suffers special damage from the interference with the public right.[268]

Finally, there must be no discretionary reason for a declaration to be refused. The discretionary bases upon which declarations may be refused are varied. If the question raised is abstract, theoretical, or hypothetical, this is a reason to refuse the declaration.[269] There must also be a real and justiciable question which the court can resolve. In other words, the dispute must involve a determination of a legal controversy concerning rights, liabilities, and interests of a kind that the courts protect. Courts do not give advisory opinions.[270] Another

---

265 See *Forster v Jododex Australia Pty Ltd* (1972) 127 CLR 421, 435–36 (Gibbs J).

266 *Russian Commercial and Industrial Bank v British Bank for Foreign Trade Ltd* [1921] 2 AC 438, 448.

267 *Meadows Indemnity Co Ltd v Insurance Corporation of Ireland Ltd* [1989] 2 Lloyd's Rep 298. Cf the recent Australian case, *Hobart International Airport Pty Ltd v Clarence City Council* [2022] HCA 5; (2022) 399 ALR 214, in which the majority found that a non-party to a lease was entitled to a declaration regarding its terms (Edelman and Steward JJ dissenting).

268 [1903] 1 Ch 109.

269 *Mellstrom v Garner* [1970] 1 WLR 603.

270 *Gouriet v Union of Post Office Workers* [1978] AC 435, 501 (Lord Diplock), 483 (Lord Wilberforce).

discretionary ground for refusing to award a declaration is that the declaration would not have utility for the claimant or practical value for the broader public.[271] As with specific relief, a declaration is likely to be refused where it cannot be clearly and precisely expressed.[272]

A declaration may also be refused if the claimant seeks to take advantage of their own wrongdoing. This occurred in *Puttick v Attorney-General*,[273] where the plaintiff sought a declaration that her marriage was valid, but she had procured the marriage using forged documents; hence, the declaration was refused.

Nominal Damages

Nominal damages are not compensatory but are intended to vindicate rights.[274] They were defined by Halsbury LC in *The Mediana*:

> 'Nominal damages' is a technical phrase which means that you have negatived anything like real damage, but that you are affirming by your nominal damages that there is an infraction of a legal right which, though it gives you no right to any real damages at all, yet gives you a right to the verdict or judgment because your legal right has been infringed. But the term 'nominal damages' does not mean small damages.[275]

Typically, nominal damages are awarded for common law wrongs actionable per se, such as trespass to land,[276] defamation,[277] and breach of contract,[278] where there is no need to show loss. The court signals, by awarding a token amount, that the defendant has committed a wrong. For example, in *Marathon*

---

271 *Dairy Farmers Co-operative Milk Co Ltd v Commonwealth* (1946) 73 CLR 381.

272 See *Global Finance Management (NSW) Ltd v Rooney* (1994) 36 NSWLR 122, 136.

273 [1980] Fam 1, 22.

274 Normann Witzleb and Robyn Carroll, 'The Role of Vindication in Torts Damages' (2009) 17 Tort L Rev 1, 7.

275 [1900] AC 113, 116.

276 See, eg, *Armstrong v Sheppard & Short Ltd* [1959] 2 QB 384.

277 See, eg, *Grobbelaar v News Group Newspapers Ltd* [2002] UKHL 40 [2002] 1 WLR 3024, although these could be better categorised as 'contemptuous damages'.

278 See, eg, *Sunrock Aircraft Corporation Ltd v Scandinavian Airlines System Denmark-Norway-Sweden* [2007] EWCA Civ 882; [2007] 2 Lloyd's Rep 612, [35] (Lord Justice Thomas, with Lord Justice Ward and Lord Justice Well agreeing).

Asset Management LLP v Seddon,[279] an award of £1 was made against each of the defendants.

A claimant who receives nominal damages may not feel that their rights have been vindicated. Previously, nominal damages were a peg upon which to hang orders for costs, but now courts have the discretion to depart from the rule that costs follow the event, so a claimant who receives nominal damages may have to pay the defendant's costs.[280] Indeed, the award of a nominal fee could be seen as contemptuous. Sometimes, as discussed below, courts use them in this way.

Burrows has argued that nominal damages are an anomaly and should be abolished in favour of declarations.[281] There is strength to this argument. However, there may still be a limited role for nominal damages, as they may be awarded in rare cases where the fact of loss is shown but evidence as to its quantum is not provided, in which case the award is not in the nature of a declaration or a vindication of rights but reflects a problem of proof.[282] There may also still be a role for nominal damages in the arena of 'contemptuous damages', discussed briefly below.

Contemptuous damages

In some cases, when the court awards a nominal sum, the award is a rebuff for the claimants and indicates that the action should never have been brought in the first place.[283]

Awards of 'contemptuous damages' are usually made in defamation cases where the claimant was technically defamed, but the judges or the jury take the view that the claimant had a bad character or was undeserving of protection. In *Grobbelaar v News Group Newspapers Ltd*,[284] the court arguably awarded contemptuous damages (notwithstanding the fact that most of the judges referred to the award as 'nominal damages'). The former Liverpool Football Club goalkeeper, Bruce Grobbelaar, sued *The Sun* for libel in relation to allegations that he had fixed matches for bribes. The allegations were tech-

[279] [2017] EWHC 300 (Comm), [2017] ICR 791 [283] (Leggatt J).

[280] *Anglo Cyprian Trade Agencies v Paphos Wine Industries Ltd* [1951] 1 All ER 873.

[281] Andrew Burrows, *Remedies for Torts, Breach of Contract, and Equitable Wrongs* (4th edn, OUP 2019) 503.

[282] James Edelman, *McGregor on Damages* (21st edn, Sweet & Maxwell 2021) [12–004]–[12–005], citing *Dixon v Deveridge* (1825) 2 C & P 109, 172 ER 50; *Twyman v Knowles* (1853) 13 CB 222.

[283] Stephen M Waddams, *The Law of Damages* (5th edn, Canada Law Book 2012) [10.40].

[284] [2002] UKHL 40, [2002] 1 WLR 3024.

nically libellous because Grobbelaar's attempts to match-fix were ultimately unsuccessful; however, there was nonetheless taped evidence that he had agreed to fix matches. Grobbelaar was initially awarded £85,000, but on appeal, the House of Lords slashed his award to £1 and ordered him to pay *The Sun's* costs, estimated at £500,000. Lord Bingham observed that the tort of defamation 'affords little or no protection to those who have, or deserve to have, no reputation deserving of legal protection', and that '[i]t would be an affront to justice if a court of law were to award substantial damages to a man shown to have acted in such flagrant breach of his legal and moral obligations'.[285]

It follows that a claimant who is awarded contemptuous damages is likely to have to pay the defendant's costs.[286]

As Burrows argues, it is difficult to see how a declaration could achieve the 'double-edged sword' effect of vindicating the claimant's rights while simultaneously admonishing the claimant, and thus contemptuous damages continue to have a role.[287]

Apologies

An apology may vindicate the claimant's right, but it may also be a form of redress and solace for emotional harm.[288] The claimant feels vindicated because it is an acknowledgement that they did not deserve to be wronged. There may also be a declaratory and deterrent function which educates the public about the wrongdoing in question.[289] It can be counterproductive to deter parties from apologising, and it can leave the claimant feeling worse if no apology is made because a defendant is afraid that an apology might be regarded as an admission of liability.

There is an ongoing debate over the legal effect of apologies, and whether apologies should have any place in the law at all. Currently, section 2 of the Compensation Act 2006 (England and Wales) provides:

> An apology, an offer of treatment or other redress, shall not of itself amount to an admission of negligence or breach of statutory duty.

The law of Scotland provides for a broader ability to apologise in the Apologies (Scotland) Act 2016. Section 1 states:

---

285 ibid [24].

286 *Martin v Benson* [1927] 1 KB 771.

287 Andrew Burrows, *Remedies for Torts, Breach of Contract, and Equitable Wrongs* (4th edn, OUP 2019) 504.

288 Robyn Carroll, 'Apologies as a Legal Remedy' (2013) 35 Syd L Rev 317, 337.

289 ibid 339.

> In any legal proceedings to which this Act applies, an apology made (outside the proceedings) in connection with any matter—
>
> (a) is not admissible as evidence of anything relevant to the determination of liability in connection with that matter, and
> (b) cannot be used in any other way to the prejudice of the person by or on behalf of whom the apology was made.

The legal proceedings covered are mostly civil proceedings.[290] An apology is defined by the Apologies (Scotland) Act 2016 as follows:

> any statement made by or on behalf of a person which indicates that the person is sorry about, or regrets, an act, omission or outcome and includes any part of the statement which contains an undertaking to look at the circumstances giving rise to the act, omission or outcome with a view to preventing a recurrence.

There has been a recent consultation in 2024 to ascertain whether the law of England and Wales regarding apologies in civil proceedings was adequate.[291] The particular concern in that consultation was to better facilitate apologies in proceedings involving child sexual abuse by institutions.[292]

In the United States, some hospitals have encouraged apologies when there has been a medical mistake, leading to positive outcomes for both doctors and patients.[293] Usually, patients want an apology; some pecuniary acknowledgement of inconvenience, pain, and extra medical costs; and an assurance that the mistake will not happen again. Instead of denying mistakes, hospitals use mistakes as a learning opportunity and improve procedures. The acknowledgement of the mistake helps ensure that similar mistakes do not happen again. A scheme dealing with this specific situation would be possible under the NHS Redress Act 2006 (UK), which allows for the Secretary of State to establish a scheme where aggrieved patients could receive civil recourse without going to court, but no such scheme has been established.

In other instances, particularly in the tort of defamation, an apology may be a reason to reduce the amount of damages payable. Section 1 of the Libel Act 1843 (c. 96, 6 and 7 Vict) states:

> In any action for defamation it shall be lawful for the defendant (after notice in writing of his intention so to do, duly given to the plaintiff at the time of filing or

290 Apologies (Scotland) Act 2016, s 2.
291 Ministry of Justice, Reforming the Law of Apologies in Civil Proceedings in England and Wales (8 April 2024 to 3 June 2024).
292 ibid [35]–[44].
293 Daniel Shuman, 'The Role of Apology in Tort Law' (2000) 83 Judicature 180, 184.

> delivering the plea in such action), to give in evidence, in mitigation of damages, that he made or offered an apology to the plaintiff for such defamation before the commencement of the action, or as soon afterwards as he had an opportunity of doing so, in case the action shall have been commenced before there was an opportunity of making or offering such apology.

Finally, in some jurisdictions, such as Australia, it is worth noting for comparison that courts have been given a statutory power to order the defendant to make an apology for discriminatory acts.[294] However, no Australian courts have ordered an apology in a purely private law context.[295] As Robyn Carroll has noted, there are two broad perspectives regarding legally ordered apologies:

> One perspective is that the law has no role to play because the apology is a moral act that will have no worth or value if it is offered as a legal requirement or for legal purposes. Another perspective, more instrumental in nature, is that the law has a role to play in creating opportunities for apologies to be offered that achieve some social or psychological benefit.[296]

The difficulty is that a coerced apology is not likely to be genuine, it interferes with the autonomy of the defendant, and it has freedom of speech implications. However, some scholars have argued that the vindicatory and exemplary effects of such an apology outweigh the detriments.[297] In practice, Australian courts have been extremely reluctant to order defendants to apologise.[298]

---

[294] The Federal Court of Australia is empowered to order an apology for breaches of anti-discrimination acts pursuant to s 46PO(4) of the Australian Human Rights Commission Act 1986 (Cth).

[295] Robyn Carroll, 'Beyond Compensation: Apology as a Private Law Remedy' in Jeff Berryman and Rick Bigwood (eds), *The Law of Remedies: New Directions in the Common Law* (Irwin Law 2010) 342.

[296] ibid 349.

[297] For a detailed discussion of the policy issues, see Carroll, ibid 352–76; Robyn Carroll, 'Apologies as a Legal Remedy' (2013) 35 Syd L Rev 317, 337–46.

[298] See Katy Barnett and Sirko Harder, *Remedies in Australian Private Law* (3rd edn, CUP 2024) [16.10]–[16.13].

9. Disgorgement of gain

DISGORGEMENT OF GAIN AND ACCOUNTS OF PROFITS

This chapter discusses the account of profits, the main remedy effecting disgorgement of gain, namely the stripping of profit from a wrongdoer. The primary rationales of the account of profits have been identified as deterrence and prophylaxis (ie, preventing a defendant from gaining from wrongdoing).[1] Deterrence looks not to the dispute in question, but to effecting specific deterrence (changing the future conduct of the specific defendant) and general deterrence (changing the future conduct of other potential defendants). The rationale is that if the defendant is stripped of their gain (or part of it), this will have a deterrent effect on those who wish to commit similar wrongdoing in the future. However, while deterrence of wrongdoing is central to accounts of profit for equitable breaches (particularly breach of fiduciary duty), the rationale for accounts of profit for intellectual property infringements is to prevent the defendant from being unjustly enriched. This underlines the difficulty of separating out unjust enrichment and gain-based relief for wrongdoing. The distinction between compensation for loss, disgorgement, and restitution will now be discussed.

---

[1] James Edelman, *Gain-Based Damages: Contract, Tort, Equity and Intellectual Property* (Hart 2002) 83–86; Sarah Worthington, 'Reconsidering Disgorgement for Wrongs' (1999) 62 Mod LR 218; Irit Samet, 'Guarding the Fiduciary's Conscience – A Justification of a Stringent Profit-Stripping Rule' (2008) 28 OJLS 763; Matthew Conaglen, *Fiduciary Loyalty: Protecting the Due Performance of Non-Fiduciary Duties* (Hart 2010); Robert Cooter and Bradley Freedman, 'The Fiduciary Relationship: Its Economic Character and Legal Consequences' (1991) 66 NYULR 1045; Peter Devonshire, *Account of Profits* (Thomson Reuters 2013) 58–59; Elise Bant and Jeannie M Paterson, 'Effecting Deterrence through Proportionate Punishment: An Assessment of Statutory and General Law Principles' in Elise Bant, Wayne Courtney, James Goudkamp and Jeannie M Paterson (eds), *Punishment and Private Law* (Hart 2021) 255, 276–84. Cf Lionel Smith, 'Deterrence, Prophylaxis and Punishment in Fiduciary Obligations' (2013) 7 J Eq 87; Lionel Smith, 'Fiduciary Relationships: Ensuring the Loyal Exercise of Judgement on Behalf of Another' (2014) 130 LQR 608, 627.

The Distinction Between Compensation, Disgorgement and Restitution and the Nature of Gain-Based Remedies

Notions of compensation, restitution, and disgorgement permeate judicial and academic commentary and sometimes cause confusion. These are all distinct concepts, but sometimes there is confusion between them.

Compensation

Compensation focusses on the loss or damage suffered by a claimant as a result of a defendant's wrong. The claimant suffers a loss, and the defendant pays damages to make good that loss. As noted in Chapters 2 and 3, compensatory damages are the default remedy in contract and tort. In tort, they aim to put the claimant in a position as if the wrong had never occurred (reliance loss). In contract, they aim to put the claimant in a position as if the contract had been performed (expectation loss).

Restitution

Unfortunately, the term 'restitution' is used in two ways. First, it is used to describe the 'giving back' of a gain made at the claimant's expense. In other words, the claimant suffers a loss, and the defendant makes a correlative gain. Restitutionary remedies involve a reversal and return of the value of the gain to the claimant. This is the way 'restitution' is used in this book, to describe a 'giving back'. Therefore, restitution focusses both on the loss of the claimant and the correlative gain of the defendant.

However, confusingly, 'restitution' is also sometimes used to describe the 'giving up' of a gain made by the defendant even though there has not been a correlative loss on the part of the claimant.[2] It is preferable not to use the word 'restitution' to describe this kind of remedy. It is better to conceive of this kind of remedy as effecting disgorgement (ie, a gain can be given up, even though there is no necessary loss on the part of the claimant).

Restitution is also distinct from compensation for loss. There is not necessarily a gain on the part of the defendant when compensation for loss is awarded. If I negligently run you down with my car, I do not make a gain.[3] Simply, you suffer loss by reason of my negligence. However, if you give me £500 because you mistakenly think it is my birthday, I am unjustly enriched at your expense,

---

[2] The distinction between 'giving up' and 'giving back' was developed in Peter Birks, *An Introduction to the Law of Restitution* (revised edn, Clarendon Press 1989) 12.

[3] Note, however, that corrective justice scholars argue that the defendant makes a 'normative gain' in this situation: see, eg, Ernest Weinrib, *The Idea of Private Law* (2nd edn, OUP 2013), and other works by corrective justice scholars.

and I must make restitution to you of the gain I received. Subtractive unjust enrichment of the second kind will be discussed in Chapter 10.

Disgorgement

Disgorgement focusses on the gain the defendant has made as a result of their breach of duty. The defendant must give up that gain and will then, in essence, be in the same position as if they had never breached the duty. This removes incentives to breach and deters further breaches (generally and specifically). There is no need for the claimant to have suffered a loss (by contrast to both compensation and restitution), only for the defendant to have made a gain. Therefore, remedies which effect disgorgement are an exception to the rule that the claimant cannot be left in a better position than if the wrong had not occurred.

The Account of Profits

The account of profits is an equitable remedy that generally effects disgorgement. It strips the defendant of their net profit, subject to allowances and discretionary bars to relief. Sometimes, the account of profits can also include the reversal of a gain that originally belonged to the claimant, or which should have belonged to the claimant.[4]

Accounts of profit are typically available for breaches of equitable obligations (eg, breach of trust, breach of fiduciary duty). Sometimes, they are awarded where third parties are made personally liable as if they were fiduciaries, for knowing assistance of breach of fiduciary duty or knowing receipt of property in breach of fiduciary duty (known as accessorial liability).[5] Accounts of profit are also available for intellectual property infringement and for passing off, either under equity's auxiliary jurisdiction or pursuant to statute. To be liable as an accessory to a tort, it is necessary that the accessory knew the essential facts that made the act wrongful, even if the tort was one of strict liability.[6] Furthermore, an accessory to a tort or equitable wrong can be liable to account only for the profit that he himself has made.[7]

---

4 *Murad v Al-Saraj* [2005] EWCA Civ 959 [85] (Arden LJ).

5 See, eg, *Ancient Order of Foresters in Victoria Friendly Society Ltd v Lifeplan Australia Friendly Society Ltd* [2018] HCA 43, (2018) 265 CLR 1. Cf *Lifestyle Equities CV v Ahmed* [2024] UKSC 17, [2025] AC 1 (no accessorial liability for trademark infringement).

6 *Lifestyle Equities CV v Ahmed* [2024] UKSC 17, [2025] AC 1 (trademark infringement).

7 ibid [158]–[169].

Historically, equitable accounts of profit have not been available for other common law causes of action (namely, contract and torts) unless the tort involved an infringement of intellectual property rights. English law has now contemplated the possibility that an account of profits may be available exceptionally for breach of contract and for some torts, but this remains controversial.

Equity

The account of profits is well-suited for preventing equitable wrongdoing, as Sarah Worthington has observed:

> The aim is to exact particular standards of conduct in the protected relationships; to this end, the relevant law is concerned with proscribing certain activities, not with precluding particular outcomes. The appropriate remedial response for breaches of these equitable obligations is disgorgement because this is the remedy which best supports the legal obligation being enforced.[8]

The proscriptive fiduciary duties include a duty not to conflict with the interests of beneficiaries, not to profit by reason of their position, and profit-stripping responds precisely to a breach of those duties. It follows that if a trustee makes an unauthorised gain through breach of trust, including by misusing trust property,[9] the trustee will be required to disgorge the profit.

In the broader fiduciary context, an account of profits may be awarded where a fiduciary accepts unauthorised remuneration,[10] misappropriates a profit-making opportunity that arises out of the fiduciary obligation,[11] or takes a bribe to act against the beneficiary's best interests.[12] A breaching fiduciary will be required to disgorge profits even if the breach was bona fide, even if the beneficiary was unlikely, unwilling, or unable to make the profits themselves, and even if the beneficiary was left better off by reason of the breach.[13]

---

[8] Sarah Worthington, 'Reconsidering Disgorgement for Wrongs' (1999) 62 Mod LR 218, 237.

[9] *Foskett v McKeown* [2001] 1 AC 102.

[10] Fiduciaries must generally act gratuitously unless payment is authorised.

[11] *Keech v Sandford* (1726) T Sel Cas 61, 25 ER 223; *Regal (Hastings) Ltd v Gulliver* [1967] 2 AC 134; *Warman International Ltd v Dwyer* (1995) 182 CLR 544; *Ancient Order of Foresters in Victoria Friendly Society Ltd v Lifeplan Australia Friendly Society Ltd* [2018] HCA 43, (2018) 265 CLR 1.

[12] *Lister v Stubbs* (1890) 45 Ch D 1; *Sinclair Investments (UK) Ltd v Versailles Trade Finance Ltd* [2011] EWCA Civ 347, [2012] Ch 453. The availability of proprietary remedies over bribes will be considered in Ch 11.

[13] *Boardman v Phipps* [1967] 2 AC 46; *Bhullar v Bhullar* [2003] EWCA Civ 424, [2003] 2 BCLC 241.

The calculation of an account of profits has two stages. At the first stage, the defendant simply provides an account to the claimant of their financial affairs in relation to the breach, to identify the profit (if any). At the second stage, if a profit has been identified, it will be stripped from the defendant. Such profits are generally the defendant's net profits, rather than the defendant's gross receipts.[14]

In assessing net profit, courts have traditionally made allowances for certain expenses incurred by the defendant.[15] This may be effected by a consideration of the defendant's specific disbursements, such as expenditures of money and other capital, as well as the value of skilled labour of the defendant;[16] or by means of an allowance that is more of an 'all things considered' calculation.[17]

In cases of breach of fiduciary duty, an account of profits is available even if the fiduciary could have made the profit without committing a breach.[18] The breach need only be 'a cause' of the gain and does not have to be the predominant cause.[19] In *CMS Dolphin Ltd v Simonet*, Collins observed that, while there were 'no firm rules for determining which is the relevant profit', there must be 'some reasonable connection between the breach of duty and the profits for which the fiduciary is accountable'.[20]

A fiduciary cannot escape liability to account by showing that the principal, if asked in advance, would have authorised the fiduciary's conduct. In

---

[14] *Patel v London Borough of Brent* [2003] EWHC 3081, [2004] 3 PLR 1 [29]; *Regal (Hastings) Ltd v Gulliver* [1967] 2 AC 134, 154 (Lord Wright); *O'Sullivan v Management Agency & Music Ltd* [1985] QB 428, 458 (Lord Justice Dunn). See Peter Devonshire, *Account of Profits* (Thomson Reuters 2013) 11.

[15] Matthew Harding, 'Justifying Fiduciary Allowances' in Andrew Robertson and Tang Hang Wu (eds), *The Goals of Private Law* (Hart 2009) 346–47.

[16] *Brown v Litton* (1711) 1 P Wms 140; 24 ER 329; *Yates v Finn* (1880) 13 Ch D 839; *Chirnside v Fay* [2006] NZSC 68, [2007] 1 NZLR 433 [153] (Tipping J).

[17] *Brown v De Tastet* (1821) Jac 284; 37 ER 858; *Featherstonhaugh v Turner* (1858) 25 Beav 382, 53 ER 683; *Lord Provost of Edinburgh v Lord Advocate* (1879) 4 App Cas 823; *Phipps v Boardman* [1964] 1 WLR 993; *O'Sullivan v Management Agency & Music Ltd* [1985] QB 428.

[18] *Industrial Development Consultants Ltd v Cooley* [1972] 1 WLR 443, 453; *Novoship (UK) Ltd v Mikhaylyuk* [2014] EWCA Civ 908, [2015] QB 499 [110].

[19] Charles Mitchell, 'Causation, Remoteness, and Fiduciary Gains' (2006) 17 KCLJ 325, 332; *Fexuto Pty Ltd v Bosnjak Holdings Pty Ltd (No 2)* (1998) 29 ACSR 290, 297.

[20] [2001] EWHC Ch 415, [2002] BCC 600 [97]. See also *Novoship (UK) Ltd v Mikhaylyuk* [2014] EWCA Civ 908, [2015] QB 499 [96]: the gain must simply be 'within the scope of [the] duty of loyalty'.

Murad v Al-Saraj,[21] Mr Al-Saraj and the Murad sisters entered into a joint venture agreement to purchase a hotel, in which they agreed on how to divide the profits of the venture. As joint venturers, they owed each other fiduciary duties. However, Mr Al-Saraj breached his fiduciary duty because, although on paper he was contributing £500,000 to the purchase, he had a secret deal with the vendor which rendered that contribution largely illusory. This was a fraudulent failure to disclose a conflict of interest. Notwithstanding this, the Murad sisters gave evidence that, if Mr Al-Saraj had disclosed the conflict of interest, they would still have invested in the scheme, but they would have wanted the profits to be divided differently. Consequently, Mr Al-Saraj argued that he should not have to disgorge all of his profits, on the basis that he would have retained some of those profits anyway. A majority of the English Court of Appeal (Arden and Jonathan Parker LLJ) required Mr Al-Saraj to disgorge all his profits, (and would have required him to do so even if he had acted in good faith). This was justified on the basis that, first, courts do not speculate about the actions the claimant could have taken if the breach of duty had not occurred;[22] and secondly, to reflect the deterrent and prophylactic nature of the fiduciary obligation.[23] Lady Justice Arden admitted that the rule was 'rigid and inflexible'.[24] Lord Justice Clarke dissented and would have accepted Mr Al-Saraj's argument.[25]

For wrongs other than breach of fiduciary duty, the causation requirement is unclear, but for these wrongs it seems to be necessary to consider at least whether the defendant would have made the profit 'but for' the breach.[26] With regard to dishonest assistance in a breach of fiduciary duty, the English Court of Appeal has gone further and held that an assistant who has no fiduciary duties needs to account for profits only if the breach and the assistance were the effective cause of the profit and not just the occasion for the assistant to make the profit.[27]

---

21 [2005] EWCA Civ 959. See Mitchell McInnes, 'Account of Profits for Breach of Fiduciary Duty' (2006) 122 LQR 11.

22 There are overlaps with the *Brickenden* principle, *Brickenden v London Loan & Savings Co* [1934] 3 DLR 465, discussed in Ch 6.

23 *Murad v Al-Saraj* [2005] EWCA Civ 959, [59]–[85] (Lady Justice Arden); [101]–[111] (Lord Justice Parker).

24 ibid [81] (Lady Justice Arden).

25 ibid [154]–[159] (Lord Justice Clarke), relying on the Australian case, *Warman International Ltd v Dwyer* (1995) 182 CLR 544, 561–62 ('*Warman*').

26 Graham Virgo, *The Principles of the Law of Restitution* (3rd edn, OUP 2015) 434.

27 *Novoship (UK) Ltd v Mikhaylyuk* [2014] EWCA Civ 908, [2015] QB 499 [114].

Of course, there is a possibility that a breach may cause both loss to the claimant and gain to the defendant. In such circumstances, the claimant must elect to receive either equitable compensation or an account of profits.[28] The claimant must have sufficient information to make an informed choice between the two for the election to be valid.

In *Tang Man Sit v Capacious Investments Ltd*,[29] the plaintiff suffered losses, but the defendant had also made gains as a result of breach of trust. At first, the plaintiff, Capacious Investments Ltd, only knew about the defendant's secret profit of HK$1.8m, gained when the defendant rented out certain houses that should have been assigned to the plaintiff. Later, the plaintiff discovered that they had also suffered two losses: one loss of HK$7.9m (representing the rental amount the plaintiff could have received if the houses had been properly rented out); and one loss of HK$11m (being the loss caused by the wrongful use and occupation—ie, the difference between the actual market value of the houses and the value if the houses had been in good condition and free from encumbrances). The plaintiff obtained summary judgment in which they obtained both profit and loss. At that point, they had elected to take the profit, as they did not know about the loss, and they thought they were entitled to both profit and loss. They were not bound by that choice because at that stage, the choice had not been made with full knowledge of gains and losses or with knowledge of the necessity to make such a choice. The Privy Council held that the plaintiff was entitled to elect to take the remedy which gave the highest return. Lord Nicholls, for the Privy Council, said that the plaintiff could not claim both the gain (HK$1.8m) and the first loss (HK$7.9m), because both were caused by the same breach of trust (a failure to pay rental in the manner required by the trust deed).[30] The plaintiff was entitled to elect between the gain and the first loss and choose the highest amount. While in this case, the loss was greater than the gain, in other cases, a breach will give rise to more gain than loss.[31] The second loss (HK$11m) was caused by a different breach (a failure to rent out the properties in a proper way, causing damage to the properties), and accordingly, there was no overlap with the gain.

The account of profits is subject to equitable allowances and to the usual bars to relief.

---

[28] See Stephen Watterson, 'An Account of Profits or Damages? The History of Orthodoxy' (2004) 24 OJLS 471, arguing that the requirement to elect is a relatively recent phenomenon.

[29] [1996] AC 514 (PC) (Lord Nicholls).

[30] ibid 522.

[31] See, eg, *Warman International Ltd v Dwyer* (1995) 182 CLR 544.

Intellectual property

Although the account of profits first became available for intellectual property breaches through the auxiliary jurisdiction of equity, these awards are now partly ruled by legislation.[32] However, the legislation does not prescribe detailed rules on how the account should be taken, and courts still use equitable principles. Moreover, an account of profits may be awarded for equitable breaches of confidence,[33] and for the tort of passing off,[34] neither of which is supported by statute. The accounts of profits governed by statute retain characteristics reflecting their equitable origins.

In *Lifestyle Equities CV v Ahmed*,[35] the Supreme Court said that where a trader has made profits by infringing a trademark or passing off, the profit for which the infringer must account is not the entire profit made from selling the article itself, but the profit made from selling it under the trademark.

As with accounts of profits for breach of fiduciary duty, a claimant must elect between damages and an account of profits, with full knowledge of the choice.

Historically, an account of profits was generally ancillary to an injunction for intellectual property law breaches.[36] In other words, the claimant was only entitled to an account if they could also show they were entitled to an injunction. Today, it is no longer necessary to show this.[37]

Prior to the enactment of the statute, claimants could only claim an account over profits derived from the period when it was shown that the defendant knowingly infringed the claimant's intellectual property, reflecting the idea

---

[32] Copyright, Designs and Patents Act 1988, s 69(2) (copyright), s 229(2) (design rights), s 1911(2) (performer's property right); Trademarks Act 1994 (UK), s 14(2); Patents Act 1977 (UK), s 61(1)(d).

[33] *Attorney-General v Observer Ltd* [1990] 1 AC 109, 262, 266, 286; *Peter Pan Manufacturing Corporation v Corsets Silhouette Ltd* [1964] 1 WLR 96; *Seager v Copydex (No 1)* [1967] 1 WLR 923; *Seager v Copydex (No 2)* [1969] 1 WLR 809; *LAC Minerals Ltd v International Corona Resources Ltd* (1989) 61 DLR (4th) 14. Cf *Vercoe v Rutland Fund Management Pty Ltd* [2010] EWHC 424 (Ch), [2010] Bus LR 141, [341] (Sales J) (accounts of profit only available exceptionally for breach of confidence).

[34] *My Kinda Town Ltd v Soll* [1983] RPC 15.

[35] [2024] UKSC 17, [2024] 2 WLR 1297 [175].

[36] *Smith v London & South Western Railway Co* (1854) Kay 408, 69 ER 17; *Price's Patent Candle Co v Bauwen's Patent Candle Co* (1854) 4 K & J 727, 70 ER 302.

[37] Andrew Burrows, *Remedies for Torts, Breach of Contract, and Equitable Wrongs* (4th edn, OUP 2019) 342–43.

that the defendant should be stripped of only those profits it would be unconscionable to retain.[38] This is known as the 'innocent infringement defence'.[39]

However, it has been held that the statutory innocent infringement defence does *not* apply to an account of profits in England and Wales. An example of the statutory defence can be found in section 97(1) of the Copyright, Designs and Patents Act 1988 (UK), which provides in relation to copyright:

> Where in an action for infringement of copyright it is shown that at the time of the infringement the defendant did not know, and had no reason to believe, that copyright subsisted in the work to which the action relates, the plaintiff is not entitled to damages against him, but without prejudice to any other remedy.

Sections 191J(1) and 233(1) of the same Act also provide for an 'innocent infringement' defence for a performer's property right and a primary infringement of a design right.

Lord Burrows has argued extrajudicially that all intellectual property rights should be treated in the same way regarding whether dishonesty, negligence, or no fault is required for an account of profits to be available.[40] In *Colbeam Palmer Ltd v Stock Affiliates Pty Ltd*,[41] Windeyer J in the High Court of Australia said that an account of profits should only be available where there has been conscious infringement. The justification for this was that it would be unconscionable for the defendant to retain the profits where they knew of the claimant's rights.

However, in *Lifestyle Equities CV v Ahmed*,[42] Lord Leggatt for the UK Supreme Court said that an account of profits *should* be treated differently from an award of damages. His Lordship said:

> A central purpose of intellectual property rights is to encourage and reward creativity and innovation by enabling the owner of the right to enjoy the fruits of its exploitation. That purpose is promoted by allocating profits made from exploiting the right to the owner, including where the right is infringed by commercial use made without the owner's consent. For this purpose it does not matter whether the infringement is deliberate or innocent. The reason for redirecting the profits to the

---

38 *Edelsten v Edelsten* (1863) 1 De GJ & S 185; 46 ER 72; *Moët v Couston* (1864) 33 Beav 578; 55 ER 493; *Slazenger & Sons v Spalding & Bros* [1910] 1 Ch 257.

39 *Colbeam Palmer Ltd v Stock Affiliates Ltd* (1968) 122 CLR 25, 43 (*'Colbeam'*).

40 Andrew Burrows, *Remedies for Torts, Breach of Contract, and Equitable Wrongs* (4th edn, OUP 2019) 342–43.

41 (1968) 122 CLR 25, 34–35.

42 [2024] UKSC 17.

> owner of the right is not to punish or deter wrongdoing. It is to achieve the goals which the right exists to further. [...]
>
> Seen from this perspective, ordering an account of profits against an innocent infringer is in fact easier to justify than awarding compensatory damages. Whereas an award of damages may make the infringer worse off than if the infringement had not occurred, an account of profits does not have this effect. The effect is simply to put the infringer back in the same position financially as if no infringement had taken place. It is hard to see how an innocent infringer can legitimately object to such restitution. Thus there is no irrationality in the approach adopted in the Copyright, Designs and Patents Act 1988 of establishing a defence based on lack of knowledge to a claim for damages but not to a claim for an account of profits. But I find it hard to see how the converse approach could be justified. As, therefore, lack of knowledge is no defence to a claim for damages for infringement of a trade mark, it should not defeat a claim for an account of profits.[43]

In that case, the defendant directors of a company had infringed the claimant company's trademark. They were not liable to personally account for profits as accessories because they did not have knowledge of the essential facts that would render them liable, notwithstanding the fact that trademark infringement was a strict liability tort insofar as primary liability was concerned.[44] Lord Leggatt said that a distinction between damages and accounts of profits must be carefully drawn. If multiple defendants cause loss to the claimants, they can be severally liable, and the losses can be apportioned. Conversely, his Lordship said that profits could only be given up by that defendant who received them; otherwise, the defendant is punished and not put back in a position as if they had not breached.[45]

Torts and 'waiver of tort'

From the eighteenth to the early twentieth century, when a proprietary tort gave rise to both gain and loss, claimants were said to be able to 'waive' the tort (ie, give up an action for compensatory damages) in favour of an action for money had and received (a restitutionary remedy). 'Waiver' suggests that the right to sue in tort is entirely relinquished, but this is misleading. Instead, the claimant elected between a compensatory remedy and a gain-based remedy. This often occurred where the defendant sold the claimant's property without authority. Courts allowed the claimant to maintain an action for money had and received over the proceeds of sale of the property on the basis that there had been an 'implied contract' between the claimant and the defendant.[46] As

---

43 ibid [155]–[156].

44 ibid [135]–[137].

45 ibid [161].

46 See, eg, *Oughton v Seppings* (1830) 1 B & Ad 241, 109 ER 776; *Chesworth v Farrah* [1967] 1 QB 407; *Lamine v Dorrell* (1706) 2 Ld Raym 1216, 92 ER 303.

discussed in Chapter 10, the notion of an 'implied contract' has now been debunked, as has the notion of 'waiver of tort'.[47]

There is some suggestion that an award which strips the defendant of profits might be available for some proprietary torts, particularly trespass to land, and conversion of goods, if one accepts that the 'waiver of tort' analysis is actually a means of obtaining disgorgement via another means, as seems to be implied by Lord Nicholls in *Attorney General v Blake ('Blake')*.[48] However, it seems that nuisance does not give rise to this kind of award, as it protects not possessory rights, but simply the right to quiet enjoyment. Outside the proprietary torts, the availability of awards effecting disgorgement is unclear, with the balance of English authority suggesting that it is unavailable.

Exceptionally, as noted above, the common law tort of passing off can support an account of profits, but this is because it involves intellectual property rights, which have always given rise to accounts of profits in equity's auxiliary jurisdiction.

Breach of contract

It has been suggested that courts award accounts of profit for breach of contract in highly exceptional circumstances in English law, as established in *Blake*,[49] an unusual case involving the 'notorious traitor', George Blake. Blake's contract of employment with the British Secret Intelligence Service included an undertaking pursuant to the Official Secrets Act 1911 (UK) not to divulge any information gained as a result of his employment, either in the press or in book form, without consent. These obligations continued after the period of service concluded. In 1959, Blake was exposed as a double agent for the Soviet Union, and in 1961, Blake was sentenced to 42 years' imprisonment. In 1966, he escaped prison and fled to Moscow. In 1989, Blake wrote his autobiography, *No Other Choice*,[50] and entered a publishing contract with Jonathan Cape Ltd. Blake had not sought permission from the British Government or intelligence services before publishing it. Blake had been paid about £60,000 of the moneys owing to him under the publishing contract. A further £90,000 remained in the jurisdiction. The British Government sought to recover it. At trial, they were unsuccessful in relying upon breach of fiduciary duty or breach of confidence to support an account of profits.[51] However, on appeal, a majority of the House of Lords found that the British Government was entitled to an account of profits over the profits derived from Blake's breach of contract.

47 *United Australia Ltd v Barclays Bank Ltd* [1941] AC 1.
48 [2001] 1 AC 268.
49 ibid.
50 George Blake, *No Other Choice* (Jonathan Cape 1990).
51 *Attorney-General v Blake* [1997] Ch 84.

Lord Nicholls delivered the principal speech and created a test which came to be known as the 'legitimate interest' test:

> Normally the remedies of damages, specific performance and injunction, coupled with the characterisation of some contractual obligations as fiduciary, will provide an adequate response to a breach of contract. It will be only in exceptional cases, where those remedies are inadequate, that any question of accounting for profits will arise. No fixed rules can be prescribed. The court will have regard to all the circumstances, including the subject matter of the contract, the purpose of the contractual provision which has been breached, the circumstances in which the breach occurred, the consequences of the breach and the circumstances in which relief is sought. A useful general guide, although not exhaustive, is whether the plaintiff had a legitimate interest in preventing the defendant's profit-making activity and, hence, in depriving him of his profit.[52]

Lord Hobhouse dissented and concluded with a 'note of warning' that the consequences of introducing such an innovation into commercial contracting would be 'very far reaching and disruptive'.[53]

While *Blake* has not been the disruptive disaster predicted by Lord Hobhouse, the attempts by English courts to apply *Blake* subsequently indicate that the legitimate interest test 'remains hopelessly ill-defined and difficult to apply'.[54] In *One Step Support Pty Ltd v Morris-Garner*,[55] while Lord Reed did not explicitly overrule *Blake*, his Lordship said that the situations in which the case would be relevant would be very narrow, and he disapproved of the way in which Lord Nicholls in *Blake* had interpreted *Wrotham Park*.[56]

In the context of contract law, it is suggested that an account of profits is a 'tertiary remedy' which should be available only if both compensatory damages for loss and specific relief are inappropriate or unavailable, and if the defendant has made a profit (possibly cynically).[57] Katy Barnett has suggested that most contract cases should not give rise to an account of profits, but that there are two classes of cases where disgorgement may be justified:

---

52 *Blake* [2001] 1 AC 268, 285.

53 ibid 291.

54 Ralph Cunnington, 'The Measure and Availability of Gain-Based Damages for Breach of Contract', in Djakhongir Saidov and Ralph Cunnington (eds), *Contract Damages: Domestic and International Perspectives* (Hart 2008) 235.

55 [2018] UKSC 20, [2019] AC 649 ('*One Step*').

56 ibid [72]–[82] (Lord Reed). See also *Prudential Assurance Co Ltd v Revenue and Customs Commissioners* [2018] UKSC 39, [2018] AC 929.

57 Although cf *Blake* [2001] 1 AC 268, 286, which says a cynical breach is not necessary.

(1) 'Second sale' cases: Alice contracts with Boris for the supply of property, goods, or services. The contract is of a kind which is specifically enforceable. Boris sees an opportunity to sell the property, goods, or service to Conrad for a greater profit. Boris breaches his contract with Alice and sells to Conrad for a profit. Typically, the contract between Alice and Boris is no longer specifically enforceable, but there is a profit for Boris to disgorge.
(2) 'Negative covenant' cases: Boris promises Alice that he will not do a specific thing which relates to Alice's best interests, but Boris breaches the contract and goes ahead and does the very thing he has contracted not to do, making a profit. These cases include contracts where there is a concurrent fiduciary duty. Generally, there must be some kind of extra interest deserving of protection.[58]

Despite *Blake*, an award of an account of profits for breach of contract is likely to be rare, particularly in light of Lord Reed's comments in *One Step*.

Allowances for Skill and Effort

An account of profits is subject to a discretionary allowance for skill and effort.

Breach of fiduciary duty

An allowance for skill and effort is available for defaulting fiduciaries who acted honestly and in good faith. This is established by two cases.

In the first case, *Boardman v Phipps*,[59] Boardman acted as a solicitor for a trust and advised the trustees on investment strategy and the running of a business. He also invested in the business. He informed two out of the three trustees of his conflict of interest but did not inform the third because she was suffering from dementia. It was found that Boardman had breached his fiduciary duty by failing to fully disclose his conflict of interest, and that an account of profits was justified by the prophylactic and deterrent nature of fiduciary law. Nevertheless, it was clear that his breach had been honest and in good faith. He was therefore awarded a liberal remuneration for skill and effort.[60]

---

[58] Katy Barnett, *Accounting for Profit for Breach of Contract: Theory and Practice* (Hart 2012) 86.

[59] [1967] 2 AC 46. In effect, a majority of the House of Lords confirmed the decision of Wilberforce J in *Phipps v Boardman* [1964] 1 WLR 993 to award a liberal allowance.

[60] ibid 104 (Lord Cohen), 112 (Lord Hodson).

In the second case, *Guinness plc v Saunders*,[61] there was a failure to disclose a conflict of interest by a director of a company who facilitated a takeover bid. The director was not entitled to an allowance for skill and effort.[62] Lord Goff confirmed *Boardman v Phipps* and said that an allowance for skill and effort was confined to 'those cases where it cannot have the effect of encouraging trustees in any way to put themselves in a position where their interests conflict with their duties as trustee'.[63]

These two cases can be contrasted with the High Court of Australia's decision in *Warman International Ltd v Dwyer*,[64] in which an employee named Dwyer breached both his contract of employment and the fiduciary duty he owed to his employer, by redirecting his employer's business to a personal enterprise. Dwyer was employed by an Australian company, Warman International Ltd ('Warman'), which distributed Italian gearboxes in Australia. Both Dwyer and the Italian gearbox manufacturer, Bonfiglioli, were unhappy with Warman's inefficiency, and together they established a new company to be the Australian distributor. The new company made a vastly greater profit than the amount Warman lost because of the breach. Even though Dwyer's breach was both deliberate and dishonest, the High Court of Australia awarded Dwyer an allowance for skill and effort notwithstanding this.[65] Notably, in the subsequent case, *Ancient Order of Foresters in Victoria Friendly Society Ltd v Lifeplan Australia Friendly Society Ltd*,[66] another case involving employees redirecting their employer's business to another, no allowance was made in the context of a fraudulent and deliberate breach of fiduciary duty.

The normative basis for the allowance for skill and effort has been contested. Some courts and academics have suggested that allowances are made because the profit obtained by the defendant is insufficiently causally connected to the breach.[67]

---

61 [1990] 2 AC 663.

62 ibid 689–96 (Lord Templeman), 700–702 (Lord Goff).

63 ibid 701.

64 (1995) 182 CLR 544.

65 ibid 562.

66 [2018] HCA 43, (2018) 265 CLR 1.

67 *Regal (Hastings) Ltd v Gulliver* [1967] 2 AC 134, 144–45 (Lord Russell), 153 (Lord Macmillan); *Chan v Zacharia* (1984) 154 CLR 178, 199 (Deane J); *Warman International Ltd v Dwyer* (1995) 182 CLR 544, 562; *Murad v Al-Saraj* [2005] EWCA Civ 959; [2005] All ER (D) 503 [72]–[79] (Lady Justice Arden). See also J Edelman, *Gain-Based Damages: Contract, Tort, Equity and Intellectual Property* (Hart 2002) 104–05, 171–72; G Virgo, *The Principles of the Law of Restitution* (4th edn, OUP 2024) 557; G Virgo, 'Restitutionary Remedies for

It is certainly true to say that courts should distinguish between profits that arise directly because of the breach and profits that do not. But this should not be confused with allowances, which recognise the defendant's skill and effort *despite* the fact that their acts were legally responsible for causing the gain. We have argued elsewhere that this is a matter of apportionment rather than an allowance.[68]

Other courts and academics have suggested that if the profit is 'too remote' from the breach of fiduciary obligation, then this justifies an allowance.[69] However, Matthew Harding has objected that remoteness 'tells us nothing meaningful about how allowances may be justified', because it does not provide clear criteria for when allowances will be allowed.[70]

Principles of desert can also justify allowances, on the basis that the defendant expended time and skilled labour, which deserves recognition. Because desert gives rise to a claim of propriety (ie, it is 'proper' in the circumstances), not to an entitlement (ie, a right), it seems to be a good explanation for a discretionary allowance.[71] However, because desert is personal and specific, it seems appropriate that the defendant must justify to the claimant why the former deserves an allowance against the latter.

A desert-based analysis does not accommodate the utilitarian concerns of law-and-economics scholars who seek to encourage entrepreneurial skills in society and ensure that accounts of profit are not overly deterrent.[72] For example, it seems likely that the allowance for skill and effort to Dwyer in the *Warman* case was awarded because Dwyer was more efficient and a better manager than Warman.

It has also been suggested that allowances are intended to prevent unjust enrichment, like counter-restitution and the principles of *restitutio in integrum*

Wrongs: Causation and Remoteness' in CEF Rickett (ed), *Justifying Private Law Remedies* (Hart 2008) 301, 309–10, 325–26.

68 Katy Barnett and Sirko Harder, *Remedies in Australian Private Law* (3rd edn, CUP 2024) [17.72]–[17.73].

69 *Warman* (1995) 182 CLR 544, 561. See also Andrew Burrows, *The Law of Restitution* (3rd edn, OUP 2011) 688–89; Ross Grantham and Charles Rickett, *Enrichment and Restitution in New Zealand* (Hart 2000) 486–87.

70 Matthew Harding, 'Justifying Fiduciary Allowances' in Andrew Robertson and Tang Hang Wu (eds), *The Goals of Private Law* (Hart 2009) 349.

71 ibid.

72 See, eg, Frank Easterbrook and Daniel Fischel, 'Contract and Fiduciary Duty' (1993) 36 J L & Econ 425.

in rescission, so that the claimant is not unjustly enriched by the receipt of services.[73]

Allowances and intellectual property breaches

Defendants in intellectual property infringement cases are clearly entitled to a variety of allowances reflecting costs of material, wages, and other costs arising from the manufacture and sale of infringing goods. The court's generosity in relation to the allowance will depend in part on whether the defendant believed that they had a bona fide right to use the intellectual property or not.[74]

Apportionment is frequently adopted in accounts of profits for copyright or patent infringement, so that the profit is split between that resulting directly from the infringement and that from other sources.[75] In *Colbeam Palmer Ltd v Stock Affiliates Pty Ltd*,[76] an apportionment was carried out by ascertaining the profits made from the infringing goods and then by ascertaining what proportion of those profits was made from the infringing use of the trademark. Justice Windeyer explained that the profit '[…] is thus not the profit [the infringer] made from selling the article itself but, […] the profit made in selling it under the trade mark'.[77] On the other hand, if the entire profit made from selling the product is attributable to the use of the infringed intellectual property, then the entire profit will be disgorged.

Allowances for accounts of profit for common law breaches

If disgorgement is to be awarded for breach of contract and possibly tort, it is clear that an allowance for skill and effort should be made in some circumstances. This would in some measure address the concern of law-and-economics scholars that 'efficient' breaches of contract would be prevented by an award of disgorgement damages.

Apportionment also affects the quantum of disgorgement, as in *Vercoe v Rutland Fund Management Ltd*,[78] which involved the breach of a negative covenant dealing with confidentiality in a contract to exploit certain business

---

[73] Elise Bant and Michael Bryan, 'Defences, Bars and Discretionary Factors' in Elise Bant and Michael Bryan (eds), *Principles of Proprietary Remedies* (Thomson Reuters 2013) [11.80], [11.140]. Cf Graham Virgo, *The Principles of the Law of Restitution* (4th edn, OUP 2024) 557.

[74] *Redwood Music Ltd v Chappell & Co Ltd* [1982] RPC 109.

[75] *Colbeam* (1968) 122 CLR 25, 42–43; *Dart Industries Inc v Décor Corporation Pty Ltd* (1993) 179 CLR 101, 121; *Potton Ltd v Yorkclose Ltd* [1990] FSR 11, 16.

[76] *Colbeam*, ibid..

[77] ibid, 37.

[78] [2010] EWHC 424 (Ch); [2010] Bus LR 141.

opportunities, as well as a breach of confidence. Mr Justice Roth awarded a 'reasonable fee' based on the amount that the claimants would have accepted from the defendants to be released from their contractual obligations. The parties agreed that a reasonable fee award was an appropriate measure,[79] although they disagreed as to the quantum. It would have been unfair to strip the entire gain from the defendants given that they had expended risk, money, and effort.

Discretionary Bars to Relief

The discretionary factors and bars to relief operate in relation to accounts of profit awarded for equitable causes of action. The position is less clear regarding accounts of profit for breaches of intellectual property rights. Finally, the applicability of bars to relief to gain-based awards for common law wrongs is controversial unless such awards are Lord Cairns' Act damages. However, it is arguable that the courts effectively take such bars into account and that, for example, delay is one reason for courts choosing a reasonable fee award rather than an account of profits.

Hardship

The discretionary defence of hardship militates against the award of any equitable remedy. It is unlikely, however, that this bar will operate to prevent a court from awarding an account of profits, as, in most cases, stripping a defendant of a gain received in breach of duty would not cause hardship—it would simply put the defendant in the same position as if the breach of duty had not occurred.

Lack of clean hands

The defence of lack of clean hands may militate against the award of an account of profits. This may explain why English courts only award allowances for skill and effort to those fiduciaries who breach their duties honestly and in good faith.

Laches: delay and acquiescence and delay and prejudice

Delay and acquiescence are difficult to categorically define, in part because acquiescence is often used in a way that overlaps with delay.[80] 'Mere' delay does not preclude the award of an equitable remedy.[81] There must be delay and

---

[79] ibid [286].

[80] *Orr v Ford* (1989) 167 CLR 316, 338 (Deane J).

[81] *Lindsay Petroleum Co v Hurd* (1874) LR 5 PC 221, 239–40.

acquiescence on the part of the claimant or delay and prejudice to the defendant or third parties.

In English law, if the claimant 'stands by' and allows the defendant to make a profit, an account of profits may still be awarded for breach of fiduciary duty.[82] This is in contrast to Australian law, where the New South Wales Court of Appeal has held that a decision to 'stand by' may render an account of profits inequitable.[83]

Delay and acquiescence may have a greater impact on the availability of accounts of profit for infringement of intellectual property rights, tort, and breach of contract. In particular, delay and acquiescence may be a reason for a court to award a reasonable fee rather than a full account of profits.[84]

---

82 *Recovery Partners GP Ltd v Rukhadze* [2023] EWCA Civ 305; [2023] Bus LR 646 [67]–[81] (appealed to UKSC on different grounds).

83 *Murdoch v Mudgee Dolomite & Lime Pty Ltd (in liq)* [2022] NSWCA 12, (2022) 398 ALR 658 [216]–[217] (Leeming JA, with whom MacFarlan and Gleeson JJA agreed).

84 Although cf *Pell Frischmann Engineering Ltd v Bow Valley Iran Ltd* [2009] UKPC 45, [2011] 1 WLR 2370 where the 'reasonable fee' outstripped the actual profit made, despite the plaintiff's delay and acquiescence.

10. Restitution and giving back

PERSONAL REMEDIES FOR UNJUST ENRICHMENT

Unfortunately, at the present time, writing a definitive account of the law of unjust enrichment in common law systems is akin to nailing a cloud to the wall. The field has been radically reshaped by the writings of academics over the last 40 years, but the success of this reshaping of the law continues to be questioned. We do not propose to get into theoretical debates about the nature of unjust enrichment law in this book, or to adopt a particular theory of our own. We simply seek to outline, as best we can, the lineaments of the current law in England and Wales, and to explain how and why the controversy has arisen.

The Nature of Unjust Enrichment and Debates About its Place in Private Law

The definition of 'remedy' used in this book encompasses a court order replicating a preexisting right,[1] not merely a response to civil wrongdoing. Consequently, the definition we use encompasses restitutionary remedies that respond to unjust enrichment. These remedies differ from remedies responding to wrongs (namely, breach of contract, tort, or equitable wrongs). Restitutionary remedies for unjust enrichment do not fit easily into an Austinian division between primary and secondary rights.[2] As a result, the cause of action and the remedy overlap, and they were famously difficult to untangle when the common counts were still used.[3] Today, it could be said that unjust enrichment is the cause of action (in that the four steps outlined below must be fulfilled)

1 Following Rafal Zakrzewski, *Remedies Reclassified* (OUP 2005).

2 A structure outlined in John Austin, *Lectures on Jurisprudence*, vol 2 (R Campbell ed, Thoemmes Press 2002), Lecture XLV, 787–800. For how unjust enrichment does not follow this structure, see Peter Birks, 'Rights, Wrongs and Remedies' (2000) OJLS 1, 28.

3 Andrew Burrows, 'Judicial Remedies' in Andrew Burrows (ed), *English Private Law* (3rd edn, OUP 2013) [21.08].

and restitution is the remedy that responds to that unjust enrichment (in that the claimant must be given the objective value of the enrichment to reverse it). It is necessary to identify an 'unjust factor' which necessitates the return of the value received, and thus, this remedy shares a kinship with rescission, considered later in this chapter.

A restitutionary remedy can be personal or proprietary. Peter Birks said that personal remedies return the 'value received', whereas proprietary remedies return the 'value surviving'.[4] In this chapter, we do not propose to become entangled in complex questions as to when a party may be entitled to a proprietary remedy for unjust enrichment. The focus of this chapter is on personal remedies which seek to reverse transfers of value from the claimant to the defendant.

As noted in Chapter 9, the discussion here is further complicated by the fact that 'restitution' has two possible meanings.[5] In the sense discussed in this chapter, 'restitution' is concerned with reversing transfers of value. If the defendant has gained at the claimant's expense, and a relevant 'unjust factor' can be identified, they must give back what they gained (or the monetary value of the gain). Hence, restitution involves the 'giving back' of a gain made at the claimant's expense. However, as discussed in Chapter 9, 'restitution' is also sometimes used to describe the 'giving up' of a gain made by the defendant where the claimant has suffered no corresponding loss. This is better understood as 'disgorgement'.

Much of the confusion in this area stems from the historical origins of restitutionary claims. Before the enactment of the Judicature Acts in the late nineteenth century, the common law in the narrow sense allowed for certain claims (the 'common counts') on the basis of an 'implied contract' or 'quasi-contract.'

The common counts were based on the action of *indebitatus assumpsit*, a common law form of action alleging that the defendant owed a debt to the claimant in the absence of an express promise or contract.[6] There were three kinds of common counts:

1. action for money had and received (for money);
2. *quantum meruit* (for the value of services); and
3. *quantum valebat* (or *quantum valebant*) (for the value of goods).

---

[4] Peter Birks, *An Introduction to the Law of Restitution* (revised edn, Clarendon Press 1989) 12.

[5] ibid.

[6] James Edelman and Elise Bant, *Unjust Enrichment* (2nd edn, Hart 2016) 9–10.

Traditionally, the cause of action and the remedy were the same: the claimant pleaded an action for money had and received and, if successful, that action returned the money. These forms of action are still used in some common law jurisdictions, including, it seems, in Australia.

The common counts operated in the following way. Suppose that the claimant paid money to the defendant by mistake. The claimant would plead an action for money had and received. The court would say that there was an 'implied contract' according to which the defendant 'promised' the claimant to pay back the money, and the court would award an action for money had and received. This rested on a fiction that the claimant and the defendant had made a contract, although they had not.[7]

Courts across the common law world have since rejected the 'implied contract' analysis.[8] However, it became necessary to establish an alternative coherent framework to explain the outcome of these cases.

First, in 1936, the American Law Institute's *Restatement of Restitution* organised the law of quasi-contract and constructive trusts into a coherent body of law by categorising them as instances of restitution (in both the sense of 'giving back' and 'giving up').[9] Then, in 1966, Robert Goff (later Lord Goff) and Gareth Jones published *The Law of Restitution*,[10] which drew a diverse range of cases together on the basis that they were intended (whether explicitly or implicitly) to prevent or reverse unjust enrichment. They expressly refuted 'quasi-contract' as a basis for these decisions. Third, in 1985, Peter Birks published *An Introduction to the Law of Restitution*,[11] seeking to present a coherent and unified vision of this area of law as grounded in notions of unjust enrichment, and drawing on civilian law and Roman law taxonomies. Birks had a profound influence on the law of England and Wales in particular.

---

[7] See, eg, *Sinclair v Brougham* [1914] AC 398, which upheld the fiction.

[8] *Deglman v Guarantee Trust Co of Canada* [1954] SCR 725; *Pavey & Matthews Pty Ltd v Paul* [1987] HCA 5, (1987) 162 CLR 221; *Lipkin Gorman v Karpnale Ltd* [1991] 2 AC 548.

[9] American Law Institute, *Restatement of Restitution: Quasi-Contract and Constructive Trusts* (American Law Institute 1936); Warren A Seavey and Austin W Scott, 'Restitution' (1938) 54 LQR 29. See now American Law Institute, *Restatement (Third) of Restitution and Unjust Enrichment* (American Law Institute 2011).

[10] Robert Goff and Gareth Jones, *The Law of Restitution* (Sweet & Maxwell 1966). Now up to its tenth edition: Charles Mitchell, Paul Mitchell and Stephen Watterson, *Goff & Jones: The Law of Unjust Enrichment* (10th edn, Sweet & Maxwell 2022).

[11] Peter Birks, *An Introduction to the Law of Restitution* (Clarendon Press 1985). A revised edition was published in 1989.

Many eminent scholars have since published texts in this area.[12] However, other equally eminent scholars have recently questioned whether a unitary approach to unjust enrichment is appropriate and argued that the law should be again disaggregated into discrete categories.[13]

The rubric adopted in this book to understand these cases is that of Birks, who proposed a four-step approach to these cases. Later, this was adopted in case law:

1. Has the defendant been benefited, in the sense of being enriched?
2. Was the enrichment at the claimant's expense?
3. Was the enrichment unjust?
4. Are there any defences?[14]

Although this four-step approach has been accepted in English courts since 1991,[15] since 2017, it has also been emphasised that relief will not be given simply because a set of facts can be fitted into the rubric, without supporting authority for relief in that category of case.[16] It appears that the four-step test is otherwise over-inclusive.

In any case, in the discussion below, the law will still be discussed according to Birks' four-step rubric, with the caveat that this has been questioned.

---

[12] See, eg, Peter Birks, *Unjust Enrichment* (2nd edn, OUP 2005); Andrew Burrows, *The Law of Restitution* (3rd edn, OUP 2011); Graham Virgo, *Principles of the Law of Restitution* (3rd edn, OUP 2015); James Edelman and Elise Bant, *Unjust Enrichment* (2nd edn, Hart 2016); Charles Mitchell, Paul Mitchell and Stephen Watterson, *Goff & Jones: The Law of Unjust Enrichment* (10th edn, Sweet & Maxwell 2022).

[13] Robert Stevens, 'The Unjust Enrichment Disaster' (2018) 134 LQR 574; Lionel Smith, 'Restitution: A New Start?' in Peter Devonshire and Rohan Havelock (eds), *The Impact of Equity and Restitution in Commerce* (Hart 2019) 91; Lionel Smith, 'Unjust Enrichment' (2020) 66 McGill LJ 165; Robert Stevens, *The Laws of Restitution* (OUP 2023).

[14] *Banque Financière de la Cité v Parc (Battersea) Ltd* [1999] 1 AC 221, 227 (Lord Steyn).

[15] *Lipkin Gorman (a firm) v Karpnale Ltd* [1991] 2 AC 548.

[16] *Investment Trust Companies v Revenue and Customs Commissioners* [2017] UKSC 29, [2018] AC 275, [40]–[42]; *Swynson Ltd v Lowick Rose llp* [2017] UKSC 32, [2018] AC 313 [22], [110]–[112]; *Skandinaviska Enskilda Banken AB (Publ) v Conway* [2019] UKPC 36, [2020] AC 1111 [79]–[80]; *Terna Energy Trading doo v Revolut Ltd* [2024] EWHC 1419 (Comm), [2024] Bus LR 1401 [23]–[29].

Enrichment and restitutionary remedies

In order to show that there has been an enrichment, it must be shown that the defendant has received a benefit from the claimant. Moreover, the defendant must have chosen to receive the benefit from the claimant. The restitutionary remedy responds to the unjust enrichment (and typically reflects the value of the enrichment).

It has been said in this context that 'enrichment' is a legal term of art.[17] Historically, there were three main kinds of enrichment a defendant might receive at the claimant's expense: money, services, and goods. These remain forms of enrichment, although, as discussed below, money and services dominate.

Money was historically an enrichment for which the common count of the action for money had and received was available. In *BP Exploration Co (Libya) Ltd v Hunt (No 2)*, Robert Goff J said: 'Money has the peculiar character of a universal medium of exchange.'[18] It is difficult to say that one is not enriched by money, and it is generally presumed that the defendant chose to be enriched.[19] The defendant will also be enriched by the value of money over time (ie, interest earned on money which should have been in the claimant's hands).

Goods were historically an enrichment for which the *quantum valebat* was available, which required the defendant to pay the claimant the fair value of goods. Any role for unjust enrichment has largely been superseded by sale of goods legislation, which provides an easier mechanism for recovering the value of goods.

Services were historically an enrichment for which *quantum meruit* was available (*quantum meruit* means 'as much as he deserves'). It remains the case that services may constitute an enrichment that gives rise to a restitutionary remedy.

However, services can be difficult to value. Moreover, as will be discussed below, a claimant may argue that the services were worthless or unwanted.[20]

Courts start from the position that a defendant who accepted services from the claimant must have derived some value from them. Hence, in *Benedetti v Sawiris*, Lord Clarke said that the starting point will be that the defendant received the market value of the services, with the burden of proof then

---

17 *Barnes v Eastenders Cash & Carry plc* [2014] UKSC 26, [2015] AC 1 [100].

18 [1979] 1 WLR 783, 799.

19 Michael Bryan, 'Equity and Restitution' in Patrick Parkinson (ed), *The Principles of Equity* (2nd edn, LBC 2003) [406]; James Edelman and Elise Bant, *Unjust Enrichment* (2nd edn, Hart 2016) 55.

20 See, eg, *Brenner v First Artists' Management Pty Ltd* [1993] 2 VR 221.

shifting to the defendant to prove that the claimant received a lesser or no benefit.[21] In that particular case, Mr Benedetti had already been paid the objective market value of the share acquisition services he provided to Mr Sawiris and did not establish an entitlement to further profits from the takeover deal.

In the Australian case *Brenner v First Artists' Management Pty Ltd*, where the plaintiff acted as a manager for the singer Daryl Braithwaite in the absence of a clear contract, Byrne J outlined six helpful guiding principles as to how to measure the value of services:[22]

(1) The exercise presupposes that no contract exists, and hence the measure is different from that undertaken for damages for breach of contract.
(2) Ordinarily, the plaintiff should be given the fair value of the work actually done, calculated at a reasonable rate.
(3) Where the parties had a contract, but for some reason it was ineffective or no longer on foot, the agreed price is evidence of the appropriate remuneration for the service, but it is not determinative.
(4) Often it is appropriate to apply an hourly rate to the time the plaintiff took in performing the services.
(5) Where it is impossible to assess the number of hours or itemise the precise services performed, the court can make a 'global assessment' and adjust this according to what can be proven.
(6) Where it is customary for the services concerned to be recompensed with a commission, the court may have regard to what a reasonable commission would be and apply it.

Point (3) above must be treated with care, as if there is a contractual arrangement which is for some reason unenforceable, the precise relevance of the contract price is still unclear.

As noted above, it is always possible to say of services that a recipient never wanted them. Birks called this 'subjective devaluation', but that term is unfortunate, as the inquiry as to whether the defendant wanted the services is objective.

A situation where the claimant could argue that they never wanted the service can be illustrated by the following hypothetical. Suppose that a driver has stopped their car at the traffic lights and a person approaches with a squeegee, water, and detergent. The driver shakes their head at the window washer and mouths the word 'No'. Despite this, the person washes the windscreen of the car. The mere fact that the driver has received a service does not establish that

21 *Benedetti v Sawiris* [2013] UKSC 50, [2014] AC 938, [34].
22 *Brenner v First Artists' Management Pty Ltd* [1993] 2 VR 221, 262–64.

they have been unjustly enriched. The law respects the driver's autonomy by allowing the driver to argue that they never wanted the benefit. Therefore, this is a defence to a claim for the value of services.

There are at least three different ways in which a claimant can argue that the defendant did want the services after all and should be made to pay for the benefit of them:

(1) The claimant could argue the enrichment is an 'incontrovertible benefit' – in other words, no reasonable person could argue that the defendant is not enriched. For example, in *Cressman v Coys of Kensington (Sales) Ltd*,[23] Coys sold the defendant a secondhand car for £20,290. However, mistakenly, Coys left a personalised number plate on the car (TAC 1), belonging to the former owner, which was worth £15,000. By the time the company discovered the mistake, the defendant had registered the car in his name. The court found that the number plate was an 'incontrovertible benefit'.[24]
(2) The claimant could establish that the defendant objectively chose the benefit.
(3) The claimant could establish that the defendant chose to retain the benefit despite the fact that they had an opportunity to reject it (which Birks called 'free acceptance').

However, Lord Burrows, writing extrajudicially, has argued that a failure to reject may only signify indifference to the service rather than a positive choice to accept.[25] Consequently, free acceptance might only be established where the defendant was under a duty to reject the benefit (for example, if the claimant asked them whether they wanted the service, and the defendant did not reject it).

Some enrichments may not fit into the old forms of action (for example, the use of the claimant's land), but a restitutionary remedy for the reversal of that gain would be awarded under the broader four-point rubric, where the claimant would be given the fair rental value of the defendant's use if it could be established that the gain was at the claimant's expense, that the relevant 'unjust factor' could be established, and no defences applied.[26]

23 [2004] EWCA Civ 47, [2004] 1 WLR 2775.
24 ibid [33]–[40].
25 Andrew Burrows, *The Law of Restitution* (3rd edn, OUP 2011) 57.
26 James Edelman and Elise Bant, *Unjust Enrichment* (2nd edn, Hart 2016) 46–49.

At the claimant's expense

The defendant must be unjustly enriched at the expense of the claimant. In other words, unjust enrichment involves subtractive restitution: the defendant has received something from the claimant and the remedy restores the value of what the defendant has received. In *Kleinwort Benson Ltd v Birmingham City Council*, Morritt LJ explained:

> [T]he words 'at the expense of the plaintiff' on which the authority placed such reliance do not appear in a statute and should not be construed or applied as if they did. In my view they do no more than point to the requirement that the immediate source of the unjust enrichment must be the plaintiff.[27]

James Edelman and Elise Bant have explained:

> The best approach to 'at the expense of' is to conclude that value received by a defendant will be at the plaintiff's expense if it is received by a transaction or a series of transactions that are sufficiently linked to an initial transaction with the plaintiff.[28]

In equity, a claimant may 'trace' property belonging to them, or an exchange product for the property, into the hands of the defendant or third parties when there has been a breach of fiduciary duty.[29] In some instances, the remedies which arise from the process of tracing[30] (whether personal or proprietary) have been argued to be restitutionary in nature.[31] However, the more complex

---

27 [1997] QB 380, 400.

28 James Edelman and Elise Bant, *Unjust Enrichment* (2nd edn, Hart 2016) 89–90.

29 *In re Hallett's Estate* (1879) 13 Ch D 696.

30 In *Boscawen v Bajwa* [1996] 1 WLR 328, 334, Lord Millett said:

> Tracing properly so called, however, is neither a claim nor a remedy but a process. Moreover, it is not confined to the case where the plaintiff seeks a proprietary claim; it is equally necessary where he seeks a personal remedy against the known recipient or knowing assistant. It is the process by which the plaintiff traces what has happened to his property, identifies the persons who have handled or received it, and justifies his claim that the money which they handled or received (and if necessary which they still retain) can properly be regarded as representing his property.

31 See especially *Lipkin Gorman v Karpnale Ltd* [1991] 2 AC 548, which involved tracing. Cass was a partner at a firm of solicitors, Lipkin Gorman. In breach of fiduciary duty, he withdrew £323,222 from the solicitors' client trust account when he was not entitled to do so. He took the money to the Playboy Club for the purposes of gambling and lost it. Lipkin Gorman successfully claimed

position of 'tracing' and how that process fits with unjust enrichment will not be considered in this book.[32]

Unjust factors

Before a court will award a restitutionary remedy for unjust enrichment, the claimant must establish an 'unjust factor' which requires the defendant to reverse the transfer of value. Comparatively uncontroversial examples of 'unjust factors' include the following:

- failure of consideration (meaning a failure of the purpose of the bargain which has led to the defendant's enrichment);
- mistake (encompassing both mistake of fact and mistake of law);
- compulsion (including duress);
- undue influence; and
- illegality.[33]

Other unjust factors may possibly give rise to restitutionary remedies, but their status is more controversial.[34]

There is an ongoing debate in unjust enrichment scholarship as to whether the trigger of a claim in unjust enrichment ought to be 'unjust factors' or the absence of a legal justification for the transfer of value from the claimant to the defendant ('absence of basis').[35] The 'absence of basis' model is used in many civilian systems, particularly in German law, and has been adopted in Canada.[36] In England, the identification of 'unjust factors' remains the dominant approach, even if the precise list of unjust factors is contested.

---

against the Playboy Club on the basis that they were unjustly enriched by the receipt of the money (subject to a change of position defence).

32 The issue must be mentioned because the first case to recognise unjust enrichment in English law was *Lipkin Gorman v Karpnale Ltd* [1991] 2 AC 548.

33 However, the status of 'illegality' as a vitiating factor is questioned in Andrew Burrows, *The Law of Restitution* (3rd edn, OUP 2011) 488.

34 eg, 'ignorance': ibid 403–34.

35 Birks first advocated an 'unjust factors' approach in Peter Birks, *An Introduction to the Law of Restitution* (revised edn, Clarendon Press 1989), but later moved to advocate for an 'absence of basis' approach in Peter Birks, *Unjust Enrichment* (2nd edn, OUP 2005).

36 Eg, *Garland v Consumers' Gas Co* [2004] SCC 25, [2004] 1 SCR 629 [38]–[47].

Defences

Defences to a claim for restitution are only dealt with briefly here. They are mentioned because they help to clarify how certain aspects of personal and proprietary rescission have been analysed by restitutionary scholars.

It was established in *Lipkin Gorman v Karpnale Ltd* that the main restitutionary defence is a change of position.[37] This defence is established if the defendant shows that they have irreversibly changed their position to their detriment in good faith in reliance upon the receipt of the benefit.[38] Thus, the defendant will not be obliged to make restitution to the extent that the change is irreversible. The rationale behind this defence has been said to be the need to uphold the security of transactions. In other words, parties can be relatively sure in most circumstances that transactions will not be readily unwound.

As will be discussed later in this chapter, for equitable rescission to be awarded, both parties must be able to make substantial *restitutio in integrum* (ie, 'restore the other to their original position'). The adjustments that courts make in achieving 'practical justice' can be seen as operating in a manner similar to a good faith change of position defence. Moreover, in a case where a claimant exercises a proprietary power to rescind, the courts may take account of the extent to which certain property cannot be returned. Again, this can be said to resemble a change of position defence.[39]

There are other defences to a claim in unjust enrichment.[40] However, a detailed consideration of these defences is beyond the scope of this book.

The Relationship Between Contract and Restitution for Unjust Enrichment

Usually, remedies for unjust enrichment arise because a contract is void, unenforceable, discharged by frustration, rescinded or terminated for breach. Consequently, there is an issue as to how contract and restitution for unjust enrichment should interact. If a contract was previously in existence, but it is

---

[37] *Lipkin Gorman v Karpnale Ltd* [1991] 2 AC 548, 558, 568, 578–80.

[38] James Edelman and Elise Bant, *Unjust Enrichment* (2nd edn, Hart 2016) 332.

[39] Elise Bant, 'Trusts, Powers and Liens: An Exercise in Ground-Clearing' (2010) 4 J Eq 286, 303; Elise Bant, '*Restitutio in Integrum* and the Change of Position Defence: Lessons from Rescission' (2007) RLR 13, 33.

[40] James Edelman and Elise Bant, *Unjust Enrichment* (2nd edn, Hart 2016) ch 15. They consider the following defences: good consideration, impossibility of counter-restitution, bona fide purchaser for value without notice, estoppel, ministerial receipt, delay, resolution of disputes, and passing on.

unenforceable for some reason, to what extent should the court have regard to its terms in establishing the proper value to be returned to the claimant?

The problem is particularly acute where the claimant has entered into a 'losing contract', where the fair value of the benefit provided is much greater than the contract price. A vivid example of this issue can be found in the Californian case *Boomer v Muir*.[41] The defendant head contractor was building a dam, and the plaintiff was a subcontractor, paid in instalments by the defendant. The plaintiff accurately alleged that the defendant had not provided sufficient materials to allow him to meet the contractual deadline and walked out by reason of the defendant's breach of contract. At the time, about US$20,000 was owing to the plaintiff, according to the contract. The plaintiff sued the defendant, claiming a *quantum meruit* for the value of work done. The court awarded the plaintiff a *quantum meruit* in the sum of US$258,000, over ten times the contract price.

There are two interlinked issues raised by such cases. First, there is a question of whether courts should undermine the contractual allocation of risk between the parties by awarding a restitutionary remedy. At one extreme, it might be argued that unjust enrichment is entirely separate from contract law and that the contractual risk allocation is irrelevant. At the other extreme, it might be argued that we should not allow unjust enrichment to undermine the parties' contractual allocation of risk.

Second, and relatedly, there is a question as to whether the measure of restitution should be limited by a contractual 'ceiling'. If such a ceiling had been applied in *Boomer v Muir*, the plaintiff would have been able to recover only US$20,000, notwithstanding that the market value of the services was vastly higher.

The current position in English law appears to be that the contract may provide evidence of the value of the services, and it should possibly be regarded as a cap on liability, contrary to *Boomer v Muir*.[42] Therefore, English courts are concerned not to unduly undermine the contractual allocation of risk.

RESCISSION

Where a claimant enters into a transaction (including a contract, a will, a disposition to a trust, a gift, or a conveyance), but the transaction is subject to a vitiating factor such as duress or misrepresentation, it is possible for the transaction to be reversed or 'set aside', using the remedy of rescission. 'The basic

---

[41] 24 P 2d 570 (Cal App 1 Dist, 1933). See also *United States v Zara Contracting Co*, 146 F 2d 606 (1944); *Re Montgomery's Estate*, 6 NE (2d) 40 (1936).

[42] *Taylor v Motability Finance Ltd* [2004] EWHC 2619 (Comm) [26].

objective of the relief given upon rescission is to restore the parties to their original positions or, where rescission occurs in equity, as near to those positions as may be.'[43]

There is no requirement for the party seeking to rescind to suffer loss; it is only necessary to identify a vitiating factor. Which vitiating factors apply depends upon whether the rescission occurs at common law (in the narrow sense) or in equity; the latter has a much broader range of factors that entitle a claimant to rescind.

A transaction that can be rescinded is not voided; rather, it is rendered 'voidable', which means that the transaction will remain valid and effective *unless and until* the claimant elects to exercise the right to rescind.[44] However, after a contract is rescinded, it 'is treated in law as never having come into existence',[45] although courts recognise that it previously existed until the election to rescind occurred.[46] Once rescinded, the contract is extinguished as if from the beginning (*ab initio*) and any unperformed obligations under the contract are also consequently extinguished.[47]

Unfortunately, the word 'rescission' has been used inaccurately to describe the situation where a party to a contract elects to terminate and treat the contract as no longer binding upon them after the other party breaches, or to describe the situation where a provision in a contract allows for one or both parties to treat the contract as no longer binding upon the occurrence of a specified event. This is *not* rescission, because the contract is not void *ab initio*; only obligations not yet due at the time of the breach or triggering event fall away: the terminated contract is determined *de futuro* rather than *ab initio*.[48]

As Bant has noted, it is unfortunate that courts sometimes use the word 'rescission' to describe a right to terminate a transaction which discharges the parties from future performance but does *not* affect accrued rights under the contract.[49] Rescission is entirely different from termination for breach of contract, because it extinguishes the contract *ab initio*, such that all obligations under the contract are no longer in existence. In this chapter, we only consider rescission according to the proper meaning of the word.

---

43 Dominic O'Sullivan, Steven Elliott and Rafal Zakrzewski, *The Law of Rescission* (3rd edn, OUP 2023) [13.01].

44 ibid [1.04].

45 *Johnson v Agnew* [1980] AC 367, 393 (Lord Wilberforce).

46 *Mackender v Feldia AG* [1967] 2 QB 590, 603 (Diplock LJ).

47 *McDonald v Dennys Lascelles Ltd* (1933) 48 CLR 457, 476–77 (Dixon J).

48 Dominic O'Sullivan, Steven Elliott and Rafal Zakrzewski, *The Law of Rescission* (3rd edn, OUP 2023) [1.06].

49 Elise Bant, 'Reconsidering the Role of Election in Rescission' (2012) 32(3) OJLS 467.

As noted in Chapter 8, rescission is sometimes said to be a self-help remedy, particularly if the right holder gives notice of their election to rescind to the other party, and the parties restore each other to their prior positions without the intervention of the court.[50] However, rescission can also be regarded as a judicial remedy (particularly where equitable rescission of an executed contract is granted). The availability of rescission on terms in equity means that, arguably, the right to rescind only arises once the court orders it upon the specified terms, and not when the party seeking to rescind the contract asserts it. Consequently, some argue that equitable rescission in equity's exclusive jurisdiction (where the vitiating factor is not fraud or duress) is always the act of the court.[51] Janet O'Sullivan has argued that rescission should *always* be the act of the court.[52]

As noted at the outset of this chapter, rescission has also been analysed as a restitutionary remedy by some scholars.[53] There is a clear kinship between restitutionary remedies for subtractive unjust enrichment and rescission: in both cases, a vitiating factor must be identified, and the parties must return the benefit or value of the benefits they have received from the other. Arguably, something resembling a defence of good faith change of position in reliance upon the receipt exists in both doctrines. However, rescission can be distinguished from subtractive restitution for unjust enrichment because it requires the claimant to elect to rescind the transaction.[54]

Types of Rescission

Rescission operates differently depending on whether it is available at common law (in the narrow sense) or in equity. Equitable rescission is more flexible than common law rescission and is better able to accommodate and adjust

---

50 *Halpern v Halpern (No 2)* [2006] EWHC 1728 (Comm), [2007] QB 88, [26].

51 JD Heydon, Mark J Leeming and Peter G Turner, *Meagher, Gummow and Lehane's Equity: Doctrines and Remedies* (5th edn, LexisNexis 2015) [25-115]; Dominic O'Sullivan, Steven Elliott and Rafal Zakrzewski, *The Law of Rescission* (3rd edn, OUP 2023) [12.11]–[12.24].

52 Janet O'Sullivan, 'Rescission as a Self-Help Remedy: A Critical Analysis' (2000) 59 Camb LJ 509.

53 See, eg, Nyuk Yin Nahan, 'Rescission: A Case for Rejecting the Classical Model?' (1997) 27 UWALR 66; Louis Proksch, 'Rescission' in Patrick Parkinson (ed), *The Principles of Equity* (2nd edn, LBC 2003) [2506]; Elise Bant, 'Trusts, Powers and Liens: An Exercise in Ground-Clearing' (2009) 3 J Eq 286.

54 See Elise Bant, 'Reconsidering the Role of Election in Rescission' (2012) 32 OJLS 467. Bant argues compellingly that election could also operate in unjust enrichment law.

to changes which occurred after the transaction was concluded. The range of vitiating factors is also wider for equitable rescission. Each form of rescission will be considered in turn.

Legal rescission

Common law or legal rescission is generally available only where there is fraud[55] or duress.[56] It is available only for contracts, and not for gifts.

Pivotally, for legal rescission to be possible, the parties must be restored *precisely* to their pre-transaction position ('complete *restitutio in integrum*'). The stringent nature of this requirement is illustrated by two cases, *Hunt v Silk*[57] and *Blackburn v Smith*.[58] In each case, an interest in land (a lease and fee simple title respectively) was transferred to the plaintiff, who took possession of the land. Each plaintiff sought to rescind the transaction for fraud, but rescission was barred because each of the plaintiffs had briefly taken possession of the land. The plaintiffs could not 'give back' this use of the land, and hence complete *restitutio in integrum* was impossible.

Equitable rescission

Equitable rescission is much more generous than legal rescission. First, the grounds for rescission are wider than those recognised at common law. Fraudulent misrepresentation[59] is a basis for rescission, but so are negligent and innocent misrepresentation,[60] undue pressure,[61] undue influence,[62] unconscionable conduct[63] and breach of fiduciary duty.[64] The position of mistake in

---

55 *Load v Green* (1846) 15 M & W 216; 153 ER 828; *Clarke v Dickson* (1858) El Bl & El 148; 120 ER 463; *Clough v London and North Western Railway Co* (1871) LR 7 Ex 26; *Car & Universal Finance Co Ltd v Caldwell* [1965] 1 QB 525; *HIH Casualty and General Insurance Ltd v Chase Manhattan Bank* [2003] UKHL 6, [2003] 1 All ER (Comm) 349, [98] (Lord Hobhouse).

56 *Whelpdale's case* (1604) 5 Co Rep 119a; 77 ER 239; *Enimont Overseas AG v RO Jugotanker Zadar (The Olib)* [1991] 2 Lloyd's Rep 108, 118; *Dimskal Shipping Co SA v International Transport Workers Federation (The Evia Luck)* [1992] 2 AC 152, 165; *Halpern v Halpern (No 2)* [2006] EWHC 1728 (Comm), [2007] QB 88.

57 (1804) 5 East 449, 102 ER 1142.

58 (1848) 2 Ex 782, 154 ER 707.

59 *Derry v Peek* (1889) 14 App Cas 337, 374 (Lord Herschel).

60 *Redgrave v Hurd* (1881) 20 Ch D 1; *Hayward v Zurich Insurance Co* [2016] UKSC 48, [2017] AC 142.

61 *Lloyd's Bank v Bundy* [1975] QB 326, 338–39 (Lord Denning).

62 *Allcard v Skinner* (1887) 36 Ch D 145.

63 *Lloyd's Bank v Bundy* [1975] QB 326, 337 (Lord Denning).

64 *Holder v Holder* [1968] 1 Ch 353, 398; *Pitt v Holt* [2011] EWCA Civ 197, [2011] 3 WLR 19, [100] (Lloyd LJ).

the law of England and Wales is unclear:[65] it seems that mistake may now render a contract entered into under mistake void at common law. However, equity can set aside mistaken gifts and mistaken dispositions to trusts.[66]

Second, rescission in equity is available not only for contracts but also for gifts and other transactions.

Third, the parties need not be restored precisely to their original position: 'substantial *restitutio in integrum*' is sufficient. Courts state repeatedly that the aim of equitable rescission is to achieve 'practical justice' for both parties.[67] Hence, if the plaintiffs in *Hunt v Silk*[68] and *Blackburn v Smith*[69] (mentioned above) had claimed equitable rescission, the court would have ordered the plaintiffs to return the interest in land to the defendants and the defendants to return the purchase price to the plaintiffs. To reflect the fact that the plaintiffs had taken possession of the land, the court would have reduced the amount payable by the defendants to reflect the fair value of the plaintiffs' limited use of the land, thus effecting substantial *restitutio in integrum.*

Fourth, equitable rescission may be ordered 'on terms' as part of the process of accomplishing 'practical justice'. Moreover, the court can make financial adjustments (such as the payment for the use of the land mentioned in the paragraph above) as part of the process of restoring the parties to their precontractual position.

The Requirement of Restitutio in Integrum

The aim of rescission is to restore the parties to the position they were in before the transaction took place. As Rimer J said in *Shalson v Russo*, 'It involves a giving and taking back on both sides.'[70]

It is first necessary to ascertain what has been exchanged by both parties under the voidable transaction and, to the extent possible, to seek the return of the subject matter of the transaction to each party. As noted earlier, common law requires 'complete *restitutio in integrum*' whereas equitable rescission requires only 'substantial *restitutio in integrum*'. If the subject matter of

---

65 *Great Peace Shipping Ltd v Tsalviris Salvage (International) Ltd* [2002] EWCA Civ 1407, [2003] QB 679 rejecting *Solle v Butcher* [1950] 1 KB 671.

66 *Pitt v Holt* [2011] EWCA Civ 197, [2011] 3 WLR 19.

67 *Erlanger v New Sombrero Phosphate Co* (1878) 3 App Cas 1218, 1278–79; *Alati v Kruger* (1955) 94 CLR 216, 223; *O'Sullivan v Management Agency & Music Ltd* [1985] QB 428, 458, 466, 471.

68 (1804) 5 East 449, 102 ER 1142.

69 (1848) 2 Ex 782, 154 ER 707.

70 *Shalson v Russo* [2003] EWHC 1637 (Ch), [2005] Ch 281 [122] (Rimer J).

the transaction cannot be returned in the same form, common law rescission will be unavailable.

For equitable rescission, if the subject matter of the transaction cannot be returned, or if one party has derived a benefit which has not been paid for, the court will order a financial adjustment reflecting the value of the benefits received. It is then necessary to value the benefits and deduct them from the value the other party is required to return.

However, there comes a point where the situation has changed so greatly that not even equity can effect substantial *restitutio in integrum*, in which case rescission will be unavailable in equity too. The longer the time that has elapsed since the transaction and the greater the changes that have occurred to the property, the more difficult it is to achieve even substantial *restitutio in integrum*.

An example can be found in the case of *Clarke v Dickson*,[71] where the shares that were the subject matter of the transaction changed substantially in nature after the transaction had occurred. The shares in the company were converted from shares on a 'cost book' basis to shares in a 'joint stock corporation'; the mine the company exploited had been worked; and the plaintiff had received dividends from the investment. Finally, three years later, the shares (and the company) became worthless. Crompton J used the vivid analogy of a butcher who sought to rescind a contract for the sale of cattle after having slaughtered the cattle and sold the meat: 'If the rule of law were as the plaintiff contends, that butcher might, upon discovering fraud on the part of the grazier who sold him the cattle, rescind the contract and get back the whole price: but how could that be consistent with justice?'[72] The butcher would not be able to return the cattle in the same form in which they had been when the grazier sold them. Although *Clarke v Dickson* was a case of attempted common law rescission, it is likely that, even if equitable rescission had been sought, it would have been refused because the shares (and the company) had changed too greatly.[73]

An example of a case where an adjustment was made to accommodate changes in circumstances is *Erlanger v New Sombrero Phosphate Co*.[74] The plaintiff company sought to rescind a contract for the purchase of a phosphate mine when it discovered eight months after the sale of the mine that the defendant, Mr Erlanger, also a promoter of the company, had failed to disclose that he had bought the land for half the price for which he later sold

---

[71] (1858) El Bl & El 148, 120 ER 463.

[72] *Clarke v Dickson* (1858) El Bl & El 148, 155; 120 ER 463, 466.

[73] See also *Thomas Witter Ltd v TBP Industries Ltd* [1996] 2 All ER 573, 587, where the nature of the business run by a company changed fundamentally after the transaction, and rescission was declined.

[74] (1878) 3 App Cas 1218.

it to New Sombrero Phosphate Co. The question was whether the court could accommodate the fact that the plaintiff had made profits from the exploitation of the mine. It was found that the plaintiff company could return the mine to Mr Erlanger in exchange for a refund of the purchase price, as long as it also accounted to Mr Erlanger for any profits it had made from the mine while working it. The House of Lords found that the promoters of the company owed a fiduciary duty to investors. Lord Blackburn said, '[...] the practice has always been for a Court of Equity to give this relief whenever, by the exercise of its powers, it can do what is practically just, though it cannot restore the parties precisely to the state they were in before the contract'.[75] To the extent that there was any deterioration of the property,[76] or a possible liability to a third party,[77] this will be reflected in the amount required to be returned to the defendant.

The Australian case, *Brown v Smitt*,[78] also suggests that improvements to the subject matter of the contract can be accounted for, as long as they are 'not mere matters of taste or personal enjoyment'.[79] In that case, the plaintiff made certain improvements to the land after purchase, but before discovering the defendant's misrepresentation, and was entitled to adjustments reflecting this.[80] However, the plaintiff was not entitled to consequential losses flowing from the misrepresentation; only the immediate consequences of the transaction can be reversed.[81]

If the party seeking to rescind the transaction cannot make substantial *restitutio in integrum* to the defendant, the transaction cannot be set aside, even if the vitiating factor is clearly established.[82]

Election

A person entitled to rescind a transaction has a choice between affirming and rescinding it. The person seeking to rescind must elect to do so, and a failure to do so will mean that the transaction remains on foot. Ordinarily, a person seeking to rescind a contract or gift will elect when they give notice to the

---

75 ibid 1278.

76 *Erlanger v New Sombrero Phosphate Co* (1878) 3 App Cas 1218, 1278; *Lagunas Nitrate Co v Lagunas Syndicate* [1899] 2 Ch 392, 457.

77 *Spence v Crawford* [1939] 3 All ER 271, 283 (Lord Thankerton).

78 (1924) 34 CLR 160.

79 ibid 165 (Knox CJ, Gavan Duffy and Starke JJ).

80 ibid.

81 ibid 167.

82 *Clarke v Dickson* (1858) El Bl & El 148, 120 ER 463; *Spence v Crawford* [1939] 3 All ER 271, 288–89 (Lord Wright); *Halpern v Halpern (Nos 1 and 2)* [2007] EWCA Civ 291, [2007] QB 195.

other contracting party of an intention to set aside the transaction. The decision to affirm or disaffirm the transaction is generally final. It is not possible to 'hedge your bets' and choose each way.

How to make an election to rescind

An election to rescind may be communicated in several ways. It is sufficient for the rescinding party to clearly show that they no longer want to be bound by the transaction. Methods of an election to rescind include clear communication of an intention to disaffirm the contract;[83] conduct incompatible with a subsisting contract, such as demanding repayment of a purchase price; an attempt to repossess goods sold under a contract;[84] non-performance of a contractual obligation where the other party is aware this may constitute an unequivocal intention to disaffirm the transaction;[85] or serving a writ on the other party seeking rescission.[86]

A party entitled to rescind does not need to immediately choose to affirm or rescind the contract, but if a bona fide third-party purchaser obtains an interest in the subject matter of the transaction, or the other party is prejudiced by the rescinding party's delay, this may be a reason for the court to refuse to allow the rescinding party to exercise their right. Moreover, delay may also constitute affirmation, as discussed below.

Usually, an election to rescind must be communicated to the other party. However, in exceptional circumstances, this will be unnecessary. Such circumstances were present in *Car & Universal Finance Co Ltd v Caldwell*,[87] when the defendant sold his Jaguar car to a rogue. The rogue sold the car to dealers who had notice of his fraud. In a series of transactions, the car was ultimately sold to the plaintiff, a bona fide purchaser for value without notice. The English Court of Appeal had to consider whether the defendant was required to communicate his intention to rescind to the rogue—unsurprisingly, the

---

83 Dominic O'Sullivan, Steven Elliott and Rafal Zakrzewski, *The Law of Rescission* (3rd edn, OUP 2023) [11.03]. See, eg, *Shuman v Coober Pedy Tours Pty Ltd* (1994) 175 LSJS 159: demand for 'restitution of the contract price' for a fossil wrongly believed by both parties to be a dinosaur bone was a valid election to rescind.

84 *Re Eastgate* [1905] 1 KB 465; *Car & Universal Finance Co Ltd v Caldwell* [1965] 1 QB 525, 555, 558. Note this must be exercised very carefully to avoid trespass to goods or conversion and would only work for common law rescission where title is revested in the claimant upon election.

85 Dominic O'Sullivan, Steven Elliott and Rafal Zakrzewski, *The Law of Rescission* (3rd edn, OUP 2023) [11.07].

86 *Clough v London and North Western Railway Co* (1871) LR 7 Ex 26, 35.

87 [1965] 1 QB 525.

rogue had given a false name and could not be found—or whether it was sufficient for the defendant to have communicated his intention to rescind to the police and the Automobile Association, and to have asked those authorities to repossess the car if they found it. The Court held that, while it was ordinarily necessary to communicate an intention to rescind to the other party, in cases where a rogue had deliberately absconded, it was sufficient to make it known to the world that the contract was rescinded and to attempt to repossess the car (the defendant had gone searching for it once he discovered the fraud).[88] Although this case has been criticised, and it may be limited to cases of fraud, it remains good law.[89]

The consequences of an election to rescind

Election gives rise to different proprietary consequences, depending on whether rescission is sought in common law or in equity.

At common law, election effects an *immediate* re-vesting of title to the person who seeks to rescind, and the other party has no title. Hence, in *Car & Universal Finance Co Ltd v Caldwell*,[90] the defendant's election to rescind meant that title to the car immediately re-vested in him. As a result, from that moment onwards, the dealers (who were not bona fide purchasers for value without notice) had no title in the car, and the operation of the principle of *nemo dat quod non habet* ('no one can give what they do not have') meant that they could not pass title to the plaintiff.[91] This immediate re-vesting of property in the original owner only applies to contracts for goods.[92] Title to real property and intangible property cannot be recovered in this way by common law rescission.

The proprietary consequences of common law rescission can provide a defendant with a defence to a claim of a proprietary tort. In other words, if a defendant used the self-help remedy of recaption to recover their property, the defendant could defend themselves from a claim in conversion by the claimant by responding that they were simply taking possession of a good to which they again had title by reason of the election to rescind. Another consequence of

---

88 [1965] 1 QB 525, 550–51, 555, 558–59.

89 See Dominic O'Sullivan, Steven Elliott and Rafal Zakrzewski, *The Law of Rescission* (3rd edn, OUP 2023) [11.37]–[11.40].

90 [1965] 1 QB 525.

91 *Lewis v Averay* [1972] 1 QB 198, where the ultimate bona fide purchaser of a car was successful in gaining title.

92 Dominic O'Sullivan, Steven Elliott and Rafal Zakrzewski, The Law of Rescission (3rd edn, OUP 2023) [14.21]–[14.28], [16.04].

common law rescission is that the party seeking to rescind may have an action in conversion.[93]

The effect of an election to rescind in equity is different. Where an executory contract is voidable for a purely equitable ground, such as undue influence, breach of fiduciary duty, or unconscionable dealing, it will be rescinded by notice to the other party and is effectively nullified.

If legal title to an asset has been transferred pursuant to a transaction voidable in equity, an election to rescind operates to confer equitable title to the asset on the rescinding party, pursuant to a constructive trust. Hence, in *Lonrho plc v Fayed (No 2)*, Millet J said:

> A contract obtained by fraudulent misrepresentation is voidable, not void, even in equity. The representee may elect to avoid it, but until he does so the representor is not a constructive trustee of the property transferred pursuant to the contract, and no fiduciary relationship exists between him and the representee.[94]

This is sometimes described as a 'proprietary power'.[95] Although the term has not yet gained judicial acceptance, it is a useful descriptor. As Millet J indicates, it is important to distinguish between the position of the title of the party seeking to rescind both prior to the election and after the election has occurred.

Prior to election, under a 'proprietary power', the party seeking to rescind simply has a 'mere equity', an inchoate proprietary right that can easily be extinguished, even by the mere fact that a bona fide purchaser for value without notice has obtained an equitable interest in the property.[96] However, after the rescinding party has made an election to rescind, they are conferred with a 'full-blown' equitable title to the property pursuant to a constructive trust.[97]

---

93 Louis Proksch, 'Rescission' in Patrick Parkinson (ed), *The Principles of Equity* (2nd edn, LBC 2003) [2503]; JD Heydon, Mark J Leeming and Peter G Turner, *Meagher, Gummow and Lehane's Equity: Doctrines and Remedies* (5th edn, LexisNexis Butterworths 2015) [25–060].

94 [1992] 1 WLR 1, 12, citing *Daly v Sydney Stock Exchange Ltd* (1986) 160 CLR 371, 387–90 (Brennan J).

95 The term is taken from Elise Bant, 'Trusts, Powers and Liens: An Exercise in Ground-Clearing' (2009) 3 J Eq 286, who in turn builds on Birke Häcker, *Consequences of Impaired Consent Transfers* (Mohr Siebeck 2009); Birke Häcker, 'Proprietary Restitution after Impaired Consent Transfers: A Generalised Power Model' (2009) 68 Camb LJ 324.

96 *Latec Investments Limited v Hotel Terrigal Pty Ltd* (1965) 113 CLR 265, 277, 284, 290–91, citing *Phillips v Phillips* (1861) 4 De G F & J 208; 45 ER 1164.

97 *Latec Investments Limited v Hotel Terrigal Pty Ltd* (1965) 113 CLR 265, 277, 290–91, citing *Stump v Gaby* (1852) 2 De GM & G 613, 42 ER 1015. Note that in *El Ajou v Dollar Land Holdings plc* [1993] 3 All ER 717, 734, Millett J

In other words, one party holds legal title, but it is now subject to the rescinding party's equitable interest, which may entitle the rescinding party to seek to have the property returned pursuant to a court order, by winding up the trust. However, it is important to note that courts also sometimes choose to award a less intrusive remedy such as a lien or no remedy at all, depending upon the presence of discretionary bars to relief.

The reasons behind the election requirement

Election primarily protects the interests of innocent defendants, and courts are less sympathetic towards fraudulent defendants. Hence, in *Spence v Crawford*, Lord Wright explained:

> The court will be less ready to pull a transaction to pieces where the defendant is innocent, whereas in the case of fraud the court will exercise its jurisdiction to the full in order, if possible, to prevent the defendant from enjoying the benefit of his fraud at the expense of the innocent plaintiff.[98]

Election also protects third parties who might have gained a competing interest in an asset transferred pursuant to a voidable transaction without being aware of the proprietary interest of the party seeking to rescind.

Rescission Must be Total

The traditional position at common law and in equity is that rescission must be total. The claimant can elect to rescind or affirm a transaction but cannot do both.

Generally, a claimant may not rescind part of a transaction and affirm another: it is an 'all or nothing process'.[99] Nor may a claimant rescind one contract out of a series. English law does not permit 'partial rescission'.[100] There are powerful reasons for this. In *Myddleton v Lord Kenyon*, Longborough LC said:

> The relief prayed is not to set aside the deed as null and void; but to declare, that all the trusts are void after that for payment of the debts; leaving all those parts to stand, and obtain their full effect so far as the payment of the debts goes. The species of relief it is totally incompetent to the Court to give. The deed may be set aside *in*

---

characterised the trust so arising as a 'resulting trust' not a 'constructive trust', but this has not been generally taken up.

98 [1939] SC (HL) 52, 77.

99 *TSB Bank plc v Camfield* [1995] 1 WLR 430, 436 (Nourse LJ).

100 *TSB Bank plc v Camfield* [1995] 1 WLR 430; *Castle Phillips Finance v Piddington* [1995] 1 FLR 783; *Molestina v Ponton* [2002] 1 Lloyd's Rep 271.

> *toto*. Any bargain, the parties enter into with each other, may be declared null, and set aside, upon grounds of undue practice or influence exerted, mistake. [...] These grounds would entitle the Court to set it aside *in toto*: but I cannot make a new bargain for the parties; or force them into a new agreement upon those things, which are matter of absolute will, and depending totally upon the consent and temper of the parties. I cannot make a new family settlement. No judge is competent to such an act. [...] This Court, if it was to go farther, and to substitute other terms, would make itself the *moderator* of the private affairs of all the families of England.[101]

By contrast, Australian courts have shown themselves willing to award partial rescission,[102] but the difficulties they have faced in doing so (particularly in *Bridgewater v Leahy*)[103] suggest that English courts should not follow suit.

Discretionary Factors and Bars to Relief

The ordinary equitable bars to relief apply to equitable rescission. Thus, where rescission would inflict undue hardship on the defendant, it will not be awarded, or a court may choose to award a lesser proprietary remedy such as a lien. Similarly, if the claimant has acted unconscionably, they will not be entitled to rescind.

The following bars to rescission will be considered in more detail:

- impossibility of complete restoration;
- affirmation;
- delay;
- intervening third-party rights;
- executed contracts and innocent misrepresentation; and
- damages in lieu of rescission.

Impossibility of complete restoration

It flows from the requirement of *restitutio in integrum* that rescission will be barred in equity where it is impossible to substantially restore the parties to their original positions.[104] This bar operates only when the claimant is unable to restore the defendant.

In *Spence v Crawford*, Lord Wright said:

---

[101] (1794) 2 Ves 391, 408; 30 ER 689, 698–99.

[102] See especially *Vadasz v Pioneer Concrete (SA) Pty Ltd* (1995) 184 CLR 102.

[103] (1998) 194 CLR 457. See criticisms in Peter Watts, 'Partial Rescission: Disentangling the Seedlings but Not Transplanting Them' in Elise Bant and Matthew Harding (eds), *Exploring Private Law* (CUP 2010) 427.

[104] *Erlanger v New Sombrero Phosphate Co* (1878) 3 App Cas 1218, 1278.

> [I]f a plaintiff who has been defrauded seeks to have the contract annulled and his money or property restored to him, it would be inequitable if he did not also restore what he had got under the contract from the defendant. Though the defendant has been fraudulent, he must not be robbed, nor must the plaintiff be unjustly enriched, as he would be if he both got back what he had parted with and kept what he had received in return.[105]

As noted previously, common law requires 'complete *restitutio in integrum*', whereas equitable rescission only requires 'substantial *restitutio in integrum*'.

Affirmation

When a contract is voidable by reason of a vitiating factor, the party seeking to rescind must elect whether to avoid or affirm the contract. Affirmation involves a choice to leave the contract in question on foot and, potentially, take action under it (including suing for damages, seeking specific performance, and so forth). If the party entitled to rescind has affirmed the contract, they can no longer rescind it. Affirmation must be unequivocal.[106]

A clear choice to affirm the contract cannot be made by a party who still operates under a vitiating factor such as duress or undue influence or is still unaware that the other party has made a misrepresentation. Thus, the party resisting rescission must show that the other party has made such a choice since the vitiating factor ceased to operate.

The claimant must also know of circumstances that gave rise to the right to rescind and that they had a legal right to rescind before any affirmation can be made.[107] Alternatively, as in *Allcard v Skinner*, the claimant may decide not to investigate their rights once they know of the circumstances.[108]

Affirmation is linked to delay as a delay in bringing a claim after becoming aware of the vitiating factor may constitute affirmation of the contract, as occurred in *Allcard v Skinner*. This will be discussed below.

Laches: delay and acquiescence and delay and prejudice

Delay may be a bar,[109] but by itself, delay is not enough—something more is needed before rescission will be barred—namely, either acquiescence on the part of the claimant or prejudice with respect of the defendant or third parties.

Delay with acquiescence is related to, and overlaps with, the bar of affirmation for the purposes of rescission. As noted earlier, the right to rescind is lost

---

105 1939 SC (HL) 52, 77.

106 *Clough v London and North Western Railway Co* (1871) LR 7 Ex 26, 34 (Mellor J).

107 *Evans v Bartlam* [1937] AC 473, 479 (Lord Atkin).

108 (1887) 36 Ch D 145, 188 (Lindsey LJ), 192 (Bowen LJ).

109 *Leaf v International Galleries* [1950] 2 KB 86.

when the claimant unequivocally manifests an intention to affirm the transaction. Once the claimant becomes aware of the right to rescind and is free of any vitiating factor, failure to rescind in a reasonable time (ie, acquiescence) may be taken as evidence of an intention to affirm the contract.[110]

A case where proprietary rescission was denied because of delay and acquiescence occurred in *Allcard v Skinner*.[111] Miss Allcard, the plaintiff, had joined a Protestant religious order known as the 'Sisters of the Poor'. The order observed a rule of poverty which required the member to give up all her property to her relatives, to the poor or to the sisterhood, with the latter strongly encouraged. Within three days of joining, Allcard executed a will in favour of Miss Skinner, the lady superior of the order, and after she inherited a large amount of property, she transferred several large sums of money and railway stock to Skinner. Some 10 years later, Allcard left the sisterhood to join a Catholic order and revoked her will, but did not demand the return of her property until six years after she had left the sisterhood. Then she sought to rescind the transaction on the basis that Skinner had exercised undue influence. The court found that there was a presumed relationship of undue influence arising from the relationship of spiritual advisor and acolyte, and that the defendant failed to rebut this presumption on the facts. However, Allcard could not assert a proprietary interest against Skinner because of her delay and acquiescence in bringing her claim.

Delay with prejudice is concerned with the prejudicial effects of delay to the defendant or third parties. The classic example of prejudice is where the defendant has reasonably acted to their detriment in reliance on the claimant's delay. It is somewhat related to the bar of impossibility of *restitutio in integrum*.[112] Bant has therefore argued that delay in this sense requires consideration of factors which make it resemble a change of position defence in unjust enrichment.[113]

Intervening third-party rights

Rescission has traditionally been barred where a third party, who is a bona fide purchaser for value without notice, acquires rights in the subject matter of a voidable contract. If the defendant transfers the subject matter of the contract to an innocent third party, before the contract is rescinded by the original victim, good title passes. This means that *restitutio in integrum* between the

110 ibid.

111 (1887) 36 Ch D 145.

112 Dominic O'Sullivan, Steven Elliott and Rafal Zakrzewski, *The Law of Rescission* (3rd edn, OUP 2023) [24.01].

113 Normann Witzleb, Elise Bant, Simone Degeling and Kit Barker, *Remedies: Commentary and Materials* (7th edn, LBC 2020) [2.155].

original parties is impossible and rescission has been held to be barred on this basis unless the third party's interests can be adequately safeguarded.

In some cases where the defendant has sold some or all of the assets received under the impugned transaction, the claimant may recover the proceeds of resale as part of the process of *restitutio in integrum*. This has been established in cases involving land[114] or shares.[115]

The more difficult question is whether the defendant can be ordered to pay for the value of the asset even if the proceeds of sale are no longer in the defendant's hands. Birks called the idea that the defendant must pay for the value of the asset 'pecuniary rescission'.[116] A possible example of pecuniary rescission can be found in the Australian case *Hartigan v International Society for Krishna Consciousness Inc.*[117] The plaintiff gave her family home and some cattle as a gift to the International Society for Krishna Consciousness, then joined a community at New Govardhana Farm. The Society sold the plaintiff's home and used the proceeds to pay off debts, among other things. The plaintiff later left the movement for Krishna Consciousness and sought to rescind her gift on the basis of presumed undue influence. Bryson J found that there was presumed undue influence arising from the relationship of spiritual advisor and acolyte. His Honour was prepared to rescind the transaction, but the property had been sold to a bona fide purchaser for value without notice, and the Society no longer had the proceeds of sale. Notwithstanding this, the Society was ordered to pay back the value of the house, represented by the proceeds of sale plus interest from the date of commencement of the hearing. Bryson J said: 'I see no injustice in restoring the defendant to the relative position of indebtedness which it would have been in if it had not received the proceeds of sale.'[118] The defendant unsuccessfully sought to rely on various bars to relief, including that the receipt of the Murray Blue cattle had inflicted hardship on them because of their unpleasant temperament. Bryson J noted that the plaintiff's delay and difficulty in funding litigation was 'directly connected with the impoverishing nature of the gift,'[119] and was not inclined to bar relief on this basis, although he did ensure interest was only charged from the commencement of the hearing.

---

114 *Blackham v Haythorpe* (1917) 23 CLR 156.

115 *New Sombrero Phosphate Company v Erlanger* (1877) 5 Ch D 73, 125; *Lagunas Nitrate Company v Lagunas Syndicate* [1899] 2 Ch 392, 434.

116 Peter Birks, 'Unjust Factors and Wrongs: Pecuniary Rescission for Undue Influence' (1997) RLR 72.

117 [2002] NSWSC 810.

118 ibid [98].

119 ibid [103].

Some argue that pecuniary rescission is, in fact, a form of equitable compensation,[120] and it has been described as such in older cases.[121] Alternatively, it has been argued that pecuniary rescission is a restitution of the value of a benefit conferred.[122] Arguably, a restitutionary analysis fits better with these cases: the defendant would be unjustly enriched if they were allowed to keep the value of the benefit they received.

However, regardless of the justification, as O'Sullivan, Elliott, and Zakrzewski have observed, there are still questions to be answered if pecuniary rescission is to be routinely awarded, including how courts deal with the difficulty in calculating the value of the thing transferred when it has changed since the date of the original transaction; whether pecuniary rescission is given in lieu of setting aside the contract or whether the contract has to be set aside before pecuniary rescission is granted; how courts ensure that defendants who were not reprehensible are not unduly prejudiced; and the impact on the rules of property law.[123]

Executed contracts and innocent misrepresentation

Previously, a contract for the sale of land that had been executed (ie, the land has already been conveyed or registered) could not be rescinded for innocent misrepresentation.[124] The conveyance bar has been statutorily abolished for all kinds of contracts in England and Wales.[125]

Damages in lieu of rescission

In circumstances where the vitiating factor is a non-fraudulent misrepresentation, section 2(2) of the Misrepresentation Act 1967 (UK) allows for damages in lieu of an order for rescission:

> Where a person has entered into a contract after a misrepresentation has been made to him otherwise than fraudulently, and he would be entitled, by reason of the misrepresentation, to rescind the contract, then, if it is claimed, in any proceedings arising out of the contract, that the contract ought to be or has been rescinded, the court or arbitrator may declare the contract subsisting and award damages in lieu of rescission, if of opinion that it would be equitable to do so, having regard to the nature of the misrepresentation and the loss that would be caused by it if the

[120] Tim Akkouh, 'Equitable Compensation Where Rescission is Impossible' (2002) 16 TLI 151.

[121] See, eg, *McKenzie v McDonald* [1927] VLR 134.

[122] Peter Birks, *Unjust Enrichment* (2nd edn, OUP 2005) 226–28.

[123] Dominic O'Sullivan, Steven Elliott and Rafal Zakrzewski, *The Law of Rescission* (3rd edn, OUP 2023) [15.27]–[15.32].

[124] *Seddon v Northern Eastern Salt Company* [1905] 1 Ch 326.

[125] Misrepresentation Act 1967 (UK), s 1(b).

> contract were upheld, as well as to the loss that rescission would cause to the other party.

This is only possible in circumstances where entry into the contract has been induced by a non-fraudulent misrepresentation, and the claimant is still entitled to rescind the contract.[126] If rescission is barred, damages will not be available.[127]

126 *Government of Zanzibar v British Aerospace (Lancaster House) Ltd* [2000] 1 WLR 2333, 2342 (Raymond Jack QC).
127 *William Sindall plc v Cambridgeshire County Council* [1994] 1 WLR 1016, 1044 (Evans LJ).

11. Proprietary remedies

PROPRIETARY REMEDIES

All of the remedies we have so far considered in this book have been personal remedies, ie, attaching to the person of the defendant, with the exception of the proprietary power which arises after an election to rescind is made in equity.

In *Trustee of the Property of FC Jones and Sons (a firm) v Jones*,[1] Millett LJ distinguished between proprietary remedies and proprietary claims. Proprietary claims are those claims based on the defendant's receipt of an asset in which the claimant has a proprietary interest. For a proprietary claim, there can be two kinds of remedy: a proprietary remedy which attaches to particular property in the defendant's hands; or a personal remedy which responds to the fact that the defendant received the claimant's property, but which obliges the defendant to pay the claimant a certain sum of money.

This chapter seeks to explain proprietary remedies, ie, remedies which attach to certain property, not to the person of the defendant. This may be unfamiliar to any civilian readers, as civilian systems tend not to have proprietary remedies. However, the common law does not have a *rei vindicatio*; hence, it had to develop other mechanisms.[2]

The proprietary remedies are primarily equitable in nature; that is to say, they were developed in the Court of Chancery before the Judicature Acts. Often, the mechanism of the *trust* has been used to create proprietary liability. Ordinarily, express trusts arise because someone creates them: a settlor settles legal ownership of property on a trustee for the benefit of beneficiaries or declares themselves as legal owner and trustee of a trust for beneficiaries.

However, equity developed other species of trusts, namely, resulting trusts and constructive trusts, which are traditionally viewed as being imposed by

1 [1997] Ch 159, 168.

2 NJ McBride, '*Vindicatio*: The Missing Remedy?' (2016) 16 SAcLJ 1052. Cf Roman law: Paul du Plessis, *Borkowski's Textbook on Roman Law* (6th edn, OUP 2020) 75.

order of the court, not by agreement of the parties.[3] The effect is ultimately to give the claimant a proprietary interest in the property, subject to the trust.

It is impossible to give a definitive description of proprietary remedies in a chapter such as this. First, to do the subject full justice, it would be necessary to write an entire book. Second, as with the law of unjust enrichment, there is considerable academic debate about the extent to which proprietary remedies should be available, the categorisation of such remedies, and the normative bases upon which they are imposed. It is fair to say that this area of the law lacks a coherent structure, and the principles governing the imposition of proprietary remedies can often only be ascertained on a case-by-case basis. What is attempted here is not a definitive account, but an overview to help understand a difficult and controversial topic. Further guidance on the specifics of trusts should be sought from textbooks and treatises on equity and trusts.[4]

The Nature of Proprietary Remedies and their Advantages for a Claimant

Proprietary remedies have several well-known advantages over personal remedies, which make them attractive for a claimant. First, the essence of a proprietary right is that it is exigible against the rest of the world. An equitable proprietary remedy can be enforced against anyone except a good faith purchaser for value without notice of the claimant's equitable proprietary rights. A constructive trust may also allow a claimant to follow and trace any transfers of value out of the defendant's hands and into the hands of third parties.

Second, some proprietary remedies, including the constructive trust, allow claimants to receive any appreciation in the value of the claimed property. For example, if I am awarded a constructive trust over a painting that was worth $100,000 but has now appreciated in value to $200,000, I will be able to claim the painting (and hence the appreciation in value). However, proprietary remedies are worthless if the property is destroyed or devalued. Presume that in the example above, the painting instead was revealed to be a fake, and worth $10. It would not be worth my while to claim a proprietary remedy over it. Therefore, a claimant must choose between proprietary and personal remedies

---

[3] See, eg, in relation to constructive trusts, *Air Jamaica v Charlton* [1999] 1 WLR 1399, 1412 (Lord Millett).

[4] Eg, Jamie Glister and James Lee, *Hanbury & Martin Modern Equity* (22nd edn, Sweet & Maxwell 2024); Graham Virgo, *The Principles of Equity and Trusts* (5th edn, OUP 2023); John McGee and Steven Elliott (eds), *Snell's Equity* (34th edn, Sweet & Maxwell 2020); Paul Matthews, Charles Mitchell, Jonathan Harris, Sinéad Agnew, *Underhill and Hayton Law Relating to Trusts and Trustees* (20th edn, LexisNexis 2024).

carefully, depending on the value and nature of the property, and whether any potential defendants are insolvent.

Third, proprietary remedies can allow a claimant to reclaim specific property, which may be important where the property has personal value.

Fourth, a proprietary remedy has distinct advantages for a claimant when the defendant is bankrupt or insolvent. A constructive trust or a resulting trust entitles the claimant to recover property to which the defendant has title, not only against the defendant but also as against the defendant's unsecured creditors. In other words, a constructive trust effectively converts a creditor from an unsecured creditor to a secured creditor by taking the asset out of the pool that can be distributed to creditors. A lien secures the claim and gives a claimant true priority in insolvency. By contrast, a personal remedy simply entitles the claimant to share *pari passu* (rateably) with other unsecured creditors.

This fourth aspect is controversial because it renders the property unavailable for distribution to unsecured third-party creditors in insolvency. On one hand, it can be argued that it is irrelevant if third-party creditors are adversely affected by the award of a constructive trust, and that property rights should prevail over personal rights; on the other hand, it can be argued that it is unfair for the claimant to obtain an advantage over unsecured creditors by removing assets from the pool available for distribution.

Types of Proprietary Remedy

Elise Bant has helpfully suggested that proprietary remedies should be divided into three categories: constructive and resulting trusts, proprietary powers, and liens.[5] These categories will be used in this book.

Constructive and resulting trusts

When a constructive or resulting trust is imposed, the defendant is ordered by the court to hold specific property on trust for the claimant as beneficiary. Both constructive trusts and resulting trusts are traditionally thought to be imposed by operation of law[6] (ie, independently of the parties' agreement). The trust is a 'bare trust', meaning that there is no expectation that the defendant will manage the property for the claimant, in contrast to an express trust. However,

---

[5] Elise Bant, 'Trusts, Powers and Liens: An Exercise in Ground-Clearing' (2009) 3 J Eq 286.

[6] However, note William Swadling, 'Explaining Resulting Trusts' (2008) 124 LQR 72, where it is argued that the resulting trust is a species of express trust. This analysis has been accepted by Justice Gordon and Justice Edelman of the High Court of Australia in *Bosanac v Commissioner of Taxation* [2022] HCA 34, (2022) 275 CLR 37 [104]–[113].

the claimant may wind up the trust pursuant to *Saunders v Vautier*,[7] and the defendant must convey the property to the claimant when requested. Austin W Scott explained: 'He is not compelled to convey the property because he is a constructive trustee; it is because he can be compelled to convey it that he is a constructive trustee.'[8] In other words, it is a mechanism for ensuring that ownership passes. As a consequence, some commentators have suggested that courts should simply issue an order to convey, rather than using the mechanism of trust, to simplify the process.[9]

Bant has described trust rights as 'the most durable and intrusive' equitable proprietary interests.[10] For a claimant, trust rights have many advantages. They are enforceable against third parties other than a bona fide purchaser for value without notice of legal title. They encompass any proportionate increase in the value of the property to which they attach.[11] Trusts may also provide a basis for a claimant to trace property (or its exchange products) into the hands of third parties.[12]

However, as noted earlier, the most distinctive advantage for a claimant arises when the defendant becomes bankrupt or insolvent. Once the defendant's property is subject to a trust, it no longer 'belongs' to the trustee; hence, it is unavailable for distribution to creditors. The timing is crucial. If a trust arises before the defendant becomes insolvent, then the asset subject to the trust will not be available for distribution, but if it arises after the defendant has become insolvent, other proprietary interests are likely to have priority. Other jurisdictions (such as the United States, New Zealand, and Australia) have 'remedial constructive trusts', which arise when the court orders them to arise and which are subject to the court's discretion.[13] Conversely, in the

---

7 (1841) 4 Beav 115, 49 ER 282.

8 Austin Scott, *The Law of Trusts* (3rd edn, Little and Brown 1967) [462].

9 Elise Bant, 'Trusts, Powers and Liens: An Exercise in Ground-Clearing' (2009) 3 J Eq 286; William Swadling, 'The Fiction of the Constructive Trust' (2011) 64 CLP 399; Elise Bant and Michael Bryan, 'Constructive Trusts and Equitable Proprietary Relief: Rethinking the Essentials' (2011) 5 J Eq 171; Elise Bant and Michael Bryan, 'Specific Restitution without Trusts' (2012) 6 J Eq 1.

10 Bant, ibid 294.

11 See, eg, *Foskett v McKeown* [2001] 1 AC 102.

12 See, eg, *Attorney-General for Hong Kong v Reid* [1994] 1 AC 324 (PC); *Twinsectra Ltd v Yardley* [2002] UKHL 12, [2002] 2 AC 164; *FHR European Ventures LLP v Mankarious* [2013] EWCA Civ 17, [2013] 3 WLR 466.

13 eg, in Australia, see *Muschinski v Dodds* (1985) 160 CLR 583, 614–15 (Justice Deane), which proposed the 'institutional-remedial' constructive trust. Nonetheless, Ying Khai Liew has argued that, in fact, most trusts in Australian law are institutional: see Ying Khai Liew, 'Constructive Trusts and Discretion in Australia: Taking Stock' (2021) 44 MULR 936. See also Ying Khai Liew,

United Kingdom, remedial constructive trusts have not been recognised.[14] Constructive trusts are institutional in that they arise from the moment that the cause of action creating them arises, and resulting trusts arise at the time when the contribution to the purchase price is made. In *Westdeutsche Landesbank Girozentrale v Islington London Borough Council*, Lord Browne-Wilkinson explained:

> Under an institutional constructive trust the trust arises by operation of law as from the date of the circumstances which give rise to it: the function of the court is merely to declare that such trust has arisen in the past. The consequences that flow from such a trust having arisen (including the potentially unfair consequences to third parties who in the interim have received the trust property) are also determined by rules of law, not under a discretion. A remedial constructive trust, as I understand it, is different. It is a judicial remedy giving rise to an enforceable obligation: the extent to which it operates retrospectively to the prejudice of third parties lies in the discretion of the court.[15]

Specific situations when constructive trusts and resulting trusts will be awarded are considered in the discussion of the criteria for the imposition of awards of proprietary remedies below. It should be emphasised that the word 'constructive' does not mean that the court 'constructs' a trust. Professor Scott noted:

> It is sometimes said that when there are sufficient grounds for imposing a constructive trust, the court 'constructs a trust'. The expression is, of course, absurd. The word 'constructive' is derived from the verb 'construe,' not from the verb 'construct' [...] The court construes the circumstances in the sense that it explains or interprets them; it does not construct them.[16]

Therefore, particular fact patterns give rise to a constructive trust.

A constructive trust may also be imposed as a remedy when a claimant follows or traces into assets. Tracing allows the beneficiary of a fiduciary duty to impose a proprietary remedy over their property or an exchange substitute in either the hands of the defendant or a third party, subject to the defence of a bona fide purchaser for value without notice. In *Foskett v McKeown*,[17] a

---

Rationalising Constructive Trusts (Hart 2017), in which he introduces the concept of replicative, reflective, and transformative constructive trusts. It is the third species which provides the court with the most discretion.

[14] *Re Polly Peck International plc (No. 2)* [1998] 3 All ER 812, 823 (Lord Justice Mummery), 830 (Lord Justice Nourse).

[15] [1996] AC 669, 714 ('*Westdeutsche*').

[16] Austin Scott and William Fratcher, *Scott on Trusts,* vol 5 (4th edn, Aspen 1989) [462.4].

[17] [2001] 1 AC 102.

constructive trust was awarded over the proceeds of a life insurance policy where the premiums had been partly paid for with trust money, which had been misappropriated by the policyholder before his death. The beneficiaries of the trust (investors in a real estate development) were entitled to a constructive trust over the proceeds of the insurance policy in the proportion to which their money had contributed to the premiums. The advantage of obtaining a constructive trust as a remedy through tracing is that the claimant will take any proportionate increase in value and will have priority in insolvency.

Unfortunately, the words 'constructive trust' and 'constructive trustee' are sometimes used to describe accessorial liability for breach of trust.[18] In saying that the knowing recipient or knowing assistant of a breach of fiduciary duty is a 'constructive trustee', courts simply mean that the recipient or assistant is subject to the same personal remedies *as if they were* a trustee. Such confusing terminology should not be used for accessorial liability, because it suggests that a proprietary remedy is present.[19] The principles governing accessorial liability for breach of trust and breach of fiduciary duty are beyond the scope of this book.

Proprietary powers

As discussed in Chapter 10, the right to rescind a contract because of a vitiating factor constitutes a proprietary power. The term 'proprietary power' has not yet gained judicial acceptance, but it is a useful descriptor. The use of the word 'power' indicates that before the claimant elects to rescind, they have only a potential proprietary interest, but once the election to rescind occurs, a fully vested proprietary interest (a constructive trust) comes into being.[20] The equitable power to rescind is also described in case law as a 'mere equity'.[21]

An unexercised proprietary power is more fragile than a vested trust right. Neither common law nor equitable proprietary powers can survive if legal title to an asset is obtained by a bona fide purchaser for value without notice. An

18 *Barnes v Addy* (1874) LR 9 Ch App 244. For a discussion, see, eg, Charles Harpum, 'The Stranger as Constructive Trustee' (1986) 102 LQR 114, 267.

19 William Swadling, 'Constructive Trusts and Breach of Fiduciary Duty' (2012) 18 T&T 985, 986–87; *Dubai Aluminium Co Ltd v Salaam* [2002] UKHL 48, [2003] 2 AC 366, [141] (Lord Justice Millett).

20 The term is taken from Elise Bant, 'Trusts, Powers and Liens: An Exercise in Ground-Clearing' (2009) 3 J Eq 286, who builds in turn on Birke Häcker, *Consequences of Impaired Consent Transfers* (Mohr Siebeck 2009); Birke Häcker, 'Proprietary Restitution after Impaired Consent Transfers: A Generalised Power Model' (2009) 68 Camb LJ 324.

21 See, eg, *Latec Investments Limited v Hotel Terrigal Pty Ltd* (1965) 113 CLR 265.

unexercised equitable right to rescind is defeated even by a subsequent bona fide purchaser of the equitable estate.[22] It is unclear whether proprietary powers survive the bankruptcy or insolvency of the person who holds the asset that is the subject of the power.

Equitable liens and charges

Liens exist both at common law and in equity. The common law lien allows a person (the creditor) to retain possession of property to secure repayment of a debt by another person who has legal title to the property (the debtor). For example, the garage owner's lien arises over the car of a customer when a mechanic has repaired it. The mechanic obtains a lien over the car for the value of the unpaid work and may retain possession of the car until the work is paid for. A common law lien does not generally give the creditor (such as the garage owner) a right to sell the property.[23] It only allows the creditor the right to retain possession of the property until the debt is paid.

In contrast to a common law lien, equitable liens do not require possession by the creditor. The court imposes them upon property in the hands of the debtor. They can be distinguished from equitable charges, a species of equitable security interest that arises by agreement.

Furthermore, an equitable lien gives the creditor the right to seek an order for a judicial sale of the property to which the lien attaches to satisfy the debt owed. The proceeds of the sale are then used to pay the amount owed, including interest and costs. However, liens do not encompass any subsequent increase in the value of the property; they are fixed at a certain amount secured by the lien.

An example of an equitable lien arising by operation of law is the vendor's lien, the counterpart to the constructive trust arising in favour of the purchaser upon entry into a specifically enforceable contract of sale. Once the vendor has transferred title to the property into the purchaser's name, the vendor will generally have an equitable lien over the property to the extent that the purchase price remains unpaid. Other instances where liens will arise include a 'fruits of litigation' lien (where a solicitor has a lien over money recovered by a client to secure costs and disbursements) and a liquidator's lien.

The lien arises when the events creating it occur.[24] Like the constructive trust, a lien is enforceable against whoever holds legal title to the property to which it attaches, unless that person is a bona fide purchaser for value of the legal title without notice of the lien.

---

22 *Latec Investments Limited v Hotel Terrigal Pty Ltd* (1965) 113 CLR 265.

23 Robert Chambers, *An Introduction to Property Law in Australia* (4th edn, LBC 2019) [12.30], noting some statutory exceptions to this.

24 Elise Bant, 'Trusts, Powers and Liens: An Exercise in Ground-Clearing' (2009) 28 J Eq 286, 304.

A lien over an asset confers a true priority on insolvency. At common law, the trustee in bankruptcy must pay off the debt before they can get the asset back from the creditor. In equity, once the debt is satisfied out of the sale of the asset, the remainder of the proceeds of the sale go back into the pool of funds available for distribution to creditors.

As Robert Chambers notes, the equitable lien preserves the defendant's freedom to choose how to repay the claimant.[25] The defendant may be able to discharge the debt secured by the lien with other funds and retain the asset. As a result, the lien preserves the defendant's autonomy to a greater degree than a vested trust interest.

A lien may also be imposed when a claimant traces into assets. For example, in the Australian case *Scott v Scott*,[26] a lien was awarded over a house which a trustee had purchased using trust assets in breach of trust. The beneficiaries of the trust were entitled to a lien reflecting the proportionate contribution of trust moneys towards the price of the house. The High Court of Australia indicated that it would have been willing to consider awarding a constructive trust, but only a lien was sought by the plaintiffs.[27] Unlike a constructive trust, a lien will not capture any increase in value after the date of judgment, but the holder of a lien will still have priority in insolvency.

Criteria for the Award of Proprietary Remedies

Unfortunately, the criteria for awarding proprietary remedies are far from clear. Somewhat discouragingly, for example, constructive trusts have been described as 'a vague dust-heap for the reception of relationships which are difficult to classify or which are unwanted in other branches of the law'[28] and as a 'rag-bag of instances having little in common'.[29]

At the very least, two basic criteria must be met for the award of a proprietary remedy:

(1) The defendant must hold identifiable property to which the proprietary remedy can attach.

---

25 Robert Chambers, 'Resulting Trusts in Canada (Part II)' (2002) 16 TLI 138, 143–44.

26 (1963) 109 CLR 649.

27 ibid 661–64.

28 Edward Sykes, 'The Doctrine of Constructive Trusts' (1941) 15 Aust LJ 171, 175.

29 Robert P Austin, 'Constructive Trusts' in Paul D Finn (ed), *Essays in Equity* (LBC 1985) 196.

(2) The cause of action giving rise to liability must be established (eg, the elements of breach of fiduciary duty must be made out before a constructive trust can be awarded).

Several animating principles have been said to govern the imposition of proprietary remedies, including unconscionability, unjust enrichment, and wrongdoing, but none can explain all cases. Gbolahan Elias has argued that constructive trusts achieve a variety of aims, including the perfection of incomplete transactions, the restitution of gains, and reparation for wrongdoing.[30] The same could be said of proprietary remedies more generally.

Any scheme seeking to divide proprietary remedies into categories is necessarily fraught with peril. As Pill LJ noted in the Court of Appeal judgment in *FHR European Ventures LLP v Mankarious*, '[c]onsideration of the views of commentators and practitioners generally on the subject of constructive trusts [...] reveals passions of a force uncommon in the legal world'.[31] Despite this warning, we proceed to walk where angels fear to tread, and to divide proprietary remedies into categories that reflect different aims: namely, whether the court seeks to perfect incomplete transactions, reverse unjust enrichment, or respond to wrongdoing.[32] We recognise in doing so that others may have different opinions on how these cases can be categorised and what the normative or animating principles behind proprietary remedies are.

Proprietary remedies and unconscionability

In *Westdeutsche*, Lord Browne-Wilkinson said that unconscionability was the general principle behind the imposition of all constructive trusts,[33] and that the defendant's conscience must be 'touched' before a constructive trust can be imposed.[34] 'Unconscionability' encompasses the notion that equity imposes a proprietary remedy where it would be unconscionable for the legal titleholder to deny the claimant's proprietary interest.

However, unconscionability only lies behind all constructive trusts in the most general sense.[35] In part, this is because 'unconscionability' is a slippery word which may have a multiplicity of meanings and aims, including

30 Gbolahan Elias, *Explaining Constructive Trusts* (Clarendon Press 1990).

31 [2013] EWCA Civ 17, [2014] Ch 1 [61].

32 Taking inspiration from, but not exactly replicating, the scheme suggested by Elias in Gbolahan Elias, *Explaining Constructive Trusts* (Clarendon Press 1990).

33 [1996] AC 669, 705. Cf Ying Khai Liew, '"Unconscionability" and the Case Against Lumping: Three Case Studies' (2021) 27 T&T 118.

34 [1996] AC 669, 714.

35 Graham Virgo, *The Principles of Equity and Trusts* (5th edn, OUP 2023) 308–09.

protection of the vulnerable, protecting the integrity of bargaining processes, enforcing reasonable expectations, and preventing substantive unfairness.[36]

In this context, however, some have argued that unconscionability has a settled meaning: conduct will be unconscionable where the claimant had a reasonable expectation of receiving property and this has been defeated by the defendant's conduct, and an equitable principle supports the imposition of a constructive trust.[37]

Ultimately, the notion of unconscionability as a touchstone of proprietary liability confuses more than it illuminates, unless there is greater specificity about precisely what aspect of the transaction makes it unconscionable. In some cases, a proprietary remedy is imposed for reasons of perfection: in other words, the defendant has promised the claimant an interest in property and then reneged on it or failed to complete a transfer of the interest. In other cases, a proprietary remedy is (arguably) imposed to reverse unjust enrichment, where the defendant has unjustly gained property at the claimant's expense. Finally, in other cases, proprietary remedies are imposed to deter wrongdoing and effect disgorgement of profit where the defendant has committed a wrong and gained without a corresponding loss on the part of the claimant. Accordingly, the discussion of trusts will proceed on that basis below.

Proprietary remedies and perfection

Elias says that some constructive trusts are imposed with the aim of 'perfection' when a defendant has chosen to dispose of their property in favour of the claimant.[38] Trusts that fall under this category arise when the claimant had a reasonable expectation of receiving property and the defendant reneges or otherwise fails to complete the transaction. However, the defendant need not display moral turpitude for a proprietary interest to be imposed. On the other hand, in some (but not all) instances, there may be detrimental reliance on the part of the claimant, which makes it unjust for the defendant to depart from the expectation. Proprietary interests arising on this basis include:

- where a fiduciary obtains property, or an opportunity which ought to have been the principal's, in breach of fiduciary duty;[39]

---

[36] Patrick Parkinson, 'The Conscience of Equity' in Patrick Parkinson (ed), *The Principles of Equity* (2nd edn, LBC 2003) [201].

[37] Michael Bryan, Vicky Vann and Susan Barkehall Thomas, *Equity & Trusts in Australia* (3rd edn, CUP 2022) [23.9].

[38] Gbolahan Elias, *Explaining Constructive Trusts* (Clarendon Press 1990) 4, 10–16.

[39] *Keech v Sandford* (1726) Sel Cas T King 61, 25 ER 223; *Boardman v Phipps* [1967] 2 AC 46.

- where a fiduciary misappropriates property from the principal in breach of fiduciary duty;[40]
- where there was a common intention for the parties to hold the property in a way not reflected in the legal title;[41]
- where there is a specifically enforceable contract for the sale of land[42] or unique goods;[43]
- in cases of incomplete gifts;[44]
- in cases of mutual wills[45] and 'secret' trusts;[46] and
- in some cases of equitable estoppel, but only where such a remedy would be appropriate.[47]

Proprietary remedies and unjust enrichment

Another way of understanding the imposition of proprietary remedies is through an unjust enrichment analysis.[48] However, unjust enrichment scholars concede that unjust enrichment cannot provide a complete explanation for all proprietary remedies.[49] Nevertheless, it seems clear that a proprietary remedy is sometimes imposed where the defendant would be unjustly enriched if they were entitled to retain legal title to the property.

Circumstances in which a proprietary remedy might be imposed for this reason include:

- where property has been acquired by reason of a mistake;[50]

---

40 *Black v S Freedman & Co* (1910) 12 CLR 105; *Westdeutsche* [1996] AC 669, 716 (Lord Browne-Wilkinson). Cf *Shalson v Russo* [2003] EWHC 1637 (Ch); [2005] Ch 281, [110] (Lord Justice Rimer) on the problems of this analysis.

41 *Stack v Dowden* [2007] UKHL 17, [2007] AC 366; *Jones v Kernot* [2011] UKSC 53, [2011] 3 WLR 112.

42 *Lysaght v Edwards* (1876) 2 Ch D 499. See *Englewood Properties Limited v Patel* [2005] EWHC 188 (Ch), [2005] 1 WLR 1961 [40]–[43].

43 *Holroyd v Marshall* (1862) 10 HL Cas 191, 209; 11 ER 999, 1006 (Lord Westbury LC).

44 *Re Rose* [1952] Ch 499.

45 *Birmingham v Renfrew* (1937) 57 CLR 666, 689–91; *Re Goodchild* [1997] 1 WLR 1216; *Olins v Walters* [2008] EWCA Civ 782, [2009] Ch 212.

46 *Re Boyes* (1884) 26 Ch D 531.

47 *Thorner v Major* [2009] UKHL 18, [2009] 1 WLR 776.

48 See, eg, Peter Birks, *Unjust Enrichment* (2nd edn, OUP 2005) 302; Andrew Burrows, *The Law of Restitution* (3rd edn, OUP 2011) ch 8.

49 Birks, ibid 301.

50 *Chase Manhattan NA v Israel-British Bank (London)* [1981] Ch 105 ('*Chase Manhattan*'). *Chase Manhattan* seems to suggest such a trust would arise upon receipt, but subsequently, it has been held that the recipient must know of the

- where a transaction can be set aside because of undue influence or duress;[51]
- where a transaction can be set aside because of the unconscionable nature of the bargain;[52]
- where there is a failure of consideration (ie, a failure of the purpose of the bargain which has led to the defendant's enrichment);[53] and
- possibly resulting trusts, insofar as these have been analysed as arising from an 'absence of an intention to benefit' on the part of the claimant towards the defendant.[54]

The cases in which proprietary remedies have been awarded for unjust enrichment mostly involve the reversal or rescission of an impugned transaction. As noted in Chapter 10, the remedy of rescission is amenable to a restitutionary analysis. Vitiating factors bear a distinct similarity to 'unjust factors', and it seems that the goal in either instance is to prevent the defendant from being unjustly enriched at the claimant's expense.

However, it is difficult to establish any firm rules, as the proprietary response in cases of rescission varies, and the cases are highly fact-specific. Where a transaction can be set aside because of vitiating factors, a variety of remedies have been imposed, including full constructive trusts (or sometimes resulting trusts), proprietary powers, liens, or no remedy at all. Bant and Bryan argue that a proprietary power model can explain these cases.[55] Where the defendant has taken the claimant's asset, it remains in the hands of the defendant, it is unique, and the claimant has elected to seek its return, Bant and Bryan argue that the claimant should be entitled to 'specific restitution' (via a constructive trust or an order to convey). However, where the asset has been exchanged for another asset, the claimant should be entitled to the value of the asset secured

---

receipt: see *Westdeutsche* [1996] AC 669, 715 (Lord Browne-Wilkinson) and *Wambo Coal Pty Ltd v Ariff* [2007] NSWSC 589, (2007) 63 ACSR 429. *Pitt v Holt* [2011] EWCA Civ 197, [2011] 3 WLR 19, [215] indicates that the mistake must relate to the payment and must not simply be a mistake about tax consequences of setting up a trust.

51 *Toman v Toman* [2009] NZHC 1000 [15]–[16].

52 cf *Hart v O'Connor* [1985] AC 1000 (PC) (contract not rescinded).

53 *Burgess v Rawnsley* [1975] Ch 429 (resulting trust). Cf, in Australia, *Muschinski v Dodds* (1985) 160 CLR 583 (constructive trust).

54 Peter Birks, 'Restitution and Resulting Trusts' in Stephen Goldstein (ed), *Equity and Contemporary Legal Developments* (Sacher Institute 1992); Robert Chambers, *Resulting Trusts* (OUP 1997).

55 Elise Bant and Michael Bryan, 'A Model of Proprietary Remedies' in Elise Bant and Michael Bryan (eds), *Principles of Proprietary Remedies* (Thomson Reuters 2013) [12.160]–[12.180].

by a lien.[56] Bant and Bryan also argue that equitable discretionary considerations, including hardship, laches, and third-party considerations, should be taken into account by courts.[57] It should be observed that some unjust enrichment scholars such as Birks take a monist view and frown upon any form of discretion.[58] However, like Bant and Bryan, we take the view that discretion is appropriate, as long as the criteria according to which discretion is exercised are clear.

A full constructive trust (or a resulting trust) is more likely to be awarded in cases where there are no third-party interests or other equitable bars to relief, and where the claimant has a special interest in the property. By contrast, a proprietary power may be more appropriate where third-party interests need to be accommodated and there is an inability to effect complete proprietary *restitutio in integrum*, as discussed in Chapter 10. A lien may be more appropriate if the claimant has no particular attachment to the asset, the asset is not the claimant's original asset, and the imposition of a constructive trust over the defendant's asset would impose hardship on the defendant by giving the claimant an asset for much less than it was worth. Finally, a claimant who has unduly delayed in seeking rescission may obtain no remedy at all, as in *Allcard v Skinner*.

A final point should be made about resulting trusts. These are either 'presumed' or 'automatic'.[59] The former is generally thought to arise when it is presumed that the contributing party did not intend to make a gift or a disproportionate contribution to the purchase price of certain property. The latter arises when an express trust fails. Some scholars have suggested that a resulting trust should be imposed wherever there is an 'absence of an intention to benefit' on the part of the claimant towards the defendant, as a restitutionary remedy.[60] However, this has not been taken up by the courts, with the possible exception of Lord Millett's speech in *Twinsectra Ltd v Yardley*,[61] where his Lordship stated that where a lender provides a borrower with money to be spent for a specific purpose, the money is held on a resulting trust for the lender

---

56 ibid [12.190].

57 Elise Bant and Michael Bryan, 'Defences, Bars and Discretionary Factors' in Elise Bant and Michael Bryan (eds), *Principles of Proprietary Remedies* (Thomson Reuters 2013) ch 11.

58 Peter Birks, 'Three Kinds of Objection to Discretionary Remedialism' (2000) 29 UWALR 1.

59 *Re Vandervell's Trusts (No 2)* [1974] Ch 269.

60 Peter Birks, 'Restitution and Resulting Trusts' in S Goldstein (ed), *Equity and Contemporary Legal Developments* (Sacher Institute 1992); Robert Chambers, *Resulting Trusts* (OUP 1997).

61 [2002] UKHL 12, [2002] 2 AC 164.

from the outset; the beneficial interest in the money remains with the lender throughout, subject to a power on the part of the borrower to spend it for the specified purpose.[62] Conversely, it has been suggested that the resulting trust is in fact a species of an express trust.[63]

Proprietary remedies and wrongdoing

Finally, some proprietary remedies are imposed because of wrongdoing on the part of the defendant, although, again, this does not explain all cases and primarily operates to disgorge gains made through wrongdoing.

Constructive trusts are readily awarded in the context of a breach of fiduciary duty or for other equitable wrongs such as breach of confidence. Courts are prepared to award a constructive trust over an asset obtained in breach of fiduciary duty in two circumstances: (1) where the fiduciary has misappropriated or stolen property belonging to the principal; and (2) where the fiduciary was under a duty to acquire the property for the principal, if the fiduciary chose to acquire it at all. These trusts can also be justified according to principles of perfection—in other words, the claimant had a reasonable expectation of receiving property and this has been defeated by the defendant's conduct. There is a corrective rationale here: the fiduciary has taken something that was the principal's (or ought to have been the principal's) and thus should return the property to the principal. However, there is a deterrent, profit-stripping rationale to these cases as well, placing them in the category of constructive trusts designed to respond to wrongdoing.

In *FHR European Ventures LLP v Cedar Capital Partners LLC*,[64] the UK Supreme Court held that whenever an agent has received a bribe or secret commission in breach of his fiduciary duty to his principal, the agent holds the bribe or secret commission on trust for the principal. Unusually, Lord Neuberger overruled his own prior decision as a Court of Appeal judge in

---

62 ibid [93]–[100].

63 William Swadling, 'Explaining Resulting Trusts' (2008) 124 LQR 72. This analysis has been accepted by Justice Gordon and Justice Edelman of the High Court of Australia in *Bosanac v Commissioner of Taxation* [2022] HCA 34, (2022) 275 CLR 37, [104]–[113].

64 [2014] UKSC 14, [2015] AC 250 ('*FHR*'). The same view was taken in *Attorney-General for Hong Kong v Reid* [1994] 1 AC 324 (PC), but the English Court of Appeal took the opposite view in *Lister & Co v Stubbs* (1890) 45 Ch D 1. Commentators were also divided; see Peter Millett, 'Bribes and Secret Commissions' [1993] RLR 7; Peter Millett, 'Proprietary Restitution' in Simone Degeling and James Edelman (eds), *Equity in Commercial Law* (LBC 2005) 309; William Swadling, 'Constructive Trusts and Breach of Fiduciary Duty' (2012) 18 T&T 985, 997–99.

Sinclair Investments (UK) Ltd v Versailles Trade Finance Ltd,[65] where it was held that a proprietary interest should never be awarded over a gain made as an (indirect) result of fiduciary wrongdoing. His Lordship explained his change of opinion in *FHR* by saying:

> Clarity and simplicity are highly desirable qualities in the law. Subtle distinctions are sometimes inevitable, but in the present case, as mentioned above, there is no plainly right answer, and accordingly, in the absence of any other good reason it would seem right to opt for the simple answer.[66]

The claimants in *FHR* sought to invest in the hotel industry. They asked Mr Mankarious and his consultancy business, Cedar Capital (the defendants), to act as their agents. The defendants recommended that the plaintiffs should buy a share in the Monte Carlo Grand Hotel. Unknown to the claimants, the defendants received a €10 million commission from the Monte Carlo Grand Hotel for finding a purchaser. The terms of the agreement between the hotel and the defendants had provided that the defendants would disclose the commission to the claimant purchasers, but they did not. Thus, the property was sold for €211.5 million, and the defendants received their €10 million commission. The claimants sought to obtain the secret commission. The question was whether the plaintiffs were entitled simply to a personal remedy (an account of profits) or a proprietary remedy (a constructive trust). If the claimants were entitled to a proprietary remedy, ie, a constructive trust, it would be enforceable even in insolvency, and it would allow the plaintiffs to trace into the defendants' accounts and investments. The Supreme Court awarded a constructive trust on the basis that a certain rule was required.

One of the authors of this book has suggested that the extreme, inflexible positions taken by the UK Supreme Court are not ideal and that the Australian discretionary approach is preferable in the context of proprietary remedies over bribes, mindful that any discretion exercised must be clearly structured and predictable.[67] Of course, if the English courts were to adopt this approach, it would be at odds with the institutional constructive trust approach preferred by the English courts, but it would be a narrow exception.

---

65 [2011] EWCA Civ 347, [2012] Ch 453 ('*Sinclair Investments*').

66 *FHR* [2014] UKSC 14, [2015] AC 250 [35]. See also Lord Neuberger, 'The Remedial Constructive Trust – Fact or Fiction' (paper delivered at the Banking Services and Financial Law Association Conference, Queenstown, New Zealand on 10 August 2014) [28]–[29], [39].

67 Katy Barnett, 'Distributive Justice and Proprietary Remedies Over Bribes' (2015) 35 LS 302. See the approach taken by the Full Federal Court of Australia in *Grimaldi v Chameleon Mining NL (No 2)* [2012] FCAFC 6, (2012) 200 FCR 296, [569]–[584].

Discretionary Factors and Bars to Relief

Discretionary factors operate in relation to remedial constructive trusts, but often they do not seem to operate in a structured fashion. Rather, they operate in a general 'Is this fair?' manner. Relevant factors include hardship, delay, and lack of clean hands. The court may also consider the impact of a proprietary award on third parties, but the extent to which they do this varies. It is unclear whether a court will take into account the impact of a proprietary award on third-party creditors when there is insolvency, with some cases saying that the effect on third-party creditors is irrelevant, and others saying that it militates against the award of proprietary relief.

Where a remedy is granted in response to a right to rescind, the discretionary factors and bars to relief are the same as those discussed in Chapter 10 with regard to rescission. Where the bars to relief operate, the court is less likely to award a full constructive trust and more likely to award a proprietary power, a lien, or no relief at all.

The Need For More Defined Criteria

Unfortunately, it is distinctly unclear when a proprietary remedy will be awarded. This is not ideal because it means that litigants find it difficult to predict what remedy will be imposed, and the impact of proprietary remedies in insolvency, in particular, means that greater certainty is needed. Presently, we can only analogise from the circumstances where proprietary awards have been made in the past.

It is suggested that the reasons for imposing proprietary remedies are complex and reflect a raft of concerns. Regardless of the approach taken, it would be advisable to have more specific criteria indicating what remedy is appropriate in which circumstances, and also to have greater clarity with regard to the timing of proprietary remedies, the effects of proprietary remedies in insolvency, and the enforceability of proprietary remedies on third parties.

Index